by Charles de Gaulle

The War Memoirs of Charles de Gaulle:
The Call To Honor
Unity
Salvation

Memoirs of Hope:
Renewal
Endeavor

Charles de Gaulle
Memoirs of Hope: Renewal and Endeavor

Translated by Terence Kilmartin

Simon and Schuster • New York

Contents

Publisher's Note

Memoirs of Hope was to consist of three volumes, respectively entitled:

> *Le Renouveau* 1958–1962
> *L'Effort* 1962–1965
> *Le Terme* 1966–1969

The present volume includes *Le Renouveau* (*Renewal*), and the first two chapters of *L'Effort* (*Endeavor*), which were completed before the author's death.

Part I

RENEWAL

1958–1962

Institutions

༈

France has emerged from the depths of the past. She is a living entity. She responds to the call of the centuries. Yet she remains herself through time. Her boundaries may alter, but not the contours, the climate, the rivers and seas that are her eternal imprint. Her land is inhabited by people who, in the course of history, have undergone the most diverse experiences, but whom destiny and circumstance, exploited by politics, have unceasingly moulded into a single nation. This nation has embraced countless generations. At this moment it contains several. It will give birth to many more. But by reason of its geography, of the genius of the races which compose it, and of its position in relation to its neighbors, it has taken on an enduring character which makes each generation of Frenchmen dependent on their forefathers and pledged to their descendants. Unless it falls apart, therefore, this human amalgam, on this territory, at the heart of this world, comprises a past, a present and a future that are indissoluble. Thus the State, which is answerable for France, is in charge, at one and the same time of yesterday's heritage, today's interests, and tomorrow's hopes.

The obligation is a vital one, which in the event of national crisis is sooner or later forced upon the community. At that point, the legitimacy of a governing power derives from its conviction, and the conviction it inspires, that it embodies national unity and continuity when the country is in danger. In France, it was as a result of war that the Merovingians, the

3

Carolingians, the Capetians, the Bonapartes, the Third Republic all received and lost this supreme authority. The authority with which, in the depths of disaster, I in my turn was invested during the course of our history, was recognized first of all by those Frenchmen who refused to give up the fight, then gradually, as events took their course, by the population as a whole, and finally, after much hostility and bitterness, by every government in the world. It was thanks to this that I was able to lead the country to salvation.

She was seen to have re-emerged from the abyss as an independent and victorious State; in possession of her territory and her empire; receiving the surrender of the Reich alongside Russia, America and England; formally accepting, on an equal footing with them, the capitulation of Japan; disposing, by way of compensation for war damage, of the economy of the Saar and coal dues from the Ruhr; acceding, as one of the "Big Five", to the rank of founder member of the United Nations Organization and member of its Security Council with the right of veto.

Although, after all the humiliations and hardships endured in servitude, it might have been thought that our people were doomed to political, social and colonial upheavals culminating in totalitarian Communism, it soon became evident that, in spite of a few isolated incidents and disturbances, de Gaulle was acclaimed everywhere; that no armed force remained outside the regular formations; that the law was functioning normally; that the public service was run by qualified officials; that far-reaching reforms had nipped the threat of revolution in the bud; that our overseas dependencies awaited patiently and confidently the emancipation promised and already begun; that everywhere and in every field the new regime had introduced order, progress and liberty.

Our economy might have seemed condemned to prolonged – some thought permanent – paralysis as a result of the terrible human and material devastation which we had suffered: the destruction of our railways, our ports, our bridges, our means of transport and communication and a large number of our

4

buildings; the financial ruin resulting from the huge levies imposed by the Germans on our natural resources, our capital equipment, our Treasury; the prolonged uprooting of several million Frenchmen, prisoners, deportees, refugees; and the crushing burden of reconstruction imposed upon us by so much damage to persons and property. Nevertheless, the work of recovery was already in full swing. In the midst of the ruins, economic activity had started up again. By hook or by crook, the elementary needs of the population were satisfied. The absentees were reintegrated, not without difficulties, but without serious upheavals. The increase in revenue, the harsh "national solidarity" tax and the huge success of the 1945 loan, brought us close to budgetary equilibrium and made us creditworthy. In short, a few months after victory, the State was on its feet, unity re-established, hope revived, France in her place in Europe and the world.

In achieving all this, I had enjoyed the massive support of popular opinion. By contrast, the various political, social and economic interest groups which had rapidly returned to the limelight were very lukewarm in their approval. No sooner had the enemy departed than they bombarded me with a multiplicity of recriminations of every sort and on every subject, but I met with no obstacle on their part which prevented me from doing what had to be done as long as the immediate fate of the country was at stake. Once this had been assured, however, all the pretensions, ambitions and blandishments of the past were flaunted in front of the French people, as though the unbelievable misfortunes which they had recently brought down upon its head had been forgotten overnight.

For the parties had reappeared, to all intents and purposes with the same names, the same illusions and the same hangers-on as before. While displaying towards my person the respect which public opinion demanded, they lavished criticisms on my policies. Without disputing the value of the services I had contrived to render in the course of shattering events and on the whole in their absence, they all clamored for a return to what they regarded as normal, in other words their own rule, claiming that it was for them to control the levers of power.

It must be said that no current of opinion in the opposite direction manifested itself among the public. Indeed, to judge by what was said or written in every social circle, from every platform, in the name of every group, in the columns of every newspaper, it was as though nothing and no one represented the country save the discordant factions which were doing their best to divide it.

Now, while I was convinced that sovereignty belongs to the people, provided they express themselves directly and as a whole, I refused to accept that it could be parcelled out among the different interests represented by the parties. Of course, the latter should, in my view, contribute to the expression of opinions and consequently the election of the deputies who would debate and vote the laws within the parliamentary assemblies. But in order that the State should be, as it must be, the instrument of French unity, of the higher interests of the country, of continuity in national policy, I considered it necessary for the government to derive not from parliament, in other words the parties, but, over and above them, from a leader directly mandated by the nation as a whole and empowered to choose, to decide and to act. Failing this, the multiplicity of viewpoints which is peculiar to our people by reason of our individualism, our diversity, the ferment of discord which is the legacy of our misfortunes, would once again reduce the State to being no more than a stage for the confrontation of amorphous ideologies, sectional rivalries, semblances of domestic and external action without continuity or consequence. Having attested that victory had been won for the nation thanks only to an authority which rose above all its divisions, and gauging the magnitude of the problems facing it in the present and the future, I saw that henceforth my great battle would be to endow it with a Republic capable of matching up to its destiny.

However, I was obliged to recognize the fact that, once the danger was past, such a renovation was feasible only at the cost of new and harsh experiences. This was all the more certain because, the constraints of the Occupation and the Vichy regime having for so long crushed French liberties, the old and so-called democratic political game was regaining its lost luster; so much so that many of my erstwhile companions, who only recently, as leaders of the Resistance, had denounced the parties, were now trying to obtain leading positions within them. Moreover, in starting up again, all the electoral organizations went out of their way to swear that they deplored the old abuses and would henceforth be careful to avoid them. After the dictatorship of the enemy and his accomplices, I had not the slightest intention of establishing my own. Since I was also anxious to drown the threat of Communism, then immediate and powerful, in universal suffrage, and had called upon the people to elect a National Assembly, I had to face the fact that the latter would inevitably belong to the parties, that incompatibilities would at once arise between it and me, that we would be in total disagreement on the subject of the Constitution which was to replace that of the defunct Third Republic, and that, consequently, the authority, however arithmetically legal, which replaced mine would be devoid of national legitimacy.

From the moment the guns stopped firing, I had decided on my line of action. Short of ostracizing the elected representatives, assuming the characteristics of a new oppressor succeeding others, and destroying myself by adopting a position which the general trend of opinion in France and the whole of the West would soon have made untenable, I must, for whatever length of time was necessary, let the party system display its noxiousness once more, determined as I was not to act as a cover or a figurehead for it. So I would depart, but intact. In this way, when the time came, I could once more be the country's refuge, either in person or through the example which I should have left behind. Meanwhile, with an eye to the future, and before the Assembly had been elected, I introduced the referendum system, made the people decide that henceforward its direct approval would be necessary for a Constitution to be valid, and thus created the democratic means of one day founding a good one myself, to replace the bad one which was about to be concocted by and for the parties.

For twelve years, then, their system went through its paces once more. While the skein of parliamentary intrigues, maneuverings and defections twined and untwined unremittingly in the precincts of the Palais-Bourbon and the Luxembourg,[1] fed by the motions of congresses and caucuses, urged on by newspapers, conferences and pressure-groups, seventeen prime ministers, representing twenty-four ministries, tenanted the Hôtel Matignon[2] in turn. These were: Félix Gouin, Georges Bidault, Léon Blum, Paul Ramadier, Robert Schuman, André Marie, Henri Queuille, René Pleven, Edgar Faure, Antoine Pinay, René Mayer, Joseph Laniel, Pierre Mendès-France, Guy Mollet, Maurice Bourgès-Maunoury, Félix Gaillard, Pierre Pflimlin – all men of worth and undoubtedly qualified for the affairs of State (six of the seventeen had been my ministers, four others would be later), but one after the other deprived, by the absurdity of the regime, of any real grip on events. How often, watching them from a distance struggling with the impossible, had I grieved over this waste! Whatever any of them tried to do, the country and the outside world witnessed the shameful spectacle of "governments" formed on the basis of compromise, attacked from all sides as soon as they were installed, split asunder by internal discord and dissent, overthrown before long by a vote which more often than not reflected only the impatient appetite of candidates for portfolios, and leaving in the intervals between them a vacuum which sometimes lasted several weeks. Moreover, during these interludes, the boards on which this comedy was staged witnessed the entrances and exits of a variety of would-be premiers, either "consulted" or "sounded out" or "designated", before one of them took over the reins. In the Elysée Palace,[3] Vincent Auriol and then René Coty, Heads of State who seemed power-

---

[1] Homes, respectively, of the National Assembly and the Senate (or Council of the Republic, as it was called under the Fourth Republic).

[2] Official residence of the French Prime Minister.

[3] Official residence of the President of the Republic.

less to intervene whatever their concern for the public good and the dignity of the nation, resignedly presided over the convolutions of this absurd ballet.

Nevertheless, as events followed their course and as life could not remain aloof from them, the country was often subject to other influences besides those which should have been exercised by the political authorities. In domestic matters, the civil service, the technologists and the military dealt of their own accord with urgent matters as they arose. As for foreign affairs, notwithstanding the appearances of diplomatic representation and occasional ministerial velleities, in the last resort the outside world determined and obtained what it wanted from France.

It is true that, in the economic sphere, consumer demand, following on a long period of scarcity, and the vast requirements of reconstruction automatically stimulated great activity, to which the Planning Office, which I had set up before my departure, strove to give direction. Thus, agricultural and industrial production increased steadily. But it did so at the cost of purchases from abroad which were not counterbalanced by exports, and of wage increases without corresponding improvements in productivity. Failing to put its house in order, the State paid the deficits. The credits received under the Marshall Plan and those which, in addition, were constantly solicited from Washington, the gold reserves of the Bank of France which had been put in safe keeping during the war in Martinique, the French Sudan and the United States and which I had preserved intact, and above all the budget deficit, in other words inflation, financed the disequilibrium. But the result of it all was the chronic decline in the value of the franc, the paralysis of trade, the exhausting of our credit, in short the growing threat of monetary and financial bankruptcy and economic collapse. Periodically, of course, the timely action of certain ministers, such as Antoine Pinay and Edgar Faure, brought some alleviation. But after their departure confusion reigned once more.

In such circumstances, nothing whatever was done in the social sphere to add to what my government had effected at the time of the Liberation. In the face of endless strikes, the authorities confined themselves to adding to the various kinds of remuneration percentages which were covered in reality by the issue of banknotes and Treasury bonds, and which were soon cancelled out by the continual rise in prices. It is true that social insurance, family allowances and the new rules concerning agricultural leases which I had put into force were sufficient palliatives to the miseries of poverty, sickness, unemployment and old age, for revolt to be held at bay. But as regards long-term problems such as housing, schools, hospitals and communications, delays were allowed to accumulate which seriously compromised the future.

While at home the natural resilience of our country mitigated to some extent the immediate consequences of official inadequacy, the same could not be said of its situation abroad. Everything I had accomplished by dint of arduous efforts, as regards the independence, the status and the interests of France, was immediately jeopardized. Lacking the drive and energy thanks to which we were on our feet, the regime was to all intents and purposes concerned with pleasing others. Naturally enough, it found the required ideologies to camouflage this self-effacement: the one, in the name of European unity, liquidating the advantages which victory had gained us; the other, on the pretext of Atlantic solidarity, subjecting France to the hegemony of the Anglo-Saxons.

Thus, the re-establishment of a central German administration in the three Western zones had been accepted, in spite of the absence of genuine guarantees. Then, the European Coal and Steel Community had been inaugurated, under an agreement which, without offering us the means of restoring our devastated mines, exempted the Germans from having to provide us with fuel deliveries and gave the Italians the wherewithal to equip themselves with a large-scale iron and steel industry. Similarly, France's lien on the economy of the Saar had been abandoned, together with the autonomous State which had been created in that territory. Again, the creation of a European Defence Community had been agreed upon – and would have been put into effect had not a national spasm of revolt exorcized it at the last moment – although it meant depriving victorious France of the right to have an army, merging the military forces, which she would nevertheless have to raise with those of defeated Germany and Italy (England for her part refusing to accept such an abdication) and handing over the command of this stateless assemblage lock, stock, and barrel to the United States of America. By the same token, once the declaration of principle known as the Atlantic Alliance had been adopted in Washington, the North Atlantic Treaty Organization had been set up, under the terms of which our defence and hence our foreign policy disappeared in a system directed from abroad, while an American generalissimo with headquarters near Versailles exercised over the old world the military authority of the new. Finally, at the time of the Suez affair, the expedition which London and Paris undertook against Nasser had been mounted in such a way that the French forces of every kind and at every level were placed under the orders of the British, and the latter had only to decide to recall theirs at the behest of Washington and Moscow for ours to be withdrawn as well.

But it was above all in the evolution of relations between metropolitan France and the overseas territories that the indecision of the State made itself felt – all the more acutely because all the colonized peoples were simultaneously stirred by a vast movement towards independence. The relative weakening of England and France, the defeat of Italy and the subordination of Holland and Belgium to the designs of the United States; the effect produced on the Asians and Africans by the battles fought on their soil for which the colonizers had needed their support; the dissemination of doctrines which, whether liberal or socialist, equally demanded the emancipation of races and of individuals; and the wave of envious longing aroused among these deprived masses by the spectacle of the modern economy – as a result of all these factors the world was faced with an upheaval as profound, though in the opposite direction, as that which had unleashed the discoveries and conquests of the powers of old Europe. It was clear that the distant domination on which the empires were founded had had its day. But might it not be possible to transform the old dependent relationships into preferential links of political, economic and cultural co-operation?

As early as January 1944, speaking in the name of France at the Brazzaville Conference, I had indicated the necessary change of direction in this vast field, and then, in 1945, I had continued along the same lines by extending the franchise to all in Algeria, in Black Africa, in Madagascar; by ceremoniously receiving the Bey of Tunis and the King of Morocco in Paris as sovereigns entitled in their own right, by instructing d'Argenlieu and Leclerc, whom I sent to Indo-China with considerable forces, to establish themselves only in the south and not to proceed to the north where Ho Chi Minh was already in control and where my Sainteny mission was in contact with him with a view to negotiations. Although I did not delude myself that a community based on a free and contractual association could replace our empire overnight without clashes and difficulties, I nevertheless considered this great undertaking to be possible. But it would have to be carried out with determination and continuity, by a government which appeared to the peoples concerned to be really representative of that generous and vigorous France which seemed to have emerged at the time of the Liberation.

Clearly these conditions were not fulfilled by the regime of the parties. A coalition of conflicting viewpoints, each, moreover, represented by men of words rather than men of action, how could it have taken the unequivocal decisions which decolonization called for? How could it have surmounted and if necessary broken all the opposition, based on sentiment, habit or self-interest, which such an enterprise was bound to provoke? To be sure, in the midst of all its fluctuating and conflicting attitudes, some of the leading representatives of the regime took sensible and enlightened measures. But these were never carried through because of the contradictions in which the authorities floundered.

As regards Indo-China, the first notion following my departure had been to invite Ho Chi Minh to Paris to negotiate, and he himself had proved willing to do so. But later the use of force had been allowed to prevail, and a somber, distant struggle had raged for eight years in the course of which the determination to win the war had alternated with the desire to make peace without anyone being able to decide between the two. Notwithstanding the bravery and the losses among the fighting men and the meritorious efforts of the administrators in the field, the final result was a grave military reverse followed by an inevitable but humiliating political settlement.

As for the Protectorates of Morocco and Tunisia, one moment the regime inclined towards coercion, going so far as to arrest and detain in exile the Sultan Mohammed V and to put Bourguiba under house arrest, the next it tried friendly overtures, re-establishing the Moroccan sovereign on his throne, granting internal autonomy to Tunisia and even formally recognizing the independence of the two States. But, lacking the resolve to complete the transformation, it insisted on maintaining there a remnant of French authority which was undermined and disregarded, and military forces which did nothing but pocket insults.

In the territories of Black Africa and Madagascar, having held out against the growing demand for self-determination and, in particular, repressed a bloody revolt in the great island in the Indian Ocean, the regime had finally, on the initiative of Gaston Defferre, introduced an "outline law" (*loi-cadre*) which created autochthonous governments and parliaments with far-reaching legislative and administrative responsibilities; but failing a decision to carry it further, the reform remained incomplete and nugatory.

But it was on the subject of Algeria that the indecision of the regime was most cruelly exposed. Until the insurrection broke out, the successive and ephemeral ministries in Paris had done nothing but vacillate. It is true that in 1947 an Algerian Statute was adopted which provided for an assembly elected by universal suffrage, and empowered to vote the budget and debate the affairs of the territory. This was an important step in the right direction, and if only others had been taken at the time, Algeria's advance towards the control of its own affairs by its own inhabitants, and the gradual emergence of an Algerian State associated with the French Republic, would no doubt have been peacefully accomplished. Unfortunately, the hostility of a large proportion of the Algerians of French stock, together with deep-rooted administrative habit, had obstructed this evolution. Thus there had been a refusal to modify the system of separate electoral colleges – one for full French citizens, roughly a tenth of the population, and the other for everyone else – although each college elected the same number of representatives and the second was moreover subject to powerful official pressure both as regards the candidates and the results of the ballot. Having at first responded favorably to the Algerian Statute, the Moslem masses and their political leaders soon came to recognize that the reforms were spurious, and abandoning the hopes which had inspired them at the time of the liberation of France, concluded that their own liberation would never be won by legal means.

When fighting broke out on November 1 1954 and rapidly spread, the regime began to oscillate between a variety of different attitudes. Many of its leaders in fact recognized that the problem demanded a drastic solution. But when it came to taking the harsh decisions which this would entail, overcoming all the obstacles which stood in its way both in Algeria and in metropolitan France, braving the ill-will of the press and the parliamentary groups which exploited public feeling and throve on the political crises provoked by this tremendous issue – all this was too much for tottering ministries. Apart from a few gestures in the direction of negotiation, certain indirect contacts with the insurrectionary organization which had taken refuge in Cairo, spasmodic measures aimed at moderating the repression, and the nomination, almost immediately rescinded, of a Minister for Algeria, General Catroux, who was a symbol of conciliation, the regime confined itself to providing the men, money and weapons to pursue the struggle which raged in every region of Algeria and all along its frontiers. Materially it was costly, since forces totalling five hundred thousand men were required. In terms of our credit abroad it was expensive too, because the world as a whole deplored this endless tragedy. And from the point of view of the authority of the State it was utterly ruinous.

This was especially true as regards the Army. Taking upon itself not only the burden of the fighting but also the severity, and sometimes the beastliness, of the repression, closely in touch with the anxieties of the French population of Algeria and the Moslem auxiliaries, haunted by fear of another Indo-China, another military reverse inflicted on its colors, the Army, more than any other body, felt a growing resentment against a political system which was the embodiment of irresolution.

Thus in the early spring of 1958, however quiescent the mass of the French population remained on the surface, everything conspired to create a wave of anxiety. It was widely felt that stern measures were required to deal with the financial disequilibrium at home, that only the foreigner benefited from the subordinate role to which we had been reduced abroad, and above all that colonization, and in particular the colonization of Algeria, had become a millstone round France's neck. But it was becoming obvious even to the most biased observers that since the regime was incapable of resolving these problems, there was a grave risk of the issue of Public Safety arising. At the same time, there arose instinctively in many people's minds, whether expressed aloud or silently acknowledged, a growing impulse towards an appeal to de Gaulle.

I was living at the time in complete retirement at La Boisserie, at home to nobody but my family and people from the village, and going only very occasionally to Paris where I received a mere handful of visitors. However, I had done a great deal to try to change the situation before it was too late. On June 16, 1946, at Bayeux, I had outlined the sort of Constitution we required, bearing in mind the nature of our people and our times. Then, when the very different one which inaugurated the Fourth Republic was finally voted, I had sought to rally the French people round the primordial and permanent interests of France and to bring about a change of regime. But in spite of an intensive campaign of popular enlightenment, and innumerable public meetings which I attended in person in every *département* of metropolitan France and Algeria and in all the overseas territories, in spite of the vast and enthusiastic influx of membership and devoted support from every social sphere, especially the most modest, I had failed to bring it off. True, the *Rassemblement du peuple français*[1] won dramatic successes in the municipal elections of 1947, in particular in the capital, where my brother Pierre was elected Chairman of the Paris Council, a position he was to retain, unprecedentedly, for five years running. True, a third of the members of the newly-created *Conseil de la République*[2] formed themselves into an RPF "inter-group" under his presidency. But the stubborn and concerted resistance of the parties, the animosity of both the unions and the leading industrialists, who, although at odds with one another, were equally mistrustful of my plans for social reform, the hostility of almost the entire press, Parisian, provincial and foreign, the ban imposed by the government on the broadcasting of my speeches, and finally, the system of electoral alliances known as *apparentements,* which was adopted for the purpose and which falsified the representation of opinions by votes – all these succeeded in preventing the entry into the National Assembly of a sufficient number of deputies determined to change the regime. At the general election of 1951, only 125 candidates were elected under the sign of the Cross of Lorraine. Whereupon a number of them left the organization to which they owed their allegiance. It was for this reason that, soon afterwards, recognizing the trend of events, I put an end to the *Rassemblement.* For the next six years, from 1952 to 1958, I was to devote myself to writing my War Memoirs without intervening in public affairs, but never for a moment doubting that the infirmity of the system would sooner or later lead to a grave national crisis.

[1] Rally of the French People (RPF).
[2] Council of the Republic: The Senate (under the Fourth Republic).

The crisis that broke out on May 13 in Algiers did not therefore surprise me in the least. Nevertheless, I had played no part whatsoever either in the local agitation, or the military movement, or the political schemes which provoked it, and I had no connection with any elements on the spot or any minister in Paris. It is true that Jacques Soustelle, one of my closest companions during the war and later in the RPF, had been Governor-General of Algeria, appointed by Pierre Mendès-France and recalled by Guy Mollet. But he had never, either in the course of his mission or after his return, communicated with me in any way. It is true that, on a trip to the Sahara in 1957 to attend some rocket-firing exercises at Hammaguir and to visit the newly-opened oil wells at Edjele and Hassi-Messaoud, I had received Robert Lacoste, the Minister for Algeria, at Colomb-Béchar; but I did not see him again. It is true that two or three enterprising individuals, who had participated in my public activity at the time when I still engaged in it, spent their time in Algeria spreading the idea that one day the fate of the country would have to be entrusted to me. But they did so without my endorsement and without having even consulted me. It is true, finally, that after the dissolution of the *Rassemblement*, several parliamentarians who were members of it had become ministers in one or other of the successive governments. But I had had no contact with them. Nevertheless, I perceived all the signs of the growing tension not only in political circles in Paris but also in military, administrative and popular circles in Algeria.

On April 15, the Félix Gaillard ministry was overthrown. Then, for the next four weeks, Georges Bidault followed by René Pleven tried without success to extract another from the deliquescence of the regime. If, on May 12, Pierre Pflimlin seemed to have succeeded, the atmosphere was such that nobody believed it could possibly be effective. At the same time, in Algiers, the fever was mounting steadily, with the Minister for Algeria, Robert Lacoste, publicly expressing the fear of a "diplomatic Dien Bien Phu," the ex-servicemen's associations demanding that "every possible means should be taken to install

a Government of Public Safety" and General Salan, the Commander-in-Chief, cabling Paris and raising the specter of "a
reaction of despair on the part of the Army". I could no longer
doubt that the explosion was imminent.

Nor could I doubt that in this emergency I should at once
have to step into the breach. From the moment when the
Army, enthusiastically acclaimed by considerable numbers of
the local population and supported in metropolitan France
by many people who were disgusted with the regime, rose up
against the official apparatus, which, in the absence of any
movement of confidence and support from the mass of the
people, simply proclaimed its impotence and confusion, it was
clear that the country was heading straight for subversion, the
sudden arrival in Paris of an airborne vanguard, and the
establishment of a military dictatorship based on a state of
siege analogous to that which now existed in Algiers, which
would inevitably provoke in retaliation more and more extended
strikes, widespread obstruction, and active resistance on a
growing scale. In short, the prospect was one of chaos, culminating in civil war, in the presence and eventually with the participation in one way or another of foreigners – unless a national
authority, outside and above both the political regime of the
moment as well as the movement which was preparing to
overthrow it, could immediately rally opinion, take over
power and restore the State. And that authority could be none
other than mine.

I therefore felt myself to be the chosen instrument of this
fresh start, the obligation of which had fallen upon me in my
retirement. On June 18, 1940, answering the call of the eternal
fatherland bereft of any other alternative to save its honor and
its soul, de Gaulle, alone and almost unknown, had had to
assume the burden of France. In May 1958, on the eve of a
disastrous tearing-apart of the nation and faced with the annihilation of the system which was allegedly in control, de Gaulle,
now well-known, but with no other weapon save his legitimacy,
must take destiny in his hands.

I had very few hours in which to decide. For revolutions move swiftly. Nevertheless I had to choose the moment when, closing the shadow-theater, I would release the *deus ex machina*, in other words make my entrance. Should I intervene without delay in order to nip the nascent disaster in the bud, at the risk of being subsequently challenged and thwarted by people who had recovered their equanimity? Or should I wait until, events becoming violent, collective fear would guarantee me a general and prolonged assent? Weighing up these alternatives, I chose to act at once. But in that case, was I to confine myself to re-establishing in the immediate future some semblance of governmental authority, to putting the Army temporarily in its place, to finding a rough and ready compromise in order to alleviate for a while the agonies of the Algerian affair, and then retire after having given a new lease of life to a detestable political system? Or was I to seize the historic opportunity presented to me by the discomfiture of the parties to endow the State with institutions which would restore to it, in a form appropriate to modern times, the stability and continuity of which it had been deprived for 169 years? Was I to act in such a way that on this basis it became possible to resolve the vital problem of decolonization, to set in motion the economic and social transformation of our country in the age of science and technology, to re-establish the independence of our foreign policy and our defence, to make France the champion of a European Europe united in its entirety, to give her back throughout the globe, especially in the Third World, the prestige and influence which had been hers through the centuries? This, without the slightest doubt, was the goal that I could and must achieve.

So be it! Notwithstanding the doubts which I felt about myself owing to my age – sixty-seven years – the gaps in my knowledge and my limited abilities; however stiff the obstacles which I was sure to meet with among our people, volatile as always and pulled in the opposite direction by almost the whole of the political, intellectual and social élite, and in spite of the resistance which foreign states would offer to the renascent power of France, I must, to serve her, personify this great national ambition.

The first step was to take the State in hand. In this connection I had the feeling that, as things were at the moment, opposition would not hold out for long. Knowing the people with whom I had to deal, I sensed that in Algiers as well as in Paris the dominant feeling among those in charge was fear of being dragged into acts of force, and that many were looking towards me in the hope that I would be able to spare them this necessity. True, the Committees of Public Safety, consisting of officers and civilians, which appeared in Algeria on May 13, struck bellicose attitudes and took over the functions of the prefects and sub-prefects. But the military High Command gave the impression that it was not anxious to do anything irreparable. Although the Army openly condemned the impotence of the political system which threatened to have disastrous consequences for itself, and although it saw fit to take the local administration under its wing on the pretext that the struggle against the insurrection would thus be facilitated, there were powerful elements among the military who did not readily envisage the prospect of a rupture with metropolitan France, the launching of an expedition against the capital, and the seizure of power. On the edge of the wide Rubicon of the Mediterranean, senior commanders, officers and men were on the whole anxious to see in Paris a government which would be capable of assuming national responsibilities and which would spare them the hazards of indiscipline. But, convinced that the regime would never provide such a government, in their anguish they now turned to me. On May 15, General Salan, who two days earlier had had to surrender the headquarters of the *Gouvernement-Général*[1] room by room to the frenzied mob, wound up a speech from the balcony of the Forum with the cry of "Vive de Gaulle!" Thus the issue which was already at the back of everyone's mind had at last been publicly raised.

In Paris, official circles now thought of nothing else. Apart from what I gathered from the radio and the newspapers, the messages I received from my liaison officer, Olivier Guichard,

[1] Headquarters of the Governor-General and later of the Minister for Algeria. The Forum was the big square in front of it.

kept me in touch with a confused situation in which my name was in the forefront of every conversation and every calculation. The more so because, in the face of the dissidence, what was still by force of habit known as the government was already showing signs of surrender. On May 13, after the rioting in Algiers, Félix Gaillard, who had been overthrown a month earlier but who, since no new ministry had been sworn in to replace his, was still dealing with current business at the Prime Minister's office, had cabled Salan that there was no occasion to use arms against the demonstrators and had delegated civil authority in Algeria to him. During the following night, although Pflimlin's government was voted into office by the National Assembly, it was only after a debate which reflected the general confusion and by means of a minority vote, only 274 being in favor while the "Noes" and abstentions totalled 319 – a result which manifestly precluded the slightest possibility of strong measures. Indeed, on the morning of the 14th, the government confirmed General Salan in his powers and, having previously decided on the interruption of communications with Algeria, now ordered them to be restored. In the course of the afternoon, spending a few hours in the capital as I often used to do on Wednesdays, I was able to gauge, from the flow of information reaching me in my office in the Rue de Solférino, the extent of the anxieties which on every side, and from the highest to the lowest, sought assuagement from General de Gaulle.

From Colombey, on 15 May, I gave my reply. In a seven-line declaration I pointed to the degradation of the State as the cause of the threatening calamity, branded the regime of the parties with responsibility for this disastrous process, and affirmed my intention to remedy it by once more assuming – "I am ready" – the powers of the Republic.

As soon as this declaration had been launched, everyone realized that events would now take their course. True, there were signs of a stiffening of partisan opposition against me. But these were conventional gestures. In reality no one doubted that unless the situation was to drift into national catastrophe, there could be no alternative to General de Gaulle. Then the procession of consenting and even enthusiastic supporters began to form behind me, growing hourly. In fact, from then on the only problem that concerned the political apparatus was the procedure for its renunciation of power.

But speed was essential. Cautious though the High Command in Algiers still remained, all the imponderables were now in play and there was a risk that the situation might get out of hand. Although President Coty had sent a public message on the 14th to all generals, officers and soldiers serving in Algeria appealing to them "not to add to the trials of the fatherland by dividing Frenchmen," all the news suggested that tension was growing apace among the military. Moreover, the resignation the following day of General Ely, the Chief of General Staff, who exercised the highest military authority and whose sense of duty was well-known, showed that the Army as a whole no longer supported the regime. In order to commit myself further vis-à-vis the nation, and being debarred from using the radio, I summoned the press to the Hôtel d'Orsay on May 19.

On arrival in Paris, I felt how much the atmosphere had darkened in a few days. It is true that the Minister of the Interior, Jules Moch, was himself contributing towards this atmosphere. At his orders, the police had deployed massive forces round the approaches to the press conference, as if it were conceivable that de Gaulle was about to appear at the head of a brigade of shock-troops to take over public buildings. At the very moment when, having come up from Colombey incognito, with no other escort but Colonel de Bonneval, my aide-de-camp, and my chauffeur Paul Fontenil, I was on my way to meet a group of journalists, the minister was personally inspecting the long columns of armored vehicles occupying both banks of the Seine. This derisory spectacle having confirmed me in my conviction that it was high time to restore some sense of proportion to the Republic, I addressed the press in the tones of the master of the moment. And indeed, to judge from the questions that were put to me, all of them relating to what I would do in power, no one had the slightest doubt that I would

soon be there. Naturally, what I affirmed on this occasion was my determination to restore the authority of the State and the confidence of the nation. I concluded by saying that I was at the country's disposal.

Meanwhile, events were moving fast. In Algeria, where Jacques Soustelle had turned up without my having had a hand in it, the Committees of Public Safety continued to establish their dictatorship. Anxious to know what was happening and what was planned, I cabled the High Command inviting them to send someone to report to me on the situation. My message was transmitted in the normal way, without any mystery, by General Lorillot, the new Chief of Staff, with the agreement of his minister, Pierre de Chevigné. Shortly afterwards General Dulac, accompanied by several officers, arrived at Colombey to tell me on Salan's behalf that if I did not take over power as soon as possible, the High Command could not prevent a military incursion against metropolitan France. In Paris, meanwhile, official circles were still affecting to carry on the business of government and parliament. The government's "special powers" were renewed by the two Houses and a bill for constitutional reform was introduced, while the parties of the Right and the Center affected to be uneasy about my program, the parties of the Left talked of "defending the Republic", and the CGT[1] called a general strike, which, incidentally, met with very little response. But public opinion as a whole realized the futility of this game. The players themselves no longer believed in it. Some of them, by no means the least, were openly turning towards me.

Among them, for example, were Georges Bidault, who announced on May 21: "I am at the side of General de Gaulle"; Antoine Pinay, who called on me at Colombey on the 22nd and, having seen me, said to all and sundry: "The General? Why, he's a fine man!" and urged Pflimlin to meet me without delay; Guy Mollet, the Vice-Premier, who, on the 25th, seizing on some remarks which I had made about him at my press conference, sent me a letter, behind the cautious terms of which could be sensed a change of heart; and Vincent Auriol, who

---

[1] *Confédération générale du travail:* Communist-led trade unions.

wrote to me on the 26th: "It is as your Minister of State in 1945 that I am approaching you . . . and as one who, before giving you his support, requires only the assurance that you will bring back to the path of duty the officers who have disobeyed."

Events, in any case, were hastening this momentum. On May 24 a detachment from Algiers had landed in Corsica without firing a shot, and Committees of Public Safety had seized power in Ajaccio and Bastia. The police forces sent to the island from Marseilles to restore order had allowed themselves to be disarmed. If the political solution was delayed, similar operations would certainly be carried out on the mainland, and ultimately against Paris. I learned from an official source that the invasion was expected by the Ministry of the Interior on the night of 27–28th. After that, anything might happen.

I therefore accelerated the progress of common sense. On the 26th, I summoned to La Boisserie the Prefect of the Haute-Marne, Marcel Dibolt, and instructed him to go at once to Pflimlin and tell him on my behalf that the national interest required him to see me. I suggested as a meeting-place the unobtrusively situated residence of the curator of Saint-Cloud, my friend Félix Bruneau. The Prefect fulfilled his mission and the Prime Minister informed me that he would go to the appointed place that very evening.

I found Pierre Pflimlin calm and dignified. He gave me a picture of the situation in which he found himself, which was that of a pilot whose controls have ceased to respond. I told him that it was his duty to draw the obvious conclusions, and not to continue in an office which in any case he could no longer exercise, making it clear that I was ready to do the necessary thereafter. Without declaring himself explicitly on this, the Prime Minister gave me the impression that he did not rule it out. However, he begged me to use my prestige at once to bring the High Command in Algeria back to the path of discipline, acknowledging that he himself was incapable of doing so. "There could be no better proof than your request," I told him, "of the solution which the Republic requires." We parted cordially, and I returned home at dawn convinced that

Pierre Pflimlin would soon adopt the course which I had suggested to him that night.

In the morning I pressed further forward. In a new public statement I announced that I had set in motion "the regular procedure necessary for the establishment of a Republican government capable of ensuring the unity and independence of the country"; that "in these conditions I cannot countenance any action from whatever quarter which threatens public order"; and that "I expect the land, sea and air forces in Algeria to observe exemplary discipline under the orders of their commanders: General Salan, Admiral Auboyneau and General Jouhaud." Thus, leaving the soothsayers of the corridors of the Palais-Bourbon and the newspaper offices to ponder what the "regular procedure" set in motion for my accession might be, I ordered the military leaders to desist from further intervention. This they did.

The next day, May 27, was to see the regime's final effort at survival. The government pushed a constitutional reform bill through the National Assembly which, theoretically, contained sensible provisions for the reinforcement of the executive. But everyone knew that it was too late and that there was nothing more to be done. The meetings and motions which continued to proliferate among the various parliamentary groups seemed utterly unreal. Equally meaningless was the meeting of the Cabinet which sat through the night, most of its members haggard from lack of sleep, and from which several ministers had absented themselves. It was all over! In the early hours of May 28, Pierre Pflimlin told his colleagues that he was "going to have a talk with the President of the Republic". He did indeed go and tender his resignation.

There was nothing left for the regime but to put itself in my hands. Fortunately, President Coty took the required steps to see that it passed off with a modicum of dignity. This good old Frenchman, although he had for long been involved in the prevailing rites and customs, was above all anxious to serve the country. At the edge of the abyss into which it was once more in danger of being plunged, three postulates outweighed all

other considerations in his mind. The first was that, in order to save the country while preserving the Republic, it was absolutely essential to change a discredited political system. The second was that the Army must be brought back to the path of obedience without delay. The third was that only de Gaulle could bring about these things. But naturally the President was anxious that power should be handed over to me in accordance with the rules and not hurriedly jettisoned. This was, indeed, what I myself intended. When, therefore, at noon, René Coty asked me if I would agree to meet the Presidents of the two Houses, Le Troquer and Monnerville, to arrange the formalities before he himself adopted a public position, I gave a favorable answer.

The interview took place late at night in Félix Bruneau's house. Gaston Monnerville had been won over to the idea of my taking up the reins of government. All he asked of me was not to insist on the special powers which I regarded as necessary at the outset for more than six months. But André Le Troquer seemed to be appalled by the imminent change. Having been my War Minister at the time of the Algiers Committee, having walked beside me down the Champs-Elysées at the time of the liberation of Paris and stood at my side during the shooting around Notre-Dame, he would not go so far as to accuse me of wishing to be a dictator. But he declared that I could not avoid becoming one given the circumstances of my accession to power. "Therefore," he added passionately, "I am opposed to it." "Well," I said to him, "if parliament follows you, I shall have no alternative but to let you have it out with the paratroops, while I go back into retirement and shut myself up with my grief." Thereupon the meeting ended. On the way out, I informed the Secretary-General to the Presidency, Charles Merveilleux du Vignaux, who was waiting expectantly for news, that I was sorry to have put myself out for nothing and that I was returning to Colombey. I arrived there at five o'clock in the morning.

By midday René Coty had announced that he was sending a special message to both Houses of parliament. At three p.m. the message was read out to them. It contained all that needed

to be said: the necessity to change the political system; the evidence of the disintegration of the State and the threat of imminent civil war; an evocation of General de Gaulle, "the most illustrious of Frenchmen who, in the darkest years of our history, was our leader in the struggle for freedom and who, having united the nation around him, rejected dictatorship in order to establish the Republic"; an appeal to him to come and discuss with the Head of State the steps immediately necessary for a Government of National Safety, and the possibility of a profound reform of our institutions; and a pledge to hand in his resignation as President if this final attempt failed. This message, which tolled the knell, was heard in complete silence by the National Assembly and the Council of the Republic. It was communicated to me by telephone from the Elysée, and I replied that I was ready to come. I arrived via the park, not through the main courtyard, in the rather vague hope of avoiding the swarm of photographers. I got there shortly before eight p.m. So did the photographers.

René Coty greeted me on the threshold, bubbling over with emotion. Alone in his study, we reached an understanding at once. He concurred in my plan: full powers, prorogation of parliament, a new Constitution to be drawn up by my government and submitted to a referendum. I agreed to be "invested" by the National Assembly on June 1, when I would read a brief declaration without taking part in the debate. We took leave of each other amid a throng of frantic journalists and enthusiastic onlookers who had invaded the park. Afterwards I issued a statement to the effect that we had reached an agreement and on what conditions. Later, along the road which took me back to the Haute-Marne, large groups of bystanders awaited my passage, shouting "Vive de Gaulle!" through the night.

The political parties spent the whole of Friday May 30 arranging their abdication. I received visits from and acknowledged the conversion of, first of all Vincent Auriol, who offered himself as Vice-Premier in the next government, then Guy Mollet and Maurice Deixonne, who were to tell their Socialist colleagues on their return "that they had just lived through one of the great moments of their lives''. Marshal Juin, for his part, came to assure me that the Army was behind me as one man. Then above my house I watched the twilight descend on the last evening of a long solitude. What was this mysterious force that compelled me to tear myself away from it?

Everything was settled. There remained the formalities. I was resolved to go through them without appearing too off-hand. For it was right that before the country, whose equilibrium was fragile, things should be seen to happen in accordance with a regular procedure. What was taking place was certainly a profound transformation; it was not a revolution. The Republic was being renewed; it remained the Republic. It was for this reason that, although the return of General de Gaulle to the head of affairs in France was not to be compared with the enthrone-ment of the successive ministries of the dying regime, I had nevertheless agreed the details of the transition with René Coty.

On May 31, I invited the leaders of the parliamentary groups to meet me at the Hôtel La Pérouse, where I was in the habit of staying whenever I came to Paris. Only the Communists were absent. Apart from François Mitterand, who gave vent to his hostility, none of the delegates present, almost all of whom had openly opposed me for twelve years, raised any objection to my statement of intentions. Meanwhile I had begun to form the government. André Malraux would be at my side and would take over Cultural Affairs. Four Ministers of State – Guy Mollet, Pierre Pflimlin, Félix Houphouët-Boigny and Louis Jacquinot – and the Keeper of the Seals,[1] Michel Debré, representing the whole of the political spectrum with the exception of the Communists, would work under my guidance on the future Constitution. Four other parliamentarians – Antoine Pinay, Jean Berthoin, Paul Bacon and Max Lejeune – would be in charge respectively of Finance, Education, Labor and the Sahara. The ambassador Couve de Murville at Foreign Affairs, the prefect Emile Pelletier at the Interior, the engineer Pierre Guillaumat at the War Office, the governor Cornut-Gentille at the Ministry for Overseas France, would be more directly under

[1] *Garde des Sceaux:* Minister of Justice.

my wing, while I myself assumed responsibility for Algerian affairs. A little later, six members of parliament – Edouard Ramonet (Commerce and Industry), Robert Buron (Public Works and Transport), Edmond Michelet (ex-Servicemen), Roger Houdet (Agriculture), Eugène Thomas (Posts and Telegraphs), and Jacques Soustelle (Information) – and three senior civil servants – Pierre Sudreau as Minister of Construction, Bernard Chenot as Minister of Health and André Boulloche as Special Assistant to the Prime Minister, would complete the government.

On Sunday, June 1, I made my entry into the National Assembly. The last time I had been there, in January 1946, I had had to administer to Edouard Herriot, who had ventured to read me a retrospective sermon on the subject of the Resistance, the somewhat sharp and ironical rebuke which he deserved. The incident had taken place in the atmosphere of veiled hostility with which the parliamentarians regarded me at the time. Today, by contrast, I sensed that the hemicycle was bubbling over with an intense and on the whole sympathetic curiosity towards me. In my brief declaration I summed up the situation: the degradation of the State; French unity threatened; Algeria plunged in turmoil; Corsica in the grip of the contagion; the Army, having come through long and bloody trials with merit, led astray by the dereliction of the civil authorities; the international position of France undermined even among her allies. Then I indicated what I expected from the representatives of the nation: full powers, a mandate to submit a new Constitution to the country, and the prorogation of the assemblies. As I spoke, there was total silence on all the benches, as befitted the occasion. Afterwards I withdrew, leaving the Assembly to debate for form's sake. In spite of a few acrimonious speeches, notably those of Pierre Mendès-France, François de Menthon, Jacques Duclos and Jacques Isorni, which were like final convulsions, the investiture was voted by an ample majority.

It was the same, the following day, with the bills concerning emergency powers in Algeria and in metropolitan France and, the day after, with the bill concerning the Constitution which demanded a two-thirds majority. I returned to the Chamber to attend this final discussion, taking the floor several times in response to various speakers, in order to add a touch of affability to the last moments of the last assembly of the regime. The Council of the Republic having also given its approbation, parliament broke up.

If this end of an era left some bitterness in the hearts of many of its leading protagonists, a feeling of immense relief swept over the country. For my return gave the impression that things were back to normal. Instantly the storm clouds vanished from the national horizon. Now that the captain was at the helm of the ship of State, there was a general feeling that the harsh problems with which the nation had for so long been faced would at last be resolved. Indeed, the somewhat mythic aura with which my person was wont to be invested tended to encourage the idea that obstacles which everyone else had found insurmountable would simply vanish from before my path. And here I was, committed as heretofore by the contract which the France of the past, the present and the future had thrust upon me eighteen years before in order to avoid disaster; here I was, still bound by the exceptional trust which the French people reposed in me; here I was, obliged as always to be the same de Gaulle who was held personally responsible for everything that happened at home or abroad, whose every word and every gesture, even when they were wrongly imputed to him, became subjects of universal discussion, and who could not appear anywhere without exciting ardent acclamations. The high dignity of the leader combined with the heavy chains of the servant!

Having laid the foundations, now I had to build. At the Hôtel Matignon, where I now resided, the questions of the moment came crowding in on me: Algeria, finance and currency, foreign affairs, etc. But while taking these in hand, I also directed the work of constitutional reform. On this subject, which was all-important, I had laid down the basic essentials twelve years before. What was about to be produced was more or less what was known as the Bayeux Constitution, after the speech I had made there on June 16, 1946.

Michel Debré, seconded by a young team drawn from the *Conseil d'Etat*,[1] prepared the draft, which I examined stage by stage with the appointed ministers. Thereafter, advice was sought from the Constitutional Consultative Committee of thirty-nine members, including twenty-six parliamentarians, created by the same law which had decided on the revision and presided over by Paul Reynaud. I sat in with this Committee on several occasions to listen to its various suggestions and to elucidate my own ideas. Thereafter the *Conseil d'Etat* offered its observations. Finally, the Cabinet discussed the draft as a whole, each member, beginning with President Coty, putting forward his suggestions. The final text was to be submitted to the people by referendum.

In none of these discussions was any fundamental opposition raised to the changes I had for so long demanded. That the Head of State should henceforth be really the head of affairs; that he should really be answerable for France and the Republic; that he should really appoint the government and preside over the Cabinet; that he should really be responsible for appointments to the highest civil, military and judicial offices; that he should really be the head of the armed forces – in short, that all important decisions as well as all authority should really emanate from him; that he should be able of his own accord to dissolve the National Assembly; that he should have the power to submit to a referendum any government bill dealing with the working of the country's institutions; that in the event of a grave crisis, internal or external, he should be empowered to take any measures demanded by the circumstances; and, finally, that he should be elected by a college much larger than parliament – all this was accepted by each of the authorities consulted.

This was also the case as regards the institution of a Prime Minister whose function would be, together with his colleagues, to decide and direct the policy of the nation but who, being

[1] Council of State: the supreme administrative jurisdiction in France.

appointed by the President, whose role would be all-important, could clearly not act in crucial matters except on his directives.

The provisions concerning parliament elicited the same general assent, in particular those which subjected certain of its votes to the control of a Constitutional Council brought into being for this purpose; those which precisely limited the legislative domain; those which, by the blocked vote, the obligation to respect the parliamentary time-table, the abolition of interpellations in the old style and the divisions which ratified them, freed the government from the obnoxious and humiliating pressures, constraints and machinations which characterized the debates of old; those which made ministerial office incompatible with membership of parliament; those which severely limited the use of the vote of censure. Finally, as regards the overseas territories, the right which was granted to them either to remain in the Republic with a special status, or, as autonomous States, to join the Community formed with metropolitan France, or, having become independent, to associate themselves with her by contractual agreement, or to separate themselves from her at once and totally – this was accepted by all.

In effect, three major questions gave rise to exchanges of views between the Consultative Committee and me. "Will it still be possible," the deputies anxiously wondered, "for us to overthrow the government even though the latter will henceforth emanate from the President?" My reply was that a vote of censure passed by the National Assembly would necessarily entail the resignation of the government. "What," it was asked on all sides, "is the justification of Article 16 which entrusts the Head of State with responsibility for the safety of France in the event of her being threatened with catastrophe?" I recalled that, in the absence of such an obligation, President Lebrun, instead of moving to Algiers with the public authorities in June 1940, called upon Marshal Pétain and thus opened the road to capitulation, whereas it was by anticipating Article 16, that President Coty had avoided civil war when he called on parliament to abandon its opposition to the return of General de Gaulle. "Will the Community," the Committee members wanted to know, "be a federation as Félix Houphouët-Boigny suggests, or a confederation in accordance with the wishes of Léopold Senghor?" I observed that at the outset it would not fit into any particular pigeon-hole, and that the draft had provided for its gradual and painless evolution. On the whole, the text of the Constitution, as it emerged under my guidance from the work of Debré and his colleagues, from the scrutiny to which it was subjected in my presence by the Ministers of State, from the report drawn up by the Consultative Committee, from the advice given by the *Conseil d'Etat*, and from the final decisions taken by the government, conformed to what I regarded as necessary for the Republic.

However, the proof of what is written, even if it is in letters of gold, lies in its implementation. Once the new Constitution was voted, it would still have to be put into effect in such a way that it was stamped in fact with the authority and efficiency which it embodied in law. That battle would also be mine. For it was clear that when it came to the point, my conception was different from that of the adherents of the outgoing regime. The latter, while affirming that the confusion of yesterday was over and done with, were in their secret hearts counting on the old game to restore the political formations to their former preponderance, which the Head of State would be obliged to cede to them on the ground that he was a neutral arbiter. Many of them were by no means pleased, therefore, to learn of my intention to assume the burden. Faced with the actuality, they were to resign themselves at first to seeing me play the part as it was laid down and as I thought it should be played, relying on me to relieve them of the millstone of Algeria, and calculating that soon afterwards I would willy-nilly throw in the sponge. But when, having cut this Gordian knot, I undertook to unravel others, they were to complain of violations of the Constitution because it had taken a turn which did not fit in with their preconceptions and mental reservations.

The French people, for their part, greeted the Fifth Republic with no such reservations. For them it meant the inauguration of a regime which, while respecting our liberties, was capable of action and responsibility. It meant a government which would and could in actual fact resolve the problems facing it. It meant answering "Yes" to de Gaulle, in whom they put their trust because the future of France was at stake. Addressing the vast crowds in the Place de la République in Paris on September 4, in Rennes and Bordeaux on the 20th, at Strasbourg and Lille on the 21st, then the entire country over the radio on the 26th, I was conscious of an immense wave of approbation. On September 28, 1958, metropolitan France adopted the Constitution by seventeen-and-a-half million votes to four-and-a-half million. Abstentions amounted to fifteen per cent, fewer than there had ever been before.

But public feeling, however massively expressed on a crucial question which required only one answer, was bound to become dispersed when it came to the parliamentary elections (the National Assembly having been dissolved by the referendum). For in this context the habitual divergences of view, the conflicting interests of the various classes and sections of the population, the differences in local conditions, the propaganda of militants, the adroitness of candidates, would variously come into play. Yet it was essential that the vast movement of support which my appeal had just aroused should be extended on an adequate scale into the sphere of political choices and that there should be in parliament a group of deputies numerous and cohesive enough to will, to support, and to accomplish by legislative action the work of recovery which could now be undertaken.

In order to have a majority, one needs an electoral system that will produce one. This was what my government decided upon when it passed the new electoral law by virtue of its special powers, rejecting proportional representation, dear to the rivalries and vetoes of the parties, but incompatible with the maintenance of a continuous policy, and adopting quite simply the system of single-member constituencies on a second ballot. Although I refrained from taking part in the election campaign and even requested my old companions not to flaunt my name as a party label, the results exceeded my hopes. In

the new National Assembly, which contained 576 members, a loyal group under the title of the Union for the New Republic comprised 206 and constituted a nucleus compact and resolute enough to establish itself on an enduring basis beside a heterogeneous "Right" and "Center" and a much reduced "Left". As a symbol of this profound renewal, Jacques Chaban-Delmas was elected President for the duration of the legislature.

On December 21 the Presidential electors – deputies, senators, departmental councillors, mayors and a number of municipal councillors – elected the Head of State. Full though my public career had been, this was the first time that I had stood for election. For I had had no need to offer myself formally as candidate when I was twice elected Head of the Provisional Government by the National Assembly in 1945, after having led France for five years during the war by virtue of events alone. Georges Marrane, in the name of the Communists, and the doyen Albert Chatelet, on behalf of a "Union of Democratic Forces", were the other candidates. The college of seventy thousand notables gave General de Gaulle seventy-eight per cent of the votes.

On January 8, 1959, I went to the Elysée to take office. President René Coty greeted me with dignified gestures and moving words. "The first of Frenchmen," he said, "is now the first man in France." As we drove up the Champs-Elysées later, side by side, to perform the ceremony at the Tomb of the Unknown Soldier, the crowd shouted alternately "Thank you, Coty" and "Vive de Gaulle." On my return, henceforth the prisoner of my high duty, I heard all the doors of the palace closing behind me.

But at the same time I saw the prospect of a great undertaking open up before me. True, by contrast with the task which had fallen to me eighteen years earlier, my mission would be devoid of the stirring imperatives of an heroic period. The peoples of the world, and ours more than most, no longer felt the need to rise above themselves which danger enjoined upon them. For almost all – including ourselves – the immediate issue was not victory or annihilation but living standards. Among the statesmen with whom I would be discussing the problems of the world, most of the giants, whether enemies or allies, whom the war had brought to the fore had disappeared. There remained political leaders who aimed to secure advantages for their own countries, even, of course, at the expense of others, but who were anxious to avoid risks and adventures. In these circumstances, how propitious the age was to all the centrifugal claims of the vested interests of the moment – the parties, the rich, the trade unions, the press – to the utopian illusions of those who would replace our action in the world by international self-effacement, to the corrosive denigration of so many people in business, journalistic, intellectual and social circles now that they were delivered from their terrors! In short, it was in a time which on all sides was drawn towards mediocrity that I must bid for greatness.

And yet it must be done! If France in the depths of her being once more called upon me to serve as her guide, it was surely not, I felt, in order to preside over her sleep. After the terrible decline which she had suffered for more than a hundred years she must use the respite which chance had accorded her to re-establish her power, her wealth and her influence in tune with the spirit of modern times. Failing this, a catastrophe on the scale of the century might one day crush her for ever. The means of this renewal were the State, progress and independence. My duty was thus laid down, for as long as the people were prepared to follow me.

Overseas

෴

On resuming the leadership of France, I was determined to extricate her from the constraints imposed upon her by her empire and no longer offset by any compensating advantages. As can be imagined, I did not undertake it lightly. For a man of my age and upbringing, it was bitterly cruel to become through my own choice the overseer of such a transformation. Not so long ago our country had put forth an immense and glorious effort in order to conquer, administer and develop her overseas dependencies. The colonial epic had been an attempt to compensate for the loss of her distant possessions in the seventeenth and eighteenth centuries and then for her European defeats in 1815 and 1870. She appreciated the world-wide prestige won for her by proconsuls of the stature of Bugeaud, Faidherbe, Archinard, Brazza, Doumer, Gallieni, Ponty, Sarraut, Lyautey. She was conscious of the services rendered in the ranks of her army by several generations of valiant African, Malagasy and Asian contingents, their contribution to our victory in the First World War, and the part played during the Second by our overseas territories, their troops, workers and resources, in the epic of Fighting France. She took pride in the human achievement represented by the basis of modern development laid down in these rough lands as a result of the activities of countless soldiers, administrators, settlers, teachers, missionaries and engineers. What an agonizing ordeal it was to be then for me to hand over our power, furl our flags and close a great chapter of History!

Nevertheless, I could see a gleam of hope piercing the sadness. It was true that in the past the advantages we were able to reap from our colonies had seemed on balance to outweigh the sum total of their cost to us. Having obtained the submission of the native populations in one way or another, what we had to spend to maintain and administer their slow-moving, backward existence was not beyond our means, whereas the fields of opportunity and the extension of power which these possessions offered us were far from negligible. But all this had visibly changed. While progress, there as elsewhere, multiplied needs, we were obliged to bear the increasing costs of administration, public works, education, social services, health and security over vast areas while at the same time we witnessed a growing desire for emancipation which made our yoke seem heavy if not intolerable to our subjects. The more so since, in bringing them our civilization, we had established in each of these territories a centralized system prefiguring 'the nation-State in place of their former anarchic divisions, and trained native elites imbued with our principles of liberty and human rights and eager to replace us from top to bottom of the hierarchy. It should be added that this movement was hastened on by the ostentatious solidarity of the Third World with its unemancipated brethren, and by the propaganda and promises of America, Russia and China, who, though rivals, were all three in search of political and ideological clientships. In short, however much one might regret the fact, the maintenance of our authority over countries no longer willing to accept it was becoming a hazard from which we had everything to lose and nothing to gain.

But did this mean that, in allowing them henceforth to govern themselves, we should "sell out", leave them in the lurch, dismiss them from our sight and from our hearts? Clearly not. Because of their long connection with us and the magnetic attraction exercised by the angels and demons of France upon them as upon all who come into contact with her, they were disposed to maintain close links with us. Conversely, what we had already contributed towards their progress, the friendships, habits and interests resulting therefrom, and our immemorial vocation for influence and expansion, committed us to seeing them as privileged partners. If they were to speak our language and share our culture, we must help them to do so. If their raw administrations, their nascent economies, their unorganized finances, their tentative diplomacies, their rudimentary defenses, required our help to put them on their feet, we must supply it. In short, to lead the peoples of "Overseas France" to self-determination and at the same time to organize direct co-operation between them and us – these were my simple and straightforward aims.

But the realities of the situation in the territories concerned were nothing if not diverse. Some, having for long – sometimes for centuries – been merged with France, would doubtless wish to remain so, either as *départements* – Martinique, Guadeloupe, Guiana, Réunion – or with a status of internal autonomy – Saint-Pierre-et-Miquelon, French Somaliland, the Comoro Archipelago, New Caledonia, Polynesia, Wallis and Futuna. For them it was simply a question of providing an opportunity of making a choice under the terms of the new Constitution. In Black Africa, which was characterized by an extreme variety of regions, tribes and dialects, the administrative entities which we ourselves had created – Senegal, Sudan, Guinea, Mauritania, Dahomey, the Ivory Coast, Upper Volta, Niger, Congo, Chad, Ubangi and Gabon – would provide a natural framework for future States. Here, there was no doubt that, prompted by their élites, the people would opt for independence. The question was whether they would do so in agreement with us, or without us, or even against us. A considerable proportion of the more advanced elements, indoctrinated to a greater or lesser extent by totalitarian blandishments, visualized emancipation not as the final stage in an evolutionary process but as a defeat inflicted on the colonizers by the colonized. That was the only sort of independence they cared about. Nevertheless, there was reason to believe that, when it came to the point, reason and sentiment would persuade most of the leaders to maintain firm links with France. It was for this, at the outset, that the Community would provide, although later it was to evolve into a series of contractual agreements.

On the other hand, Madagascar, in former times a State with its people, its language, its traditions, would certainly prefer to deal with us. Two more territories, Togoland and Cameroon placed under our tutelage by the United Nations, would wish to be released from it but would almost certainly ask for our continued aid. As for our Protectorates, whose independence had been recognized in principle – Morocco under its king and Tunisia as a republic – it was simply a question of restoring complete sovereignty to them. This I was determined to do, assuming incidentally that they would wish to remain linked with us in spirit and in practice. This was already the case with the kingdoms of Laos and Cambodia, over which we no longer held suzerainty but where I intended to maintain France's special position. And it would perhaps be the case – I proposed to work towards this end – with North and South Vietnam, whenever that country, already sorely tried and about to be terribly decimated and ravaged, emerged from its misfortunes.

Provided that we respected their emergent or reconstituted nationhoods, that we were careful not to exploit the troubles which could not fail to beset them, that we furnished them with all the reasonable support which they required, there was a chance that a vast complex, based on friendship and co-operation, might form itself round us. I wanted to seize this opportunity for France, putting aside all regrets for the past, overcoming all prejudices, remoulding our relationships with our former subjects who would now become our partners.

But what of Algeria? There we were faced, not with a situation to be settled by amicable agreement, but with full-scale tragedy; a French tragedy as much as a local one. Algeria assumed an importance in our national life beyond comparison with that of any other of our dependencies. We had conquered it, after the long and somber episodes of the Berber era, at the cost of an enormous military effort in which both sides had fought bravely and suffered heavy losses. Even then we had had to suppress many subsequent revolts. Thus we were all the more gratified to have become the masters of a land which had cost us so dear. Moreover, thanks to Algeria, our position in Africa and the Mediterranean was powerfully reinforced. It had served as a base from which to launch our penetration of Tunisia, Morocco and the Sahara. More recently, in addition to recruiting once again a number of excellent *tirailleurs* from its inhabitants, we had formed our Liberation Government there and, with our allies, mustered a considerable proportion of the means of our victory. The million Frenchmen who had settled there had achieved a remarkable economic development of the country thanks to their own abilities, the help of capital from metropolitan France, and the support of the administration, while a magnificent infrastructure had been created by French money, French technology and local labor. And now we had found deposits of oil and natural gas which could make good our grave deficiency in sources of energy. For a variety of reasons, therefore, the French people were inclined to regard the possession of Algeria as valuable and, moreover, well-earned. True, it was not without uneasiness and some impatience that they endured the costly struggle that was being waged there, and if they had condemned the Fourth Republic, it was above all because it had failed to extricate them from it. But they thought that de Gaulle, now that he was at the helm, would find some means of ending it at the minimum cost.

For the settlers, the maintenance of the *status quo* seemed vital, whatever the cost to France. Living in the midst of an Arab and Kabyle population which outnumbered them by ten to one and was increasing at a faster rate, they were haunted by the fear that if France ceased to govern, to administer, to repress, they themselves would be ineluctably submerged, dispossessed, driven out. Moreover, their own society and that of the Moslems, though juxtaposed, remained in practice totally estranged from one another. Those who called themselves *pieds-noirs*, born or brought up in a conquered land, proud of what they had achieved – not without risk and by dint of their own efforts; secure in their privileges of status, education, employment and wealth; in possession of all the most important agricultural, industrial and commercial enterprises, monopolizing almost entirely the higher echelons in every field, including the liberal professions, naturally supported by the civil service; and confident that in any case the Army would once again restore order for their benefit, had always held themselves above and apart from the more or less submissive masses who surrounded them. Any reform tending towards equality between the two categories of citizen seemed to them a grave threat. In their eyes, the only conceivable outcome of the tragedy for which Algeria had now been the stage for several years was the crushing of the insurrection and the maintenance of what they called "French Algeria", that is, the confirmation of our direct authority and their own supremacy. It was for fear of being abandoned that they had supported the May 13 movement against the previous regime. It was in order to alter the semblance of French domination without modifying it in reality that they now affected to favor integration. In fact they saw it as a means of warding off the evolution towards equality of rights and Algerian autonomy, of not only avoiding being engulfed by ten million Moslems but of submerging them instead among fifty million Frenchmen. In this way, encouraged by long experience, they thought that with a firm Governor-General, reliable prefects and above all the presence of powerful police and security forces, their situation would remain unchanged. This was what they expected and would if necessary demand from General de Gaulle, believing him to be a strong man but incapable of conceiving that he could be strong in a cause other than their own.

Their intransigence was matched by that of the now determined and in some cases armed Moslems. After long years of resignation, punctuated by periodic outbreaks of rebellion, years during which notables concerned about their property or hankering after jobs and honors, ex-servicemen loyal to the brotherhood of arms, and a few people with careers in the public service or politics had given the French their more or less sincere support; years during which they had cherished and then lost one illusion after another as regards their acquisition of full civil rights and an autonomous status for Algeria, the Moslems as a whole were now sympathetic to the National Liberation Front[1] and the insurrection, even if they did not take part in it. Moreover they were well aware that if the plight of their fathers had left the world indifferent, there was now a vast wave of sympathy and sometimes active support for their cause abroad. This was the case with their neighbors in North Africa and the other Arab countries. But elsewhere, too, there was a considerable body of opinion in their favor which was regularly expressed in the United Nations Assembly. Furthermore, since the French Republic had renounced its sovereignty in Indo-China in 1954, since parliament had passed an outline law[2] in 1956 granting wide autonomy including autochthonous councils of government and elected assemblies to every territory in Black Africa as well as to Madagascar, and since Tunisia and Morocco had finally been emancipated from Paris in 1957, the Algerians were confident that in the long run, provided they themselves opened the breach, their independence was a foregone conclusion.

Nevertheless, while some suffered agonies in the *djebels*[3] where they lay in ambush, and others all manner of indignities in the towns and villages where they were kept under surveillance, and while they cursed those Frenchmen who aimed to keep them under the yoke, they did not despair of France. Differentiating between the latter and the former, they still, in spite of everything, felt an attachment for a nation naturally humane and historically generous, and hoped to remain associated with it once they were liberated. This feeling was evident in the lack of hatred as a rule displayed in their attitude towards our officers – humane, straightforward men – and our soldiers – upright and disinterested youths. And now the advent of General de Gaulle, whom they too were prepared to regard as the symbol of a France haloed by their hopes, seemed to presage

[1] *Front de libération national* (FLN).
[2] *Loi-cadre.*
[3] Mountains.

43

a new era. Scarcely had Salan and others publicly cried "Vive de Gaulle!" than Moslems everywhere joined in demonstrations with the French, something they had never done spontaneously, not even the day before.

The Army, for its part, and especially the generals and senior officers, expected much from my return. For, at grips with the rebellion, their constant preoccupation had been to avoid a political stab in the back. They dreaded the collapse of governmental authority, pressure from foreign powers, a mood of abdication on the part of a public weary of the military and financial commitment and shocked by deplorable incidents during the repression which were exploited in certain circles – all of which threatened to undermine military operations in the field and ultimately to cause some grave reverse. The restoration of national authority, they felt, would give them the time and the means to win the war and would discourage the enemy. As for the political solution which was to crown their victory, broadly speaking they conceived it as a new winning-over of Algeria to France, with a vast program of economic, social and educational development on the part of the mother country by way of compensation. What it saw for itself on the spot inspired the Army with sympathy for the sufferings and miseries of the people and a fierce resentment against a colonial regime which left them so destitute. But above all, whatever the personal calculations of certain of its leaders and the mischief fomented in its midst by a small batch of fantasy-spinning and ambitious officers, the army was conscious of the need to be commanded by the State. Hence, for the moment, it was thankful to see me govern France and to entrust me with the Algerian question.

From the moment I took the helm, I was up to the eyes in the problem. Needless to say, I approached it with no strictly predetermined plan. The facts I had to go on were too varied, too complex, too shifting for me to be able to decide in advance on the precise details, the phasing and the timing of the solution. In particular, how was one to discover at that time which Algerians could or would fall in with it when it came to the point? But the main outlines were clear in my mind. Indeed, as early as June 30, 1955, when the insurrection was at its height, I had said at a press conference in reply to questions on the subject: "No other policy but one which aims at replacing domination by association in French North Africa can be valid or worthy of France."

In the first place, I excluded from the realm of possibility all idea of the assimilation of the Moslems into the French population. Perhaps this might have been conceivable a hundred years earlier, provided it had then been possible to transplant several million Frenchmen to Algeria and an equal number of Algerian immigrants to France; all the inhabitants of the combined nation thus enjoying the same laws and the same rights. Perhaps it might still have been attempted after the First World War, in the proud flush of victory. Perhaps, after the Second, in the spirit of the Liberation, the gradual establishment of an autonomous Algeria evolving of its own accord into a State attached to France by federal ties, a solution adumbrated by the still-born Statute of 1947, might have been feasible. Now it was too late for any form of subjection. The Moslem community, by reason of its ethnic origins, its religion, its way of life, and because it had for so long been treated as inferior, held at a distance, fought against, had developed too powerful and too prickly a personality to allow itself to be dispersed or dominated, especially at a time when, all over the world, people were taking their destiny into their own hands. Integration, then, was in my view no more than an ingenious and empty formula. But could I, on the other hand, contemplate prolonging the *status quo?* No! For that would be to keep France politically, financially and militarily bogged down in a bottomless quagmire when, in fact, she needed her hands free to bring about the domestic transformation necessitated by the twentieth century and to exercise her influence abroad unencumbered. At the same time, it would condemn our forces to a futile and interminable task of colonial repression, when the future of the country demanded an Army geared to the exigencies of modern power. On the essential point, therefore, my mind was made up. Whatever the dreams

45

of the past or the regrets of today, whatever I myself had undoubtedly hoped for at other times, there was in my view no longer any alternative for Algeria but self-determination.

But having decided to accord her this right, I would do so only on certain conditions. First of all it must be France, eternal France, who alone, from the height of her power, in the name of her principles and in accordance with her interests, granted it to the Algerians. There could be no question of her being compelled to do so by military setbacks, or prevailed upon to do so by foreign intervention, or induced to do so by partisan and parliamentary agitation. We would, therefore, put forth the effort required to make ourselves masters of the battlefield. We would pay no attention to any overtures from any capital, to any offer of "good offices", to any threat of "agonizing reappraisal" in our foreign relations, to any debate in the United Nations. When the moment came, it would not be some fortuitous assembly of deputies but all our people who would vote the necessary changes. Furthermore, should it prove desirable, particularly for Algeria itself, that some Frenchmen should remain there, it would be for each of them to decide individually, our army guaranteeing their freedom and security until they had chosen one way or the other where they would settle. Finally, for the mutual advantage of France and Algeria, treaties would have to be drawn up between them providing for preferential relations, notably as regards civic status, trade, cultural agreements, and the exploitation of Saharan oil and gas. Believing as I did that the "French Algeria" for which I heard people clamoring in the early days of my administration was a ruinous Utopia, I nevertheless hoped to ensure that, in the sense in which France had always remained in some degree Roman ever since the days of Gaul, the Algeria of the future, by virtue of the impress which she had received and would wish to preserve, would in many respects remain French.

Such was my strategy for the realization of this policy. As for my tactics, I should have to proceed cautiously from one stage to the next. Only gradually, using each crisis as a springboard for further advance, could I hope to create a current of consent powerful enough to carry all before it. Were I to announce my intentions point-blank, there was no doubt that the sea of ignorant fear, of shocked surprise, of concerted malevolence through which I was navigating would cause such a tidal wave of alarms and passions in every walk of life that the ship would capsize. I must, therefore, maneuver without ever changing course until such time as, unmistakably, common sense broke through the mists.

On June 4, almost as soon as I had come to power, I flew to Algiers. I was accompanied by three ministers, Louis Jacquinot, Pierre Guillaumat and Max Lejeune, by General Ely, whom I had reinstated as Chief of General Staff, and by René Brouillet, my special adviser for Algerian affairs. General Salan, surrounded by the principal civil and military leaders, welcomed me at Maison-Blanche airport. As I drove through the city I was greeted with frenzied cheers all along the route. At the Summer Palace, the representatives of the various corporate bodies and public authorities were presented to me in accordance with tradition and I listened to an address from the Committee of Public Safety which was read to me by General Massu. Then I went to the Admiralty to greet the Navy. At about seven in the evening I arrived in the Forum.

When I appeared on the balcony of the *Gouvernement-Général* an unbelievable surge of cheering rose up from the vast crowd gathered in the square. Then in a short speech I tossed them the words, seemingly spontaneous but in reality carefully calculated, which I hoped would fire their enthusiasm without committing me further than I was willing to go. Having shouted "I have understood you!" in order to establish emotional contact, I evoked the May 13 movement, to which I attributed two of the noblest motives: renovation and fraternity. I took cognizance thereof, and declared that France would accordingly grant equality of rights to all Algerians irrespective of their community. Thus, the differences in civic status and the separate electoral colleges were swept away at a single blow, so that within a stated period the Moslem majority would at any rate be able to make itself felt as such. Thus the necessity was affirmed to "open doors which have hitherto been closed to many . . . to give the means of livelihood to those who have lacked them . . . to recognize the dignity of those who have been deprived of it . . . to guarantee a motherland to those who may have doubted that they had one." In the reconciliation between the two communities, of which Algiers that evening was setting the example, I called for the participation of "all the inhabitants of the towns, the *douars*,[1] the plains and the *djebels*, and even those who, through despair, have felt it their duty to wage upon this soil a struggle which is undoubtedly cruel and fratricidal but whose courage I recognize. Yes! I, de Gaulle, open the doors of reconciliation to them too!" Meanwhile I did not neglect to confer upon the Army, "which is carrying out a magnificent task of understanding and pacification," a public token of my confidence.

A frenzied ovation greeted my words. Yet the prospect which they opened up by no means gratified the desires of the mass – three-quarters French – of my listeners in the Forum. But a wind had stirred to which, momentarily, no one offered any resistance. All realized that this time it was France herself who spoke, with all her authority and generosity. All saw that, after the great convulsion we had just come through, the State had risen to assert itself. All felt that, whatever happened, de Gaulle had the duty and the right to solve the problem. In Constantine, where the audience was principally Moslem, in Oran, where the French were largely predominant, in Mostaganem, where the two communities were evenly balanced, my message was the same: no more discrimination between Algerians no matter who they were! This was tantamount to saying that the day would come when the majority amongst them could decide the destiny of all. It was by this means that Algeria would remain in her own way French, and not by virtue of a law imposed upon her by force.

Independently of these encounters with the masses, the immediate facts of the Algerian situation were outlined to me by the many notables and delegations I received. If the

[1] Arab encampment of tents.

Algerians of French stock were, as a group, Frenchmen first and foremost who, while prepared to influence, not to say coerce, the mother country, would not in fact tolerate being separated from it, they were nonetheless highly susceptible to the intrigues of their activists. The latter, though apparently split into disparate and often rival groups, seemed to be exploiting the prevalent anxiety and unrest for political ends which went beyond the boundaries of Algeria. Taking advantage of the violent agitation which they excelled at fomenting among these excitable Mediterranean crowds, they organized networks and commando units which could lead to subversion not only on the spot but also farther afield. Not surprisingly they found some sympathizers in the Army, theorists of direct action leading to the seizure of power, if necessary through intermediaries. Needless to say, these trouble-makers were in touch with similar elements in metropolitan France. Meanwhile, several incidents revealed to me their methods and intentions. For instance at the Forum, the ministers Jacquinot and Lejeune were secretly locked in an office to prevent them from appearing on the balcony. Again, during my speech in Oran, in the midst of the applause and the shouts of "Vive de Gaulle!", claques here and there in the audience raised loud, rhythmic chants of "The Army to power!" and "Soustelle! Soustelle!" to the point where I had to interrupt my speech to order them to be quiet. Yet again, as I was giving an audience to the executive of the Committee of Public Safety before leaving for Paris, some of its members vehemently adjured me to proclaim "integration" and held out the threat of a riot, which led me to inform them that, in that eventuality, they would go straight to gaol.

The Moslems, whether assembled to hear me speak or encountered individually, made no secret of the respect and the hope my person inspired in them, but remained very guarded on the basic question. It was clear that, apart from a few whose devotion was sincere and moving, and excluding those whose official position or electoral mandate outwardly ranged them with the loyalists, the decision they had collectively taken was: hold out and never surrender.

As for the Army, after the turmoil into which it had been plunged, my arrival on the spot restored it to normal. Receiving reports from the local commanders wherever I went, invariably calling the officers and often the NCOs together in order to say a few words to them and question several of their number, I had no difficulty in discovering what they were thinking. By and large, this great body of men, by nature concerned with the short run rather than the long, clung to the idea that France should keep possession of Algeria, symbol of her ancient power, a land impregnated with glorious memories. Beneath the uniformity of the military attitude, however, I discerned three different tendencies among my interlocutors. For some, "French Algeria" was a veritable mystique. Taking the wish for the deed, these men were convinced that they had only to will it and assert it for their solution to become a reality and for the population to "swing" in the direction they desired. For others, in whom the trust they reposed in me was paramount, it was simply a matter of following me now as in the past. For others, finally, and these were no doubt the majority, now that the country had a government which could be called a government and was prepared to govern, it was for it to decide, and for the Army, no matter what the feeling in its ranks, to obey. The conclusion I drew was that, in the last analysis, this was what it would do.

In the meantime, the military situation gave the Army no cause for anxiety. In particular, the protection of civilian lives and property was assured as efficiently as possible by the five hundred thousand men it maintained in Algeria. Its combat forces – Foreign Legion paratroops, armored units, *tirailleurs*, commandos – composed mainly of volunteers and stoutly led, periodically mounted offensives against the *fellaghas*[1] in one or other of the mountain or forest areas where they were entrenched, employing large-scale artillery barrages and aerial bombing. The engagements were often fierce and prolonged, owing to the difficulty of the terrain and the stubbornness of the adversary. Most of the other units, largely composed of national

[1] Algerian guerrillas.

servicemen, protected centers of population, lines of communication, strategic points, ports and airdromes; escorted convoys combed suspected areas, or seconded police operations. "Barrages", consisting of defense-works covered with mines, obstacles, barbed-wire entanglements, were established and permanently manned along the frontiers with Tunisia and Morocco – thanks to which the rebel forces who had taken refuge with their neighbors were prevented from infiltrating into Algeria until we ourselves freely allowed them back after peace had been concluded. The Air Force carried out unremitting reconnaissance and ground support, patrolled the territory and provided transport and liaison facilities. The Navy prevented the landing of arms and reinforcements for the rebels by the constant vigilance of its escort and patrol vessels. In addition to their operational missions, our forces lent their men and their resources to a variety of economic, social, educational and medical tasks on behalf of the population. On this vast apparatus, effective in preventing the situation from worsening but incapable of solving the insoluble, a wealth of ingenuity, conscientiousness and patience was expended.

As a result of these unsparing efforts, life went on in Algeria. Although in certain mountainous areas – the Aurès, the Nementchas, the Hodna, the Bibans, the Ouarsenis, the Dahra, the Daia and Tlemcen mountains, the Saharan Atlas, etc. – pockets of insurrection were continually re-forming as soon as they were dispersed; although from these bases innumerable attacks and depredations were carried out by guerrilla bands; although the resistance, whether active or passive, enjoyed everywhere the support and subsidies of the population, the fact was that over by far the greater part of the territory shooting was rare, in the countryside as a whole it was only by night that it was dangerous to go out, and in the towns, thanks to the curfew, there was no fighting apart from isolated incidents. Moreover, those of the *fellaghas* who were organized in regular formations, and whose number at no time exceeded thirty thousand, had the greatest difficulty in arming themselves with rifles, grenades and occasionally machine-guns and mortars, and did not have a single piece of artillery, a single tank or a single aircraft at their disposal. Thus the fields were cultivated. Transport and communications functioned normally. Offices remained open. Schools were full of children. Shops served their customers. Farmers, workers, dockers, miners, clerks, officials, all went about their daily tasks. Out of a million and a half people of French stock, civilians and servicemen, then on Algerian soil, of whom an average of seventy died each day, ten at the most were killed as a result of the insurrection. In Algeria there was not, nor ever would be, a general uprising.

General Salan, as Commander-in-Chief and acting head of the civil authority, accompanied me on my tour of inspection. As a career soldier, he was naturally well-informed on service matters, and by virtue of his experience as well as natural inclination completely at home amid the complex of intelligence activities, secret contacts with the enemy, decoy operations to hoodwink them and traps set for their leaders, which are the traditional adjuncts of colonial expeditions. As for the military operations themselves, spread out as they were over different zones, he was only too glad to leave the conduct of them to the Army corps commanders. He was naturally less at home in the field of civil administration, the management of the economy and the control of finance; but in dealing with them he had the assistance of a team of officials thoroughly experienced in local affairs. It was above all the political side of his task which absorbed him, meddling and maneuvering among the eddies and currents which stirred the Algerians of French stock, and endeavoring to penetrate and influence the movements of opinion in Moslem circles. Naturally greatly affected by what had taken place in Paris, he seemed to feel a mixture of relief at having been saved from the unknown and regret at not having succumbed. However, he observed towards me an attitude of discipline which appeared genuine, and offered no objection to the hints I gave him of my intentions regarding Algeria, which, I was sure, in no way conformed to his views. In short, there was something slippery and inscrutable in the character of this capable, clever and in some respects beguiling figure which seemed to me to accord ill with the certitude and rectitude demanded by a high and honorable responsibility. But, already, I was thinking of finding him another job before long.

I returned to Paris on June 7. The following week saw the implementation of the agreements with Tunisia and Morocco which I had proposed to their Heads of State on the 3rd and under which our troops were withdrawn from their territories, with the exception of Bizerta in the former and Meknes, Port-Lyautey, Marrakesh and Agadir in the latter. At the beginning of July I returned to Algeria accompanied by Pierre Guillaumat and also Guy Mollet. The latter had gone there as Prime Minister in 1956 and his presence had raised such a storm of threats from the *pieds-noirs* that he had been forced to recall his Minister for Algeria, General Catroux, appointed only a week before. Now, in spite of some booing in Algiers which he stood up to gallantly, he took part in my tour, which was mainly devoted to military outposts, without mishap. After these two visits I was to return to Algeria on six further occasions up to December 1960, traversing the entire country several times. What Head of State or Government had done as much since 1830, although few of them had been septuagenarians? But in order to reach a decision, there too, there above all, I had to see and hear, be seen and heard.

It was for this reason that, in August, I betook myself to Black Africa. Pierre Pflimlin, Minister of State, Bernard Cornut-Gentille, Minister for Overseas France, and Jacques Foccart, my special adviser for African and Malagasy affairs, flew with me. My purpose was to explain to our territories the significance of the forthcoming referendum; to emphasize that to vote "Yes" meant sovereignty combined with continued association with metropolitan France, and to vote "No" meant to break off all ties. It was inevitable that the impression my visit made and the speeches I delivered would have a powerful influence on the attitude of the educated minority and the reaction of the masses, and consequently on the result.

Having stopped off on August 21 at Fort-Lamy, where President Toura Gaba promised me that yet again Chad would follow me without question, I proceeded to Madagascar. Philibert Tsiranana, the head of the Council of Government, was there to welcome me with Jean Soucadaux, the High Commissioner, at his side. What emerged from our conversations, as well as from the applause in the representative Assembly which I addressed beforehand, was that there was every chance that the response of the great island would be affirmative. But the fervor of the multitude gathered in the stadium in Tananarive to listen to me was enough to convince me finally. A storm of cheering broke out when, pointing to the historic royal residence, last inhabited by Queen Ranavalo, on the neighboring hill, I declared: "Tomorrow you will be a State once again, as you were when the palace of your kings up there was inhabited by them!"

It was Brazzaville's turn to welcome me next. Whether in the seething suburbs of Bas-Congo and Potopoto, in the beflagged streets of the city center, or around Government House where the notables came to me, in front of the Case de Gaulle where I stayed, or in the Eboué Stadium near the Cathedral of St Anne where I delivered my speech, the entire capital was delirious with enthusiasm. Nevertheless, political circles in the Federation were not entirely convinced. While the Abbé Fulbert Youlou, the mayor of Brazzaville, and his friends had already decided to vote "Yes", Barthélemy Boganda, President of the Grand Council of Equatorial Africa, was making a show of reluctance. But, according to the High Commissioner, Yvon Bourges, there was no doubt which way the territories would go. In the end Boganda, who was the hero and guide of Ubangi, and Léon M'Ba, the ruler of Gabon, confirmed this to me just before my departure, each speaking in the name of his country and with the same warmth as I had encountered in the Congo.

Then on to Abidjan. There, too, the welcome was magnificent, under the aegis of President Houphouët-Boigny with the rousing support of the entire population. For this country, like the man who led it, had no hesitations, as it demonstrated to me when I spoke to a vast audience in the Géo André Stadium. But if, thanks to its leader, the Ivory Coast was on the right road, and if the same was true of Upper Volta and Dahomey, governed respectively by Ouezzin-Coulibali and Sourou-Migan Apithy, while the Mauritanian vote under the guidance of Moktar Ould Daddah was certain to be favorable, the High Commissioner, Pierre Messmer, informed me that in the rest of West Africa the outcome was highly uncertain. No doubt the *Rassemblement démocratique africain,* which was the dominant if not the only party in the various territories – with the exception of Senegal – would incline on the whole towards voting "Yes." But there was a distinct risk of a reverse trend in those places where the Head of Government, with a politically active entourage and intent on playing the champion of orthodox Marxism and anti-imperialism, was preparing to flaunt a "No" which would be tantamount to a ukase.

This was the case in Guinea – as the young, brilliant and ambitious Sekou Touré made me well aware. No sooner had I landed at Conakry airport than I found myself surrounded by the trappings of a totalitarian republic. There was nothing insulting or hostile to me personally, but from the airport to the center of the town the crowd, evenly distributed in well-drilled battalions along both sides of the road, obeyed as one man the orders of its leaders, shouted with one voice "Independence!" and waved innumerable banners inscribed with that one word. The women were lined up in front in their hundreds, each group wearing dresses of the same cut and color, and all, as the procession passed by, jumping, dancing and singing to order.

The "working session" took place in the territorial Assembly where the Premier had assembled his militants. In a peremptory tone he delivered for my benefit a speech which was tailored for propaganda purposes and punctuated with rhythmic outbursts of cheers and applause. The gist of it was that Guinea, hitherto oppressed and exploited by France, would refuse any solution other than independence pure and simple. I replied calmly and bluntly that France had done much for Guinea and that one obvious sign of this was the fact that the orator I had just heard had spoken in excellent French; that she was proposing a Community of self-governing nations based on mutual co-operation

55

and that, despite her already heavy commitments, she would provide aid to those who became members of it; that Guinea was completely free to vote "Yes" or "No"; that if she voted "No" it would mean severance; that France would certainly put no obstacles in her way, but that naturally she would draw her own conclusions.

In the course of the meeting I had afterwards with Sekou Touré and during the reception which I gave in Government House, I took the opportunity of re-stating the position. "Make no mistake," I told him. "The French Republic you are dealing with is no longer the one you knew, which preferred expediency to decision. For the France of today, colonialism is finished. She is, therefore, indifferent to your retrospective reproaches. Henceforth, she is willing to lend her support to the State which you are about to become. But she is perfectly prepared to be relieved of it. She lived for a long time without Guinea. She will live for an equally long time if she is severed from her. In that event, it goes without saying that we shall immediately withdraw our administrative, technical and educational assistance and cease to subsidize your budget. I must make it quite clear to you that in view of the ties which have united our two countries, a formal 'No' in response to the interdependence which France offers you will mean that relations between us will lose their friendly and preferential character among the countries of the world." Next day, returning to the airport by the same route as before, I did not see a living soul. The same enforced discipline which yesterday had peopled it with a dense crowd had today emptied it completely. Thus I was in no further doubt as to what would emerge from the ballot-boxes. To Sekou Touré, who came to see me off, I said: "Good-bye, Guinea!"

The atmosphere in Dakar was tense. The Premier, Mamadou Dia, and a number of politicians failed to turn up to welcome me. The crowds which thronged the route from one end of the town to the other were dotted with angry, vociferous groups. Lamine-Gueye, the mayor, who was at my side, was shattered and appalled. On the Place Protêt where I was to speak, there was a waving mass of banners and placards and fierce shouting in support of independence. Promptly taking the bull by the horns, I addressed the shouting, jostling crowd below me as follows: "First of all, a word to the placard-bearers! If they want their own brand of independence, let them take it on September 28! But if they don't take it, then let them do what France is proposing: create a Franco-African Community! Let them do it in complete independence, independence for Africa, independence for France! Let them do it with me, for better or for worse! Let them do it on the terms which I have outlined unequivocally, in particular the other day in Brazzaville, terms whose sincerity I will not allow to be questioned! We live in an age of efficiency, that is, an age of organized groupings. We do not live in an age of demagogy. Let the demagogues go back where they came from, where they are awaited!" As I spoke, the banners were furled and the shouts died down. When I went on to expatiate on the subject of Franco-African co-operation as it would be inaugurated by the new Constitution, I was widely applauded. Leaving the rostrum, I saw the faces of the delegates and officials lit up with optimistic smiles.

In fact, after my departure, the Senegalese political groups, which had at first been strongly opposed to the project, nearly all came round to it. At the same time the affirmative vote of the Sudan seemed assured, in spite of the reservations of its political guide Madeira Keita. Lastly, in Niger, where Djibo Bakari, the head of the government, in collusion with Sekou Touré, wanted to inveigle the masses into voting "No" but had failed to secure dictatorial powers in time, a vigorous swing in public opinion left him out on a limb. Soon afterwards, he was forced to flee to Ghana, and Hamani Diori took over the leadership of the country.

Returning to Paris on August 29 after another visit to Algiers, I concluded from my journey that with the sole exception – would it be permanent? – of Guinea, all our colonies in Black Africa, together with Madagascar, were determined to remain linked to France while at the same time becoming their own masters. But I could also see that it was high time we set them upon the road; that to refuse or even to postpone this step would be to invite serious clashes; that, on the other hand, in taking it we would be inaugurating a fruitful and exemplary undertaking.

The constitutional referendum, a triumph in metropolitan France, was even more so overseas. Guinea apart, all the Black African territories and Madagascar voted "Yes" with majorities in excess of ninety-five per cent. In December, the same figures were recorded for my own election as President of the Community.

In Algeria, the issue was naturally not the same. For as things still stood there could be no question of the referendum establishing self-determination. Nevertheless, without prejudice to the ultimate status of Algeria, it was a splendid opportunity to introduce a single electoral college there, to give the vote to women as well as men for the first time and to provide the Moslems with a chance of showing, without compromising themselves, that they had no desire to break with France and were confident of General de Gaulle's intentions. In spite of the orders to abstain issued by the Front, the fact was that out of four and a half million registered voters three and a half million took part in the ballot; that the "Noes" were infinitesimal in number; that although in the villages the authorities used their influence to see that people went to the polls, such pressure could have played no part in the big urban centers, where the percentages were nevertheless the same as in the countryside; and lastly, that the Electoral Control Commission – set up for the occasion under the high-principled chairmanship of the former French ambassador to the United Nations, Henri Hoppenot, composed of individuals chosen for their impartiality and with inspectors stationed in every sector – reported that the flow of Moslem voters to the polling stations was general, that everywhere they voted freely and often, in doing so, said "It's for de Gaulle!" The parliamentary elections in November, despite a lower poll and the fact that there were no candidates from the Front and, consequently, none elected, provided similar evidence.

However, I had not waited for these election results in Algeria, or for the manifold interpretations to which they inevitably gave rise, before pushing matters forward as far as present circumstances would allow. My immediate objectives were first, to bring Algiers completely under the authority of Paris, secondly, to show the rebels that France was aiming at peace, a peace which she would ultimately wish to conclude with them and which she counted on to preserve her ties with Algeria, and thirdly, to reinforce our military presence in such a way that nothing that happened in the field would interfere with our decisions.

In order that the authority of the State should be exercised in an orderly way, everything of importance connected with Algeria was dealt with under my chairmanship by a special Cabinet committee consisting of the ministers, including, of course, the Minister, the senior officials and the generals directly concerned, with René Brouillet, and later Roger Moris, in the co-ordinating role of Secretary-General. The measures I was to adopt were, therefore, decided on in the light of full background knowledge.

It was thus that the sort of parallel government which the Algiers Committee of Public Safety had presumed to exercise locally since May 13 disappeared from the scene. In July, this Committee having declared itself opposed to the projected municipal elections – which were indeed expressly designed to put an end to its interference in municipal affairs – and Salan having not only sanctioned this but even forwarded me the text of the Committee's proclamations, I publicly called the Delegate-General to account and let it be known that since the areopagus of May 13 had no right to exercise any authority, its motions had no validity, neither legal nor administrative. Passing through Algiers in August, I refused to meet a delegation from the Committee. In October I ordained that all officers and officials should cease to be members of it. They withdrew at once. Overnight, the Committee and its offshoots lost the semblance of official authority which they had arrogated to themselves. In December, General Salan was recalled to France and appointed Inspector-General of the Armed Forces. In January, that post having been abolished, he became military governor of Paris. Paul Delouvrier replaced him as Delegate-General, and General Challe as Commander-in-Chief. These appointments put an end to the confusion of civil and military authority, and by restoring the primacy of the former, re-established the prefects in their functions.

Nor did I lose any time before making it known to the political leadership of the insurrection that the road to negotiation would be open as soon as they acknowledged the necessity of that course. As early as June 12, I had summoned Abderrahmane Farès, president of the defunct Algerian Assembly, who had not declared himself publicly but was known to have kept in touch with Ferhat Abbas, president of the committee which was soon to call itself the Provisional Government of the Algerian Republic.[1] I proposed there and then to Farès that he should enter my government as Minister of State. He would be there to participate in measures relating to the fate of Algeria, just as Houphouët-Boigny was there to advise on matters concerned with the future of Black Africa. As I expected, Farès reserved his answer "until he had consulted certain persons." Accordingly, he went to Switzerland with my approval and returned a fortnight later. He then told me that although he was greatly honored by my offer, he was unable to accept it. He also put forward certain views, making no secret of the fact that they were those of his friends abroad, the gist of which was that negotiations could one day be entered into on the question of the political and military conditions for a cease-fire, without a prior recognition of Algeria's independence but on the understanding that that would be the ultimate objective. Shortly afterwards, I saw Farès again. "I should like you to know," I told him, "that if the occasion arises we are prepared to talk about everything. But first of all we must talk. Therefore, if ever someone qualified to do so were to come to France, he would find all the discretion and protection he required." At that time

[1] *Gouvernement provisoire de la république algérienne* (GPRA).

there was no further communication from either side. But is a good action ever wasted?

Perhaps the proposal for "a soldiers' peace"[1] which I put forward with full publicity during a press conference on October 23, would not be wasted either. I suggested that this could be done either by local cease-fires arranged between the combatants, or by an agreement negotiated between the French government and the "external organization" which directed the rebellion. It is true that the "Provisional Algerian Government", whose internal dissensions at the time precluded any other attitude but passive intransigence, greeted my offer with a blank refusal. But this conciliatory proposal on the part of France left a deep impression on people's minds.

The same had been true of the Constantine Plan, announced a few days earlier. This title covered a series of development measures which, taken together, were infinitely more far-reaching than anything that had yet been done at one blow. After detailed studies carried out on the basis of a report drawn up by the Councillor of State, Roland Maspetiol, the government had taken the necessary decisions and set aside the necessary credits in order to bring about a total transformation in the living conditions of the Algerian Moslems within five years.

On the economic and social plane, specific targets were laid down for the industrial and agricultural expansion of Algeria during those five years: the distribution of Saharan gas over the entire country and, using this means of power, the establishment of large combines, whether chemical, as at Awzew, or metallurgical, such as the iron and steel works at Bône; the provision of roads, ports, telecommunications, hospitals; the re-housing of a million people; the allocation of two hundred and fifty thousand hectares of cultivable land to Moslem farmers; the creation of four hundred thousand new jobs. In the field of education, elementary schooling would be extended to two-thirds of the boys and girls of Algeria over the same period, and made universal by the end of the following three years. In the public

[1] *La paix des braves.*

service in metropolitan France, it would be obligatory for one out of every ten young people entering the administration, the judiciary, the Army, the teaching profession, the public utility services, to be Arab or Kabyle and, in Algeria itself, there would be a notable increase in the proportion of Moslems employed in these branches. In order that the Plan should acquire a meaningful name, it was in Constantine, in the Place de la Brèche, that I announced these measures to the general public, emphasizing that they would be the fruit of co-operation between metropolitan France and Algeria. Speaking of the future, I declared that "it cannot be determined in advance and on paper", but that, in any event, "Algeria's future will be built on twin pillars: her own personality and her close solidarity with France."

No sooner was the Plan announced than it was put into general execution, under the active direction of Delouvrier. I followed its progress attentively. In December, I visited the oil installations at Edjelé and Hassi-Messaoud and saw how the construction of the pipeline to Bougie was progressing. I also inspected the iron and steel works at Bône.

Meanwhile, there was no relaxation in the military effort. Nothing could have been more disastrous than some untoward incident in which we came off worst; and as long as there were still pockets of active and organized resistance in several areas, an ill-starred encounter with serious losses in men and equipment was always a possibility. In such a case, there was no doubt that the insurrection would immediately flare up on every side. In appointing General Challe as Commander-in-Chief and in separating military action and civilian affairs at the top level, I expected operations to take a dynamic turn which would result in our undisputed mastery of the field. Challe was particularly well qualified to succeed in this. Before he left for Algiers, I studied with him and approved his plan of action, which consisted in concentrating the requisite forces for an offensive against each of the rebel pockets in turn, reducing them one after another and subsequently occupying the sites, however inhospitable, where they might be able to re-form. It involved withdrawing selected units from the *quadrillage*[1] system, reorganizing them, reinforcing them with men and material and, above all, providing them with a massive quantity of helicopters. Thanks to the diligence of the Minister of Defence, Pierre Guillaumat, everything was ready in time for the opening of the new and decisive phase in the spring of 1959.

Public opinion was unaffected by these military measures, which were naturally secret. On the other hand, the direction imparted to the political evolution of Algeria was beginning to create a stir. The trend which was gradually revealed by my actions and my words not only dismayed the local partisans of integration but at the same time, in France itself, perturbed a number of people belonging to the "Right" and the "Center" who in this, as in everything else, were instinctively in favor of the *status quo*. But those who called themselves "Left-wing" were equally reluctant, albeit for different reasons, to express their approval, the Communist Party systematically denying that de Gaulle intended to end the war, while the rest, in any case divided among themselves on the subject, forbore to give me their confidence, let alone their praise, even though at heart they were for the most part pleased at the turn of events. Among the "Gaullists", of course, it would not have done openly to doubt that the path being followed was the right one. But the apprehensions even within my own government were no less real for not being expressed aloud. Needless to say, as usual I received no support whatever from the press, which confined itself to its habitual acrimony, criticism and ratiocination. As for the Moslems, the majority greeted my initiatives with an obdurate silence, not from indifference – as the referendum proved – but from caution; the only voices raised being either those of the propagandists of the "Front" abroad, or the few faithful supporters of "French Algeria" in Paris. The rest of the world, I might add, although it followed my actions with close attention and some surprise, was divided between scepticism as to my sincerity or my chances of success – this was the tendency in the West – and hostile mistrust on the part of official circles

[1] Grid system of territorial defence against guerrilla activity.

in the Third World and the totalitarian bloc. At home, the antagonism and doubts were certainly not sufficiently vocal or co-ordinated to present any real obstacle to me; abroad, there was resigned acceptance of my freedom of action. But when it came to serving the interests of France, France alone, France as a whole, an impetus strong enough for the purpose could only come from me.

In the meantime, throughout the years 1959 and 1960, the African territories and Madagascar were forming themselves into states. All of them chose to do so on the basis of democracy save totalitarian Guinea who, once outside our orbit and deprived of our support, did not hesitate to have recourse to the aid proffered by foreign States – the Soviet Union, the United States, Germany, Great Britain, Ghana – all of whom, for various reasons, were equally gratified to see her estranged from France. Our former colonies in the dark continent, to-gether with the great island in the Indian Ocean, thus became republics, each voting itself a Constitution, electing a President and a parliament, forming an administration. This assumption of sovereignty took place everywhere without undue incident, in the habitual euphoria of new departures. It must be said that we helped considerably to get things under way, the Community playing its supporting and transitional role in this respect. The "Executive Council" composed of Heads of State, which was to settle the many questions raised by the transfer of power, met in Paris under my presidency in February, March, May and September of 1959. In July, I convened a meeting of the Council in Tananarive. The demonstrations in the capital proved to me how grateful Madagascar was to France for restoring her former independence while at the same time helping her to make her way in the future. On the occasion of this journey, I revisited French Somaliland and the Comoro Archipelago, overseas territories of the Republic which gave enthusiastic expression to their joy at having chosen to remain so. I also went back to Réunion, our ancient île Bourbon, still passionately French in the depths of the Indian Ocean and prepared to demonstrate it yet again in unforgettable fashion.

The "Senate of the Community," composed of delegates from our Parliament and of elected African and Madagascan representatives, which opened in my presence in the Luxembourg Palace in July, gave certain political elements in France and the overseas countries the opportunity of debating subjects of common interest. On July 14 in the Place de la Concorde, thirteen Heads of State received from my hands the "flag of the Community" and attended a march-past of our troops and theirs. Gradually, then, without hesitating to ask for and to follow our advice, the young governments assumed their responsibilities. Indeed, at their request, we continued to maintain a number of officials, technicians, teachers, doctors and officers in the ranks of their administrations.

The emergence of these nations, almost all new-fledged, each containing elements of very different ethnic groups within frontiers which had been drawn up during the colonial period simply for purposes of partition between European States or for administrative convenience, could, with the disappearance of our old "Federations" of West Africa and Equatorial Africa, have led to a haphazard balkanization. But regional groupings were formed among neighbors which we ourselves helped to create and foster. For instance the Equatorial Customs Union between Congo-Brazzaville, the Central African Republic, Chad and Gabon, soon to be joined by Cameroon, was signed in Paris in January 1959, and in April the "Council of the Entente", comprising the Ivory Coast, Dahomey, Niger and Upper Volta, and later Togo, established technical and economic co-operation between countries stretching from the Sahara to the Bight of Benin. It is true that the attempt to merge Senegal and the Sudan into a federation known as Mali was to fail because the liberal and democratic leaders in Dakar were afraid of being stifled by the Marxists of Bamako; Senghor, the President of the Federal Assembly, broke with Modibo Keita, the Head of Government, and Senegal resumed its former name while the Sudan kept that of Mali. But subsequently the "Organization of the Senegal River States" was set up, in which Senegal, Mali, Mauritania and even Guinea were to co-operate. In addition to this, in many other African regions, river navigation, access to the sea, the building of roads and railways, were the subject of multilateral agreements negotiated with our help. Throughout our former territories, the airlines were operated by a single company, *Air-Afrique*. Later, the *Organisation commune africaine et malgache* was created, which all the French-speaking countries except Guinea were to join, including even Rwanda and the former Belgian Congo.

But, not unexpectedly, as the new States established themselves *de facto* and *de jure*, they were more and more inclined to assert their individual personalities. Wisely, in defining their relations with us, our Constitution had provided not only at the outset for the "Community" formula, which placed foreign affairs, currency, defense, the Court of Cassation[1] and higher education in the common domain, but also, with an eye to the future, the "association" formula, whereby co-operative agreements in every sphere, notably those above, would be enshrined in special treaties. By the end of 1959, it was "association" that the new Republics, one after another, came to propose to us.

The first to do so were Madagascar and Mali, the latter at the time still a union of Senegal and Sudan. As this transformation was legally valid and in no way undermined our interests, merely altering the form without affecting the basis of Franco-African solidarity, we willingly accepted it. On December 11, after calling at Nouakchott, I arrived at Saint-Louis to preside over the Executive Council of the Community on the following day. There, warmly supported by the Prime Minister, Michel Debré, who was at my side, I made it known publicly that France was ready to accede to these requests. But I said to the assembled Heads of State, as the pilgrims of Emmaus said to the traveller: "Abide with us. The day is far spent. Night is falling upon the world." On December 13, speaking to the Mali General Assembly in Dakar, I announced officially that we, the French nation, sanctioned the change from Community to Association, and this was the signal for moves in the same direction on the part of the other States. Meanwhile, although the United Nations

[1] *Cour de Cassation:* Appeal Court.

had, with our consent, rescinded our trusteeship over Togoland and Cameroon, recognized their complete international
sovereignty and admitted them as members, both countries had
decided to maintain the closest possible links with us by means
of special agreements. The year 1960 was thus to be devoted to
the signing of treaties of co-operation in the fields of economic
affairs, education, culture, defense, communications, civic
status and property rights, etc. with fourteen different States of
which six, Madagascar, Senegal, Congo-Brazzaville, Chad,
Central African Republic and Gabon, nevertheless wished to
remain titular members of the Community. The text of the
constitution embodying these various changes of status was
submitted to parliament in May.

Thus, between France on the one hand and a sizeable part of
Africa and Madagascar on the other, an assemblage of men,
territories and resources was built up, whose common language
was French, which in terms of currency constituted a "franc
area", in which goods of every kind were exchanged on a preferential basis; in which there was regular consultation on
political and diplomatic matters; in which each was pledged to
help the others in case of danger; in which sea and air transport
and the telegraph, telephone and radio networks were co-
ordinated; in which every citizen, wherever he came from and
wherever he went, knew and felt himself, far from being a
stranger, to be welcome, esteemed, and to a large extent at
home.

In order that these new relationships should be sealed at the
summit and should accord with what was for me a duty, an
honor and a pleasure, I maintained friendly personal relations
with the Heads of State. A general secretariat for the Community, and later for African and Malagasy Affairs, headed
successively by Raymond Jannot and Jacques Foccart, was the
working body, the organ of liaison with the government, and
the communications center through which I kept in touch with
these matters. In particular, the official visits to Paris which the
Heads of State were invited to make and the frequent calls they
paid on me when they were in France, were arranged there.

Between July 1960 and June 1962, all of them were solemnly received in state. In addition, I had nearly two hundred meetings with one or another of them.

In this way I came to know extremely well and, I may add, to appreciate highly, Modibo Keita, Maurice Yameogo, Hubert Maga, Sylvanus Olympio, Fulbert Youlou and David Dacko, at that time the Heads of State of Mali, Upper Volta, Dahomey, Togo, the Congo and the Central African Republic respectively. But those who, by reason of circumstance and force of personality, were destined to remain Heads of State as long as I myself, became my intimates.

There was Houphouët-Boigny of the Ivory Coast, a first-class political brain, familiar with all the problems not only of his own country but also of Africa and the entire world, who enjoyed exceptional authority at home and unquestionable influence abroad and wielded them in the cause of reason. There was Philibert Tsiranana, who displayed immense good sense and perseverance in leading Madagascar along the path of modern progress, in developing the great island's links with the African continent while preserving its separate identity, and in sheltering it from Asiatic intrusions. There was Léopold Senghor, the steadfast ruler of turbulent Senegal, responsive to all the arts, and above all the art of politics, and as proud of his negritude as of his French culture. There was Hamani Diori, President of Niger, who, mirroring his country's landscape with its mixture of desert and savanna, knew how to reconcile the long view with practical common sense in his policies at home and abroad. There was Ahmadou Ahidjo, magisterially surmounting the ethnic, religious, linguistic and economic complexities of Cameroon thanks to his wisdom in domestic affairs and his cautious attitude towards the outside world. There was Léon M'Ba, a model of fidelity in his attachment to France and his devotion to Gabon which, before his death, he was to see emerge from crushing poverty and advance towards prosperity. There was François Tombalbaye, whose mission it was to hold Chad together amid the swirling currents sweeping across the heart of Africa and whose febrile intensity made him equal to the task. There was Moktar Ould Daddah, who exercised limitless ingenuity in order to induce us to extract Mauritania's mineral riches from beneath her impoverished soil without compromising her proud and solitary nature. All in all, these African and Malagasy peoples whom France, in colonizing, had exposed to all the demons, good and evil, of modern times, attained human freedom and national sovereignty without any serious upheaval. Perhaps the friendly relations which General de Gaulle maintained with their Heads of State had something to do with this.

Nevertheless, their accession to independence with the concurrence of France could not fail to have profound repercussions on the Algerian situation. The feeling that it was part of a general evolution, and one which could turn out satisfactorily after all, gave people food for thought. No doubt a large proportion of the settlers and certain Army men on the spot, together with those in metropolitan France who encouraged their demands, were more than ever inclined to rely upon intransigence to ward off the inevitable. But in Moslem circles people asked: "Might not France do for us what she is doing for the Blacks?" The same idea gripped popular feeling at home. As for me, aware as I was of the psychological and political realities in our former dependencies, of the revolts we should have had to face had we refused to accept what was both equitable and ineluctable, of the prospects of fruitful co-operation which had opened up before us there, I was confirmed in the conception I had already formed of the Algerian problem and its solution. Whatever happened, above all else I must extricate France from a costly burden of responsibilities and losses which would otherwise become increasingly onerous, while the reciprocal benefits which she drew therefrom in the past were now but a hollow pretense. But what a long road lay ahead before this goal could be reached! And moreover I must proceed step by step.

The year 1959 was spent in gaining ground. When I arrived at the Elysée on January 8 to take up my duties as President of the Republic, I evoked in my inaugural address the Algeria of the future, "peaceful, transformed, developing by herself her own personality in close association with France". That same day, I took certain conciliatory measures. Seven thousand Moslems interned in Algeria were released. Every rebel under sentence of death was reprieved. Ben Bella and his companions, who had been arrested at Maison-Blanche airport after the aircraft taking them to Cairo had been diverted to Algiers, were transferred from the Santé Prison to the Île d'Aix in Brittany, where henceforth they were kept in honorable confinement. The veteran champion of independence, Messali Hadj, who had been kept under house arrest in metropolitan France, was released unconditionally. During my first press conference at the Elysée on March 25, in reply to a questioner who asked me if Algeria would remain French, I replied: "France, while endeavoring to achieve pacification, is working towards a transformation which will enable Algeria to find her new personality." Shortly afterwards, in an interview with the editor of the *Echo d'Oran*, Pierre Laffont, I said: "What the activists and their supporters want is to preserve 'father's Algeria'.[1] But 'father's Algeria' is dead. If they do not understand that they will die with it." Addressing the throngs on each of my successive journeys through the South-West, the Center, Berri, Touraine, the Massif Central, I missed no opportunity of making the same point. At Saint-Etienne, for example, I said: "I make no prejudgment about the Algeria of tomorrow. . . . But we must hope that a human transformation comes about there, and comes about in conjunction with France." Meanwhile, following the municipal elections held in May on the basis of a single electoral college, Moslems had gained control of a large number of Algerian communes, notably in Algiers itself, and formed a considerable majority of the newly returned Algerian senators.

As might be expected, my statements and the facts that accompanied them shook the foundations of what had appeared inviolate. The result was a hardening of the opposition in Algiers, which reaffirmed that "the only solution is the total extermination of the outlaws or their unconditional surrender"

[1] *l'Algérie de papa.*

and endeavored to organize noisy demonstrations, in particular for the anniversary of May 13. On the Moslem side, a few positive signs began to emerge. Thus in Beirut on May 1 Ferhat Abbas declared: "We are ready to meet General de Gaulle on neutral ground, without prior conditions. . . . We are prepared to have discussions with the French Government. . . . We do not rule out the possibility of sending a National Liberation Front delegation to Paris." The majority of the new Moslem senators declared publicly that "they entirely supported my policy". The deputy for Bône, Chibi Abdelbaki Mosbah, set forth a motion calling for a "peace and reconciliation commission" to be set up in Algeria which would mediate between the two camps. Ali Khodja, Chairman of the Departmental Commission of Algiers, publicly expressed the hope that talks would be opened with the National Liberation Front "with a view to a cease-fire". In French political circles, although there was no rush to emulate my attitude and vocabulary openly, the fundamental trust reposed in me by a large segment in parliament, and opportunist calculations on the part of many others, resulted in the prevailing opinion that "de Gaulle should be left to get on with it". Only the Communists, prejudiced as always, and at the other end of the spectrum, the increasingly isolated and impassioned groups haphazardly united by traditional attachment to "French Algeria," or local vested interests, or bitterness dating from the Vichy era, withheld their assent. But among the general public, the feeling was gaining ground that de Gaulle was following the right course in trying to find a way out of a situation which everyone wanted to see ended. This profound popular feeling was certainly only rarely and very inadequately expressed by those who lived by speaking and writing, but in fact it had an increasing effect in forming opinion.

Against this background, General Challe opened his offensive against the rebel strongholds. The initial phase, in March and April, took place in the Oran region, where General Gambiez was in command. It was launched against the Frenda massif and the Dahra hills in the western sector of the Ouarsenis, and resulted in the destruction of over half the *katibas*[1] concealed there. In May and June, in the Algiers region, under the command of General Massu, the eastern Ouarsenis and the heights which surround the capital in the neighborhood of Médéa, Blida and Miliana were, in turn, the scene of fierce fighting. There, again, the outcome was satisfactory. Great Kabylia and Lesser Kabylia – the "twins" – were the next to be attacked. As this was one of the most important enemy sanctuaries, encroaching on both the Algiers and Constantine commands, the responsibility of General Massu and General Olié respectively, General Challe himself took over the direction of the operation. He did so with much authority, method and effectiveness. The operation opened with a surprise attack resulting in the penetration in depth of the Hodna, a vast mountain range in which from crest to crest, from ravine to ravine, from forest to forest, the rebels of the two Kabylias were able to keep in touch with their brethren in the Aurès and the Nementchas. When this had been completed, the Kabyle stronghold was besieged in its turn.

At the end of August, I visited the troops and their commanders in the west, the center and the east of Algeria. Pierre Guillaumat and General Ely accompanied me. Challe and Delouvrier awaited me on the spot. On the 27th, I arrived at Saïda, from which central point I went by helicopter to various outposts in the Ouarsenis and the Dahra to make contact with units now established in the heart of the mountains. On the 28th I did the same in the eastern Ouarsenis and the Hodna between M'Sila and Bordj-Bou-Arréridj. On the 29th, off again, this time by car, to inspect the barrage right along the Tunisian frontier from Tébessa to the sea. On the 30th, after passing through Tizi-Ouzou, I was in Great Kabylia, first of all at Tizi-Hibel where the reserve units for "Operation Binoculars" were stationed, then on the Chellata pass in the Djurdjura mountains. It was there that the famous rebel leader Amirouche had been killed in the spring. It was there, too, at an altitude of

---

[1] A company of about one hundred men: the basic field unit of the Algerian rebel army.

5,500 feet, that Challe had set up his command post, a forest of radio aerials by means of which he was kept in touch with the movements and skirmishes of the *commandos de chasse*,[1] the paratroops and the legionaries scattered among the peaks and slopes of these unbelievably furrowed and rugged mountains. He was thus able to direct helicopter-borne reinforcements held in permanent readiness, to any point where they were needed at a moment's notice. After a final halt at the Col des Chênes, I returned to Paris.

As always, direct contact with the men on the spot had clarified my mind on facts which none of the reports had sufficiently illuminated. It was clear to me now that, provided our courage did not fail us, the insurrection was and would remain powerless to gain mastery over Algeria. It was no less evident that resistance could and would be indefinitely prolonged and renewed in appropriate areas thanks to the widespread collusion of the population. In this connection, I had been struck by a number of pointers. Everywhere I went upcountry, the peasants rounded up and brought before me by the military had exhibited an exaggerated deference though remaining mute and inscrutable. On the other hand at Tizi-Ouzou, an urban center too populous for its inhabitants to be rounded up to order, there was almost nobody to be seen in spite of the loud-speakers which had announced my arrival. In one Kabyle village which I had been taken to visit, and in which manifestly every effort had been made to turn it into a model one, my entry into the communal hall was greeted with cheers, the local councillors were profuse in their obeisances and the schoolchildren chanted the *Marseillaise*. But just as I was leaving, the Moslem town clerk stopped me, bowing and trembling, and murmured: "*Mon Général*, don't be taken in! Everyone here wants independence." At Saïda, where the heroic Bigeard introduced me to a commando unit composed of ex-*fellagha* prisoners-of-war who had been won over, I caught sight of a young Arab doctor attached to their group. "Well, Doctor, what do you think of it all?" "What we Arabs want, and what we

---

[1] Mobile units of about one hundred men used for tracking down guerrillas.

need," he replied, his eyes filled with tears, "is to be responsible for ourselves instead of others being responsible for us." Hence, I was more certain than ever that, in spite of our crushing superiority in military means, it would be a futile waste of men and money to try to impose "French Algeria", that peace could result from political initiatives tending in a different direction, and that France could and should take them.

In addition to this it had been borne in upon me that to carry on a meaningless struggle indefinitely would be to put the very soul of our Army in jeopardy, and with it our national unity. The nature of our operations tended in effect to divide our forces into two increasingly distinct components. While the main body of over four hundred thousand men was employed in occupying the towns and villages and manning the frontier defences, offensive operations were carried out by specialized troops. Challe had first of all assigned the 10th and 25th Parachute Divisions and the helicopter-borne Air Commandos to this task. A little later he added the *tirailleurs* and legionaries of the 11th Infantry Division. Together they made up a total of forty thousand fighting men, scarcely more than the *katibas* who opposed them. These shock troops, composed of volunteers and regulars splendidly equipped, constantly engaged in lone actions, attracting to their ranks an elite corps of officers and NCOs, came to look upon their fighting role as a special prerogative. Both officers and other ranks were justly proud of it. For it was a struggle which, undeniably dangerous, often frustrating, and sometimes exhausting, involved continual stalking, hunting, tracking, beating, flushing, taking cover, pursuing, closing in for the kill, with no lack of variety or technical appeal. It was also a sort of crusade in which, against that isolated background, the values attendant upon risk and action were developed and affirmed. Deeply responsive and sympathetic though I was to this concentration of military qualities, I could not help seeing how tempting it could be for a leader of warped ambition to make use of it one day as an instrument of political adventure.

It was, therefore, by deliberate design that I revealed the next stage of my plan to the officers of the "Forces of Intervention" assembled to meet me at Challe's headquarters, knowing full well that my words would be carefully noted and spread abroad. Having expressed lively satisfaction at what my inspection had revealed to me as regards the military situation, I went on to say that "although the success of the operations in progress was essential whatever happened, the Algerian problem would not be solved thereby . . . that it could not be solved until we eventually reached an understanding with the Algerians . . . that we would never reach an understanding unless they themselves desired it . . . that the era of European administration had run its course . . . that we were faced with this tragic situation at a time when all the colonized people of the world were throwing off the yoke . . . that we must act in Algeria only for Algeria and with Algeria and in such a way that the world realized this . . . that it was in the interests of France, which were the only interests we should consult." I concluded: "As for yourselves, mark my words! You are not an Army for its own sake. You are the Army of France. You exist only through her, for her and in her service. It is I who, in view of my position and my responsibilities, must be obeyed by the Army in order that France should survive. I am confident of your obedience and I thank you for it in the name of France." In saying this I was giving my audience an inkling of my intention to recognize Algeria's right to self-determination. I was also demanding their discipline in advance. Later, in the presence of the Defence Minister, the Chief of General Staff and the Delegate-General in Algeria, I told the Commander-in-Chief precisely what I was soon to announce publicly. Challe replied: "It's feasible!" and assured me that I could count on him whatever happened.

On September 16, 1959, France, through me, announced her intention to place Algeria's destiny in the hands of the Algerians. In my view, this destiny could consist either of complete secession from France, who would then "cease to provide Algeria with so many benefits and so many millions", would henceforth do nothing to help her to avoid "poverty and chaos", and would "take the necessary measures to regroup and resettle those Algerians who wished to remain French"; or else "Francization", by which "the Algerians would become an integral part of the French people," enjoying complete equality of political, social and economic rights, "residing wherever they pleased in any of our territories"; or else "the government of Algeria by the Algerians", a government supported by French aid, based on universal suffrage, by all means including "the present political organization of the insurrection" but without allowing it "the right to impose itself with knife and sub-machine-gun". I pointed out that Algeria would not be in a position to govern itself until pacification had made further progress, no doubt stretching over a number of years, and that, in the meantime, France would continue her efforts to bring about the economic transformation of the country.

The decisive step had been taken. Undoubtedly, before everything was settled, there would be more delays, more fighting, more crises, more bargaining. But France had proclaimed that it was for the Algerians, that is to say the Moslems, to choose what their future should be; she had no intention of deciding for them under the cloak of "French Algeria"; she foresaw and accepted the fact that Algeria would become a State and, once this had been achieved, she was equally prepared to dissociate herself completely from it or to offer it her co-operation. At a press conference on November 10, I confirmed the position I had adopted. I reiterated the offer already made to the leaders of the insurrection to discuss with the French government, in complete security, "the political and military conditions for an end to the fighting". At the same time, I cited a few statistics relating, first of all, to pacification: half as many monthly exactions and half as many civilian victims as there had been two years earlier; secondly, to investments directly financed by the French Treasury: two hundred billion old francs over the year, three hundred billion in the following year; thirdly, to the development of the country by comparison with the situation before the rebellion: agricultural production increased by fifty per cent, electricity consumption, foreign trade and schooling doubled, four times the number of houses built, five times the number of roads, and ten times the number of factories; and fourthly, to the bringing of the oil pipe-line from the Sahara to the port of loading at Bougie which would henceforth secure for Algeria the basic financial resources she had always lacked.

As a catalyst thrown into boiling liquid precipitates crystallization, so the position I had taken over self-determination provoked a radical division of opinion among the public. In metropolitan France there was overwhelming approval. I received proof of this in the course of a visit I made to the Nord and the Pas de Calais at the end of September. Wherever I referred to my decision, the crowds went wild with enthusiasm. Ministers, to whom I had outlined it in Cabinet on August 26 on the eve of my military inspection tour in Algeria, and explained it in detail on September 16 before making my public pronouncement, had proved, in the main, extremely favorable. On October 16, the National Assembly, in which the Prime Minister had opened a debate on the subject which he himself had asked to be put to the vote, expressed its confidence by a huge majority. At the same time, however, all those bent upon wrecking my plans redoubled their virulent opposition.

The activists in Algeria, inciting and exploiting the feelings of the local population of French stock, were already talking of revolt in the public palavers they held and the tracts they distributed. A "French National Front" was organized semi-clandestinely, under the leadership of Ortiz. "We need a Charlotte Corday!" an orator shouted at one meeting, and was loudly applauded. The principal organ of the *pieds-noirs*, the *Echo d'Alger*, which in the articles of its editor, Alain de Sérigny, had hitherto displayed a moderate attitude towards me, now adopted a tone of the utmost hostility. A fair number of Algerian deputies poured out bitter diatribes. In the melting-pot of Algiers life, both officers and civil servants indulged in contacts which were detrimental to their loyalty. "There are ways," the whisper in offices and messes went, "of forcing the General to to see the error of his ways." In France itself, Georges Bidault and a few members of parliament founded the Committee for

French Algeria, which forthwith provided a platform for the usual agitators of the so-called "extreme Right". In December, the ex-Premier undertook a lecture tour of Algeria which further stirred up passions. In Paris, the speeches and articles in which Marshal Juin – born in Bône, married in Constantine and a veteran of the African army – expressed his sorrow and General Weygand took the opportunity to give vent to old Vichy resentments, nourished the animosity of certain social, political, journalistic and military circles. In short, by the beginning of 1960, as national support grew more pronounced, the storm clouds were gathering on the Algerian horizon.

The storm did indeed break. The incident which caused the thunderbolt to strike was an interview which a German journalist had obtained in January with General Massu, army corps commander in Algiers, where he was very popular. In the course of the interview this valiant soldier, my old comrade, caught off guard, had been foolish enough to rail against my policy. Although I understood the distress it must cause a man of his kind (was I, its begetter, any happier about it?), although I made every allowance for the influence of his immediate circle, although I took into account his partial disclaimer and above all the protestation of loyalty he had taken it upon himself to publish, I felt that his outburst could not go unpunished. He was recalled to Paris, never to return to Algiers. Meanwhile, at a conference on Algeria which Challe attended at the Elysée on January 22, I informed him of Massu's transfer. In spite of the objurgations of the Commander-in-Chief, who warned of the risks of an explosion and talked of resignation, I stood by my decision.

The civilian and military activists in Algeria did in fact seize upon this pretext to put their prearranged plans into action. On the 23rd, Pierre Lagaillarde, the young firebrand deputy and leader of the students' union, occupied the university at the head of a large group of demonstrators many of whom belonged to the Territorial Defence Units, a sort of *pied-noir* militia created in 1954, and were armed and in uniform. Lagaillarde himself wore the uniform of a reserve officer. There they established a stronghold, digging themselves into the faculty buildings and cellars, throwing up barricades, observing military discipline and swearing to turn the campus into a "French Algeria" redoubt. Meanwhile the word went out to the population to assemble the following afternoon, a Sunday, on the "Plateau des Glières"[1] in the center of the city to demonstrate solidarity with the "defenders" of the university and put pressure on the authorities.

The latter, however, took steps to clear the "Plateau", where a considerable crowd, almost entirely French, had gathered. Two columns, one of *gardes mobiles*, the other of paratroops, were to converge on the square and disperse the demonstrators. The first column discharged its mission, but as it debouched into the square it came under fire from armed groups, suffering heavy casualties, both dead and wounded, and replied with a burst of machine-gun fire which wounded several civilians. The paratroops had meanwhile failed to intervene, and this at once created the impression that the loyalty of at least one section of the security forces was now in doubt. Thereupon, with the Algiers cauldron boiling over, the agitation and unrest spread to France and even into the government itself. Believing as I did that the immediate objective of the rioters was simply to force me to renege on self-determination, I was determined to lance the abscess, make no concessions whatever and obtain complete obedience from the Army.

I indicated as much briefly over the radio on January 25, describing the previous day's events as "a stab in the back for France", expressing my confidence in Delouvrier and Challe, and declaring that "I shall do my duty". The next few days were heavy with suspense. General Challe, who had at first reacted as a leader should, publicly condemning the disorder, declaring his intention to quell it, calling up powerful reinforcements, throwing a cordon of troops around the university to isolate it from the population, later modified his attitude, became engrossed in consultations with Army and civilians, did

---

[1] The Plateau des Glières (in the Savoy Alps) was the scene of a savage battle between the French Resistance and the Germans in 1944.

nothing to subdue Lagaillarde and his companions, and allowed them to communicate with the town as much as they pleased. He also gave Paris to understand that it was going to be necessary to compromise. He said as much to Michel Debré, who arrived in Algiers together with Pierre Guillaumat during the night of the 25–26th, and had it repeated by a bevy of colonels assembled for the purpose. He sent two or three of them to me at the Elysée the following day so that I too should hear it. In the end, after Paul Delouvrier, for fear of being swept away in the general uproar, had decided to leave Algiers on January 28 for Reghaia whence he addressed a moving appeal to the city, the Commander-in-Chief left his command post and followed the Delegate-General. That same day he gave General Ely, who went to see him on my instructions to lay down his course of action, every indication of irresolution. Meanwhile the security forces wavered; a sort of saturnalia developed on the barricades surrounding the university, with insurgents, civilians and soldiers all intermingling; and Algiers, strike-bound, without transport, shops closed, seemed to be sliding into anarchy. However, without discounting the possibility that the worst might happen, I had the impression that in all this there was more of an attempt to intimidate me than any real eagerness to cross swords. Having let the agitation "stew in its own juice" for a few days, I sensed that the moment had come to bring the affair to an end and dispel all illusions.

So on January 29 I once more appeared at the microphone and on the television screen. I had donned my uniform. I first of all confirmed that "the Algerians will have the right to decide their own destiny" and that "self-determination, as defined by the Head of State, decided on by the government, approved by parliament, adopted by the French nation, is the only possible outcome." I then addressed myself to "the Algerian community of French stock" in order to calm its fears, to the Army in order to call upon it to observe discipline and to give it strict orders to see that "force remains in the hands of the law", and finally "to my old and beloved country", France, in order to "ask her to give her support whatever happens." I ended by saying: "Since the guilty men who dream of usurping power are using as a pretext the decision I have taken concerning Algeria, let it be understood everywhere, let it be understood clearly, that I shall never go back on it!"

The effect was instantaneous. In France, there was every indication of general approval. In Algiers, where my speech had been heard during a thunderstorm which seemed symbolic, every Frenchman realized that the adventurers must either surrender or go to such extremes that few would be ready to follow them. Without more ado, the men in command made up their minds. On Saturday January 30, General Gracieux, appointed to the command of the Algiers sector by Challe, was given strict orders by General Crépin, Massu's successor, to clear the precincts of the university, and thus blockaded the rebels; seeing which, a number of them came out and gave themselves up. The remainder, summoned to do likewise, laid down their arms and asked to be allowed to enlist in regular units. With the exception of their leaders, they were permitted to do so. By February 1 it was all over. Lagaillarde was arrested and sent to Paris for trial. Similar action was taken in the case of several ring-leaders, including Alain de Sérigny and the ex-deputy Demarquet. Ortiz escaped to Spain. Algiers calmed down and the Army resumed its task of pacification.

The proclamation of self-determination, the revolt of the Barricades and the demonstration of the authority of the State marked a decisive turning-point in the painful saga of the Algerian settlement. Thenceforward, however severe and dramatic the obstacles that still lay ahead, there was no longer any doubt that a solution could be found, that it must inevitably lead to the emancipation of Algeria by France and some form of association between the two countries, and that it would not result in the rupture of our national unity. Bearing in mind the free choice made by the overseas territories which remained within the Republic, what had been achieved in Black Africa and Madagascar, what was happening in relation to Morocco and Tunisia, what was still going on in Laos and Cambodia, and the glimpse of what might one day be possible in Vietnam, it was clear that the evolution from colonization to modern co-operation now had every chance of being accomplished in such a way that France would not only be relieved of what had become an unjustifiable burden but offered the promise of fruitful co-operation in the future.

Destiny had entrusted me with this momentous task. As happened to those men who likewise in the course of our history were called upon to enforce the supreme interest of the nation, as had already happened to me in other circumstances, I was obliged, in order to achieve my aim, to coerce and sometimes punish other Frenchmen who opposed it but whose first impulse may have been well-intentioned. I was obliged to overcome the anguish which gripped me as I deliberately put an end to a colonial domination which was once glorious but would henceforth be ruinous. I was obliged, against great odds, to carry the national ambition into other fields. I knew that France called upon me to perform this task. I believed I had the ear of the people. When the time came, I would ask them whether they thought me right or wrong. And their voice would then for me be the voice of God.

Algeria

෴

My decision to grant the Algerians the right to be their own masters had laid down the path to be followed. The liquidation of the revolt of the Barricades had shown that the Army was loyal to its duty once I gave the necessary orders from the pinnacle of the State. I saw better than ever what had to be done. I doubted less than ever that it was my duty to accomplish it. But I needed as much as ever the support of the French people.

Certainly, on the Algerian side, the Moslem masses were confirmed in the belief that only from General de Gaulle could they expect justice and peace. But they thought it without saying it. The leaders of the National Liberation Front declared themselves in principle ready to enter into negotiations. But they still refused to make a move, bogged down as they were in their suspicions, their haggling and their divisions. In France everything led me to believe that the nation relied on me alone to achieve a solution. But it could not prove this unless it was given an opportunity to express itself. In opposition circles, the upholders of French Algeria were certainly not capable of forcing me to maintain the *status quo*, nor the Communists of compelling me to grovelling surrender. But the prospect of free self-determination exacerbated the fury of the former and aroused among the latter the same systematic hostility which they evinced towards me in all circumstances. The parties, while at heart recognizing that I was on the right track and must be allowed to pursue it, were reluctant to blazon the fact and continued to lavish criticisms and reservations. Almost all the political elements which had rallied round me in the cause of national renewal continued to give me their steadfast support. But many of them found the cup a bitter one. Most of the officials and military who, whether in Paris or on the spot, were responsible for the execution of policy felt that my authority was necessary and must be obeyed. But Algerian illusions died hard. The ministers undoubtedly complied with my directives. But most of them did so resignedly. Michel Debré himself adopted each of my initiatives with complete loyalty and was in any case aware that in matters of state reason must prevail. But he suffered and did not hide the fact. On the morning when I showed him, before delivering it, the speech in which I predicted that "one day there will be an Algerian Republic", he could not contain his chagrin.

In this vast and painful operation, my responsibility was consequently indivisible. So be it! But in the absence of a sufficiently powerful momentum to carry the country towards the goal, and in view of the continuing possibility of resistance, I would have to proceed not by leaps and bounds but step by step, launching each stage myself only after having thoroughly prepared the ground and conditioned public opinion beforehand. Constantly I would have to strive to remain master of the situation without allowing the cross-currents of politics, the acrimonies of the press, the pressures from abroad, the feelings of the Army, or the ferment among the local population to deflect me from my path. At two vital moments, in order to create a situation on which there could be no going back, I was to call upon the people to approve my decisions above and beyond the maneuverings, the obstructions and the compromises. In short, I would play my cards in such a way as gradually to reconcile the feelings of Frenchmen with the interests of France while avoiding a rupture in national unity.

For the moment, after the crisis in Algiers, I was concerned with consolidating present gains. Parliament, summoned to an extraordinary session on February 2, 1960, was requested to vote the government special powers to make changes in administrative and judicial procedure and in the personal status of individuals in the light of recent events. These powers were voted at once, the Socialists indeed specifying that they must be exercised at the personal discretion of the President of the Republic, which did not prevent them from later denouncing my "personal power." Two members of the government were relieved of their duties. The first of these was Jacques Soustelle. From 1940 until I withdrew from public life twelve years later, this gifted man, this brilliant intellectual, this passionate politician had stood beside me. My withdrawal from political activity had left him on his own. Appointed Governor-General of Algeria soon after the outbreak of the insurrection in 1954, he had witnessed the horrors of the massacres and been the recipient of the adjurations and acclamations of the *pieds-noirs*. Having become their champion, he had also become the champion of "French Algeria" as they envisaged it. If, by reason of our old companionship, I had nevertheless brought him into the government – the killers of the FLN having then attempted to assassinate him – the turn which events had taken made it impossible for me to keep him there any longer. Bernard Cornut-Gentille, less openly committed but inclined towards the same views, also left his ministerial post. In addition, since Pierre Guillaumat was now to assume responsibility for our scientific, atomic and space programs, Pierre Messmer became Minister for the Armed Forces. Needless to say, I kept Algerian affairs directly under my wing. The special committee which had been set up to deal with them with Bernard Tricot as its Secretary-General decided in particular on the transfer of certain senior officials and military commanders, the dissolution of the Territorial Units which at the time of the "Barricades" had been elements of disturbance, not to say revolt, and the suppression of the Psychological Warfare Bureaux which had been created with the intention of keeping the High Command informed of the state of mind of the population but which, at the instigation of a few activist military theoreticians, had become hotbeds of sedition and agitation.

85

From March 3 to 7, 1960, accompanied by my ministers Messmer and Terrenoire and Generals Ely, Lavaud and Challe, I went to inspect the Army in Algeria. From east to west, at the most sensitive points in the most active zones – Hadjer Mafrouch, Catinat, Col de Tamentout, Batna, Menaa, Barika, Aumale, Souk-el-Khemis, Ouled-Moussa, Bir-Rabalou, Boghari, Paul-Cazelles, Tiaret, Zenata, Zarifete, Côte 811, Souani and Montagnac – I heard the reports and gave my instructions on the spot, spending my days and my nights among the troops, not stopping in any town and excluding all newspaper correspondents from my escort. For I intended the journey to have an exclusively military character. But this was to reckon without the faculty for invention and interpretation of the press. In accordance with its all-too-frequent propensity to consider every event on the lowest level and for its story value, it dubbed General de Gaulle's contacts with the fighting forces a "tour of the messes" (*tournée des popotes*). But in addition to this, failing to perceive that, while leading France towards disengagement, I also wanted our forces to remain masters of the territory until such time as I deemed it advisable to withdraw them, it represented the rousing words which I addressed to the combat units as a sudden reversal of my policy. For, quite naturally, I told these soldiers who were risking and sometimes laying down their lives for "the honor of French arms" that the struggle was not yet over, that it might continue for many more months, and that as long as it lasted the adversary must be everywhere sought out, reduced and conquered. It is true that I also said that the eventual outcome would be an "Algerian Algeria", by the decision and with the support of the French nation, which made my aim quite clear. But the tendentious reporting of my visit momentarily created some political and journalistic ebullition and provoked warlike declarations on the part of the leaders of the National Liberation Front which added a few extra thorns to the asperities of my task.

Meanwhile, the cantonal elections took place in Algeria at the end of May. The event was an important one, because for the first time the departmental councils were renewed on the basis

of a single electoral college, because the government intended
to draw from them commissions of Algerian representatives
which would assist the authorities at every level, and above all
because the instructions not to vote addressed to the Moslems
by the FLN and to the Europeans by various activist organizations provided a test of public opinion. The eventual poll was
fifty-seven per cent of registered voters, a very high proportion
considering the number of absentees and the very moderate
interest which this sort of election arouses anywhere at any
time. The Moslems voted overwhelmingly for the candidates
who supported the policy of General de Gaulle. If the *pieds-noirs*
mostly gave their votes to "French Algeria" candidates, an
appreciable number who regarded themselves as liberals voted
the other way. I concluded from all this that the time had come
to take a further step towards peace.

On June 14, speaking to the nation about its general progress, I declared: "The spirit of the century has also altered the
circumstances of our action overseas and led us to put an end
to colonization. . . . It is perfectly natural for people to feel
nostalgia for the empire that was, just as we may sigh for the
soft glow of oil-lamps, the splendor of sailing ships, the charm
of the days of the horse-drawn carriage. But alas, no policy
worthy of the name can ignore the realities." Then I came to the
burning question: "And what of Algeria? Ah! I have never
thought that I could solve overnight this problem which has
been with us for a hundred and thirty years. . . . But on September 16 the straight and clear road which must lead to peace was
opened up. . . . Self-determination for the Algerians as regards
their own destiny is the only possible outcome of a complex and
tragic situation." And I concluded: "Once more, in the name
of France, I turn to the leaders of the insurrection. We await
them here in order to seek with them an honorable end to the
fighting which still drags on. . . . After which, everything will
be done to ensure that the Algerian people can express their
choice in tranquillity. The decision will be theirs alone. But
I am sure that they will take the one that common sense
dictates: to bring about, in conjunction with France and in

co-operation between the two communities, the transformation
of Algerian Algeria into a prosperous and fraternal country."

On June 20, Ali Boumendjel and Mohammed Ben Yahia
arrived at Melun, where the prefecture had been made available to them. I was sufficiently aware that those who sent them
owed an appearance of intransigence to the feelings of their
militants, the cohesion of their own committee and the curiosity
of the world audience not to expect any agreement to emerge
from this first contact. Besides, the FLN leadership had publicly
specified that its two emissaries were coming merely to settle
the conditions under which a delegation led by Ferhat Abbas,
"President of the Provisional Government of the Algerian
Republic", would later meet the French government. These
conditions, as outlined by Boumendjel and Ben Yahia to their
interlocutors, Roger Moris, Secretary-General for Algerian
Affairs, and General de Gastines, must imperatively include
direct talks between Ferhat Abbas and General de Gaulle and
an assurance that the negotiators who established themselves in
our country, even – why not? – in the capital, could see whom-
soever they pleased, make any public speeches or declarations
they wished, and bring into the discussions Ben Bella and his
fellow-detainees on the Île d'Aix, who would be released for the
purpose. They naturally received the reply that none of this
could even be considered until the fighting and the outrages
ceased, and that, in particular, General de Gaulle would never
confer with the rebel leader as long as his soldiers were being
fired on in Algeria and his civilian compatriots murdered in
the very streets of Paris. But we were ready to settle the terms
and conditions for a cease-fire there and then, and subsequently
those for self-determination, on the assumption and in the
expectation that this would be voted by the French and the
Algerians. If, on their side, the FLN delegates were prepared to
enter into such negotiations, they would be guaranteed every
facility for communicating with Tunis. The discussions continued for a week without achieving any results, save one, which
in my view was not inconsiderable: representatives of the rebels
had openly solicited and obtained an invitation to metropolitan

France and had conversed at length with representatives of the government. They took leave of each other courteously, both sides expressing the intention to meet again.

At a press conference on September 5 I explained clearly where we were going, in what spirit and with what hopes. Having given details of what had been achieved from the point of view of the administration of local affairs – in the communes by the municipal councils of which the mayors were now in the great majority Moslem, in the *départements* by the thirteen departmental councils all of whose presidents were Moslems, and in the regions by the commissions of representatives, three-quarters of whose members would be Moslem – I spoke of the future as it would shortly emerge from the votes of the Algerian people: "Whatever happens, I believe that they will want Algeria to be Algerian. In my view, the only question that arises is whether this Algeria will be Algerian against France . . . or in association with her." As for the procedure whereby the Algerians would be invited to voice their decision, I affirmed that it should be discussed "with all shades of opinion", which clearly meant that the government would negotiate with the FLN. Then I moved into a higher key: "I am not so blind, or so unjust, as to ignore the importance of that agitation of wounded spirits, or awakened hopes, which led to the insurrection in Algeria. . . . While condemning the attacks against civilians, while regarding the sporadic ambushes to which the fighting has now been reduced as nothing but a waste of time, suffering and blood. . . . I nevertheless recognize the courage displayed by the combatants. . . . More, I am convinced that once the last skirmishes are over, the wind that will blow through strife-torn Algeria will be a wind of fraternity and peaceful co-operation. . . ." I ended the press conference as follows: "On every side I hear it said that 'only de Gaulle can solve the problem. If he cannot, no one can.' Well then, let me get on with it!"

Two months later, I intervened yet again. I was actually on the point of fixing the date for the referendum, and its approach gave rise to a ferment of agitation. In Tunis, where they had established themselves, the leaders of the insurrection rejected the result in advance, declaring that no vote in Algeria would be valid as long as the French Army remained in the country. In metropolitan France, there was a spectacular increase in the number of FLN attacks on Frenchmen or Moslems who supported Messali Hadj. In Algiers, *pied-noir* activists were planning anti-de Gaulle demonstrations to take place on Armistice Day. Moreover, the bitterness which marked the budget discussions in France for the first time since 1958 was an indication of the intense impatience and anxiety of the French people. But in a broadcast to the nation on November 4 I deliberately appeared full of resolution and assurance. "Having resumed the leadership of France," I said, "I have decided in her name to pursue a course which will lead from government of Algeria by metropolitan France to an Algerian Algeria. That means an emancipated Algeria . . . an Algeria which, if the Algerians so wish – and I believe this to be the case – will have its own government, its own institutions, its own laws." I repeated that "the Algeria of tomorrow, as decided by self-determination, can be built either with France or against her," and that France "will abide by the result of the ballot, whatever it may be." I renewed my invitation to the leaders of the external organization of the rebellion "to take part, without restrictions, in discussions concerning the forthcoming referendum, then in the campaign itself, which will be conducted in complete freedom, and finally in the supervision of the ballot," the sole condition being that "we should come to an agreement to stop killing one another." But I categorically rejected their claims to assume power by virtue of the sub-machine-gun alone, after France had withdrawn her troops and before the destiny of Algeria had been decided in advance by universal suffrage, on the ground that they were already to all intents and purposes "the government of the Algerian Republic". Such a Republic "will one day exist, but has never yet existed." Then I attacked those elements in our country who were bent on "fomenting trouble and whipping up public feeling. . . . Thus we see two rival packs, one on the side of sterile reaction, the other of ignoble abandonment, snarling and snapping in opposite directions, each of which would lead France and Algeria to catastrophe." Nor did I spare the outsiders who took up propagandist attitudes on the question: "While the Soviet empire, which is the most savagely imperialist and colonialist power ever known, strives to extend its domination, while Communist China prepares to follow its example, while enormous racial problems bedevil many parts of the world, America in particular, not only do we find threatening statements being hurled against France by the oppressors of the East but tendentious criticisms appearing in the free world. . . . In the face of these attempts at incitement both from within and from without . . . the State stands firm! . . . There is a government, which I appointed and which is fulfilling its task with exemplary ability and devotion. . . . There is a parliament, which debates, legislates and supervises. . . . The executive power and the legislative power are now completely separate, thus guaranteeing the government the necessary freedom of action. . . . There is a Head of State on whom the Constitution imposes a duty which is paramount." I ended: "The Republic is on its feet. The country's leaders are at their posts. The nation will be called upon to decide from the depths of its being. Frenchwomen, Frenchmen, I am counting on you. You can count on me!" I had spoken in the same vein on my visits to our provinces during the course of the year: Languedoc in February, Normandy in July, Brittany in September and the Alps at the beginning and end of October. All of them had given me their fervent approbation.

Meanwhile, those to whom my warnings were addressed reacted according to their fashion. The leaders of the National Liberation Front issued a statement on the referendum: "Its purpose is clearly to impose a predetermined status on Algeria . . . with the object of preventing the Algerian people from declaring themselves for independence." They therefore called on Moslems to abstain. In France, the Communists declared: "To vote 'Yes' is to say 'No' to peace!" The activists made their opposition felt everywhere. In Algeria, they formed themselves into the French Algeria Front, corresponding to the National Front for French Algeria in metropolitan France, and at once enrolled more than two hundred thousand supporters. In Algiers, massive disaffection among civil servants had been feared as a result of my speech. Yet only one resigned his post, admittedly one of the most important, and was instantly recalled. But many others openly expressed their disagreement. On November 11, a raging mob appeared in the streets, pillaged various buildings and stoned the security forces. The following day saw the first of the series of plastic bomb explosions, this time by the *ultras*. In Paris, Marshal Juin let it be known that "despite a friendship of fifty years' standing with General de Gaulle, he must protest, both in his capacity as the highest dignitary in the Army and as an Algerian, against the idea of deserting our Algerian brothers." In San Sebastian, whither his calculations had already led him, General Salan declared to the press: "I say No! to this Algerian Algeria. . . . From now on, every man must face up to his responsibilities. . . . The time for evasions is over." At the trial of the ringleaders of the revolt of the Barricades – Lagaillarde, Susini, Demarquet, Perez, Ronda – which had just opened, the military tribunal, with an indulgence which bordered on complicity, immediately gave the accused bail, thus enabling them to escape to Spain whence they could return secretly to Algeria at their leisure.

Nevertheless, I continued to hasten things forward. On November 16, my decision to proceed some time in early January with the referendum through which the people of France would or would not grant the right of self-determination to the Algerians was taken in Cabinet, where, shortly afterwards, the text of the question was drawn up and the date fixed. Meanwhile, I had received a number of prominent Algerians, notably several recently-elected Moslems – mayors of important towns, senators, presidents of departmental councils. All of them gave me clearly to understand that the final solution could only be achieved by agreement with the National Liberation Front and that otherwise no Algerian government would be possible. On November 22 Louis Joxe was appointed Minister of State for Algerian Affairs, so that henceforth the government, in his person, could come and go regularly between Paris and

Algiers. On the following day Paul Delouvrier, the Delegate-General, whose loyalty had never for one moment faltered but who professed extreme weariness, was replaced by Jean Morin. On December 5, before I issued the decree convoking the electors, Michel Debré presented the government's Algerian policy to the National Assembly at the beginning of a two-day debate on the subject. Finally, on December 8, I flew once more by Caravelle to Algeria where I intended to visit several centers of population and talk to Army officers. Louis Joxe and Pierre Messmer accompanied me. Wherever I went, Jean Morin presented me with the facts and introduced me to the people on the civil side, and General Crépin did the same on the military side. Six months earlier Crépin had replaced Challe who had become Commander-in-Chief of Allied Forces in Central Europe.

My inspection tour was a turbulent one. In Algiers and Oran, which, as it happened, I had not planned to visit, the French Algeria Front had ordered a general strike and the closing of all shops. Sunday December 11 was to be a day of bloodshed in both cities, when rival processions of Europeans and Arabs clashed and the police were driven to open fire. From the moment I arrived, on the 9th, at Aïn-Témouchent in the Oran region, I noted the hostile attitude of many *pieds-noirs*. If the welcome at Tenezara and Tlemcen seemed more friendly, it was because the Arabs had not been prevented from taking part. But in the Algiers region on the following day, at Blida, Cherchel, Zeddine and Orléansville, I found the atmosphere oppressive. The Europeans watched me go by in silence, while the Moslems did not dare to leave their homes. In Kabylia, on the other hand, where the Europeans were fewer in number, the population was on the streets. At Tizi-Ouzou, for example, in contrast to the reception I had been given the previous year, a considerable crowd of Kabyles gathered in front of the town hall to hear and to applaud me. It was the same at Akbou. I then proceeded to the Constantine region by way of Bougie, where violent clashes broke out between the two communities around the prefecture which was my residence for the night. On the

93

12th, having passed through Sétif and Télergma, I was in the Aurès mountains, cradle and stronghold of the insurrection. Here, at Arris, at Kef-Messara, at Biskra, as I went through the streets on foot, I found myself escorted by enthusiastic crowds. On December 13 I travelled the length of the defence barrage on the Tunisian frontier from Tébessa to Bône without hearing a shot fired. At Ouenza I visited the iron-ore mines which were working at full capacity and where the miners welcomed me with open arms. Finally, on the airfield at Bône, I met the last group of officers under the auspices of General Gouraud, who had introduced me to those in the Constantine region as my tour proceeded, as Gambiez had done in the Oranais and Vézinet in the Algiers region. They had all heard what I had to say to them, clearly enough for them to understand that Algeria was going to be granted self-determination, firmly enough for them to realize that I, their chief, had decided upon my goal and would not be deflected from it, and loudly enough for them to realize what a national disaster the defection of the military would be and, conversely, the exemplary value of their discipline. As I left Algerian soil, the last words of farewell were from Gouraud. "*Mon Général*," he said, greatly moved, "I can answer for myself and for my subordinates!"

Everything that I had seen, heard and absorbed during those five days had left me with a clear impression of the realities of the Algerian situation just as the vote on self-determination was about to tear away the final veils. The war was all but over. Military success was achieved. Operations had been reduced to next to nothing. Instead, politics dominated the scene, and in this respect the two communities were further apart than they had ever been: the Moslem masses convinced that they had the right to independence and would obtain it sooner or later, the Europeans for the most part resolved at all costs to deny it to them. There was, therefore, a growing danger that terrorism and revolt would change direction. In these circumstances, it was to be anticipated that the activists of "French Algeria", no matter how extreme their actions, would enjoy the support of the *pieds-noirs* and widespread connivance from the local police,

94

civil service and judiciary. It was also to be expected that incidents of unforeseeable gravity might arise from the acts of certain military units a section of whose officers considered Algeria to be an indispensable French possession. On the other hand, I was in no doubt that in the last resort the Army as a whole would remain disciplined and that the mass of the French people would follow me. Above all, it was abundantly clear to me that if the situation dragged on our country could expect nothing but trouble and perhaps misfortune; in short, it was time to put an end to it.

I addressed the nation on three further occasions before the referendum. Who, after all, is better placed to explain how matters stand than the man who carries the burden of responsibility? On December 20 I declared: "The French people are being called upon to say whether they agree, as I propose, that the peoples of Algeria should choose their own destiny. . . . Thus, France is about to take the decision to give it her formal consent. She will take it in accordance with her tradition, which is to liberate others when the moment has come. . . . She will take it in the hope, which her interests dictate, of being able to deal in the future, not with an inorganic and rebellious Algeria but with a peaceful and responsible one. I therefore ask Frenchmen and Frenchwomen for a frank and overwhelming Yes." I returned to this point in my end-of-year message on December 31: "I ask you to give the proposal which is being submitted to you an immense majority. First, because it is common sense. . . . But also because if, by some misfortune, the country's response were to be negative, or indecisive, or marred by many abstentions, who knows what consequences might result from this impotence, this discord! If, on the other hand, the referendum is positive and unmistakable, then the whole nation, and its government, its parliament, its administration, its army, will have no further doubts as to the path to be followed and the goal to be reached. Then the Algerians will really have been shown the way ahead. Then the world will really see that France knows her own mind." So that there should be no ambiguity on my own account, I added that whether or not I carried on with my task would depend on the nation's vote. And it was on the same note that I concluded my final appeal on January 6: "Frenchwomen, Frenchmen . . . the truth is – and who is not aware of it? – that the matter is one between you, each man and woman among you, and me."

On January 8, 1961, the nation gave me the massive and unequivocal response I had asked for. Out of twenty-seven and a half million registered voters, over twenty-one million people voted. Fifteen and a half million voted "Yes", five million voted "No"; in other words, a majority of seventy-six per cent. The result was all the more striking in that the "No" which had been passionately advocated by the supporters of "French Algeria" and the Communist Party provided an opportunity for every sort of dissatisfaction and discontent to express itself. In Algeria, out of 4,760,000 registered voters 2,800,000 went to the polls – a remarkable proportion (fifty-nine per cent) of the electorate in a region where the leaders of the insurrection had called for a boycott and where at least a million men were away from their communes. 1,920,000 said "Yes" – 70 per cent of the poll – 790,000 said "No."

It was done! The French people had given the Algerians the right to decide their own fate. There was no doubt that they would choose independence. It remained for us to ensure that they did so at a time of our choice and that the accession of their territory to the rank of sovereign State was promulgated by us. A final referendum would, therefore, be necessary. But we French might well ask ourselves whether it would not be best if it were to lead us deliberately to abandon Algeria as a "sea of troubles", to withdraw our administration, our teachers, our economic activities, our credits, our forces; to concentrate those of the inhabitants who wished to remain French around Algiers and Oran; to send the Algerians living in France back where they came from; to watch from afar and with indifference the fate of a country which would no longer concern us; in short, to act as though, in the fields of colonization as in love, "victory lies in flight". After all, such a total separation, though disastrous for Algeria, would not be disastrous for us, and I found myself seriously considering it. Nevertheless, when all was said and done, I could not help thinking that there was a better solution: to arrive at a mutually preferential association between France and Algeria.

In this connection, nothing that might be devised and, when the time came, voted upon would have any reality without the primary participation of those who were fighting for independence. For it was with them that the vast majority of Algerians now identified themselves, even if not all of them by any means openly supported them. In short, the National Liberation Front must be induced to come to terms with us, so that once the fighting was finally over, the citizens of both countries could be called upon to decide by their vote not only on the establishment of an independent Algeria but a contractual arrangement for its relations with France.

I had no doubt of course that before such negotiations could be successful or even get under way, we were bound to meet with much prejudice, equivocation and haggling from the other side. We were well enough informed through various channels about the organization which called itself the GPRA[1] to realize that it would be contrary to its nature to arrive swiftly at constructive decisions. Not that there were any doubts among the leaders of the insurrection as to the necessity for a future Algerian State to enjoy preferential relations with France. Even while brandishing the standard of revolt, men like Ferhat Abbas, Belkacem Krim, Boumendjel, Ben Khedda, Boulharouf, Ahmed Francis, etc. were too imbued with our ideas, too bound up with our values, too aware of the geographical, historical, political, economic, intellectual and social ties between their country and ours, not to want a future of co-operation. But the mistrust which they felt towards the French authorities as they had known them in the past, the doubts raised in their minds by what they read in our press as to the sincerity and stability of my government, their own lack of practical experience, and the internal rivalries which beset them ever more bitterly as the prospect of real power drew nearer – all these encouraged

[1] See p. 60, n. 1.

them to cling to wordy propagandist attitudes. They dreaded
the confrontation and the precise commitments which genuine
negotiations would entail.

Yet how much longer could they avoid them? Whatever they
might say about it, the vote of January 8 was a decisive factor
which had put the ball firmly into their court. They knew, moreover, that world opinion was already drawing the obvious
inferences from it. They were aware of the fact that the governments of Tunisia and Morocco, whose co-operation was
essential for the maintenance of the units they had formed outside Algeria as well as for their links with the internal resistance,
were impatient to see an end to the fighting. They realized
that even the guerrillas in the *djebels* had begun to ask themselves
why their terrible ordeals dragged on now that General de
Gaulle's proposals had rendered them superfluous. Already,
in June 1960, the leaders of what the rebels called Wilaya iv, in
other words the Algiers region, had made overtures with a view
to a local cease-fire. I had arranged for their delegates – two
"military", Si Salah and Si Lakdar, and one "political," Si
Mohammed – to come to Paris in the greatest secrecy and had
received them myself with due courtesy. Having met me and
heard what I had to say, they had been very anxious to come
to some arrangement, very confident of being able to carry
most of their comrades with them and, despite my warnings,
quite convinced that they could obtain the tacit consent of the
leaders of the FLN. It is true that after several months of coming
and going across the mountains and, doubtless, the intervention
of the supreme leadership, the "political" representative had
had the other two assassinated. But the attempt spoke volumes
for the drastic change of attitude provoked by my proposals
among the combatants.

In February 1961, in response to solicitations addressed to
us from Switzerland by emissaries of the "Front", I deemed it
advisable to send a semi-official spokesman to Lucerne; someone
of whom there could be no reason to doubt that he expressed my
point of view directly. In accordance with instructions, he would
make it clear to his interlocutors that, far from wishing France

to cling on to Algeria, my aim was to disengage her therefrom, and that this would happen in any event. It was, thus, for the Algerians, if they felt they needed her, to ensure that France continued to help them thereafter. Georges Pompidou, accompanied by Bruno de Leusse, conferred at length, on February 20 and March 5, with Ali Boumendjel and Taieb Boulharouf. After this exchange of views, we proposed and the Front agreed that real negotiations should begin at last on French soil, dealing simultaneously with the cease-fire, the conditions governing the final referendum, and the future of Algeria. Thus was initiated the series of talks which were to begin at Evian, resume at Lugrin, re-open at Les Rousses and end at Evian and which, in the space of nine months, were to result in the agreements on the basis of which the French people would unreservedly grant Algeria her independence and substitute a close partnership for the domination which had lasted one hundred and thirty-two years since her conquest. But before this point was reached, scenes of conciliation and agonizing crises were yet to alternate on the stage where the drama was being played out.

President Bourguiba, for his part, had realized at once that the referendum of January 8 opened up a prospect the consequences of which would be of cardinal importance for Tunisia. He asked to see me. On February 27 we spent the day together at Rambouillet. I was in the presence of a fighter, a politician, a Head of State, whose caliber and ambition transcended the limits of his country. From the beginning he had been the champion of Tunisian independence, a position which obliged him to overcome a number of contradictions within himself. He had constantly opposed France, to whom he was, nevertheless, attached by ties of culture and sentiment. He had overthrown the regime of the Beys in Tunis and espoused the revolution, although he believed in the value of what is permanent and traditional. Free-thinker though he was, and imbued with the ethos and manners of the West, he had identified himself with the great Arab and Islamic struggle. At present he was supporting the insurrection in Algeria, but not without some forebodings about the uncomfortable proximity of a turbulent republic. If he had sought me out, it was undoubtedly in order to indicate that he approved of what I had done to bring about Algerian negotiations and hoped to play a conciliating role during the confrontation. But his purpose was also to obtain a few advantages at a time when Algeria was about to receive many.

Habib Bourguiba began by bringing up the question of Bizerta. He demanded its evacuation. I reminded him that in 1958, on withdrawing French forces *proprio motu* from Tunisian territory, I had insisted that they should retain the naval base until further notice. This stipulation was indeed specified in the letters which we had exchanged at that time. Since then, the French had ceased to occupy the arsenal, had handed back the administration of the town to the Tunisians, and had allowed their troops to be billeted there too. In fact, the presence of our small garrison and our naval workshops was profitable for Bizerta. "In any event," I told the President, "it will not last much longer. It is true that in the present state of international tension, with Tunisia not covered by NATO and determined to remain neutral, France cannot leave a base whose location in the middle of the Mediterranean area could be of the greatest strategic importance, at the mercy of a surprise attack. But, as you know, we are in the process of equipping ourselves with atomic weapons. As soon as we have the bomb, the situation as regards our national security will alter radically. In particular, we shall have the means to protect ourselves against anything that might happen in Bizerta after our departure. You may, therefore, rest assured that we shall withdraw in about a year's time." "I accept your assurance," Habib Bourguiba replied, "and in that case I shall not insist on an immediate solution to the problem." He was to repeat this during the plenary session which we held later in the presence of Michel Debré, Maurice Couve de Murville, Mohammed Masmoudi and Sadok Mokaddem.

But the question of Bizerta was, for Bourguiba, merely a roundabout way of approaching the main issue. What chiefly concerned him was to procure for his country certain territorial extensions on its Saharan borders in the likely event of the vast desert being handed over to a sovereign Algeria. The object of this acquisitiveness was, of course, oil. Whereas none had been found on Tunisian territory, the French had discovered and were currently exploiting abundant sources close by, in the Hassi-Messaoud and Edjelé areas. Could the frontier not be modified so as to put Tunisia in possession of some oil-bearing lands? According to Bourguiba, this could be justified on the ground that the boundary between the Sahara and the south of the former Regency had been drawn in a vague and arbitrary way. But I could not accede to the President's request. The expansion of our mineral prospecting and our exploitation of Saharan oil would be an important factor in future co-operation with the Algerians. Why should we jeopardize it in advance by handing over to others land which could, on this understanding, revert to Algeria? If, moreover, we were to do so for the benefit of Tunisia, what irresistible encouragement it would give to Moroccan claims on Colomb-Béchar and Tindouf, not to mention what Mauritania, Mali, Niger, Chad and Libya might also wish to claim! When the time came, it would be in our interest to make an overall settlement for the exploitation of Saharan oil. We would certainly take into consideration the advantages which certain neighboring countries might hope to draw from this development and the possibility that they might wish to join in it. Indeed, for Tunisia's benefit we had just completed a pipe-line which would bring some of the Edjelé oil to La Skhirra, and we were about to build a refinery at the port of loading. We had also proposed that the countries bordering the Sahara should join with us, pending the time when they could do so with a sovereign Algeria, in setting up a consortium for the prospecting, financing, extraction and marketing of all gas and oil resources in the desert. But there could be no justification for dividing up the territory. Bourguiba received this refusal with some displeasure. Nevertheless, it seemed to me that our talks had been sufficiently frank and cordial for me to feel able to say as we parted: "I look forward with confidence to our future relations." He warmly concurred.

The day before, Mohammed V, King of Morocco, had died suddenly. We had been linked by a friendship of twenty years' standing. I was grateful to him in the name of France for having remained faithful to his pledges even during the darkest days of the war, and for having refused to be swayed, after our initial defeat, by Hitler's insistent encouragement to rebel or, later, by the insidious advice of Roosevelt, who at the time of the Anfa Conference urged him to denounce the Protectorate treaty. Because he came to personify the important contribution in men and resources which Morocco had brought to our victory effort, I had made him a Companion of the Liberation. For his part, the sovereign had always gratefully acknowledged the fact that in safeguarding the honor and integrity of France I had enabled Morocco to preserve hers. He appreciated the courtesy which I had shown him both in North Africa and later in Paris. He shared my wish to develop Franco-Moroccan relations into a close association between two sovereign States. Finally he was grateful to me for having expressed my sympathy and understanding at the time of his exile to Madagascar in 1953 and had never forgotten that, on receiving him discreetly on his return from Tananarive two years later, I had said to him: "Sire, you have suffered. I congratulate you on it. Those who inflicted this ordeal upon you did you a service. For one must have suffered in order to be great!" Since my return to the helm, we had resumed a relationship of mutual trust. While affording those Algerian rebels who had taken refuge on his territory only such facilities as were required by elementary Arab solidarity, he influenced the rebel leaders in the direction of peace. At all events, as long as he was on the throne I was certain that any difficulties created for us by Morocco would remain limited.

The sudden departure of Mohammed V threatened to present us with a serious problem in this connection. Agitation in Moroccan political circles gave reason to fear that the crisis of the succession might provoke grave repercussions. But nothing of the kind: the young Prince Hassan, seizing the initiative immediately, assumed his father's throne unchallenged. Sensitive though the new king was on the subject of national sovereignty, he had every intention of maintaining a special relationship with France. Altogether, there was reason to hope that on the part of Morocco, as of Tunisia, the Algerian "Front" would henceforth receive encouragement to do the right thing, in other words negotiate.

Soon after the referendum, independently of the secret contacts which were preparing the ground, public positions began to be taken up with an eye to the opening of the peace talks. On January 16, 1961, the GPRA once more expressed its willingness to enter into negotiations with the French government, though a fortnight later, on February 2, through the medium of Ferhat Abbas and Boumendjel who were on a visit to Malaysia at the time, it declared that self-determination demanded the prior withdrawal of the French Army from Algeria. In France, a number of Algerian Moslem parliamentarians, including all the senators, formed themselves for the first time into a group known as the *Rassemblement démocratique algérien* and called for the opening of official talks with the GPRA. At the same time there were various signs that a grave crisis provoked by activist elements was brewing. On January 25, General Challe announced his decision to retire because he was in conflict with government policy. In March, the military court in the "Barricades" case, in spite of the fact that the law had been flouted by the escape of the ring-leaders to Spain, pronounced scandalously lenient verdicts. The political elements in favor of "integration", led by Jacques Soustelle, set up a committee with headquarters at Vincennes whose manifesto proclaimed: "It is we who serve the law and those in power who are violating it!" In Algiers and Oran, the various extremist commandos formed themselves into the Secret Army Organization (OAS). In metropolitan France as well as Algeria, the plastic bomb outrages perpetrated by the OAS developed into a campaign of threats and punishments directed against prominent members of parliament, public servants and those responsible for law and order. Sensing that the adverse wind would continue to blow relentlessly, I myself decided to speak out, more frankly than ever before, at a press conference on April 11.

Observing that "Algeria is costing us – to say the least – more than she is worth to us", I repeated that "France envisages with the greatest composure a situation in which Algeria would cease to belong to her . . . and will offer no objection should the people of Algeria decide to organize themselves into a State which would take over responsibility for their country." I underlined my belief that "such a State would be sovereign at home and abroad." Moreover, it was not the military results achieved by the FLN which caused me to speak as I did. "In fact the rebellion, which until recently killed some fifty people a day, is now killing an average of seven or eight, of whom four or five are Moslems. . . . Nevertheless, events have confirmed me in what I have been at pains to point out for twenty years, with no pleasure, I can assure you, but in the certainty of thus serving the interests of France." After recalling what I had done to bring about decolonization, I said: "If I have done all this, it is not only because of the vast movement towards emancipation unleashed by the Second World War and its consequences from one end of the world to the other . . . but also because it seems to me contrary to the present obligations and burdens which no longer conform to the demands of her power and her prestige." I then called upon the leaders of the rebellion to negotiate. "Certainly, it is difficult for an essentially insurrectionist body to approach such questions as peace, the organization of a State and the economic development of a country with the necessary minimum of serenity and at the required level. But it remains to be seen, inasmuch as they will never achieve supremacy in the field, where our Army has the situation under control, inasmuch as they have great responsibilities owing to the influence which they exercise over the Moslems, inasmuch as they seem destined to play an important role in the launching of the new Algeria, whether these leaders will prove capable of constructive action."

The die was cast. From a score of platforms over the next few days, in the course of my journey to Aquitaine and Périgord, I renewed my proposals, which were greeted with huge public ovations. All the factors had thus been brought into play in such a way that the FLN could no longer postpone its decision to accept the challenge. But first of all I had to be prepared for the ultras to move over to the attack, taking myself and my authority as their direct targets.

In the early hours of April 22, 1961, I learned that General Challe, who had been secretly flown to Algiers in an Air Force plane, had launched a military coup. In accordance with plans drawn up in advance by a group of colonels – Argoud, Broizat, Gardes, Godard – several paratroop regiments had placed themselves under his orders, thus enabling him to arrest Jean Morin, the Delegate-General, General Gambiez, the Commander-in-Chief, General Vézinet, Commander of the Algiers region, René Jannin, the Prefect of Police, and Robert Buron, a minister who happened to be there on a tour of inspection; to seize the principal public buildings; and to obtain the support of a section of the General Staff and certain elements in the administration and the police. He had found Generals Zeller and Jouhaud already on the spot and was soon to be joined by General Salan. With these three accomplices he formed a kind of Directory, which declared a state of siege and assumed all the attributions of a government. At first glance it seemed as though the group might be able to win over a considerable section of the armed forces. Challe, after all, had commanded them recently and with brilliant success. Before him, Salan had exercised complete civil and military power in Algiers. Zeller and Jouhaud had been Chiefs of Staff of the Army and the Air Force respectively and the latter, a native of Oran, was extremely popular there. This meant that, quite apart from the attachment to "French Algeria" and the spirit of rebellion which infused certain units, they might be able to count on reflexes of obedience and personal loyalties among both officers and men in attempting to impose their authority. Moreover, by setting themselves up against myself and my government, imprisoning the representatives of public authority, and declaring that "those who have directly taken part in the abandonment of Algeria and the Sahara will be brought before a military tribunal created to deal with crimes against the security of the State", the mutineers had burnt their boats and committed themselves to extremes. Thus I did not close my eyes to the fact that this desperate venture had every chance of seizing the initial advantage in Algeria and I fully expected that its leaders would be induced to launch an expedition on Paris which, thanks to a degree of active collusion in the midst of a fairly general passivity, would attempt to overthrow the State. My mind was made up. I must quell the revolt without compromise or delay by inflexibly affirming the legitimacy that was mine and thus persuading the people to uphold the law and the Army to choose the path of discipline.

In order that this should be immediately demonstrated on the spot, Louis Joxe, Minister of State, and General Olié, who had become Chief of General Staff when General Ely had reached retiring age, were sent to Algeria, in spite of the danger, on the morning of April 22. They were to issue firm orders to wavering commanders. This was announced immediately over the radio by Michel Debré, who declared that "the government is inflexibly determined to enforce the nation's will", and that "every chief in Algeria owes obedience solely to the nation's chief: General de Gaulle." All sea and air traffic to Algeria was suspended the same day. In metropolitan France, a number of preventive arrests were made, notably of suspects in military circles. The Cabinet decreed a state of emergency and formally indicted the leaders of the mutiny by name. The next day, having consulted, in accordance with the law, the Prime Minister, the Presidents of the Senate, the National Assembly and the Constitutional Council, all of whom, in their anxiety, gave me their approval, I decided to invoke Article 16 of the Constitution. Thus, whatever happened, I would be in a position to take any action necessitated by the public danger independently and without delay. At the same time, everyone was made to realize by the example of the Head of State that there could be no trifling with duty.

However, on Sunday April 23, it seemed as though Challe had scored a few points. Some fifteen regiments, the majority of them paratroops, had rallied to his side. The self-styled "Commander-in-Chief" had managed to arrest General Pouilly, commander of the Oran region, who, hoping to make him see reason, had agreed to meet him under a safe-conduct. After a great deal of wavering General Gouraud, commander of the Constantine region, came down in favor of the revolt. Others who had joined it were General Bigot, Commander of the Air Force in Algeria, General Petit, second-in-command of the Saharan region, and the retired General Gardy, ex-inspector of the Foreign Legion. It was only with the greatest difficulty that Louis Joxe and General Olié had succeeded in getting back to Paris after passing through Tlemcen, Constantine and Bône. The OAS militia, in special uniforms, had appeared in Algiers and Oran, taking over control of police stations and prisons, freeing activist prisoners and putting other people under lock and key. Meanwhile, at eight o'clock in the evening, I appeared on the screen and at the microphone, in uniform, ready to assume my responsibilities *urbi et orbi*.

"An insurrectionary authority has established itself in Algiers by military pronunciamento. This authority has a façade: a quartet of retired generals. It also has a reality: a group of partisan, ambitious and fanatical officers. This group and this quartet know how to act fast. But their view of the nation and the world is distorted by their frenzy. Their action must lead straight to national disaster. . . . And by whom? Alas! Alas! by men whose duty, whose honor, whose calling it was to serve and to obey. . . . In the name of France I order that every means, I repeat, every means should be employed to bar the way against these men until they can be crushed. I forbid every Frenchman, and first and foremost every soldier, to carry out their orders. . . . There can be no other fate for the usurpers than that which awaits them from the full rigor of the law. . . . In face of the calamity which hangs over the nation and the danger which threatens the Republic. . . . I have decided to invoke Article 16 of the Constitution. From today I shall take, directly if need be, the measures which seem to me to be demanded by the circumstances. In so doing I am asserting, now and for the future, the republican legitimacy entrusted to me by the French nation, which I shall uphold, no matter what may happen, until the end of my mandate or until either my strength, or life itself, fail me, and of which I shall take steps to ensure the survival after I am gone. . . . Frenchwomen, Frenchmen, help me!"

Everyone, everywhere, heard my words. In metropolitan France, there was no one who did not watch or listen. In Algeria, a million transistors were tuned in. From then on, the revolt met with a passive resistance on the spot which became hourly more explicit. It is true that the government, alerted from various sides, had envisaged the possibility of a rebel irruption in the neighborhood of Paris that very evening, had warned those who could to bar the way, and had deployed all the security forces which were available in the capital. But throughout the following day there were increasing signs of Challe's discomfiture. In the Constantine region, General Gouraud's defection was not emulated by his subordinates. General Lennuyeux in Constantine, General Ailleret in Bône and General Géliot in Sétif all kept to the path of duty, as did the Air Force commander, General Fourquet. In Kabylia, General Simon had taken to the mountains to escape the mutineers. In the Algiers region, General Arfouilloux, whom Joxe on his way through had appointed corps commander in place of the captive Vézinet, was holding firm at Médéa, where he was regrouping loyal elements. Whereas, in Oran itself, General Gardy, seconded by Colonel Argoud, had been installed by the paratroops in the name of the insurrection, in Tlemcen Generals Perrotat and Foucault refused them access to the zone. In Sidi Bel Abbès, the headquarters of the Foreign Legion, General Brothier restored discipline. In Mers-el-Kébir, whither Admiral Querville, the naval Commander-in-Chief, had made his way and later, cutting short his self-questioning, wisely put to sea, the naval base had not allowed itself to be imposed upon. Not one of the warships patrolling the Algerian coast showed signs of going over to the mutiny. In Algiers itself, the *garde mobile*, assembled in its barracks, refused to accept orders from the usurpers. Meanwhile, throughout the territory, a growing number of soldiers, NCOs and officers expressed their refusal to lend themselves to the rebels' venture. As the national servicemen showed themselves hourly more determined in this respect, the rebel "quartet" announced that it would advance the date of their discharge, but without obtaining an end to the agitation. Even in the very regiments which had been the first to be dragged into the "misadventure", signs of wavering, even of recantation, began to appear. During the evening of Monday the 24th, the four rebel generals decided to appear in the Forum where the population had been summoned to hear them. Although they claimed to be confident of success, although Challe declared that they were there "to fight, to suffer, to die if need be", although the crowd cheered them, a feeling of anxiety hung over the assembly.

Without a single shot having been fired from either side, Tuesday April 25 saw the collapse of the whole and disreputable venture. In Constantine, Gouraud declared that he had been mistaken and was placing himself once more under my authority. In Oran, the paratroops withdrew from the city to return to their previous stations, Gardy and Argoud disappeared, and General Perrotat regained control of the entire army corps. All the "Nord" aircraft which, technically speaking, would alone have been capable of transporting commandos to Paris for a *coup d'état*, had taken off from Blida and Maison-Blanche and landed in metropolitan France on Government orders. In Algiers, the *zouaves* joined together "to address a motion of loyalty to General de Gaulle"; near La Redoute, Air Force recruits marched past shouting "Vive de Gaulle!"; the *gardes mobiles*, emerging from their barracks in the Tagarins district, took up positions at all the principal crossroads, liquidated the headquarters of the OAS, and resumed possession of the central police station. By nightfall the only rebel troops remaining in the Algerian capital were the 1st Parachute Regiment of the Foreign Legion who still guarded Government

House, and the remains of a rebel GHQ in the Rignot district. Towards midnight, the female announcer declared over the newly-liberated radio: "Law and order will be restored in Algeria." Shortly afterwards the "quartet", summoned by anxious civilians in the Forum, appeared on the famous balcony. As the electricity to their microphone had been cut off, the Four could not make themselves heard. In any case, what could they have said? Zeller, in mufti, disappeared into the crowd. He was to give himself up a few days later. Salan and Jouhaud, amid the last of the legionaries who left the town singing the Edith Piaf refrain, "*Je ne regrette rien*," fled in a lorry to the Legion's camp at Zeralda. From there, the two of them went underground to lead the OAS campaign. As for Challe, after having sent an officer to announce his surrender to his minister that afternoon, he then seemed to change his mind and finally, at dawn, gave himself up to the police. He was taken immediately to Paris, where he was imprisoned in the Santé.

The collapse of this escapade henceforth rid men's minds of the specter of an Army move to take over the State or at least force it to maintain the *status quo* in Algeria. Assured as I now was of unqualified obedience of the Army and the support of the country, I was, of course, glad to see the threat removed once and for all. But I was nonetheless deeply saddened by the human waste resulting from the affair and especially by the ruin of the senior officers who had instigated it and certain of the participants. Joxe immediately returned to Algeria to reorganize the police and the administration. On Messmer, who accompanied him, devolved the cruel task of amputating, disbanding and punishing the guilty units.

But the law is the law, however severe, and justice must be done. By what process was it to be meted out to the rebel leaders? No civil court would be competent. The normal military tribunal would not be of a sufficiently high level, and moreover its behavior over the "Barricades" affair gave reason to fear that, in the circumstances, it might suffer a second lapse. For this reason a Military High Court was established under Article 16 of the Constitution to try the principal accused.

Under the chairmanship of an eminent and supremely well-qualified judge, Maurice Patin, President of the criminal division of the Court of Cassation, it consisted of nine judges, five officers and four civilians, and the Public Prosecutor at the Court of Cassation would put the case for the State. The trial of Challe, Zeller and Gouraud opened on May 29. Three days later, judgment was pronounced. The sentences imposed, fifteen years' criminal detention for the first two and ten for the third, took into account their previous service records, the fact that they had given themselves up to the authorities without there having been any loss of life, and finally the motives behind their offense which – as I knew and felt – were not entirely base.

Once the law had rung down the final curtain on this melancholy conspiracy, another year was to pass before the Algerian problem, now settled in principle, would be resolved in fact. Certainly the fighting was henceforth to be reduced to rare and minimal skirmishes. But for all that, the days that passed were to be filled with trouble and unrest. Negotiations that dragged on because of the collective uncertainty and the rival ambitions of the FLN leaders; a sudden and futile attack on our troops in Bizerta and on the Saharan border at the orders of the President of the Tunisian Republic; numberless crimes perpetrated by the OAS with the object of creating a secret rule of terror in Algeria which would spread to metropolitan France; acts of reprisal by the Moslems, especially in Algiers and Oran, against those who were massacring them; and finally, on the part of the French political parties, an animosity which had lost all restraint now that the phantom of military subversion had vanished and the outcome was in sight – such were the themes which were to occupy the country's public life as well as my own existence during this period. But I was well-armed against these adversities: my breast-plate was the unambiguous support of the French people, my sword the certainty that I was taking the only valid course.

On May 20, 1961, the two delegations met in Evian. Louis Joxe led the government delegation, Belkacem Krim that of the

Front. The day before, in order to emphasize that the objective was peace, I had taken several significant steps. Our troops were ordered to observe a month's truce, which meant that they would suspend all offensive operations and restrict themselves, if attacked, to repulsing their assailants. An entire Army division and several Air Force squadrons were recalled to metropolitan France. Six thousand of the ten thousand Moslems convicted in Algeria for acts of rebellion were freed. Ahmed Ben Bella and his fellow-prisoners left the Île d'Aix and were installed in the Château de Turquant. During the nine months the negotiations lasted, in four official phases interspersed with semi-official contacts, we were unfailingly explicit, patient and firm – an attitude which indeed reflected the character of Louis Joxe, who was entrusted with the conduct of the talks. He was passionately eager to reach an agreement, but was determined to make it a valid and therefore a reasonable one. Since his arduous duties as Secretary-General to the Government and later as Minister had placed him for twenty years at the center of the spectrum of public affairs, he was profoundly conversant with all the many questions, political, economic, financial, social, administrative, educational and military, involved in the construction of an Algerian State on the basis of the French State and their subsequent close co-operation. Being a humane man, he was at pains to ensure that the agreements concluded should pay due consideration to civic rights, especially those of the Europeans, which would be seriously jeopardized by the transfer of power. Being devoted to the cause of national renewal, he was anxious to ensure that the emancipation of Algeria bore the stamp of France's generosity and dignity.

But if we were to consent to grant Algeria a status of association rather than abandon her to her own devices, certain conditions would have to be fulfilled. A profound osmosis, human, economic and cultural, must be brought about between the new State and ourselves; preferential trade channels must be maintained in every sphere; goods must be reciprocally imported and exported duty-free; the respective currencies must belong to the franc area; the nationals of each country must be free to enter the other at will, take up residence wherever they wished, carry on their professions there, bring in, take out or leave their belongings freely. The French community in Algeria must receive strict guarantees in respect of civic status, property rights, way of life, language, schools, etc., whether they chose, while keeping their French nationality in France, to become Algerians – in which case they would automatically have their share in the government, the administration, the judiciary – or whether they preferred to remain French citizens in Algeria, in which case they would be accorded a privileged establishment convention. France's enormous investment in the discovery, exploitation and transport of Saharan oil must remain secure for the present and must guarantee her a formal preference as regards future drilling and mining rights. The series of atomic and space tests in the desert, which were of the utmost importance, must be continued as planned, and this would entail the continued presence of our military and technical apparatus. In return for all of this, we were prepared to give exceptional aid towards the development of Algeria by granting her a large annual subsidy, by pursuing the application of our Constantine Plan, by offering her the assistance of our technicians in various fields, by opening our doors to vast numbers of her workers and students and by providing a sufficient number of teachers at every level of the educational system to ensure that the Algerian élite was moulded by French culture and that the people were taught French.

But it was our wish that the historic operation which consisted, for France, in conferring sovereignty and responsibility upon Algeria, for the latter in assuming them, and for both in maintaining a large measure of interdependence, should be accomplished with due deliberation and by democratic means. There could be no Algerian independence and no association between the two countries until after these had been voted by the French and the Algerian people. There could be no sovereign government of Algeria save that which would be duly elected there, even though this entailed a transitional period during which French authority would remain supreme. In addition, the French Army would remain in Algeria until the new State had proved its capacity to honor its commitments.

To bring all this about, we would first have to scale the mountains of mistrust and bridge the abysses of arrogance behind which the FLN entrenched themselves throughout the discussions. For in every question raised they saw an intention on our part to keep a direct grip on Algeria, or at least some pretext for intervening there, when in fact this was precisely what we wanted to be relieved of. Hence they kept producing more and more preconditions for an agreement. Invoking one after another the "legitimacy" of their authority, the unity of the Algerian nation, the integrity of the territory, they demanded variously that the cease-fire should not come into operation until all other questions had been settled, that our forces should first of all be withdrawn, that before everything else the rebel organization should take over the government of the country, that we should not demand a special status for the French community, and that we should forgo the exercise of preferential rights in the Sahara. For our part, in order to overcome this dialectic and achieve the basic objective, we deployed the irrefutable arguments afforded us by the fact that we were still in control. In order that the text of the agreement and its application should begin with the cease-fire and not with the transfer of our authority, in order that self-determination should result from a referendum, first in France and then in Algeria, and not from a mere oath once sworn on the Soummam,[1] in order that governmental power in Algeria should also derive from an election and not from a revolutionary decree, we gave our interlocutors the choice between France's generous and fruitful aid and the chaos which would be inflicted upon Algeria if we were to abandon her. In order that the rights of the *pieds-noirs* should be guaranteed in such a way as to ensure co-operation between the two communities, we raised the alternative of a regrouping of the Europeans and those Moslems who wished to remain French, in a restricted zone where they

[1] A river in Kabylia. A conference of Algerian rebel leaders was held in the Soummam valley in August 1956.

would be in the majority and which France would protect as though it were her own territory. In order to keep control of the oilfields we had developed and of the experimental bomb and rocket bases, we pointed out that we were in a position to remain in the Sahara whatever happened, possibly establishing the autonomy of that vast wilderness. In order for our Army to remain in Algeria for as long as it suited us, it was simply for us to decide, since we controlled the entire territory and the frontiers.

In short, the object of the negotiations as far as we were concerned was to persuade the FLN to accept the provisions which were essential, on the one hand for a satisfactory procedure for Algeria's accession to independence, and on the other hand for an effective association between the new State and France. Failing this, we should be driven to a total breach, while safeguarding our own interests, which clearly we had every means of doing. It was a dilemma which was inevitably to provoke innumerable clashes throughout the talks. The latter opened at Evian and were suspended on June 13. They were resumed at the Château Lugrin at the end of July, still without reaching agreement. As the discussions followed their fitful and fluctuating course, my oral and written instructions guided our delegation step by step.

At the same time, I continued to explain our aims in public. By this means, people's minds were clarified and more often than not convinced. By this means the facts, which were unfailingly distorted by the organs of information, were brought back into focus. On May 8, 1961, speaking to the country on the anniversary of V-day and a few days after the Algiers crisis, I said: "It is for the people of Algeria to take over their own affairs. It is for them to decide if Algeria is to be a sovereign State, nationally and internationally. It is also for them to decide whether this State is to be associated with France, which France is willing to accept provided she receives a valid return for her aid and provided it involves an organic co-operation between the two communities." Then I addressed the *pieds-noirs*: "In these circumstances, what a rewarding task would present itself to the Algerians of French stock! With all my heart I ask them, in the name of France, on the very day when we are commemorating a victory to which they contributed so much, to put aside outworn myths and foolish agitation which lead to nothing but misery, and to turn their courage and their abilities to the great task ahead." In an extensive tour of Lorraine, where I received a magnificent welcome, I expressed the same sentiments to many different audiences between June 28 and July 2. On July 12, I spoke to the nation once more, to a France "who is now wedded to her century": "In Algeria, our Army had to prevail in the field in order that we should retain complete freedom of decision and action. This has been achieved. We are thus in a position to take a number of pacificatory measures there, to withdraw large forces back to metropolitan France, and to cut down the length of military service by several weeks. . . . This being so, France unreservedly agrees that the Algerian people should establish a completely independent State. To this end, she is ready to organize free self-determination with all Algerian political elements, in particular those of the rebellion. She remains willing to maintain her aid to Algeria as long as the organic co-operation of the two communities is assured and her own interests are safeguarded. Failing this co-operation, she would be obliged in the last resort, in order to protect those of the inhabitants who refused to belong to a State doomed to chaos, to regroup them in a special zone and provide them with the means of settling in metropolitan France if such was their desire, leaving all the others to their own devices and forbidding them access to her territory."

Had the drama seemed to be approaching its denouement, I would then have done everything in my power to light up the stage. Of course, the clearer and more straightforward my policy appeared, the more the professional objectors presented it to readers and to voters as being tortuous and obscure. Not the least of the drawbacks of their unremitting dissent was its effect abroad. For as a result, the outside world, hitherto accustomed to seeing the French government perpetually undermined by the general spirit of resignation, was only too ready to believe that de Gaulle, assailed from all sides in his turn, would equally be unable to stand firm.

No doubt it was on this mistaken assumption that President Bourguiba suddenly ventured to demand, in a threatening letter on July 6, that France should immediately withdraw her forces from Bizerta and agree to a frontier rectification between the Sahara and Southern Tunisia. On the 18th, he went over to the attack. Tunisian troops brought up from the interior, joining forces with the town garrison and accompanied by a detachment of the Neo-Destour militia, opened fire on our soldiers, cut them off from the sea, blockaded the base installations, in particular the airfield, and obstructed the harbor entrance to deny access to our ships. Simultaneously, in the extreme south, a large Tunisian detachment crossed the Saharan frontier, surrounded our outpost at Garet-el-Hammel and occupied the area known as "frontier post 233". Bourguiba probably calculated that Paris would hesitate to mount a large-scale operation just as the Lugrin talks were about to begin, and opinion in France and abroad only wished to see the end of all fighting in North Africa. He was therefore counting on negotiations being opened on the basis of a *fait accompli*, in which case he had every chance of obtaining satisfaction. Thus the "supreme warrior" could, while there was still time, pose once more as the intransigent enemy of French colonialism in the eyes of the Arab world, and at the same time secure the cession of the coveted oil-bearing lands.

But, determined though I was to extricate our country from its overseas commitments, and conciliatory, not to say obliging, though I had been towards Tunisia, I could not permit France to be flouted. For this reason, our military rejoinder was short and sharp. On July 19, a brisk air battle over Bizerta and a paratroop descent enabled us to regain possession of the airfield, where reinforcements were subsequently landed. More arrived by sea shortly afterwards. Admiral Amman, commander of the base, was then able to lift the blockade, seize the area of the town adjoining the port, clear the harbor entrance of the hostile elements who were holding it and the wreckage which was blocking it, re-establish naval and air communications and put the sorely pressed assailants to flight. That done, a cease-fire was granted to the Tunisian Governor, and our troops turned to the assistance of the population which had been deprived of food supplies and was in a state of panic. As for the Saharan frontier, it was swiftly and brilliantly relieved by our mobile desert forces. Altogether, their futile aggression had cost the Tunisians over seven hundred wretched dead, more than eight hundred hapless prisoners and several thousand unfortunate wounded. Twenty-seven of our soldiers were killed.

It is true that in France the political parties blamed de Gaulle. All in their different ways condemned our military action and demanded the immediate opening of negotiations with Tunis, completely ignoring the aggression committed against our troops in Bizerta and the Sahara. As usual, only a few faint voices were raised in my support against these multiple demands for the line of least resistance. But knowing what such speeches and articles were worth as a yardstick by comparison with what was at stake, I took care not to halt our counter-offensive before it had completely carried the day.

Nor did the agitation at the UN or the attempt at intervention by its Secretary-General Dag Hammarskjöld induce us to modify our actions. Hammarskjöld, who was already in open disagreement with us at the time because he was interfering directly in the affairs of the Congo, sided personally with Bourguiba. He went to see him in Tunis, held friendly discussions with him, and on July 26, when the fighting was over, proceeded to Bizerta as though it was for him to settle the dispute on the spot. This move rebounded to his discomfiture. For, following instructions, our troops paid no attention to the comings and goings of the self-appointed mediator and Admiral Amman refused to see him. There was nothing left for President Bourguiba to do but write the whole thing off as a dead loss. In any case he would get over it eventually, just as the damaged friendship between France and Tunisia would one day be repaired.

As it happened, this unfortunate event had no effect on the

course of the negotiations with the FLN. But would the same be true of the sudden changes in the rebel leadership on August 27? In particular, Ferhat Abbas ceased to be President. Benyoussef Ben Khedda succeeded him. At first it might have been feared that the replacement of the former nationalist leader by someone younger and apparently more "revolutionary" would stiffen the intransigence of the GPRA. But a communiqué from the new "Premier" soon seemed to suggest the contrary. "For our part," Ben Khedda declared, "we are convinced that frank and just negotiations, which will enable our people to exercise their right to self-determination and accede to independence, can bring an end to the war and open the way to a fruitful co-operation between the Algerian and French peoples. That is what we want." It is true that a later speech by this same Ben Khedda declaring that the referendum was quite unnecessary and that "we should dispense with it" appeared to put everything back into the melting-pot. But shortly afterwards we were told that he had said it "merely for form's sake". Thus our interlocutors were gradually moving towards the goal which we had set for them.

Ferhat Abbas's disappearance from the scene put an end to some long-standing ambitions, among them one which he had entertained for twenty years concerning myself and which he had revealed to me in Algiers during the Second World War. In the course of a conversation we had at that time, he unfolded to me with passion and intelligence the political aim which he was pursuing as head of the *Union populaire algérienne*: to establish with our agreement a democratic Algerian State which would be federated with France. But first of all the fierce resistance of the settlers and the administration to any such change would have to be broken down. "Because you are who you are and because your present actions will make you all-powerful later," he told me, "you will be able to act in this direction in a way no other Frenchman has ever dared or will ever dare." But since, in the middle of the war and the terrible situation our country was in at the time, there were more urgent and imperative matters to be settled, I had listened to Ferhat Abbas

non-committally though with great interest. When I said to him
with a smile: "No doubt you see yourself as the President of the
future Algerian Republic as you conceive it?" he had replied
gravely: "I could hope for nothing better than to find myself one
day at your side, accompanying France in the name of Algeria."
Ten years later, when the rebellion had already broken out without his at first having had a hand in it, and when he, a French
member of parliament, was preparing to go to Cairo to take
over the leadership of the FLN, Ferhat Abbas had begged me
for an interview. I had refused. For what would have been the
point of such an interview at a time when, cut off from all
public affairs, I held no power whatsoever?

Some years earlier, for the same reason, I had given the same
response to Ho Chi Minh, President of Vietnam, who in 1946
had just been negotiating with the Fourth Republic at Fontainebleau and who, sensing that the hoped-for agreement was about
to perish unborn, had asked to see me urgently in my retirement.
Did they perhaps hope, these leaders of movements which were
about to sweep their people into a struggle against ours, that
before that point was reached they might find personified in me
a France unfettered by the impotent subterfuges of partisan
politicians? Might events have turned out differently if, at that
time, I had remained at the helm? But to what and for what
could I have pretended to commit France when I was not
responsible for her fate?

While the FLN, notwithstanding its change of leadership,
was now progressing towards peace, it was war to the knife that
the elements grouped under the initials OAS were now unleashing. Here was not simply a spontaneous explosion of anger
and disappointment. It was a large-scale campaign, aimed at
imposing, by dint of crime, a policy which was laughably known
as "French Algeria" but which was calculated to create an
unbridgeable gulf between the two peoples. These seditionists
hoped that by killing more and more Moslems they would
provoke the latter to step up the fighting and the terrorism from
their side too, and that the resultant atmosphere of mutual
massacre would make peace talks impossible. But in addition,

these doctrinaires of terrorism, esteeming that fear, once "the mainspring of assemblies", had now become the mainspring of society as a whole, sought by incessant outrages to intimidate public opinion and the authorities and thus force them in the prescribed direction. For more than a year, then, the OAS pursued its murderous activities, theoretically under the authority of Salan and Jouhaud, in hiding respectively in Algiers and Oran, who retained considerable influence in the administration, the police and the Army, but in reality at the behest of thugs consumed by totalitarian passion, such as Jean-Jacques Susini. It used deserters and fanatics who were the scum of the Army, particularly of the Foreign Legion units, and the underworld elements who are always brought to the surface by latent political turmoil. It exploited the illusions and the anger of the majority of the *pieds-noirs* who continued to expect what they regarded as salvation from some providential stroke of force. And, finally, it was linked with all kinds of political thieves' kitchens, networks of conspiracy and scourings of ex-"militias" which, in metropolitan France, were bent on bringing down the Republic at any price and in many cases on paying off old scores which they had been harboring against de Gaulle since 1940.

From the beginning of the Evian meetings, the principal Algerian towns, especially Algiers and Oran, were the scene of daily tragedy. The OAS killers showed a preference for the sub-machine-gun or automatic pistol against Moslems, either exterminating individuals marked down in advance or firing indiscriminately on any Moslems they came across in shops, on café terraces or on the pavement. These commandos of crime usually operated from cars, the more swiftly to escape pursuit by the police which was in any case rare and apathetic. Against fellow-Frenchmen whom they wanted to liquidate, or at least intimidate, they mainly used bazookas or bombs, whose nightly explosions – over 1500 in a few months – added to the warlike atmosphere and were greeted, from balconies draped with the OAS colors, with a general uproar of blood-curdling yells and clashing saucepan lids. On their side, the Moslems, entrenched

by night in their own districts bedecked with FLN flags, fired
at anything that looked suspicious and answered the European
uproar with a din of their own. In one year, some twelve
thousand men, women and children were slaughtered by the
OAS in the course of their *ratonnades*.[1] In addition, they killed
or wounded several hundred members of the police, the *gendarmerie* and the CRS,[2] and organized the methodical assassination of some thirty police superintendents, Army officers and
judges. Moreover, on February 23, 1962, Salan signed a document requiring the murder-gangs "to open fire systematically
on units of the *gendarmerie mobile* and the CRS." Collusion on the
part of the European population and even at various levels of
the administration and the police was such that the arrest, let
alone the conviction, of the guilty parties happened only rarely.
If, in these circumstances, the Delegate-General, Jean Morin,
and the Commander-in-Chief, General Ailleret, managed to
carry on their duties, it was because they had set up headquarters outside Algiers, at Rocher-Noir and Reghaïa respectively.

In metropolitan France, in spite of the strenuous efforts of the
Minister of the Interior, Roger Frey, and the police, plastic
bomb outrages amounted to over a thousand during the same
period. In one of these Camille Blanc, the Mayor of Evian, met
his death; another, aimed at André Malraux, blinded a little
girl. The master stroke was attempted on September 9, 1961.
Leaving Pont-sur-Seine in the middle of the night on the way
from the Elysée to Colombey, the car in which I was travelling
with my wife, my aide-de-camp Colonel Teisseire, and my
bodyguard Francis Marroux, was suddenly enveloped by a huge
flame. It was caused by the explosion of a detonating device
intended to set off a charge of ten kilograms of plastic concealed
beneath a pile of sand, much more than enough to destroy its
"target". By an extraordinary chance this charge failed to
explode.

Meanwhile, events were taking their course. At a press

[1] "Wog-bashings": *raton* is slang for Arab.
[2] *Compagnies républicaines de sécurité*: riot police.

conference a few days earlier, I had specified the conditions under which the Algerian State would be created: "Naturally, such a State can only emerge from the votes of the inhabitants. . . . This means a referendum which will establish the State, followed by elections from which the final government will emerge. . . . A provisional Algerian executive can lead the country towards this self-determination and these elections, provided that it has sufficient stability and is in harmony with us. . . . But if, in spite of what France has proposed, no agreement were to be reached, we should have to draw our own conclusions." I pointed out what this would mean: the end of our aid, and the regrouping of the Europeans. I also touched on the Saharan question: "The line we are taking is one which guarantees our interests and takes account of reality. . . . Our interests are: the unrestricted exploitation of the oil and gas which we have discovered, the use of airstrips, and communications rights. . . . The reality is the fact that there is not a single Algerian who does not believe that the Sahara ought to belong to Algeria. . . . Thus, in the Franco-Algerian debate, the question of the sovereignty of the Sahara does not have to be considered. But we must have an association which safeguards our interests. If this association and these safeguards are not forthcoming, then we shall be compelled to make some other arrangement for the future of all the stone and sand of the Sahara. . . ."

From September 20 to 24, I visited the *départements* of the Aveyron, Lozère and Ardèche, where my explanation of my policies was heard and warmly approved.

As ever, the destiny of France depended upon her soldiers. I affirmed it yet again in a radio broadcast on October 2: "For the past three years in Algeria, we have steadily drawn nearer to the goal which I laid down in the name of France. . . . But in order for this firm and clear-cut solution to be achieved, the French Army had to become and to remain master of the field. So it did, and so it still does. It was essential, it is still essential, that the Army should remain faithful to its duty. It was, and it still is. All honor to it!" My journey to Corsica and Provence between November 7 and 10 gave me a number of opportunities to enlarge on this theme, which the common sense of the majority now accepted and which was wildly applauded. On November 23 I was in Strasbourg, which was celebrating the anniversary of its liberation. A large number of officers had come to take part in the parade and to hear what de Gaulle had to say. It was about the Army that I spoke to the people of Strasbourg and, through them, to the French people as a whole. Having extolled the exploits of the Leclerc Division, I pointed out how and why the deliberate disengagement of France and her armed forces, for so long tied down in Algeria, would enable us to build up a national defense system adapted to our age. I explained what this should consist of. Thus our basic interest in terms of military power in bringing the Algerian affair to an end was made clear, and the prospect of an immense new field of activity opened up for our Army. But how could I help but bring home to my audience the degree of military self-sacrifice involved in the renunciation of all the services performed and successes achieved overseas for so very many years? Calling to mind the touching hopes which had for so long sustained the dream of "French Algeria", I said: "Everyone can understand, and no one better than I, how the hope, or rather the illusion, should have arisen in so many hearts and minds that in the ethnic and psychological sphere one can change things simply by willing them to be the reverse of what they are." But in conclusion I exclaimed: "For all that, once the State and the nation have chosen their path, the soldier's duty is irrevocably laid down. Outside that duty, soldiers are lost men. Within it, on the other hand, the country finds example and assurance."

On December 29, in my end-of-year message, I once more explained what our intentions were and observed that "it now seems possible that such will in fact be the outcome of this cruel drama." Three days later, orders were given for the recall of two more divisions and nearly the whole fighting arm of the Air Force. Finally, on February 5, 1962, I announced that the ordeal was definitely nearing its end: "Who can honestly deny that the generous and necessary task of changing the relationship based on domination which linked us to our colonies into a relationship based on co-operation ought to be accomplished where it had not yet been accomplished, namely in Algeria? . . . We are nearing the goal. . . . I am confident that, having painstakingly prepared the ground, we shall soon achieve the solution which we consider to be the best."

At this point, the decisive phase of the negotiations opened at Les Rousses. Louis Joxe, this time accompanied by two other ministers, Robert Buron and Jean de Broglie, re-established direct contact with the representatives of the FLN, Belkacem Krim, Saad Dahlab and Lakdar Ben Tobbal. For the final talks, the conference moved to Evian. The agreements were concluded on March 18, 1962. They contained everything we had wanted them to contain. First of all, there was to be an immediate cease-fire. Thereafter, once the independence of Algeria had been granted by the French people and subsequently voted by the Algerian people, they provided for a close association between France and Algeria on economic and monetary matters; far-reaching cultural and technical co-operation; a privileged status for the citizens of each of the two countries when on the other's territory; full and precise guarantees for members of the French community who wished to remain where they were; preferential rights as regards Saharan oil and gas; the continuance of our atomic and space tests in the desert; the use of the naval base at Mers-el-Kébir and of various airfields for a minimum of fifteen years; the maintenance of our Army in Algeria wherever we judged necessary for three years. For the transitional period, it was agreed that the French Republic should on the one hand appoint a High Commissioner for Algeria who would be the supreme authority, particularly as regards public order, and on the other establish an Algerian Provisional Executive which would take over the administration, organize the referendum and, assuming the public response to be positive, arrange for the election of a National Constituent Assembly from which the government would emanate. Since, in the meantime, Algerian sovereignty did not exist and consequently the Evian agreements did not constitute a treaty, the French and Algerian people would vote in the referendum on a "general declaration" by the French government which would ask the electorate to approve its text.

The same evening I announced to the nation that, subject to its endorsement, the drama was over and the problem solved. "What has just been decided," I said, "reflects three truths which are as clear as daylight. The first is that our national interest, the realities facing us in France, Algeria and the world, the traditional role and genius of our country, all demand that in our time we should wish Algeria to be self-governing. The second is that Algeria's great needs and vast desires in the matter of development require her to associate herself with our country. The third and final truth is that, above and beyond the fighting, the outrages and the suffering, and in spite of all the differences of race, religion and custom, France and Algeria share not only the manifold links forged over the hundred and thirty-two years of their communal existence, not only the memories of great battles in which the soldiers of the two countries fought side by side in our ranks for the freedom of the world, but also a kind of special and elemental attraction. Who knows, perhaps the struggle which is now ending and the sacrifice of the fallen on both sides may in the end have helped the two peoples to understand that they were made, not to fight one another, but to march together like brothers on the road to civilization." Then I affirmed that: "If the common sense solution has at last prevailed, it is due first of all to the Republic, which had the wisdom to provide itself with the institutions essential to the authority of the State. It is due also to the Army, which, at the price of many glorious dead and great and praiseworthy efforts, achieved control of the territory in every region and along the frontiers, established human and amicable relations with the population and, in spite of the nostalgia of a number of its officers and the attempts at subversion by certain misguided leaders, remained firmly in the path of duty. It is due, finally, to the French people who, thanks to the steadfast trust they have shown in him who bears the burden of State, made it possible for the solution to be brought to fruition." Two days later, in a message addressed to parliament, I gave notice that the nation would be called upon to pronounce its verdict in a referendum.

The poll took place on April 8. Two days earlier, addressing the country once more, I had asked each citizen, by voting "Yes", to make himself "the architect of an event of immense significance, because the great French task of decolonization would thereby be completed." In metropolitan France and the overseas territories, 20,800,000 people went to the polls, that is, seventy-six per cent of registered voters. 17,900,000 voted "Yes"; 1,800,000 voted "No"; 1,000,000 papers were blank or spoiled. It was a ninety-one per cent affirmative reply from those who voted.

This national near-unanimity, which settled the question once and for all and left no room for doubt as to the outcome, nevertheless failed to deter the OAS from pursuing its exactions. Once it became clear that the final negotiations were under way and that many French Algerians, foreseeing the outcome and moreover terrified by the wave of crime which had overwhelmed the country, were preparing to flee to metropolitan France, the terrorists had maintained that the exodus was tantamount to handing the country over to the enemy. To prevent people from leaving, therefore, they threatened to burn down any property left behind and even to "execute" the owners. And these threats were indeed carried out. On the other hand, once the agreements had been signed, they switched to a "scorched earth" policy. Now the Europeans must get out of Algeria at all costs and leave nothing but ruins. "Let us leave it as we found it in 1830!" was the slogan. In pursuance of this campaign of organized arson, schools, town halls, factories, shops and offices were burnt down all over the country. In Algiers, the Hôtel de Ville, the university, the oil-storage tanks and the harbor installations went up in flames.

The government had naturally foreseen that a considerable proportion of the French colony might wish to be repatriated. As early as August 1961, Michel Debré had given State Secretary Robert Boulin the task of preparing for this vast operation. In December 1961, a law was passed for the benefit of those who chose to settle in France, making temporary provision for transport, accommodation, resettlement and social security. But the repatriation could and should have been accomplished gradually, without undue haste. Moreover, in their own interest as well as that of our country, it was obviously highly desirable that many of them should remain in Algeria, where they represented the only skilled personnel in most branches of the administration and the economy. But under pressure from the OAS, nearly all the French departed, often in panic-stricken flight. In May and June 1962, an average of seven thousand people a day crowded desperately on to the boats and airplanes to Marseilles. Apart from soldiers and civil servants, there were a million Europeans in Algeria. Fewer than a hundred thousand were to remain. Thus many houses abandoned in the general panic were to change hands willy-nilly, and great quantities of goods, furniture and personal belongings were looted.

Everything comes to an end. On March 25, Jouhaud was tracked down and arrested in Oran. The Military High Court under President Bornet, in place of Maurice Patin who was ill, condemned him to death. On April 20, Salan in turn was picked up in Algiers. The High Court, however, sentenced him to life imprisonment only, sparing him the death penalty. Yet the crimes he had committed were grave in the extreme. Moreover, how could it be justified that of two sentences delivered within six weeks of each other in the same court, the less severe should be meted out to the chief culprit, who was indeed recognized as such in the wording of the sentence? My first reaction was to allow Jouhaud's case to take its course. Then, at the instance of Georges Pompidou, who was now Prime Minister, and Jean Foyer, Minister of Justice, who had used a legal subterfuge to delay the execution, I reprieved the poor man since his leader had saved his neck.

Soon afterwards, both men let it be known one after the other that they wished the OAS to cease a struggle which could no longer achieve anything. Meanwhile, in circumstances of such danger to the State, such a glaring use of double standards in such widely publicized trials made it impossible for me to maintain a tribunal which had forfeited all claim to impartiality. In any case, all the seditious generals had now been brought to trial. The Military High Court was therefore abolished. It was replaced by a simple Military Court of Justice, established by ordinance to officiate until public life returned to normal. These measures, which prompted various outbursts from politically committed lawyers, in no way shocked the French public, thankful to see an end to the Algerian dramas. This was made clear to me by the resounding acclamations I received in the Limousin and in Franche-Comté when I visited them in May and June.

The bloody turmoil in the big Algerian cities and the massive exodus of the French population did not prevent the setting up of the transitional authority provided for in the Evian agreements. Christian Fouchet, appointed High Commissioner of the French Republic, assisted by Bernard Tricot, went to Rocher-Noir from where he was to direct this final phase. No sooner had he arrived than he had to assume responsibility for law and order, more than ever disrupted by the riot on March 26 in the rue d'Islay in Algiers by a mob infuriated by Jouhaud's arrest, who could only be dispersed by the troops opening fire. I called upon President Abderrahmane Farès, who reappeared on the scene full of optimism and drive, to head the Provisional Executive. The Executive was soon constituted. Three of its members were Frenchmen, political notables of Algeria. Eight were Moslems, five of whom had been members of the FLN. Once they too were installed at Rocher-Noir, Farès and his colleagues had the task of organizing the referendum and the elections. All having taken up their posts, Louis Joxe went to Algiers to signify the government's support. Despite the continual affrays mounted by Susini's commandos and the Moslem reprisals, the economic and administrative paralysis caused by the disappearance of a large number of Europeans, and the deep divisions which had emerged in Tunis among the leaders of the FLN, notably between Ben Bella and Ben Khedda, Algeria was moving painfully towards independence.

The referendum date was fixed for July 1 and the question

was framed as follows: "Do you want Algeria to become an independent state co-operating with France on the terms laid down in the Declaration of March 19, 1962?" Suddenly, before this date, the OAS decided to give up the struggle. Using well-known French liberals as intermediaries, in particular Jacques Chevalier, the ex-mayor of Algiers, Jean-Jacques Susini made contact with the Provisional Executive and, on the pretext of bringing about a reconciliation between the two communities, offered, to the general surprise, to put an end to all violence. Similar advice was given from prison, first by Jouhaud and then by Salan. Farès accepted the proposal and an agreement was concluded. The voting therefore took place in an atmosphere of complete calm. Over ninety per cent of the electorate voted, over ninety-nine per cent of the votes recorded said "Yes", which proved that the *pieds-noirs* who still remained must have been part of the total. On July 3, I wrote to the President of the Provisional Executive that: "France solemnly recognizes the independence of Algeria." The National Constituent Assembly, to be elected on September 20, would appoint Ahmed Ben Bella as head of the first government of the Algerian Republic.

The end of colonization was a chapter in our history. In closing it, France felt a mixture of regret for what was past and hope for what was to come. But would the man who had written it for her survive the fulfilment? That was for destiny to decide! It did so, on August 22, 1962. That day, at Petit-Clamart, the car taking me to the airfield at Villacoublay with my wife, my son-in-law Alain de Boissieu and my chauffeur Francis Marroux was suddenly caught in a carefully organized ambush: a hail of bullets from automatic weapons at point-blank range, then pursuit by a car-load of gunmen. Of the 150-odd bullets aimed at us, fourteen hit our car. Nevertheless – by an unbelievable chance – none of us was hit. De Gaulle would therefore continue to pursue his path and his vocation.

The Economy

৵ৼৼ

Politics and economics are as closely linked as action and life. If the national task which I was undertaking demanded the allegiance of men's minds, it naturally presupposed that the country had the means to achieve it. What a nation earns from its resources and its labor; what it sets aside from this total income by means of its budgets in order to finance the running of the State which guides and administers it, dispenses justice, provides for its education and defense, or to maintain and develop through investment the instruments of its livelihood, or to assist its members in the hardships which progress brings in its wake; in short, what a nation is worth in the physical sense of the term and, consequently, the weight it carries in relation to others – these are the essential foundations on which its power, its influence and its greatness are based, as well as that relative degree of well-being and security which passes for happiness in this world of ours.

This has always been true. It is truer than ever today because people are ceaselessly obsessed with the desire to possess the new goods created by the modern age; because they know that in this respect their fate is directly dependent on what happens globally and what is decided at the top; because the rapid and widespread transmission of information means that individuals and nations can continually compare their own wealth with that of their fellows. Thus it is the principal object of public concern. No government can afford to ignore these realities. The ambition and the efficacy of a nation's policies are bound up with the strength and expectations of its economy.

I know this as well as anyone – and with good reason! Soon after the Liberation I had succeeded, by means of far-reaching reforms, in steering the country clear of the fatal upheavals which threatened it. Now I was to redeem it from the deplorable state to which the parties had reduced it. For ten years I was to preside over a successful achievement in terms of the country's economic and financial prosperity and progress such as it had not experienced for more than half a century. And later I was to restrain it at the last moment from plunging into disaster, at a time when a bitter and unanimous campaign directed against my authority in all the most influential circles, the morbid passivity which suddenly gripped the nation, and the neglect of their duty by almost all those who were supposedly in positions of responsibility in every sphere, had allowed it to lapse into anarchy. Hence, at the head of France, whether in calm or in storm, I was to keep economic and social problems continually in the forefront of my actions and my thoughts. I was to devote to them more than half my work, my audiences, my travels, my speeches, for as long as I was responsible for the nation's affairs – which explains, incidentally, why the accusation of indifference to such matters so obstinately levelled against de Gaulle always struck me as absurd.

It is true that in dealing with the subject my natural instinct was to try and bring it down to essentials. It is true that I would place little or no reliance on the fluctuating advice of those learned men who airily manipulate the kaleidoscope of theory. It is true that I would not succumb to the intellectual gymnastics practiced by the jugglers with doubts and reservations, the conjurers of the lecture hall and the editorial column, the acrobats of demagogy. It is true that although, in the supreme position which I occupied, it was incumbent upon me to elicit expert opinion and advice, and then to choose and decide, I did not usurp the role of those ministers and officials whose duty it was to examine, to propose and to execute in the light of the complex data with which habit and vocation had made them familiar. It is true, finally, that the results, whatever they were, would inevitably be contested in a field in which, by definition, the wishes of all are boundless and nothing ever seems adequate to anyone. But for me, in this as in every other field, no lines of retreat, no evasions, were possible, even if I had looked for them. Everything that was done by the State would be done by my authority, on my responsibility, and in many cases at my instigation, by virtue of the primordial role which the nation instinctively assigned to me, and by the normal application of the powers which the new Constitution conferred upon the head of affairs.

What guidance must I give to the economic effort so that it should measure up to the policies to which I was about to commit France? From the very beginning I felt that it was simply a matter of common sense. The country could only thrive internally and carry weight abroad if its activity was in tune with the age. In an industrial era, it must be industrial. In a competitive era, it must be competitive. In an era of science and technology, it must cultivate research. But in order to produce a great deal, and to do so on terms which would facilitate trade, in order to renew by continual invention what it made in its factories and harvested from its fields, it must undergo a profound transformation.

Not that, even as it was, its fundamental qualities were by any means to be underestimated. While wishing to bring about far-reaching changes in its structure and its habits, I nevertheless had a great deal of respect for the way in which our forefathers had moulded it over the centuries. At the moment when I resumed the government of the French people, the fact was that in spite of what they lacked in raw materials and sources of energy, and in spite of the wars which had impoverished and decimated them, the quantity and quality of their industrial and agricultural production were nothing short of remarkable. The fact was that the French people worked diligently and on the whole steadily at the traditional tasks to which they were wedded, that they provided for most of their own needs, that in some branches they sold fairly widely abroad and that their scientists and technicians were very highly regarded everywhere. The fact was that their enterprises were many and varied, as might, after all, be expected from the diversity of their race and territory and the individualism which is a feature of their national character. The fact was that, without shielding them from crises, the flexibility of their collective existence spared them the worst and often alleviated the bitterness of social strife. The fact was, in short, that as a result of their age-old efforts, their economy possessed the elements of proficiency and soundness.

Conversely, however, the same characteristics, as a result of the failure to adapt and correct them in time, were now tending to impede France's forward progress. For, ever since men have been dependent on machines and consequently governed by the laws of output and acceleration, it is no longer enough for industry, agriculture and trade to manufacture, harvest and exchange as much as before; they must manufacture, harvest and exchange more and more. It is not enough to do what one does well, one must do it better than anyone else. It is not enough to "make ends meet", one must earn enough to be able to afford the best equipment. It is not enough to maintain, in order to live, innumerable separate, small-scale enterprises; they must unite to conquer. Expansion, productivity, competition, concentration – such, clearly, were the rules which the French economy, traditionally cautious, conservative, protected and scattered, must henceforth adopt.

For a country and a regime such as ours, it goes without saying that such a metamorphosis demanded not so much a succession of decrees promulgated from on high, as a large number of specific, spontaneous and individual actions on the part of those concerned as well as the government and the administration. As Head of State, it would be for me to encourage them thereto and to keep public opinion apprised thereof, but also to give my personal attention to certain essential points. Naturally at my level this meant that I was concerned with the Plan, because it was all-embracing, because it fixed the targets, established a hierarchy of necessities and priorities, induced among the people in charge and even in the public consciousness a sense of what is global, ordered and sustained, and because it compensated for the drawbacks of freedom without sacrificing its advantages; thus I was to endow the preparation and execution of the Plan with a prestige it had hitherto lacked, by giving it the character of an "ardent obligation" and proclaiming it as mine. I was concerned with international competition, for this was the lever which could activate our business world, compel it to increase productivity, encourage it to merge, persuade it to do battle abroad; hence my determination to promote the Common Market, which as yet existed only on paper, to support the abolition of tariffs between the Six, to liberalize appreciably our overseas trade. I was concerned with the investments, private and public, which would enable us to modernize our equipment, to adapt our means of communication to the speed of the century, to provide ourselves with the housing, the schools, the hospitals, the sports facilities which progress demanded; and in the budgets of which I signed the drafts and promulgated the decrees, development expenditure would always exceed running expenditure. I was concerned with "advanced" industries – basic research, atomic development, aviation, space, computers, etc. – because their laboratories and their inventions provide a spur to progress throughout the whole of industry; thus I was to follow their activities closely, intervening on many occasions in favor of their grants, ostentatiously visiting their establishments, meeting and listening to many of their directors. I was concerned with the currency, the criterion of economic health and *sine qua non* of credit, whose soundness guarantees and promotes saving, encourages enterprise, contributes to social harmony, procures international influence, but whose weakness unleashes inflation and waste, stifles growth, provokes unrest, jeopardizes independence; I was therefore to give France a model franc whose parity was to remain constant as long as I was in power and which, in spite of the damage inflicted on our country in the spring of 1968 by a coalition of illusion, blackmail and cowardice, I was to preserve up to the end thanks to the enormous reserves of foreign currency and gold which ten years of financial confidence had accumulated in our coffers. Indeed, at the time of my departure, these reserves, in spite of the losses caused by the convulsion, were to leave four thousand million dollars at our disposal, including a net sum of two and a half thousand million, over and above the considerable credits which were immediately offered to us from all sides.

Nevertheless, for a long time I had been convinced that modern mechanized society lacks a human incentive to safeguard its equilibrium. A social system which reduces the worker – however respectably paid – to the level of a tool or a cog is, in my opinion, at variance with the nature of our species and indeed with the spirit of sound productivity. Notwithstanding the undoubted benefits which capitalism produces not only for the few but for the community as a whole, the fact remains that it carries within itself the seeds of a gigantic and perennial dissatisfaction. It is true that the excesses of a system based on *laissez-faire* are now mitigated by certain palliatives, but they do not cure its moral sickness. On the other hand, Communism, although in theory it prevents the exploitation of men by men, involves the imposition of an odious tyranny on the individual, and plunges life into the lugubrious atmosphere of totalitarianism without achieving anything like the results, in terms of living standards, working conditions, distribution of goods and technological progress which are obtainable in freedom. Condemning both these diametrically opposed systems, I believed that it was incumbent upon our civilization to construct a new one which would regulate human relations in such a way that everyone would have a direct share in the proceeds of the concern for which he worked, and would enjoy the dignity of being personally responsible for the progress of the collective enterprise on which his own future depended. Would this not be tantamount to the transposition onto the economic plane, *mutatis mutandis*, of what the rights and duties of the citizen represent in the political sphere?

It was to this end that I had in earlier days set up the system of works committees. It was to this end that subsequently, while out of office, I had made myself the champion of "association". It was to this end that, having taken the reins once more, I intended to introduce a statutory profit-sharing scheme, and did in fact do so. It was to this end that, seizing the occasion of and drawing the lessons from the evidence brought to light in the factories and in the universities by the scandals of May 1968, I was to attempt to throw the door wide open to participation in France, an attempt which was to rouse against me the determined opposition of all the vested interests, economic, social, political and journalistic, whether Marxist, liberal or diehard. This coalition, by persuading the majority of the people solemnly to repudiate de Gaulle, was to shatter there and then the possibility of reform at the same time as it shattered my power. Nevertheless, beyond all the ordeals and the obstacles, and perhaps beyond the grave, that which is legitimate may one day be legalized, that which is rightful may in the end be proved right.

The truth is that by April 1969 very few were to remember – if they ever knew – the state which the economy, the finances and the currency of France were in when I had resumed control of the country eleven years earlier.

No sooner was I installed at Matignon than Antoine Pinay outlined the situation to me. On every single score we were on the verge of disaster. The 1958 budget was to reveal a deficit of one billion two hundred thousand million francs. Our foreign debt exceeded three thousand million dollars, of which half was repayable within a year. As regards our trade balance, receipts amounted to barely seventy-five per cent of outgoings in spite of the *de facto* devaluation, known as "Operation 20%", which the Félix Gaillard government had put into effect in 1957. By way of reserves, on June 1 we had no more than six hundred and thirty million dollars' worth of gold and foreign currency, the equivalent of five weeks' imports, and all the external sources of credit, relentlessly drawn on by the previous regime, had now completely dried up. Nothing remained of the last line of credit we had been able to raise – some five hundred million dollars – which had been reluctantly granted to Jean Monnet's begging mission at the beginning of the year by the International Monetary Fund and the American banks. As for economic activity, which had for a long time remained buoyant, though still disorganized, it was now showing a marked decline as a result of the import restrictions which had had to be imposed to prevent the economy from collapsing. Finally, the commitments entered into at European and world levels to take certain trade liberalization measures before the end of 1958 so that France, like other developed countries, might begin to face competition, could not be honored. Nor did there seem much hope of honoring the pledges arising from the Treaty of Rome, which involved the first round of tariff cuts between the six member States of the Common Market on New Year's Day, 1959. All in all, it was a choice between a miracle or bankruptcy.

But might not the psychological transformation produced by my return to power make a miracle possible? Antoine Pinay thought so. If I had chosen this eminent figure, renowned for his good sense, respected for his character, popular for his devotion to the public interest, as Minister of Economic Affairs, it was because his presence at my side would strengthen the confidence which alone might save us from imminent catastrophe. During the long succession of expedients and failures which characterized the financial history of the Fourth Republic, his spell at the head of affairs in 1952, and in particular the success of the loan he had launched, had marked a definite respite. From then on he had become in the eyes of the public the symbol of sensible management. So there was a chance that, with his experience and reputation added to the weight of my national authority, the harsh measures which were immediately and absolutely necessary could be taken in a favorable atmosphere, that my government would then have time to work out a complete plan for economic recovery, and that these combined measures, which were bound to be extremely painful, would enjoy the sincere co-operation which specialized circles in the administration and in business were more willing to give to this minister than to any other.

The first thing to be done as a matter of extreme urgency was to bring some money into the Treasury coffers, in order to meet the expenses of the State without activating the banknote printing-presses. I agreed with Antoine Pinay that we should launch an immediate loan which, because de Gaulle was there and because it was he who had decided to initiate it, took on the aura of a great national enterprise. This is what I proclaimed to the country on June 13 in an address broadcast on radio and television, and I repeated it through the same channels on the 26th, representing every subscription as a gesture of confidence in our people and myself. For his part, the Minister outlined frankly and clearly the dangers we were in and how they could be obviated, and explained the terms and conditions of the loan operation. Begun on June 17 and closed on July 12, it was a triumphant success, unexampled except by the equally success- ful "Liberation" loan thirteen years earlier. 324 thousand million francs were brought in, including 293 thousand millions of "fresh money". In addition, 150 tons of gold, the equivalent of 170 million dollars, came back to the Bank of France, almost as much as in 1945 and five times more than in 1952. The resultant alleviation in the settling of public accounts and in foreign exchange was immediately noticeable. Furthermore, the effect produced by this demonstration of support for the united effort which I had called for improved France's credit. There were signs, literally overnight, of a return of some of the capital that had taken flight, and, as a result, a marked improvement in our balance of payments position. Finally, the sudden revival of optimism about the future took the edge off the innumerable and pressing claims from every sector of society which had been boiling up in the atmosphere of uncertainty and unrest.

Now, however justified they might be in principle, and what- ever promises had been wrested from the faltering hands of the previous regime, to satisfy these demands would be to lose the battle. In the last days of July my government took a series of decisions of which the least that can be said is that they challenged all particular interests for the good of the com- munity as a whole.

Thus the increases in the wages and salaries of civil servants and public employees which were due to come into effect at precisely this moment were indefinitely postponed, as were the projected increases in farm prices, although under a law passed in 1957 they were pegged to the general price index (for example, a hundredweight of corn would now sell at 113 francs less than the farmers had counted upon), while considerable reductions were imposed on retail prices. At the same time a supplementary tax amounting to some fifty thousand million francs was levied on companies and on luxury goods, petrol went up in price, and credits allocated to a number of building and development projects were reduced or suspended. As a result, estimated government expenditure for the current year was reduced by approximately six hundred thousand million francs, domestic consumption was curtailed in the interests of exports, and prices, which had risen by more than one per cent per month in each of the first six months of 1958, were to rise by only a third of this during each of the last six. Thus on the whole inflation was kept at bay, and without any drastic loss of production, signs of stabilization began to appear.

Meanwhile, since virtue is sometimes rewarded even in France, it happened that in other countries, notably the United States, there was a slowing-down of economic activity, which halted the rise in the price of raw materials, made our imports less onerous, and indirectly helped to discourage the tendency towards "overheating". It is true that, in consequence, some anxiety arose over full employment. The number of unemployed receiving unemployment benefit rose from nineteen thousand to thirty-six thousand and the average working week was reduced by half an hour. However, in the more relaxed social atmosphere which coincided with the political pause, the government induced business to pay a regular contribution equivalent to one per cent of wages for the creation of a Communal Fund for Guaranteed Wages to be managed jointly by unions and employers, which would ensure a basic wage and organize the redeployment of workers who lost their jobs.

To underline the significance of these preliminary steps

towards putting its affairs in order, I spoke to the nation. "What is being done," I said on August 1, "is to stabilize our financial, monetary, and economic situation, to halt the slide into the abyss of inflation, to secure the foundations on which we can build up our prosperity and power." Then, having declared that "I ask all sectors of the French community to share in the sacrifices," I enumerated the various government measures without concealing their severity. But I added that "it is not in vain": the 1958 budget would be closed under favorable conditions, the balance of payments had taken a turn for the better, prices were being stabilized, the value of the franc was improving. I ended by saying: "France has made a start on the road to prosperity. As long as she remains resolutely on course, I can guarantee a safe arrival."

We had dealt with the most pressing problems. But there was a great deal more to be done: steps must be taken to ensure that, without sacrificing budgetary equilibrium, the impetus was maintained and prolonged. Indeed it was with this in mind that broad provision had been made under the terms of the referendum of September 28 whereby – up to the date when the new institutions came into force, that is, January 8, 1959, the day when I took up office in the Elysée – "the government will take, by ordinances having the force of law, such measures on any subject as it may consider necessary to the life of the nation."

Greatly though I esteemed the administrators of the Treasury, I felt that the decisions to be taken were so profound and far-reaching as to transcend the horizons of the ordinary government department. After voicing some objections, Antoine Pinay came round to this view. On September 30 a commission was formed of nine highly-qualified individuals drawn from the Institute, the Inspectorate-General of Finance, the *Conseil d'Etat*, the universities, the Order of Chartered Accountants, the banking world, and industry, "to report on the French financial problem as a whole . . . and to make appropriate suggestions for the utilization of the special powers conferred upon the government by the referendum."

Its chairman was Jacques Rueff, who, by virtue of his wide-ranging mind and the nature of his training, had the subject at his finger-tips. Nothing that concerned finance, economics or currency escaped the attention of this accomplished theoretician, this experienced practitioner. Dogmatic as regards their relationships, poetic in his sense of their vicissitudes, he wished them to be free. But knowing as he did by what damaging influences they were constantly threatened, he was determined that they should be protected. The plan which he presented on behalf of his Commission to myself and to Antoine Pinay on December 8 formed a complex of measures whereby, at the cost of considerable sacrifice, a number of barriers would be swept away with the result that in rejecting artificial expedients France would recover financial stability; savings and credit would, under normal conditions, provide for the investments essential to her progress, and she would deliberately enter into competition with the great modern trading countries.

The plan in fact comprised three basic elements, all inter-related and calculated to bring about a drastic transformation of French economic activity and financial policy. The first was an all-out attack on inflation; this being merely a drug which through alternating phases of agitation and euphoria leads a society to its death. We would cure ourselves of it, first, by reducing the expenditure and increasing the revenue of the State so that budget deficits starting with that for 1959 no longer necessitated the creation of artificial means of payment; and, secondly, by squeezing domestic consumption temporarily so that instead of an excessive proportion of the national income being swallowed up thereby, savings, the well-spring of investment, would grow and production would be geared to exports. A series of harsh measures were proposed to this end: a four per cent ceiling on pay rises for public employees, a reduction in State subsidies to nationalized industries and the social security services to make good their deficits, and of price support subsidies on certain consumer goods, and the non-payment in 1959 of pensions to able-bodied ex-servicemen. At the same time, there was to be another increase in corporation tax and surtax, higher taxes on wine, spirits and tobacco, a rise of fifteen per cent in the price of gas, electricity, and transport, ten per cent in the price of coal, and sixteen per cent on postal rates. On the other hand, in order that the lowest income groups should as far as possible be spared the full impact of these extra charges, there would be a four per cent rise in the guaranteed minimum wage (SMIG), a ten per cent increase in family allowances to take effect in six months, and an immediate additional 5,200 francs for old-age pensioners.

The second group of measures outlined in the plan concerned the currency. The intention was that, after the eleven reductions in parity it had undergone since 1914, when it was still the Napoleonic "gold franc", it should be re-established on a stable and fixed basis so that the prices of our products became competitive in the world market we were about to enter. Thus a devaluation of 17·5 per cent was recommended. But it was essential that on this basis our currency should henceforward have an unalterable value not only proclaimed in France – which entailed the prohibition, as tending to advertise doubts, of all escalator clauses linking prices and wages to the cost of living with the exception of the SMIG – but also recognized abroad. The franc would, therefore, be convertible, in other words freely interchangeable with other currencies. In addition, to restore to the venerable French franc, whose losses were a reflection of our national ordeals, something of its former substance, the new franc, worth a hundred of the old, would appear in accounts and also on the obverse of coins and in the wording of banknotes.

The third set of measures aimed at the liberalization of trade. This was nothing less than a revolution. For the plan advised us to disengage France from the old system of protectionism she had practised for a century. True, in the shelter of this bulwark she had been able to amass an enormous fortune before the two world wars, and afterwards, although ruined, to re-establish her own economic existence without becoming someone else's colony. But now the system isolated and lulled her, while vast currents of trade energized the world market. Customs barriers, tariff walls, quota restrictions provided our industry, our agriculture and our trade with a certain security but also the certainty of mediocrity. Competition, on the other hand, would spur them on to take risks. There was reason to believe that, faced with the challenge, the French economy would adapt its resources, its enterprise and its methods to the demands of productivity, and make expansion abroad its criterion of success. Jacques Rueff and his colleagues proposed that forthwith, beginning on January 1, quotas should be removed on ninety per cent of France's imports from the countries of Europe, and on fifty per cent from those in the dollar area.

I accepted the experts' plan. I had in fact been kept informed of the progress of their labors by my colleagues Georges Pompidou and Roger Goetze, who were in close touch with the Commission. The technical details, rates, scales, dates, specifications, etc., I left on the whole to the experts who submitted them to me. But it was the coherence and fervor of the plan as well as its daring and ambition that won me over. In order that it should be translated into action without any compromising with the national and international reactions it was bound to provoke, I now had to take full responsibility for it. In this I was powerfully encouraged by the many moving signs of the confidence which the mass of the people, if not its elite, reposed in me and which they expressed that autumn in the September referendum, the parliamentary poll in November, and my election in December.

Although the principles and texts of the decrees were to be drawn up in the absence of parliament, political obstacles nonetheless presented themselves. The first of these was raised by the Minister for Economic Affairs and Finance himself, who came in an agitated state to tell me that he opposed Rueff's plan on two basic counts: devaluation and the new taxes. "You will appreciate," Antoine Pinay told me, "that having always condemned both, I cannot subscribe to them now." While recognizing that it would be extremely magnanimous of him

to give his consent, I urgently requested the Minister to try
and bring himself to do so in consideration of my task, my
responsibility and, consequently, my right and duty to make the
final decision. And this decision was to give effect to the plan in
its entirety, with no half-measures, including the matters in
question. Antoine Pinay was prepared to bow to these lofty
considerations. Nevertheless, when everything was settled, he
was to send me a letter in which he expressed his reservations
and doubts. But then it was the turn of the Socialist members of
the government to declare their opposition to the plan. "I
cannot," Guy Mollet told me, "agree to a devaluation and
to measures which will impose heavy sacrifices on people of
small means without even an adequate dose of State direction
[*dirigisme*] by way of compensation." In reply, I mentioned
the additional financial burdens which were to be imposed on
the rich, the provisions for avoiding hardship to the very poor,
and above all the imperative need to restore the economy to
health in view of the disastrous state in which previous governments had left our country. But Guy Mollet maintained his
opposition. Since I was in no doubt that this would become
more and more openly the Socialists' attitude as the end of the
Algerian crisis approached and as a result of the humiliating
setbacks suffered by their party in the elections, I accepted the
resignation of their Secretary-General. Eugène Thomas and
Max Lejeune also tendered theirs. Nevertheless, I asked all
three to remain at their posts until the inauguration, on January
8, of the Fifth Republic which they had helped me to found.
They did so willingly.

The decisions were taken on December 26 in the course of a
Cabinet meeting which lasted ten hours and was attended by
all the members of the government as well as Jacques Rueff
and senior Treasury officials. Leading the discussion throughout,
I gave my personal backing to each of the proposals in order to
ensure that they were adopted. The following day, the whole
plan was ratified by the Cabinet, basically in the form of an
ordinance which represented the budget for 1959, another
ordinance creating the new franc, a decree fixing its parity, and

a notification to foreign governments concerning the liberalization of trade. On the 28th, I went on the air to explain to the
country what was happening, why, and how.

Having first of all pointed out that the national task which
had devolved on me for the last eighteen years had just been
endorsed by my election the previous Sunday, I declared that
"as France's guide and as Head of the Republican State, I shall
exercise supreme authority in all the breadth it now carries and
in the new spirit which has invested me with it." For it was
the instinct for national survival which inspired the call which
was addressed to me by the French people. "They have entrusted me with their leadership because they want to be shown the
path, not indeed towards idle comfort but towards endeavor
and renewal." By virtue of my mission, and together with my
government, "I have therefore decided to put our affairs
positively and radically in order. . . . On the occasion of the
budget, we have adopted, and tomorrow we shall put into
effect, a whole range of financial, economic and social measures
which will establish the nation on a basis of truth and severity."
I added that "our country will feel itself sorely tried . . . but
the reconstruction aimed at is such that it will compensate
for all else." There followed a summary of all the points which
were later developed in detail by the Minister for Economic
Affairs and Finance. I ended by saying: "Without this effort
and these sacrifices, we would remain a country in the rear-
guard, perpetually oscillating between crisis and mediocrity.
On the other hand, if we succeed, what a leap forward on the
road which leads to the heights!"

Both in France and abroad the effect was prodigious. To the
professional opinion-mongers it seemed indeed astonishing,
after so many fragmentary, spasmodic and capricious attempts
on the part of previous governments, to see the new regime
undertake a fundamental, sustained and determined action.
Neither the parties nor the newspapers, whose malevolence
was for the moment frustrated, could deny that the plan was
coherent and far-reaching. Abroad, people were struck by the
fact that I had committed myself so deeply. But whereas the

opinions expressed beyond our frontiers continued to be favorable, a fact which was incidentally to play its part in reversing the movement of capital away from France, at home, once the shock effect had worn off, the rehabilitation of our affairs was to be carried out amid a welter of criticism from the political parties, the trade unions, and almost the entire press.

Naturally, it was the hardships inherent in the recovery program which caused the outcry. Without a single voice being raised in defense of the idea that the common good should prevail over particular interests, all these dissenters joined in denouncing the inevitable sacrifices as unjust. On the basis of this general accusation, each trade organization naturally took the opportunity of inveighing against those decisions which were allegedly damaging to its own members alone. The employers protested against the burdens imposed on industry and demanded a reduction in public spending in order to alleviate them. Small and medium firms attacked the liberalization of trade, claiming that they would thereby find themselves forced into competition which a number of them would be unable to withstand. It was the taking into account of external signs of wealth in assessing incomes which angered the representatives of management and the liberal professions. The spokesmen of commerce condemned the measures which tended to restrict the purchasing power of consumers. The trade unions raised an outcry against the reduction they foresaw in the standard of living of wage-earners as a result of price rises consequent upon devaluation and of the recession which would accompany the austerity program. The farmers' organizations were bitterly opposed to the abolition of price and wage pegging which, they claimed, would violate the principle of parity of peasant incomes. The ex-servicemen's associations complained vehemently at the suspension, partial though it was, of the pensions paid to survivors of the First World War.

All this, of course, was no more than I expected from these political and social groups. The parties, such as they were, obviously could not endorse the policies of a regime created in opposition to them, especially when these policies gave rise to the dissatisfaction on which they thrived. As for the professional organizations, since they exist and operate expressly to formulate and press claims, they cannot be expected to co-operate with authority on anything constructive, *a fortiori* if it involves constraints on their membership. Needless to say, this natural hostility of the various vested interests towards the State, especially if it shows strength, becomes bitter and systematic in the case of those dominated by the Communists, who in every instance strive to weaken the fabric of society preparatory to destroying it.

Faced with such a universal outcry, I saw myself as the engine-driver in the American film who continues to drive his train, ignoring the alarm bells being rung by frightened or ill-intentioned passengers. Throughout this crucial period my government, in spite of all challenges, made scarcely a single alteration in its decisions. Moreover, the enthusiastic popular demonstrations which marked my visits to sixteen *départements* in the South-West, the Center, Berri, Touraine and the Massif Central at this time, proved that at heart the nation was well-disposed towards the undertaking. Even the National Assembly, to which, on January 15, Prime Minister Michel Debré outlined our policy and asked for a vote of confidence, expressed its approval by a large majority. Yet again, recriminations counted for little in the face of success.

For, sure enough, success began to emerge. Six months after the promulgation of the plan, the incipient recession gave way to a marked recovery. The number of unemployed went down, the average working-week became longer. On June 30, 1959, the rise in prices, which had been expected to reach seven or eight per cent, barely amounted to three per cent. As a result, our exports had soared to an extent unknown for many a year. During this first half-year our reserves of foreign currency, which had already shown an increase at the end of 1958, went up by nine hundred million dollars, with the result that, after having paid off external debts to the tune of six hundred million, we still had one thousand five hundred million in hand. Activity on the Paris Stock Exchange reflected these good results: the index of the number of transactions of French securities doubled in the course of this period. As early as January 30 I had been able to announce to the country that the wind was favorable. "Good fortune," I said, "the blessed good fortune which our people have known from time to time, is here making a renewed appearance. A new France is resuming her historical course. But in order to provide her with a firm basis on which to build her power, we must overhaul in breadth and in depth our finances, our currency and our economy. This is what we are engaged in, to the amazement of the whole world. . . ." Then I appealed, not to the well-known and the well-off, who would undoubtedly not have listened, but to the ordinary people: "Ah! I know how hard it is on every sector of society, especially the humblest. I know that battles are invariably won by the infantry. I know that France's greatness has always been the achievement of her children as a whole." Finally, I hailed the premonitory signs of victory: "In spite of the discomforts suffered by each and every one, in spite of what workers, farmers, shopkeepers, clerks, civil servants and many ex-servicemen have to endure, the desire of the French people to avoid chaos, inflation, and beggary is clear for all to see. Already the preliminary signs of recovery are becoming visible. Whether in terms of production, wages, prices, trade, currency, or social harmony, the living conditions of the French people will be stabilized before the end of the year. On this basis, technology, hard work and saving will bring about general prosperity."

The end of 1959 and the three years which followed represented for our country a veritable triumph of expansion and stability, terms which most pundits regarded as incompatible. The expansion was considerable, since the rate of increase of the gross national product was three per cent during the second half of 1959, 7·9 per cent in 1960, 4·6 per cent in 1961, 6·8 per cent in 1962, corresponding to an average annual increase in industrial production of 5·4 per cent and in agricultural production of more than five per cent. The stability was impressive, since all the budgets were balanced, the trade balance showed a constant surplus month after month, reserves of gold and foreign currency exceeded four thousand million dollars in 1962, short- and long-term foreign debts were fully paid off by the same date, the annual increase in retail and wholesale prices was less than 3·5 per cent. Could success be more striking? It resulted, moreover, in an actual yearly increase of four per cent in the standard of living, while unemployment fell to less than 0·5 per cent of the working population. At the same time, and in spite of the fact that consumption – or, if you like, well-being – followed the progress of wages, savings-bank deposits rose by three thousand million new francs in 1958, 4500 million in 1959 and 1960, five thousand million in 1961, and six thousand million in 1962, private investments rose each year by more than ten per cent, and credits allocated by the State for development regularly amounted to at least half its expenditure.

In this way the firm foundation was laid on which to carry out the transformation of the country. But how was this to be accomplished? By brutally dismantling what already existed? This would be theoretically imaginable in a situation so serious that, in an attempt to avoid extinction, the nation submitted to the terrible surgery of a totalitarian regime which would begin by making a clean sweep and then rebuild by dint of relentless norms and implacable severity. But no catastrophe threatened France, and the Fifth Republic, although it possessed authority, was far from being a dictatorship. Power was exercised there in the context of a free democracy in which each individual and each group had rights of their own, in which everything was done openly and subject to the sanction of the ballot-box, in which the authorities used neither prison nor confiscation against recalcitrant property-owners, neither forced labor nor deportation in dealing with intractable workers and employees. For us, then, the task of the State was not to force the nation under a yoke, but to guide its progress. However, though freedom remained an essential lever in economic action, this action was none the less collective, it directly controlled the nation's destiny, and it continually involved social relations. It thus required an impetus, a harmonizing influence, a set of rules, which could only emanate from the State. In short, what was needed was State direction (*dirigisme*). I myself was resolved on it; and this was one of the reasons why I had wanted the Republic's institutions to be such that the government's means matched its responsibilities.

In practical terms what it primarily amounted to was drawing up the national plan, in other words deciding on the goals, the priorities, the rates of growth and the conditions that must be observed by the national economy, and determining the extent of the financial outlay which the State must make, the fields of development in which it must intervene, and the measures to be taken in consequence through its decrees, its laws and its budgets. It is within this framework that the State increases or reduces taxation, eases or restricts credit, regulates customs duties; that it develops the national infrastructure – roads, railways, waterways, harbors, airports, communications, new towns, housing, etc.; harnesses the sources of energy – electricity, gas, coal, oil, atomic power; initiates research in the public sector and fosters it in the private; that it encourages the rational distribution of economic activity over the whole country, and by means of social security, education, and vocational training, facilitates the changes of employment forced on many Frenchmen by modernization. In order that our country's structures should be remoulded and its appearance rejuvenated, my government, fortified by the new-found stability of the State, was to engage in manifold and vigorous interventions.

It was all the better equipped for doing so because the Prime Minister was Michel Debré. Since January 1959 the new Constitution had been in force, under the terms of which, supervised by the President of the Republic and nominated by him, the Prime Minister led the government and headed the administration. On the basis of the directives which I issued, either of my own accord or on his recommendation, he was responsible for activating the various ministries, drawing up the measures to be taken, arranging for the submission of these measures either to myself, to the Cabinet or to parliament, and finally, when they were incorporated in decrees or laws, of directing their application. Michel Debré was the first to assume this cardinal and virtually limitless role under the Fifth Republic. He set his stamp upon it, and it was a powerful and enduring one. Convinced that France needed greatness, and that it was through the State that greatness was won or lost, he had dedicated himself to public life in the service of the State and France. In this cause, his mind was open to every idea, his feelings were aroused, and often wounded, by every occurrence, his will was equal to every task. Always tense with eagerness to activate, to reform, to put right, he fought without sparing himself and endured without losing heart. Moreover, while extremely well informed about personalities and the wheels within wheels of politics, he was also a man of texts and debates, who distinguished himself in the parliamentary arena. Yet convinced, since June 1940, that de Gaulle was essential to the country, he had given me his unreserved support. However much my view of things may sometimes have pained him, never once did he withhold his dedicated and invaluable co-operation.

This was certainly the case as regards the industrialization of the country. How simple it was in theory, how difficult in practice! How obnoxious to old-established habits its realization was! Michel Debré, in agreement with me, committed the government to it up to the hilt. Clearly there could be no question of starting from scratch as had once been possible for the United States, whose population grew *pari passu* with the discovery of vast sources of raw materials, for Great Britain, bulging with coal when it was the basic prerequisite of industry, for Germany, blessed with the mineral wealth of the Ruhr and Silesia, geographically homogeneous, and traversed by great parallel navigable rivers; or as was now the case with Russia, equipped with the unimaginable resources of Siberia, with Japan, impelled by the pressure of an overflowing population, and with Italy, able to run its great northern factories with the unemployed manpower of the south. Our own economy had for a long time been limited by our possibilities, and these changed little. But although we already manufactured a great deal, and in every branch of industry, it was a question of doing so more cheaply and improving the quality of our goods. This called for modernized equipment, better organization to reduce costs, and an acceptance of the challenge of competition. To encourage expansion, investment and exports – that was to be my government's role in this field. It would be a long and arduous task, since, short of discovering new sources of wealth as had been done at other times in other countries, we had only taxes raised from day to day on the nation's profits to sustain our advances.

The Third Plan, for the period 1958–61, which had been drawn up before my return to power, obviously fell short of the possibilities opened up by the financial and monetary recovery and the demands created by the liberalization of trade. An Interim Plan was therefore put into action, boldly aiming at an average annual increase of 5·5 per cent in production and an investment program which would represent a high proportion of overall national income. On the basis of this, a variety of legislative and statutory measures were taken to relieve firms of some of the burden of re-equipment costs by fiscal means, to lower the rates at which they contracted modernization loans, to encourage them to merge, to persuade them to set up their factories and their subsidiaries in provincial areas where their presence would create opportunities for local talent and enterprise. The Fourth Plan, which was to cover the period 1962–65, aimed at accentuating this general evolution, and, in particular, set a target figure of twenty-four per cent for the growth of our economy over that period. On November 17, 1961, with my ministers in attendance, I paid a formal visit to the Economic and Social Council to hear its views and to announce the new targets for national economic expansion.

Meanwhile, by an ordinance of January 7, 1959, the door had been opened for a workers' profit-sharing scheme. Whether the agreements entered into in this connection between management and labor simply involved a percentage of the profits, or incorporated the sharing of capital and the plowing back of profits, or entailed the setting up of a company of which every manual or clerical worker was a member and shareholder, the tax exemptions guaranteed by the State were considerable. It is true that although the law thus determined the conditions under which these partnerships must operate, they nevertheless remained optional. Consequently, despite the advantages offered by such an innovation in terms of productivity and social relations, and the favorable conclusions drawn therefrom by those who tried it out, it was put into practice by only a limited number of concerns. Against it were ranged the concerted prejudices of management and unions, congealed in a state of mutual antagonism in which the former hoped to be able to maintain the bastions of their power by well-tried methods of resistance and the latter found the justification for their exclusively wage-claiming role and their refusal to exercise a new and positive one. Nevertheless a breach had been made in the wall between the classes. It is only by widening this breach that we may one day ensure that the all-important reform of participation provides modern society with the new basis for its existence.

My government, proud of taking the first steps towards this social process which could be decisive, also endeavored to anticipate the economic expansion by a program of national re-equipment and development on a scale unequalled by anything that had happened in the past. The main emphasis was on sustaining new hopes. For instance, as regards the sources of energy, annual production of gas from Lacq in the Pyrenees increased to four thousand million cubic meters and its distribution was organized to cover the whole country; Algerian oil, thanks to the completion of the pipe-lines to Bougie and La Skhirra, was now available in ever-increasing quantities – twenty-five million tons in 1962 – which saved us the necessity of buying it elsewhere for dollars and pounds; and the atomic power stations at Marcoule and Chinon began to produce electricity. Then there was the nuclear center at Cadarache, built for the study of fast breeder reactors, and the Center for Space Studies at Brétigny, which planned the launching of French satellites. As regards communications, in four years

a further two thousand kilometers of railway track were
electrified, the motorway network grew from 125 to 300 kilometers, excavation of the Mont Blanc tunnel was begun, a
program-law of April 23, 1959, initiated or speeded up extensive
work on our waterways: the widening of the Dunkirk–Lille–
Valenciennes canal, the construction of the canal du Nord, the
acceleration of the development of the Rhône, the Seine, the
Moselle, etc. Similarly with ports: extensive development of
docks, harbor approaches, graving-slips, at Dunkirk, Le Havre,
Rouen, Brest, Bordeaux and Marseilles. Similarly with airports: the construction of new runways and terminals at Orly
and in the provinces; the modernization of traffic control.
Similarly with housing: more than three hundred thousand
homes built each year, mostly from public funds. Similarly with
scientific research, whose credits were tripled, and which, in
1958, was brought under the direction of a Delegate-General on
behalf of the government, with an Advisory Council of distinguished scientists. Between 1958 and 1962 our budgets devoted seventy-five thousand million new francs to investment.
Nothing like it had ever been seen before.

Nor had a Frenchman travelling across France ever been
able to witness such vast and rapid changes. Industry had been
granted permits to build on fourteen million square meters of
land – nearly all in the provinces – and at the same time the
number of firms was reduced by amalgamation or merger by
some five thousand. In the retail sector, where, in 1958, eight
supermarkets and 1,500 "self-service" shops were in operation,
in 1962 they numbered respectively 207 and 4,000. Atomic
energy flaunted the new and mysterious apparatus of its sixteen
centers and installations. Model firms now invented, developed
and manufactured our aircraft, our helicopters, our rockets,
which were of international class. Twice as many laboratories,
some at the most advanced level, were now in operation. Different regions which had been selected to bring together on their
territory the elements of a particular advanced industry each
adopted a modern vocation: aeronautics in Aquitaine, elec-
tronics in Brittany, industries allied to gas-production at the

foot of the Pyrenees, the unloading, stockpiling and refining of petroleum products in the Marseilles region. Our ancient cities and historic townships were cluttered with building works aimed at giving them a new lease of life. Paris, for instance, its buildings cleansed of their grime yet retaining their familiar outlines, chock-full of motor cars swarming around its newly-restored monuments, had been traversed by three motorways, encircled by a ring road, and adorned with innumerable new blocks of offices and flats both within its walls and on its out-skirts.

There was a reverse side to the medal. Our industrial expansion inevitably reduced the relative importance of our agriculture. Being the man I am, how could I fail to be moved and concerned as I watched the gradual eclipse of this rustic society, immemorially established in its enduring occupations and enclosed by its traditions; this world of changeless villages, ancient churches, close-knit families, the eternal cycle of plowing, sowing and harvesting; this land of ancestral legends, folk songs and dances, of local dialects, costumes and markets; this age-old France which by its nature, its activity and its spirit was essentially rural? How could I disregard the fact that if, in our existence as a nation, the city – and above all, the capital – had always been the seat and setting of the official apparatus, the home of the arts and sciences, the principal meeting-place for commerce, the most convenient site for industry, the country nevertheless remained the source of life, the genetrix of the population, the basis of our institutions, the nation's refuge? How could I forget that through the ages, up to the end of the last century, seven out of ten Frenchmen lived on the land; that those who had left it were for the most part simply migrants who retained their roots in the soil; that at the time of my birth, in spite of the exodus towards the towns which the factories and railways had set in motion two generations earlier, more than half the inhabitants of France were still rustics; that our land produced almost all the nation's food; that our armies were for the most part made up of young countrymen, and that even during the First World War the majority of our soldiers and two-thirds of our dead were farm workers? How could I fail to realize that the French peasantry had an instinctive sense of being the very essence of France, and that the colossal mutation which reduced their social preponderance and their economic role inevitably aroused their anxiety and sadness?

To this was now added an ever-increasing concern about making a living. Gone were the days when subsistence agriculture was the rule in France, when, without ever varying what he grew on his patch of earth, the peasant mainly produced the wherewithal to feed himself and his family, and what remained was enough to supply the towns, while duties and tariffs prevented the intrusion of foreign foodstuffs. The machine had passed this way, upsetting the old equilibrium, imposing efficiency, accumulating surpluses, creating everywhere new products and simultaneously new desires, causing the peasants to feel the need to earn more, producing massive pressure from foreign goods and forcing us to offer quality in return. Thus it was the market which would henceforth dictate its laws to agriculture, namely: specialization, selection and distribution. However, since every undertaking needed sufficient scope, equipment and capital to meet these conditions, how could we maintain more than two million farms on our territory, three-quarters of which were too small and too poor to be viable but on which, nevertheless, nearly a fifth of the French population still depended for their livelihood? How, in this day and age, could the agricultural profession be left to drift along without the technical training, the organized markets, the rationalization of credit, needed to make it competitive? How could this gigantic and pre-eminently national problem be resolved peacefully unless the community as a whole accepted responsibility for it?

It was by the 1960 *Loi d'orientation agricole*, the *Loi complémentaire* of 1962, and the decrees which implemented them, that the reform was set in motion. Organizations with multiple activities and multiple initials were formed to activate it: *Sociétés d'aménagement foncier et d'établissement rural* (SAFER),

Sociétés pour le financement et le développement de l'économie agricole (SOFIDECA), *Fonds d'orientation et de régularisation des marchés agricoles* (FORMA), *Fonds d'action sociale pour l'assainissement des structures agricole* (FASASA). At the same time, the allocation of credits for water supplies, farm building, drainage, regrouping of land,[1] was generally speeded up. Basically, the aim was to help those farms which were economically viable to expand, improve their structure and adapt their production, and to encourage those which were too small to be viable to amalgamate; to persuade farmers to produce the right foodstuffs and sell them in the right way, at the right price, in the right place and at the right time; to form a network of regional markets – of which the new central market at Rungis would eventually form a part – where produce would be rationally marketed in vast quantities; to organize agricultural training and expert advice; to provide retirement pensions and encourage elderly farmers to retire; and finally, to establish a special system of social insurance for the peasants. Public credits for agriculture rose from 940 million new francs in 1958 to three thousand million in 1962. But at this price immense and drastic changes were effected. For example, during these four years, the number of farms fell from 2,200,000 to 1,900,000 while the total value of agricultural output rose from thirty-two to forty-two thousand million. This rate of progress, if maintained, would allow the whole problem to be solved in a generation. For the first time, by dint of an effort commensurate with the size of the problem, the Republic had really taken on the burden – until such time as it would begin to reap the benefit – of leading French agriculture into the modern world.

Meanwhile, the undertaking was transcending its national framework. France, which is made for a hundred million inhabitants, was able to produce from her rich and beautiful land far more food than she herself consumed. In spite of the recent growth in her population, this imbalance was growing more pronounced as every improvement in equipment, methods

---

[1] *Remembrement:* consolidation of scattered holdings to make more viable units.

and soil treatment raised crop and stock-farming yields. Therefore we must export, and in a world where agricultural
surpluses were to be had for the asking, we must do so, willy-
nilly, at prices related to the needs of our producers unless the
State was to provide them with subsidies so enormous that they
would cripple its finances. I may say that if, on resuming control
of our affairs, I embraced the Common Market forthwith, it was
as much because of our position as an agricultural country as
for the spur it would give to our industry. Certainly I was
fully aware that, in order to integrate agriculture effectively into
the Community, we should have to work energetically on our
partners, whose interests in this matter were not ours. But I
considered that this, for France, was a *sine qua non* of membership, for in an association theoretically free of national tariffs and
taxes where the fruits of the earth were alone denied free access
everywhere, in a grouping of consumers where domestic agricultural products did not enjoy preference over those from
outside, our agriculture would constitute an incubus which
would put us in a position of chronic inferiority in relation to
the others. Thus in order to impose on the Common Market, as
it developed, what we considered necessary in this respect, we
were obliged to put up a literally desperate fight, sometimes
going so far as to threaten to withdraw our membership.
Nevertheless we succeeded.

The summer of 1962 marked the end of a period in the course
of which our country made steady progress. During these four
years, the Fifth Republic had put up a performance in the
economic and social sphere of which the least that can be said
is that it was more sustained and more continuous than that of
any previous regime. No doubt it was compelled to do so, if it
was to avoid collapsing itself, by the necessity of extricating the
country from the grave situation in which it had found it at the
start. Furthermore, and in any case, the changes imposed by the
ever-increasing demands of modern progress necessitated the
ever more determined intervention of the government and
the law. But the spirit and the letter and the functioning of
the new institutions were precisely calculated to meet these

conditions. An unprecedented cohesion in the government, the presence of an impregnable majority in parliament, massive assent from the people, encouraged the State to embark on new projects and enabled it to persevere with them. It is true that the overall achievement imposed incidental hardships on everyone. But the results were tangible: for the nation, an appreciable increase in prosperity; for the individual, a marked improvement in his standard of living; for France, renewed self-confidence and a revival of respect abroad.

While the nation worked, it was for me, primarily, to give a sense of national aspiration to the whole, to demand that the common interest should transcend the routines and the pretensions of individual groups, and to show that the aim of the struggle for prosperity was not so much to make life more comfortable for such and such a category of Frenchmen as to build up the wealth, the power and the greatness of France as a whole. It was this that I had in mind on the numerous occasions when I discussed things personally with Michel Debré during the meetings we had several times a week; with Antoine Pinay as long as he remained Minister for Economic Affairs and Finance and subsequently, with his successor Wilfrid Baumgartner when, at the request of the Prime Minister, this change took place as a result of a clash not between two policies, but between two personalities; with Jean-Marcel Jeanneney, who was in charge of Industry; with Henri Rochereau and then Edgard Pisani, the successive incumbents of the Ministry of Agriculture; with Paul Bacon and Robert Buron, respectively in charge of Labor and of Public Works and Transport. It was this that characterized the audiences I gave for example to Pierre Massé, who organized the setting up of the Fourth Plan; to Jacques Brunet, Governor of the Bank of France, who kept me informed about the state of the economy, credit and currency; with François Bloch-Lainé, Director-General of the Deposit and Consignment Office, who apprised me of the loans granted to local authorities and the resources of the national savings banks; with Eric de Carbonnel, Georges Gorse, Jean-Marc Boegner, successive government representatives to the Common Market, who kept me in touch with what happened in the intervals between the meetings of ministers in Brussels, etc. It was this that inspired my decisions at the end of Cabinet meetings, the greater part of which were always given over to economic and social affairs. It was this that I expressed when I spoke about France, whether in speeches delivered via the microphone and the television screen, or at press conferences, or in hundreds of appeals addressed to the people during my travels in sixty-seven *départements* of metropolitan France, or in talks to the staff on the occasion of my visits to some eighty factories, mines, power-stations, shipyards, agricultural developments, co-operatives, markets, railway marshalling yards, road works, waterways, harbors, airfields, new towns, technical colleges, fairs, exhibitions, etc.

It is true that nothing that was said or done in the national cause disarmed the opposition of any vested interest. The socio-professional organizations, although out of conventional prejudice they accused my government of clinging to past abuses and neglecting reforms, were basically hostile to changes which threatened both to curtail the privileges of the owners and to remove substance from the claims of the unions. Certain industrialists encouraged the organs of information they controlled by means of their wealth to sow doubt and distrust, and obstructed economic progress by resisting desirable mergers and even, on occasion, preferring to sell their businesses to foreigners. The various farmers' associations intensified their protests even to the extent of unleashing gangs of militants here and there to block roads and break windows. The trade unions accused the "Gaullist regime" of trying to crush them, of being "the cat's-paw of the monopolies" and victimizing the workers. However, popular support for the intentions and the authority of General de Gaulle was so widespread and so profound that the agitation in specialized circles had comparatively little effect on the nation's work. So much so that the renovation of our economic life, though often tentative, proceeded satisfactorily; the peasant demonstrations that broke out in certain areas up to the spring of 1960 died down everywhere thereafter; and from

1958 onward, both in the public and the private sectors, for a work force of thirteen million, fewer than a million days were lost annually through strikes, that is to say eight times less than before.

On February 5, 1962, I drew the nation's attention to the progress it had made. "Nobody in the world," I said, "who is not blindly partisan can fail to recognize France's powerful development. Each one of us is struck by it when he travels through the country, even if only via the television screen. Never has so much been produced, built or taught in France. Never has the standard of living of the French people been as high as it is today. Never has any country had fewer unemployed than we have. Never have our currency and our credit been stronger than they are now, so much so that instead of borrowing we now lend to the richest. And now the great Plan, which in four years will increase our power and our prosperity by a quarter, is about to be put into operation. Certainly in all this there are still many gaps and shortcomings. Our troubles are not yet over. We know the sort of world that surrounds us and how events can influence our affairs. But why, at the very moment when our success is becoming apparent, should we begin to lose heart, like the fisherman described by Shakespeare who, finding a pearl that terrified him by its beauty, threw it back into the sea?"

I did not throw back the pearl. Nevertheless, at grips day after day with material and human realities in a sphere in which all is asperity, in which nothing is once and for all achieved, in which no one is ever remotely satisfied with what he gets, I was reminded that economic progress, like life itself, is a struggle whose course is never marked by a decisive victory. Even on the day of an Austerlitz, the sun does not emerge to light up the battlefield.

Europe

∾✤∽

War gives birth and brings death to nations. In the meantime, it never ceases to loom over their existence. For us French, the development of our national life, our political regimes and our world position from 1815 to 1870 was determined by the hostile coalition which united the nations of Europe against the Revolution, the dazzling victories and then the downfall of Napoleon, and finally the disastrous treaties which sanctioned so many battles. Thereafter, during the forty-four years of the "armed truce", it was our defeat, our secret desire to avenge it, but also the fear that a united Germany might inflict another on us, that dominated our actions at home and abroad. Although the gigantic effort put forth by our people in the First World War opened the way to renewal, we closed it upon ourselves by failing to consolidate our military victory, by forgoing the reparations which would have provided us with the means of industrializing our country and thus compensating for our enormous human and material losses, and, finally, by withdrawing into a passive strategic and foreign policy which left Europe a prey to Hitler's ambitions. Now, in the aftermath of the last conflict in which she had all but perished, on what premises was France to base her progress and her actions?

The first of these premises was that, in spite of everything, she was alive, sovereign and victorious. That was undoubtedly a marvel. Who would have thought that, after suffering an unparalleled disaster, after witnessing the subjection of her rulers to the authority of the enemy, after undergoing the ravages of the two greatest battles of the war and, in the meantime, prolonged plundering by the invader, after enduring the systematic abasement inflicted on her by a regime founded on surrender and humiliation, she would ever heal the wounds inflicted on her body and her soul? Who would not have sworn that her liberation, if it was to come, would be due to foreigners alone and that they would decide what was to become of her at home and abroad? Who, in the almost total extinction of her resistance, had not condemned as absurd the hope that one day the enemy would surrender to her at the same time as to her allies? Nevertheless, in the end she had emerged from the struggle with her frontiers and her unity intact, in control of her own affairs, and in the ranks of the victors. There was nothing, therefore, to prevent her now from being what she intended to be and doing what she wished to do.

This was all the more true because, for the first time in her history, she was unhampered by any threat from her immediate neighbors. Germany, dismembered, had ceased to be a formidable and domineering power. Italy regretted having turned her ambitions against us. The alliance with England, preserved by Free France, and the process of decolonization which had removed old grievances, ensured that the wind of mistrust no longer blew across the English Channel. Bonds of affection and common interest were bringing a serene France and a pacified Spain closer together across the Pyrenees. And what enmities could possibly spring up from the friendly lands of Belgium, Luxembourg, Holland or neutral Switzerland? Thus we were relieved of the state of constant tension in which dangerous neighbors once held us and which gravely hampered our activities.

It is true that, while France had lost her special vocation of being constantly in danger, the whole world was now haunted by the permanent fear of global conflict. Two empires, the American and the Soviet, now become giants in comparison with the old powers, confronted each other with their forces, their hegemonies and their ideologies. Both were in possession of nuclear armaments which could at any moment shake the entire world, and which made each of them omnipotent protectors in their respective camps. This perilous balance was liable to tip over eventually into limitless war unless it evolved into a general *détente*. For France, reduced in wealth and power by the conflicts in which she had been engaged over the past two centuries, dangerously exposed by her geographical position at the edge of the Old World and facing the New, mortally vulnerable by reason of her size and population, peace was obviously of vital importance. And, as it happened, circumstances now ordained that she should appoint herself its champion. For she was in the singular position of having no claims on what others possessed while they had nothing to claim from her, and of harboring no grievances on her own behalf against either of the giants, for whose peoples she cherished a traditional friendship confirmed by recent events, while they felt an exceptional attachment to her. In short, if there was a voice that might be listened to and a policy that might be effective with a view to setting up a new order to replace the Cold War, that voice and that policy were pre-eminently those of France. But only on condition that they were really her own and that the hand she held out in friendship was free.

At the same time, France now enjoyed a vast fund of interest and trust among peoples whose future was in gestation but who refused to pay allegiance to either of the rival dominations. China, endowed with such reserves of manpower and resources, that limitless possibilities were open to her for the future; Japan, re-creating an independent world role on the basis of economic strength; India, at grips with problems of subsistence as vast as her size, but ultimately destined to turn towards the outside world; a great number of old and new States in Africa, Asia and Latin America which accepted aid from either or both of the two camps for the immediate needs of their development, but refused to align themselves – all these now looked by choice towards France. True, until she had completed the process of decolonization, they bitterly criticized her, but the criticisms soon ceased when she had liberated her former possessions. It remained for her to exploit the potential of respect, admiration and prestige which existed in her favor over a large part of the globe provided that, as the world expected of her, she served the universal cause of human dignity and progress.

Thus the same destiny which had enabled France to survive the terrible crisis of the war, offered to her afterwards, in spite of all she had lost over the past two centuries in terms of relative power and wealth, a leading international role which suited her genius, responded to her interests and matched her means. I was naturally determined that she should play this role, the more so since I believed that the internal transformation, the political stability and the social progress without which she would unquestionably be doomed to disorder and decline demanded that she should once again feel herself invested with world responsibility. Such was my philosophy. What was my policy to be as regards the practical problems that faced our country abroad?

Apart from that of Algeria and our colonies, which was for us to settle on our own, these problems were of such scope and range that their solution would be a very lengthy undertaking, unless a new war should chance to come and cut the Gordian knots tied by the previous one. Hence a sustained and continuous policy was required to deal with them, and this was precisely what, in contrast to the unending shifts and changes of the past, our new institutions made possible.

But what exactly were these problems? First of all there was Germany, divided into three by the existence of a parliamentary republic in the West, a Communist dictatorship in the East, and a special status for Berlin, a prey to the internal strains imposed by this state of affairs and the principal pawn in the rivalry between the two camps. There was Europe, impelled by reason and sentiment towards unification after the terrible convulsions which had torn it apart but radically divided by the Iron Curtain, the Cold War and the enforced subjection of its eastern half to Soviet domination. There was the organization imposed on the Atlantic alliance, which amounted to the military and political subordination of Western Europe to the United

States of America. There was the problem of aid for the development of the Third World, which was used by Washington and Moscow as a battleground for their rivalry. There were crises in the East, in Africa, in Asia and in Latin America, which the rival interventions of the two giants rendered chronic and incurable. And there were the international institutions in which the two opposing camps polarized judgments on all subjects and prohibited impartiality.

In each of these fields, I wanted France to play an active part. In this poor world which deserved to be handled gently and each of whose leaders was weighed down with grave difficulties, we had to advance step by step, acting as circumstances demanded and respecting the susceptibilities of all. I myself had struck many a blow in my time, but never at the pride of a people nor at the dignity of its leaders. Yet it was essential that what we did and said should be independent of others. From the moment of my return to power, that was our rule – such a complete change of attitude on the part of our country that the world political scene was suddenly and profoundly transformed.

It is true that the Eastern camp at first confined itself to watching to see what new attitude emerged in Paris. But our Western partners, among whom up till then official France had submissively taken its place under the hegemony known as Atlantic solidarity, could not help being put out. However, they would eventually resign themselves to the new situation. It must be said that the experience of dealing with de Gaulle which some of them had had during the war, and all of them after it, meant that they did not expect this Republic to be as easy to handle as the previous one. Still, there was a general feeling in their chancelleries, their parliaments and their newspapers that the ordeal would be a brief one, that de Gaulle would inevitably disappear after a while, and that everything would then be as it had been before. On the other hand, there was no lack of people in these countries, especially among the masses, who were not at all displeased by France's recovery and who felt a certain satisfaction, or envy perhaps, when they saw her shaking off a supremacy which weighed heavily on the whole of the Old World. Added to this were the feelings which foreign crowds were kind enough to entertain for me personally and which, each time I came in contact with them, they demonstrated with a fervor that impressed their governments. On the whole, in spite of the annoyance that was felt, the malicious remarks that were made, the unfavorable articles and aggressive caricatures that proliferated, the outside world would soon accommodate itself to a France who was once more behaving like a great power, and henceforth would follow her every action and her every word with an attention that had long been lacking.

I was to find rather less resignation in what was said and written in quarters which had hitherto been looked upon as the fountainhead of French political thought. For there it had long been more or less taken for granted that our country should take no action that was not dictated to it from outside. No doubt this attitude of mind dated from the time when the dangers which threatened France forced her continually to seek support from abroad, and when the instability of the political regime prevented the government from taking upon itself the risks of major decisions. Even before the First World War, in its alliance with Russia, the Third Republic had had to undertake to respect the Treaty of Frankfurt and let St Petersburg lead the way rather than Paris. It is true that, during the long battle subsequently fought on our soil in alliance with the English, the Belgians and finally the Americans, the leading role and then the supreme command fell to the French, who in fact provided the principal effort. But was it not primarily the Anglo-Saxons' cry of "Halt!" that brought the sudden cessation of hostilities on November 11, 1918, at the very moment when we were about to pluck the fruits of victory? Were not the wishes and promises of the American President the dominant factor in the Treaty of Versailles, which admittedly restored Alsace and Lorraine to us but left the enemy's unity, territory and resources intact? And afterwards, was it not to gratify the wishes of Washington and London that the government in

Paris surrendered the guarantees we had secured and renounced the reparations which Germany owed us in exchange for specious schemes offered to us by America? When the Hitlerian threat appeared and the Führer ventured to move his troops into the Rhineland, and preventive or repressive action on our part would have been enough to bring about his retreat and discomfiture at a time when he was still short of armaments, did not our ministers remain passive because England failed to take the initiative? At the time of the Austrian Anschluss, then the dismemberment and annexation of Czechoslovakia by the Reich, from whence did French acquiescence stem if not from the example of the English? In the surrender of Vichy to the invader's law and in the "collaboration" designed to make our country participate in a so-called European order which in fact was purely Germanic, was there not a trace of this long inurement to satellite status? At the same time, even as I strove to preserve France's sovereign rights in relation to our allies while fighting the common enemy, whence sprang the reprobation voiced by even those closest to me, if not from the idea that we should always give way?

After so many lessons, it might have been thought that once the war was over, those who claimed to lead public opinion would be less inclined towards subordination. Far from it: for the leading school of thought in each political party, national self-effacement had become an established and flaunted doctrine. While for the Communists it was an absolute rule that Moscow is always right, all the old party formations professed the doctrine of "supra-nationalism", in other words France's submission to a law that was not her own. Hence the support for "Europe" seen as an edifice in which technocrats forming an "executive" and parliamentarians assuming legislative powers – the great majority of both being foreigners – would have the authority to decide the fate of the French people. Hence, too, the passion for the Atlantic organization which would put the security and therefore the policy of our country at the disposal of another. Hence, again, the eagerness to submit the acts of our government to the approval of international organizations in which, under a semblance of collective deliberation, the authority of the protector reigned supreme in every field, whether political, military, economic, technical or monetary, and in which our representatives would never dare to say "we want" but simply confine themselves to "pleading France's cause". Hence, finally, the constant fury aroused among the party-political breed by my actions in the name of an independent nation.

Nevertheless, I was to find no lack of support. Emotionally, I would have the backing of the French people, who, without being in the least inclined to arrogance, were determined to preserve their own identity, all the more so because they had nearly lost it and because others everywhere were ardently affirming theirs, whether in terms of sovereignty, language, culture, production or even sport. Whenever I expressed myself in public on these matters I felt a quiver of response. Politically, the organization which had been formed to follow me above and beyond all the old parties, and which had had a numerous and compact group elected to parliament, was to accompany me through thick and thin. Practically, I would have a stable government at my side, whose Prime Minister was convinced of France's right and duty to act on a world scale, and whose Foreign Minister displayed in his field an ability which few have equalled in the course of our arduous history.

Maurice Couve de Murville had the required gifts. Amid a welter of interlocking problems and tangled arguments he was immediately able to distinguish the essential from the accessory, so that he was clear and precise in matters which others deliberately made as obscure and ambiguous as possible. He had the experience, having dealt with many of the issues of the day and known most of the men in command in the course of a distinguished career. He had the confidence, certain as he was that the post to which I had nominated him would be his for a long time. He had the manner, being skilful at making contact by listening, observing and taking note, and then excelling, at the critical moment, in the authoritative formulation of a position from which he would never be deflected. He had the necessary faith, convinced as he was that France could survive only in the first rank of nations, that de Gaulle could put her back there, and that nothing in life was more important than working towards this goal.

This was what we were aiming for in the vast arena of Europe. I myself had always felt, and now more than ever, how much the nations which peopled it had in common. Being all of the same white race, with the same Christian origins and the same way of life, linked to one another since time immemorial by countless ties of thought, art, science, politics and trade, it was natural that they should come to form a whole, with its own character and organization in relation to the rest of the world. It was in pursuance of this destiny that the Roman emperors reigned over it, that Charlemagne, Charles V and Napoleon attempted to unite it, that Hitler sought to impose upon it his crushing domination. But it is a fact of some significance that not one of these federators succeeded in inducing the subject countries to surrender their individuality. On the contrary, arbitrary centralization always provoked an upsurge of violent nationalism by way of reaction. It was my belief that a united Europe could not today, any more than in previous times, be a fusion of its peoples, but that it could and should result from a systematic *rapprochement*. Everything prompted them towards this in an age of proliferating trade, international enterprises, science and technology which know no frontiers, rapid communications and widespread travel. My policy therefore aimed at the setting up of a concert of European States which in developing all sorts of ties between them would increase their interdependence and solidarity. From this starting-point, there was every reason to believe that the process of evolution might lead to their confederation, especially if they were one day to be threatened from the same source.

In practice this led us to put the European Economic Community into effect; to encourage the Six to concert together regularly in political matters; to prevent certain others, in particular Great Britain, from dragging the West into an Atlantic system which would be totally incompatible with a European Europe, and indeed to persuade these centrifugal elements to integrate themselves with the Continent by changing their outlook, their habits and their customers; and finally to set an example of *détente* followed by understanding and co-operation with the countries of the Eastern bloc, in the belief that beyond all the prejudices and preconceptions of ideology and propaganda, it was peace and progress that answered the needs and desires of the inhabitants of both halves of an accidentally divided Europe.

At the heart of the problem and at the center of the continent lay Germany. It was her destiny to be the keystone of any European edifice, and yet her misdeeds had contributed more than anything else to tearing the Old World apart. True, now that she was sliced into three segments, with the forces of her conquerors stationed in each, she was no longer a direct threat to anyone. But how could the memory of her ambition, her audacity, her power and her tyranny be effaced from peoples' memories – an ambition which only yesterday had unleashed a military machine capable of crushing with one blow the armies of France and her allies; an audacity which, thanks to Italy's complicity, had carried her armies as far as Africa and the Nile basin; a power which, driving across Poland and Russia with Italian, Hungarian, Bulgarian and Rumanian aid, had reached the gates of Moscow and the foothills of the Caucasus; a tyranny whose reign had brought oppression, plunder and crime wherever the fortune of war took the German flag? Henceforth, every precaution must be taken to prevent Germany's evil genius from breaking loose again. But how could a real and lasting peace be built on foundations that were unacceptable to this great people? How could a genuine union of the continent be established without Germany being a part of it? How could the age-old threat of ruin and death be finally dispelled on either side of the Rhine as long as the old enmity remained?

On the all-important question of Germany's future, my mind was made up. First of all, I believed that it would be unjust and dangerous to revise the *de facto* frontiers which the war had imposed on her. This meant that the Oder-Neisse line which separates her from Poland should remain her definitive boundary, that nothing should remain of her former claims in respect of Czechoslovakia, and that a new Anschluss in whatever form must be precluded. Furthermore, the right to possess or to manufacture atomic weapons – which in any case she had declared her intention to renounce – must in no circumstances be granted to her. This being so, I considered it essential that she should form an integral part of the organized system of co-operation between States which I envisaged for the whole of our continent. In this way the security of all nations between the Atlantic and the Urals would be guaranteed, and a change brought about in circumstances, attitudes and relationships which would doubtless ultimately permit the reunion of the three segments of the German people. In the meantime, the Federal Republic would have an essential role to play within the Economic Community and, should it ever materialize, in the political concert of the Six. Finally, I intended that France should weave a network of preferential ties with Germany, which would gradually lead the two peoples towards the mutual understanding and appreciation to which their natural instinct prompts them when they are no longer using up their energies in fighting each other.

By a stroke of good fortune, at the moment when I took up the reins once more in Paris, it happened that Konrad Adenauer, of all Germans the most capable and most willing to commit his country alongside France, was still at the head of the Bonn Government and would remain there for some time longer. This Rhinelander was imbued with a sense of the complementary nature of the Gauls and the Teutons which once fertilized the presence of the Roman Empire on the Rhine, brought success to the Franks and glory to Charlemagne, provided the rationale for Austrasia, justified the relations between the King of France and the Electors, set Germany afire with the flame of the Revolution, inspired Goethe, Heine, Madame de Staël and Victor Hugo, and in spite of the fierce struggles in which the two peoples were locked, continued to seek a path gropingly through the darkness. This patriot was aware of the barriers of hatred and distrust which the frenzied ambitions of Hitler, passionately obeyed by the German masses and their elite, had raised between his country and all its neighbors and which France alone, he knew, by offering the hand of friendship to the hereditary enemy, could succeed in breaking down. This politician, whose tenacious skill had up to now succeeded in maintaining the stability and progress of the Federal Republic, had to steer a careful course to ensure that neither the threat from the East nor the protection of the West endangered the fragile edifice of a State built from the ruins, and perceived the potential value at home and abroad of the resolute backing of the new French Republic.

As soon as he realized that my return was something more than an interlude, the Chancellor asked to see me. I received him at Colombey-les-deux-Eglises on September 14 and 15, 1958. It seemed to me appropriate to mark the occasion in some special way, and I felt that the atmosphere of a family house would be more striking than the splendor of a palace as a setting for the historic encounter between this old Frenchman and this very old German in the name of their two peoples. And so my wife and I offered the Chancellor the modest hospitality of La Boisserie.

When we were face to face, Konrad Adenauer came straight to the point. "I have come to you," he said, "because I consider that you are in a position to influence the course of events. Your personality, what you have already accomplished in the service of your country, the circumstances in which you returned to power – all this gives you the means to do so. Our two peoples are now for the first time in a position to put their relations on an entirely new basis of cordial co-operation. True, we are already on the right road in this respect. But what has been achieved so far has been due to circumstances which, though pressing enough in all conscience, are transitory by the time-scale of history: Germany's defeat and France's exhaustion. The question now is whether something more durable can be achieved. According to what you personally want and decide to do, France and Germany can either reach a genuine long-term understanding, to the immense benefit of themselves and of Europe, or else remain mutually estranged and thus doomed to oppose each other again to their joint detriment. If it is your aim to bring about a genuine *rapprochement* between our two countries, let me say that I am determined to work with you to this end, and that I myself have certain assets in this regard. I have held the office of Chancellor for eleven years, and in spite of my great age I hope to be able to do so for some time to come. The prestige I enjoy and my past record – the reprobation and contempt I showed for Hitler and his people and the maltreatment I and my family suffered at their hands – enable me to lead German policy in the desired direction. But you? What direction do you intend to give French policy?"

I told the Chancellor in reply that if we were together in my house it was because I felt that the moment had come for my country to adopt a new policy towards his. After the terrible ordeals inflicted on her as a result of Teutonic ambitions in 1870, 1914 and 1939, France now faced a Germany which had been defeated, dismantled and reduced to a pitiful international position, which entirely altered the circumstances of their relationship. Of course the French people would not readily forget what they had suffered in the past at the hands of their neighbor across the Rhine, or neglect the precautions which must be taken to safeguard their future. I had, indeed, before the end of hostilities, intended that such precautions should be physical and territorial. But in view of the momentous events which had occurred since then and the resulting situation for Germany, in view of the change of policy and outlook brought about in the Federal Republic by Konrad Adenauer's government, and in view of the overriding importance of the union of Europe, a union which above all demanded the co-operation of Paris and Bonn, I felt that we should try to reverse the course of history by reconciling our two peoples and uniting their efforts and abilities.

This said, Adenauer and I proceeded to consider how to put our aims into practice. We had no difficulty in agreeing on the fundamental principle that, instead of merging the respective policies of the two countries, as the theorists of the European Coal and Steel Community, Euratom and the European Defence Community sought to do, we should recognize that our positions were very different, and build on this fact. According to the Chancellor, there were three things which humiliated and handicapped Germany ventured to ask of France: first, to help her to recover the respect and trust of other nations which would restore her international position; secondly, to contribute towards her security *vis-à-vis* the Soviet camp, especially with regard to the threat that overshadowed Berlin; and thirdly, to recognize her right to reunification. I pointed out to the Chancellor that, in response to so many requests, France for her part had nothing to ask of Germany with respect to unity, security or rank, whereas she could certainly help to rehabilitate her erstwhile aggressor. She would do so – with what magnanimity! – in the name of the entente to be established between the two peoples, and of the balance of power, the unity and the peace of Europe. But to justify her support, she would insist that certain conditions be fulfilled on the German side. These were: acceptance of existing frontiers, an attitude of goodwill in relations with the East, complete renunciation of atomic armaments, and unremitting patience as regards reunification.

I must say that on these points the Chancellor's pragmatism reconciled him to my position. Devoted as he was to his country, he did not intend to make frontier revision the present and principal aim of his policy, knowing full well that to raise the matter would produce nothing but redoubled alarm and fury from Russia and Poland and reproachful anxiety in the West. Despite his unwavering hostility to the Communist regime and his fears of Muscovite imperialism, he by no means ruled out the possibility of a *modus vivendi*. "As early as 1955," he told me, "I paid an official visit to the Kremlin. I was the first Western Head of State or Government to have been there since the end of the war." He categorically denied that Germany had any intention of possessing atomic weapons, and was aware of the immediate threat to peace if it were otherwise. Although he longed with all his heart to see a united German State and an end to the totalitarian oppression imposed by the Communists, on behalf of the Soviets, in what he called "the Zone", I sensed in this Catholic Rhinelander, leader of a party of traditional democrats, a feeling that, in the event, the present Federal Republic might experience some uneasiness in incorporating outright the Prussian, Protestant and socialist complex of the eastern territories. In any case he agreed that, although this was a goal which Germany would never relinquish, no time limit should be set for its achievement.

We discussed Europe at length. Adenauer agreed with me that there could be no question of submerging the identity of our two nations in some stateless construction. He did, however, admit that Germany had drawn distinct advantages from the mystique of integration, and he was grateful to its French protagonists such as Jean Monnet and Robert Schuman for their gifts. But being Chancellor of a defeated, divided and threatened Germany, he naturally inclined towards a West European system which would ensure his country not only equal rights but also commanding influence, would provide powerful support against the East, and by its very existence would encourage the United States to remain in Europe and thus maintain its guarantee to Federal Germany. Adenauer set great store by this guarantee because, he said, "by providing for the security of the German people and putting them in good company, it diverts them from their obsession with isolation and the worship of power which, to their cost, drove them into Hitler's arms."

I told Adenauer that from a strictly national point of view France, unlike Germany, had no real need of an organization of Western Europe, since the war had damaged neither her reputation nor her territorial integrity. Nevertheless, she was in favor of a practical and, if possible, political *rapprochement* of all European States because her aim was general peace and progress. Meanwhile, on condition that her national identity remained unaffected, she was prepared to implement the Treaty of Rome and, further, to propose that the Six should meet

regularly to discuss joint action on all the political problems
facing the world. Difficulties would arise for the European
Economic Community from the problem of agriculture, a
solution to which was essential for France, and Britain's application for membership, which France felt must be turned down as
long as Britain remained economically and politically what she
was. On these two points, the French government was counting
on the agreement of the German government, failing which a
genuine union of the Six would be unattainable. "Personally",
the Chancellor said, "I understand your reasons very well.
But Germany on the whole is unfavorable to the agricultural
Common Market and anxious to give satisfaction to Britain.
However, since in my opinion nothing is more important than
that the union of the Six should succeed, I promise to act in
such a way that the two problems you have mentioned do not
prevent its realization. As for the idea of regular political discussions with our partners, I am entirely in favor of it."

I assured the Chancellor that we in France considered it
perfectly natural that Federal Germany should adhere unreservedly to the Atlantic Pact. How could she do otherwise? In
this age of atomic weapons, as long as she was threatened by the
Soviets, it was obvious that Germany needed the protection of
the United States. But in this respect as in others, France was
not in the same position. Hence, while continuing to belong to
the alliance formed by the Treaty of Washington for mutual
assistance in case of aggression, she planned to leave NATO
sooner or later, the more so as she intended to equip herself
with nuclear weapons which there could be no question of
integrating into the system. More than anything else, political
independence commensurate with my country's position and
aims was essential to its survival in the future. The German
Chancellor listened while I explained the reasons for this. "The
French people," I told him, "had for centuries grown accustomed to think of their country as the mastodon of Europe. It
was this sense of their greatness and the responsibilities it
entailed that preserved their unity, although by nature, ever
since the time of the Gauls, they have been inclined to divisions

and airy illusions. Now once again circumstances – by which I mean France's salvation at the end of the war, her strong institutions, and the profound upheaval which the world is undergoing – offer them the chance of fulfilling an international mission, without which they would lose interest in themselves and fall into disruption. It is my view that every country in the world, including Germany, has a great deal to lose and nothing to gain from the eclipse of France. Anything that leads my country to give up the struggle represents a grave danger to us and a serious threat to others." "I agree with you," replied Adenauer, "and I am heartily glad to see France resume her rightful place in the world. Allow me to say, however, that the German people, although their genius is different from that of the French, have a similar need for dignity. Having seen you and listened to you, I feel confident that you are willing to help Germany recover that dignity." At the conclusion of our discussions, we agreed to establish direct and special links between our two countries in every field, and not to limit them to membership of organizations which extinguished their individual personalities. From then onwards we were to remain in close personal contact.

Two months later, on November 26, I paid a return visit to Adenauer at Bad-Kreuznach, accompanied by Michel Debré and Maurice Couve de Murville. The Chancellor was seconded by the dynamic Ludwig Erhard who, making the most of the enterprise and initiative of management, the constructive co-operation of the unions and the credits provided under the Marshall Plan, had restored his country's means of production and was now presiding over a remarkable economic achievement. Heinrich von Brentano, the Foreign Minister, was also there, as convinced as his chief that an understanding with France must henceforth be a basic principle of German policy. In the course of this meeting, the two governments set out the terms of their co-operation in accordance with what had been adumbrated at Colombey-les-deux-Eglises. In particular, they agreed to put an end to the negotiations conducted by Reginald Maudling which were calculated to submerge the Community of the Six at the outset in a vast free trade area together with

England and eventually the whole of the West. At the same time, it was an opportunity for us French to assure the Germans, who were then in a state of acute anxiety, that we would oppose the change in the status of Berlin which Nikita Khrushchev was at that very moment threatening to impose.

From then until mid-1962, Konrad Adenauer and I were to write to each other on some forty occasions. We saw each other fifteen times, either in Paris, Marly or Rambouillet, or in Baden-Baden or Bonn. We spent more than a hundred hours in conversation, either in private, or with our ministers in attendance, or in the company of our families. Then, since it was my intention that the new relationship between the two nations, so long at enmity, should be solemnly consecrated, I invited the Chancellor to pay an official visit to France. Heinrich Lübke, President of the Federal Republic, had already made a discreet State visit in June 1961. Now, in July 1962, the Head of the German government made a public appearance in the squares and avenues of our capital. The welcome he received, particularly from the people in the street, testified to the esteem in which he was personally held, as well as to the fund of goodwill towards the policy of reconciliation and co-operation to which he had dedicated himself. After his Parisian reception, an impressive military ceremony took place at the camp of Mourmelon. There, General de Gaulle received Chancellor Konrad Adenauer before the colors. Standing side by side in a command car, they inspected a French and a German armored division which outvied one another in smartness and bearing. Then, with their ministers and many dignitaries around them, they watched these heavy units parade before them, while aerial formations from both countries flew overhead. The journey ended at Rheims, the symbol of our age-old traditions, but also the scene of many an encounter between the hereditary enemies, from the ancient Germanic invasions to the battles of the Marne. In the cathedral, whose wounds were still not fully healed, the first Frenchman and the first German came together to pray that on either side of the Rhine the deeds of friendship might for ever supplant the miseries of war.

Subsequently, and until the death of my illustrious friend, our relations were to progress at the same tempo and with the same cordiality. By and large, everything that was spoken, written and evinced between us was to do no more than develop and adapt to events the friendly agreement concluded in 1958. It is true that circumstances would produce some divergences of view. But these were always surmounted. Through us, the relations between France and Germany were established on foundations and in an atmosphere hitherto unknown in their history.

This co-operation between the two former enemies was a necessary but by no means a sufficient precondition for organized European co-operation. It is true that, judging merely by the spate of speeches and articles on the subject, the unification of our Continent might well appear to be a matter as simple as it was foreordained. But when the realities of needs, interests and preconceptions came into play, things took on an altogether different aspect. While fruitless bargaining with the British showed the fledgeling Community that good intentions are not enough to reconcile the irreconcilable, the Six found that even in the economic sphere alone the adjustment of their respective positions bristled with difficulties which could not be resolved solely in terms of the treaties concluded to that end. It had to be acknowledged that the so-called executives installed at the head of common institutions by virtue of the delusions of integration which had prevailed before my return, were helpless when it came to making and enforcing decisions, that only governments were in a position to do this, and then only as a result of negotiations carried out in due form between ministers or ambassadors.

In the case of the European Coal and Steel Community, for example, once it had used up the birthday presents bestowed upon it by its member States, none of them, be it said, for our benefit – French relinquishment of coke from the Ruhr, deliveries of coal and iron to Italy, financial subventions to the Benelux mines – the High Authority, although vested with very extensive theoretical powers and considerable resources, was soon overwhelmed by the problems presented by competing national requirements. Whether it was a matter of fixing the price of steel, or regulating fuel purchases from outside, or converting the collieries of the Borinage, the areopagus enthroned in Luxembourg was powerless to legislate. The result was a chronic decline in that organization, whose prime mover, Jean Monnet, had moreover resigned the presidency.

At the same time, in the case of Euratom, there seemed an irremediable disparity between the situation of France, equipped for some fifteen years past with an active Atomic Energy Commissariat, provided with numerous installations and already engaged in precise and far-reaching programs of research and development, and that of the other countries which, having done nothing on their own account, now wanted to use the funds of the common budget to obtain what they lacked by placing orders with American suppliers.

Lastly, in the case of the Economic Community, the adoption of the agricultural regulations in conjunction with the lowering of industrial tariffs raised obstacles which the Brussels Commission was unable to overcome on its own. It must be said that in this respect the spirit and terms of the Treaty of Rome did not meet our country's requirements. The industrial provisions were as precise and explicit as those concerning agriculture were vague. This was evidently due to the fact that our negotiators in 1957, caught up in the dream of a supra-national Europe and anxious at any price to settle for something approaching it, had not felt it their duty to insist that a French interest, no matter how crucial, should receive satisfaction at the outset. It would, therefore, be necessary either to obtain it *en route*, or to liquidate the Common Market. Meanwhile, determined though it was to have its way in the end, the French government was able to allow the machinery of the Treaty of Rome to be set in motion thanks to the recovery of our balance of payments and the stabilization of the franc. In December 1958 it announced that it would implement the inaugural measures which were scheduled for New Year's Day, in particular a ten per cent tariff cut and a twenty per cent quota increase.

Once initiated, the implementation of the Common Market was to give rise to a vast outgrowth of not only technical but also diplomatic activity. For, irrespective of its very wide economic scope, the operation proved to be hedged about with specifically political intentions calculated to prevent our country from being its own master. Hence, while the Community was taking shape, I was obliged on several occasions to intervene in order to repel the threats which overshadowed our cause.

The first arose from the original ambivalence of the institution. Was its objective – in itself momentous enough – the harmonization of the practical interests of the six States, their economic solidarity in face of the outside world and, if possible, their co-operation in foreign policy? Or did it aim to achieve the total fusion of their respective economies and policies in a single entity with its own government, parliament and laws, ruling in every respect its French, German, Italian, Dutch, Belgian and Luxembourg subjects, who would become fellow-citizens of an artificial motherland, the brainchild of the technocrats? Needless to say, having no taste for make-believe, I adopted the former conception. But the latter carried all the hopes and illusions of the supra-national school.

For these champions of integration, the European executive was already alive and kicking: it was the Commission of the Economic Community, made up, admittedly, of representatives nominated by the six States but, thereafter, in no way dependent on them. Judging by the chorus of those who wanted Europe to be a federation, albeit without a federator, all the authority, initiative and control of the exchequer which are the prerogatives of government in the economic sphere must in future belong to this brigade of experts, not only within the Community but also – and this could be indefinitely extensible – from the point of view of relations with other countries. As for the national ministers, who could not as yet be dispensed with in their executive capacity, they had only to be summoned periodically to Brussels, where they would receive the Commission's instructions in their specialized fields. At the same time, the mythmongers wanted to exhibit the Assembly in Strasbourg, consisting of deputies and senators delegated by the legislatures of the member countries, as a "European parliament" which, while having no effective power, provided the Brussels "executive" with a semblance of democratic responsibility.

Walter Hallstein was the Chairman of the Commission. He was ardently wedded to the thesis of the super-State, and bent all his skilful efforts towards giving the Community the character and appearance of one. He had made Brussels, where he resided, into a sort of capital. There he sat, surrounded with all the trappings of sovereignty, directing his colleagues, allocating jobs among them, controlling several thousand officials who were appointed, promoted and remunerated at his discretion, receiving the credentials of foreign ambassadors, laying claim to high honors on the occasion of his official visits, concerned above all to further the amalgamation of the Six, believing that the pressure of events would bring about what he envisaged. But after meeting him more than once and observing his activities, I felt that although Walter Hallstein was in his way a sincere European, he was first and foremost a German who was ambitious for his own country. For in the Europe that he sought lay the framework in which his country could first of all regain, free of charge, the respectability and equality of rights which the frenzy and defeat of Hitler had cost it, then acquire the preponderant influence which its economic strength would no doubt earn it, and finally ensure that the cause of its frontiers and its unity was backed by a powerful coalition in accordance with the doctrine to which, as Foreign Minister of the Federal Republic, he had formerly given his name. These factors did not alter my esteem and regard for Walter Hallstein, but the goals I was pursuing on behalf of France were incompatible with such projects.

The fundamental divergence between the way the Brussels Commission conceived its role and my own government's insistence, while looking to the Commission for expert advice, that important measures should be subordinated to the decisions of the individual States, nurtured an atmosphere of latent discord. But since the Treaty specified that during the inaugural period no decision was valid unless unanimous, it was enough to enforce its application to ensure that there was no infringement of French sovereignty. So during this period the institution took wing in what was and must remain the economic sphere without being subjected to any mortal political crisis, in spite of frequent clashes. Moreover, in November 1959, at the initiative of Paris, it was decided that the six Foreign Ministers should meet at three-monthly intervals to examine the overall situation and its various implications and to report back to their own governments, which would have the last word if the need arose. It may be imagined that ours did not allow itself to be led.

But it was not only from the political angle that the new-fledged Community had to undergo the truth test. Even in the economic sphere two formidable obstacles, secreting all kinds of contradictory interests and calculations, threatened to bar its way. These were, of course, the external tariff and agriculture, which were closely bound up with one another. True, on signing the Treaty, our partners had seemed to accept that common taxes should be imposed upon foreign goods as customs duties were reduced within the Community. But although they all recognized in principle that this procedure was essential to their solidarity, some of them were nonetheless irked by it because it deprived them of trade facilities which had hitherto been intrinsic to their existence. They therefore wanted the common external tariff to be as low as possible and in any case so elastic that their habits would not be disturbed. The same countries, for the same reasons, were in no hurry to see the Six take upon themselves the consumption and, therefore, the cost of continental farm products, nearly half of which happened to be French. For instance Germany, nearly two-thirds of whose food was imported cheaply from outside the Community in exchange for manufactured goods, would have liked to see a

Common Market for industrial goods only, in which case the Federal Republic would inevitably have had an overwhelming advantage. This was unacceptable to France. We therefore had to put up a fight in Brussels.

The battle was long and hard. Our partners, who bitterly regretted our having changed Republics, had been counting on us once again to sacrifice our own cause to "European integration", as had happened successively with the Coal and Steel Community, in which all the advantages went to others at our expense; with Euratom, for which our country put up practically the entire stake without a *quid pro quo*, and, moreover submitted her atomic assets to foreign supervision; and with the Treaty of Rome, which did not settle the agricultural question which was of paramount importance to ourselves. But now France was determined to get what she needed, and in any case her demands were consistent with the logic of the Community system. So her requirements were eventually met.

In May 1960, at our urgent insistence, the Six agreed to establish the external tariff and to adopt a timetable for the decisions to be taken on agricultural policy. In December of the same year, while urging an acceleration of the process of lowering customs barriers between them, they agreed that all imports of foodstuffs from elsewhere should be liable to an enormous financial levy at the expense of the purchasing State. And in January 1962 they adopted the decisive resolutions.

For at this date, now that the first phase of application was completed, it had to be decided whether or not, in pursuance of the terms of the Treaty, to proceed to the second phase, a kind of point of no return, involving a fifty per cent reduction in customs duties. We French were determined to seize the opportunity to tear aside the veil and induce our partners to make formal commitments on what we regarded as essential. When they proved reluctant to give way, and indeed showed signs of some disquieting reservations, I judged that now or never was the moment to take the bull by the horns. Our ministers in Brussels, Couve de Murville, Baumgartner and Pisani, made it quite clear that we were prepared to withdraw from the Community if our requirements were not met. I myself wrote in similar terms to Chancellor Adenauer, whose government was our principal antagonist in this matter, and repeated it by formal telegram on the evening of the final debate. Feeling ran high in the capitals of the Six. In France, the parties and most of the newspapers, echoing foreign opinion, were disturbed and scandalized by the attitude of General de Gaulle, whose intransigence was threatening "the hopes of Europe". But France and common sense prevailed. During the night of January 13–14, 1962, after some dramatic exchanges, the Council of Ministers of the six States formally decided to admit agriculture into the Common Market, laid down there and then a broad basis for its implementation, and made the necessary arrangements to establish the agricultural regulations on the same footing and at the same time as the rest. Whereupon the implementation of the Treaty was able to enter its second phase.

But how far could it go, in view of the difficulties which the British were doing their utmost to raise, and the tendency of our five partners to submit to their influence? It was not surprising that Great Britain should be radically opposed to the whole venture, since by virtue of her geography and therefore her policy, she has never been willing to see the Continent united or to merge with it herself. In a sense it might almost be said that therein lay the whole history of Europe for the past eight hundred years. As for the present, our neighbors across the Channel, adapted to free trade by the maritime nature of their economic life, could not sincerely agree to shut themselves up behind a continental tariff wall, still less to buy their food dear from us rather than import it cheap from everywhere else, for example the Commonwealth. But without the common tariff and agricultural preference, there could be no valid European Community. Hence at the time of the preliminary studies and discussions that led up to the Treaty of Rome, the London government, which was represented at the outset, had soon withdrawn. Then, with the intention of undermining the project of the Six, it had proposed that they should join a vast

European free trade area with itself and various others. Things had reached this stage when I returned to power.

As early as June 29, 1958, Prime Minister Harold Macmillan had come to see me in Paris. In the midst of our friendly discussions which touched upon a great many topics, he suddenly declared with great feeling: "The Common Market is the Continental System all over again. Britain cannot accept it. I beg you to give it up. Otherwise, we shall be embarking on a war which will doubtless be economic at first but which runs the risk of gradually spreading into other fields." Ignoring the overstatement, I tried to pacify the English Premier, at the same time asking him why the United Kingdom should object to seeing the Six establish a system of preference such as existed inside the Commonwealth. Meanwhile, his minister Reginald Maudling was actively engaged inside the so-called Organization for European Economic Co-operation, to which Britain belonged, in negotiations which were keeping the Six in suspense, and delaying the launching of the Community by proposing that the latter should be absorbed and, consequently, dissolved in a free trade area. Harold Macmillan wrote me a number of very pressing letters in an effort to obtain my compliance. But my government broke the spell, and made it clear that it would not agree to anything which did not include the common external tariff and an agricultural arrangement. London then appeared to abandon its policy of obstruction and, suddenly changing course, set up its own European Free Trade Association, with the Scandinavians, Portugal, Switzerland and Austria. At once, our Brussels partners dropped all their hesitations and set about launching the Common Market.

But the match had merely been postponed. In the middle of 1961 the British returned to the offensive. Having failed from without to prevent the birth of the Community, they now planned to paralyze it from within. Instead of calling for an end to it, they now declared that they themselves were eager to join, and proposed examining the conditions on which they might do so, "provided that their special relationships with the

Commonwealth and their associates in the Free Trade area were taken into consideration, as well as their special interests in respect of agriculture." To submit to this would obviously have meant abandoning the Common Market as originally conceived. Our partners could not bring themselves to do so. But, on the other hand, it was beyond their power to say "No" to England. So, affecting to believe that the squaring of the circle was a practical proposition, they proceeded to discuss a series of projects and counter-projects in Brussels with the British minister Edward Heath, which threw nothing but doubt on the future of the Community. I could see the day approaching when I should either have to remove the obstruction and put an end to the tergiversation, or else extricate France from an enterprise which had gone astray almost as soon as it had begun. At all events, as could have been foreseen, it was now clear to all that in order to achieve the unification of Europe, individual states are the only valid elements, that when their national interest is at stake nothing and nobody must be allowed to force their hands, and that co-operation between them is the only road that will lead anywhere.

In this respect what is true of economics is even truer of politics. And this is no more than natural. What depths of illusion or prejudice would have to be plumbed in order to believe that European nations forged through long centuries by endless exertion and suffering, each with its own geography, history, language, traditions and institutions, could cease to be themselves and form a single entity? What a perfunctory view is reflected in the parallel often naïvely drawn between what Europe ought to do and what the United States have done, when the latter was created from nothing in a completely new territory by successive waves of uprooted colonists? For the Six in particular, how was it conceivable that their external aims should suddenly become identical when their origins, situations and ambitions were so very different? In the matter of decolonization, which France was about to bring to a conclusion, what part could her neighbors play? If, from time immemorial, it had been in her nature to accomplish "God's work,"[1] to disseminate freedom of thought, to be a champion of humanity, why should it *ipso facto* become the concern of her partners? Germany, baulked by defeat of her hopes of supremacy, divided at present and suspected by many of seeking her revenge, was now a wounded giant. By what token should her wounds automatically be shared by others? Given the fact that Italy, having ceased to be an annex of the Germanic or the French empires, and thwarted of her Balkan ambitions, remained a peninsular power confined to the Mediterranean and naturally located within the orbit of the maritime nations, why should she throw in her lot with the Continentals? By what miracle would the Netherlands, which had always owed its livelihood to shipping and its independence to overseas resources, allow itself to be swallowed up by the land powers? How could Belgium, hard put to it to maintain the juxtaposition of Flemings and Walloons in a single entity ever since a compromise between rival powers had turned her into a State, genuinely devote herself to anything else? Lying at the center of the territorial arrangements which had succeeded the rivalries of the two great countries bordering on the Moselle, what major concern could the people of Luxembourg have other than the survival of Luxembourg?

On the other hand, while recognizing that each of these countries had its own national personality which it must preserve, there was no reason why they should not organize concerted action in every sphere, arrange for their ministers to meet regularly and their Heads of State or Government periodically, set up permanent organs to discuss politics, economics, culture and defense, have these subjects debated in the normal way by an assembly of delegates from their respective parliaments, acquire the taste and habit of examining together problems of common interest, and as far as possible adopt a united attitude towards them. Linked with what was already being practiced in the economic sphere in Brussels and Luxembourg, might not this general co-operation lead to a European policy as regards progress, security, influence, external

[1] "Les gestes de Dieu": a reference to the Frankish motto, *Gesta dei per francos*.

relations, aid to the developing countries, and finally and above all as regards peace? Might not the grouping thus formed by the Six gradually attract the other States of the Continent into joining in on the same terms? And perhaps in this way, by opposing war, which is the history of men, that united Europe which is the dream of the wise might ultimately be achieved.

Before discussing this with the German Chancellor, I had put the idea to the Italian Prime Minister. Amintore Fanfani came to visit me on August 7, 1958. I was to receive him again in December and in January. Each of these meetings made me appreciate his wide-ranging intellect, his prudent judgment and his urbanity. Through him, I saw an Italy anxious to keep in touch with everything that was afoot, willing to join in on condition that she was treated with the consideration due to a nation with a very great past and a very important future, ready to subscribe to declarations of principle which expressed good intentions, but careful not to commit herself too deeply. This was the case as regards European unity. The head of the Italian government was certainly in favor of it. He even shared the supra-national leanings bequeathed to him by de Gasperi. Yet, comfortably ignoring an obvious contradiction, he did not want anything done without England, although he was well aware that England was opposed to integration. While paying lip-service to the solidarity of the peoples of the Old World, he did not feel that this should lead them to alter their ties – however dependent – with the United States. In particular, the organization of the Atlantic alliance must on no account be modified. However, he did not spurn my plan for organized political co-operation among the Six, though he reserved judgment on the terms and conditions until these came up for discussion.

Soon afterwards, as it happened, I was to make direct contact with the Italian government and people. Our neighbors were celebrating the centenary of the Franco-Piedmontese victories of 1859. When I was invited to take part by the President of the Republic, Giovanni Gronchi, I accepted with alacrity. Couve de Murville and Guillaumat came too. Milan welcomed me on June 23 amid a storm of cheers. I met with the same enthusiasm the following day during a military parade in which French troops took part alongside the Italian Army. At Magenta too, and then at Solferino, where an enormous crowd had gathered and where I made a speech on the battlefield, fervent demonstrations left no doubt as to public feeling towards our country and General de Gaulle. In the course of the religious service the Archbishop of Milan, Monsignor Montini, the future Pope Paul VI, gave a sermon imbued with a deep affection for France. The same warmth was evident during the reception given to me at the Capitol shortly afterwards by the municipality of Rome. There could be no better proof of the aberration represented by the aggression committed against us nineteen years before on the orders of Mussolini. But nothing could be more encouraging for the future relations between the two kindred nations. President Gronchi, Prime Minister Antonio Segni and Foreign Minister Giuseppe Pella agreed on this point with myself and the ministers who accompanied me.

Nevertheless our discussions, first on the train which took us to Rome, then at the Quirinal Palace, where my wife and I were the guests of the Head of State and Signora Gronchi and where the two Presidents forgathered with members of their governments, revealed attitudes on either side which were far from identical. We French wanted to proceed towards a European Europe. The Italians set the utmost store by the maintenance of existing relations with the Anglo-Saxons. Basically, the Rome government favored integration because under cover of that mythical apparatus it could maneuver to its heart's content, because there was nothing in such a structure that could interfere with the protective hegemony of Washington, and because in any case it saw it as a temporary arrangement until the arrival of the English. Soon I was to discover that the Benelux countries took the same view. Just as French economic and social vested interests and political parties clamored for the transformation of France, but resisted any reform that altered the established order, so the unification of the Continent whose necessity was proclaimed by the ruling circles of our European partners and by our own coteries, came up against a wall of reservations, exegeses and counterbids whenever I attempted to clear the way for it. But I reflected that if Rome was not built in a day, it was in the nature of things that the construction of Europe should require protracted efforts.

In the matter of perseverance, I received the best possible reminder in the Vatican. I was received there by Pope John XXIII. The pomp and pageantry displayed for the occasion demonstrated his exceptional concern for France. He was gratified to hear what I had to say about our efforts towards national renewal, since he knew our country well and had witnessed its former political confusion at close range as Nuncio in Paris. Then, with an anxiety tempered by his natural serenity, the sovereign pontiff spoke of the spiritual perturbation inflicted on Christendom by the gigantic upheavals of the century. Among all the peoples of Europe and Asia which had been subjected to Communism, the Catholic community was oppressed and cut off from Rome. But everywhere else, under free regimes, a sort of diffuse rebelliousness was undermining, if not religion then at least its practices, its rules, its hierarchy and its rites. Nevertheless, however much anxiety this situation might cause him, the Pope saw it as no more than another in the long series of crises which the Church had faced and surmounted ever since the time of Christ. He believed that by putting into practice its own values of inspiration and self-examination it would not fail once more to regain its equilibrium. It was to this that he proposed to dedicate his pontificate. After my wife had been introduced, John XXIII gave us his blessing. We never saw him again.

Europe, for its part, had no certainty of eternal life. However, by regrouping in order to come to grips with its own problems, perhaps it too might take on a new lease of life. But with all the talk and counter-talk about unity, no plan for such a confrontation had ever been submitted to the Six. I took it upon myself to do so once it had become clear that our country was extricating herself from the Algerian problem and about to regain her freedom of action. My intention was to invite the Heads of State or Government to Paris, so that France could present her proposals in a setting commensurate with the subject. Chancellor Adenauer was the first to be informed. In July 1960 at Rambouillet, where I had invited him to stay, I announced to him my plan for a summit conference and explained to him how, in my view, the political co-operation of the Six should be run by periodic meetings of their leaders and, in the interim, by the work of permanent bodies which would prepare the ground for the meetings and follow up the decisions. He and I were agreed on the essentials. In August, I confided my plan to Jan de Quay, Prime Minister of the Netherlands, and Joseph Luns, the Foreign Minister, when they came to Paris. As expected, I found them orientated far less towards the Continent than towards America and England, and above all anxious to see the latter join the Six on no matter what terms. Much the same was true of the Belgians, Gaston Eyskens, the Prime Minister, and Paul-Henri Spaak, once again in charge of Foreign Affairs, when I received them too at the Elysée. There also the cautious Luxembourg ministers Pierre Werner and Eugène Schauss were welcomed in their turn. In the meantime, I had conferred at leisure with Amintore Fanfani, once again Prime Minister of Italy, and Antonio Segni when they came to stay at Rambouillet, and had had a further discussion with Konrad Adenauer in Bonn.

In addition, as was my wont, I saw fit to apprise the public of my plans. In the course of a press conference on September 5, I gave details of what was being undertaken. After saying that "to build Europe, which means to unite Europe, is an essential aim of our policy," I declared that to this end it was necessary "to proceed, not on the basis of dreams, but in accordance with realities. Now, what are the realities of Europe? What are the pillars on which it can be built? The truth is that those pillars are the States of Europe . . . States each of which, indeed, has its own genius, history and language, its own sorrows, glories and ambitions; but States that are the only entities with the right to give orders and the power to be obeyed." Then, while recognizing "the technical value of certain more or less extra-national or supra-national organisms," I pointed out that they were not and could not be politically effective, as was proved by what was happening at that very moment in the European Coal and Steel Community, Euratom and the Brussels Community. I insisted that, "although it is perfectly natural for the States of Europe to have specialist bodies available to prepare and whenever necessary to follow up their decisions, those decisions must be their own." Then I outlined my plan: "To arrange for the regular co-operation of the States of Western Europe in the political, economic and cultural spheres, as well as that of defense, is an aim that France deems desirable, possible and practical. . . . It will entail organized, regular consultations between the governments concerned and the work of specialist bodies in each of the common domains, subordinated to those governments. It will entail periodic deliberations by an assembly made up of delegates of the national parliaments. It must also, in my view, entail as soon as possible a solemn European referendum, in order to give this new departure for Europe the popular backing which is essential to it." I concluded: "If we set out on this road . . . links will be forged, habits will be developed, and, as time does its work, it is possible that we will come to take further steps towards European unity."

On February 10 and 11, in the Salon de l'Horloge in the Quai d'Orsay, I presided over a meeting of Prime Ministers, Foreign Ministers, higher civil servants and ambassadors of Germany, Italy, the Netherlands, Belgium, Luxembourg and France. The discussion was lively, because the doubts and misgivings were considerable. Needless to say, they all had to do with America and England. In response to my formal proposal to establish political co-operation among the Six forthwith, Adenauer gave his entire approval. Werner followed suit. Fanfani concurred, with certain reservations. Eyskens and Wigny raised no objections at first. But Luns, with some asperity, expressed all kinds of hesitations; whereupon Eyskens

adopted the same attitude. It was clear that Holland and
Belgium, small powers bordering on the North Sea, always on
their guard against the "great ones" of the Continent and
traditionally protected by the British Navy, now superseded
by the Americans, did not take kindly to a system from which
the Anglo-Saxons were excluded. But it was no less obvious
that if the western half of the Old World remained subordinated
to the New, Europe would never be European, nor would
she ever be able to bring her two halves together. However,
the prevailing impression at the conclusion of this encounter
was that Europe had taken its first steps towards unity, that
all the participants had been highly interested and gratified
to meet and deliberate together, and, in short, that we should
attempt to go further. To this end, it was agreed that there
should be a second meeting in Bonn in three months' time, and
that with a view to this next summit conference a political
commission made up of representatives of the Six should draw
up proposals in Paris for the organization of their co-operation
in every sphere.

In view of the magnitude of the obstacles, however, there
was little likelihood of immediate success. Indeed, an active
campaign to impede it was launched at once behind the
scenes. The supporters of unconditional British entry into the
economic and – should it materialize – the political Community concerted their negative efforts with those of the champions of supra-nationalism, without the evident contradiction
between the two theses in the least deflecting them from
working together to combat the French solution. When I went
to Bonn on May 20, I became aware of the commotion aroused
there by the positive attitude which the Chancellor had
adopted in my favor. Upon receiving the King and Queen of
the Belgians, who were given a whole-hearted welcome by
the Parisians at the end of the same month, I naturally took
the opportunity to express to the young sovereigns and to their
country the warm feelings of France, but I also listened to
Spaak, who accompanied them, while he repeated to me his
unfavorable views on the question of political co-operation

among the Six. At the same time, there were nothing but echoes of dubiety from Italy and of criticism from Holland.

In spite of everything, after some delay the second meeting of Heads of State and Government took place in Bonn on July 18 and 19. Each of the delegations took up a similar position as in Paris. But since Chancellor Adenauer and General de Gaulle once again expressed their firm agreement, the opposition moderated its virulence. And when the Germans took everybody off after the session for an excursion and a luncheon on the Rhine, scarcely a cloud overshadowed the European effusions. The decision taken by the conference was to proceed on the lines advocated by the French government. To this end, the Political Commission already set up under the chairmanship of Christian Fouchet was instructed to draw up the text of a formal treaty which could be ratified by a summit meeting to be held subsequently in Rome.

Caution and the proprieties had thus prevented the higher authorities from parading their differences. But they were inevitably to come to light during the proceedings of the Fouchet Commission. A single project was submitted to it – that of France. Germany continued to support it. But the determined opposition of Holland and Belgium and the calculated indecision of Italy were to ensure that it came to nothing. At one moment it had looked as though the Rome Government was coming round to the Paris–Bonn viewpoint, and this would certainly have decided the issue. On April 4, 1962, I had gone to Turin to see Amintore Fanfani again. Our discussion led me to believe that we were in agreement on the somewhat amended text of the Fouchet Plan. No doubt this was true, that day, of my interlocutor himself. For the Italian statesman had sufficient taste for great issues and sense of the higher necessities of our day to want his country to be a pillar of European unity together with France and Germany. But so simple and categorical a resolve would have been out of keeping with the political complexities characteristic of our transalpine cousins. It was for this reason that when the Foreign Ministers of the Six met in Paris on April 17

to make their governments' final positions known, Antonio
Segni turned down the French plan. This was Spaak's cue to
speak out for all the dissentients. Warmly supported by Luns,
he declared that Belgium would not sign the treaty, "even if it
suited her as it was", as long as England was not a member
of the Community. Some days later he wrote to me to say that
Belgium was ready to conclude an agreement among the Six
on condition that the Political Commission destined in our
plan to be an instrument of the Council of States was set up as
a power independent of the governments. Thus, without the
slightest embarrassment, Spaak simultaneously embraced the
two mutually exclusive theses of the supporters of Anglo-Saxon
hegemony and the champions of supra-nationalism.

From then on, things were to remain in abeyance before it
became known whether the French offer to initiate the co-
operation of the sundered Old World was to be, for history,
"some armada foundered in eternal error," or, for the future,
a fair hope riding the waves.

The World

If our neighbors had refused to respond to France's call for
the unity and independence of a European Europe, it was to
some extent because of their traditional fear of our supremacy,
but above all because, in the state of Cold War which existed
in the world, everything for them was subordinated to the desire
for American protection. Now on this point our appraisal of
the situation was different from theirs. They saw things as they
had been fifteen years before. We saw them otherwise.

After Yalta, which had enabled Stalin's Russia to annex
Central Europe and the Balkans automatically at the time of
the collapse of the Third Reich, a further extension of the
Soviet bloc was certainly to be feared, and in the event of
such an aggression the Western States of the Continent could
not by themselves offer sufficiently powerful resistance. The
Franco-British organization for European defense, adumbrated
in 1946 under the supreme command of Field-Marshal Mont-
gomery, would obviously not have sufficed. Hence nothing
could have been more justified and perhaps more salutary
than the American aid which, through the Marshall Plan,
enabled Western Europe to re-establish its means of production
and saved it from drastic economic, social and political
upheavals, while protecting its security under the atomic
umbrella. But an almost inevitable consequence had been the
inauguration of NATO, a system of security whereby

Washington controlled the defense and consequently the foreign policy and even the territory of its allies.

Among the latter, Germany, shorn of Prussia and Saxony, in a situation of immediate proximity to the totalitarians, constantly vilified by them for her past misdeeds, accused of preparing to renew them, and held in a strait-jacket by the seizure of Berlin, saw in this protectorate the guarantee of her very survival. The others, who were not directly threatened, but who rightly believed that if ever the Soviets were to reach the Rhine and the Alps they themselves would at once be doomed, considered the American guarantee essential and were, moreover, highly appreciative of the economies they were able to make in their military budgets as a result of the reinforcements in troops, ships and aircraft and the gifts of war material provided by the United States. Of course, from time to time, a pang of regret for their erstwhile independence troubled the hearts of these proud and ancient peoples. But the usefulness and convenience of the Atlantic hegemony in the world, whatever the United States might think fit to do there, quickly brought them to heel. Thus it never happened that a government belonging to NATO took an attitude that diverged from that of the White House. If the idea of European integration found so much favor with our partners, it was largely because a stateless system, incapable by its very nature of having its own defense or foreign policy, would inevitably be obliged to follow the dictates of America. If, in the absence of a supra-national technocracy, they were anxious to see the Community join with the British Commonwealth, it was because that path also led to the protectorship of Washington. Conversely, if my plan for a European Europe had not yet come to fruition, it was because it would have conduced towards the freeing of the Old World, and this was something that the latter dared not risk.

In 1958 I considered that the world situation was very different from what it had been at the time of the creation of NATO. It now seemed fairly unlikely that the Soviets would set out to conquer the West, at a time when all the Western nations were back on an even keel and making steady material progress. Communism, whether it rises from within or irrupts from without, has little chance of taking root without the help of some national calamity. The Kremlin knows this very well. As for imposing the totalitarian yoke on three hundred million recalcitrant foreigners, what would be the point of trying, when it was difficult enough to hold down a third as many people in the satellite countries? Moreover, in accordance with the perennial alternation which governs their history, it was towards Asia rather than towards Europe that the Russians must now turn their attention on account of the ambitions of China, provided that the West did not threaten them. Above all, what madness it would be for Moscow, as for anyone else, to launch a global conflict which might end, amid the bombs, in wholesale destruction! But if one does not make war, one must sooner or later make peace. No regime on earth, however oppressive, is capable of maintaining indefinitely in a state of war-like tension peoples who believe they will not have to fight. Everything, therefore, led me to believe that the East would feel more and more strongly the need and the attractions of a *détente*.

On the Western side, too, the military conditions of security had altered profoundly in twelve years. For, from the moment when the Soviets had acquired the wherewithal to exterminate America, just as the latter had the means to annihilate them, it was unimaginable that the two rivals would ever come to blows except as a last resort. On the other hand, what was to prevent them from dropping their bombs in between their two countries, in other words on Central and Western Europe? For the Western Europeans, NATO had thus ceased to guarantee their survival. But once the efficacy of the protection had become doubtful, why leave one's destiny in the hands of the protector?

Finally, something had recently happened to alter France's international role. For this role, as I conceived it, precluded the Atlantic docility which yesterday's Republic had practised during my absence. In my view, our country was in a position to act on its own in Europe and the world, and must so act because, morally speaking, this was an essential motive force for its endeavors. Naturally this independence presupposed the possession of modern means of deterrence to ensure France's security. So she must acquire them.

My aim, then, was to disengage France, not from the Atlantic alliance, which I intended to maintain by way of ultimate precaution, but from the integration realized by NATO under American command; to establish relations with each of the States of the Eastern bloc, first and foremost Russia, with the object of bringing about a *détente* followed by understanding and co-operation; to do likewise, when the time was ripe, with China; and finally, to provide France with a nuclear capability such that no one could attack us without running the risk of frightful injury. But I was anxious to proceed gradually, linking each stage with overall developments and continuing to cultivate France's traditional friendships.

As early as September 14, 1958, I hoisted my colors. In a memorandum addressed personally to President Eisenhower and Mr Macmillan, I called in question our membership of NATO which, I declared, was no longer adapted to the needs of our defense. Without explicitly casting doubts on the protection afforded to continental Europe by the British and American bombs, my memorandum pointed out that a genuine organization of collective defense would need to cover the whole surface of the earth instead of being limited to the North Atlantic sector, and that the world-wide character of France's responsibilities and security made it essential for Paris to participate directly in the political and strategic decisions of the alliance, decisions which were in reality taken by America alone with separate consultation with England. France's accession to this summit would be all the more appropriate because the Western monopoly of atomic weapons would very soon cease to belong exclusively to the Anglo-Saxons, now that we were about to acquire them. I therefore proposed that the alliance should henceforth be placed under a triple rather than a dual direction, failing which France would take no further part in NATO developments and would reserve the right, under Article 12 of the treaty which had inaugurated the system, either to demand its reform or to leave it. As I expected, the two recipients of my memorandum replied evasively. So there was nothing to prevent us from taking action.

But circumstances decreed that we should act with circumspection. We did not yet possess any bombs. Algeria still held our Army, our Air Force and our Navy in its grip. We did not know what direction the Kremlin would eventually take in its relations with the West. For the moment there was Nikita Khrushchev's disquieting threat to conclude a separate peace with East Germany and hand over the fate of Berlin to the Pankow Communists – which, for the Soviet Union, would be tantamount to controlling it themselves – and thus obliging America, Great Britain and France, whose forces occupied the Western sectors of the city, either to defend it, in other words to accept the risk of conflict, or to abandon it, in other words to suffer a disastrous political defeat and military humiliation. We, therefore, proposed to take appropriate steps in the direction of Atlantic disengagement while at the same time maintaining our direct co-operation with the United States and Britain.

In March 1959 our Mediterranean fleet was withdrawn from NATO. Shortly afterwards came the ban on the introduction of atomic bombs into France by the American forces, whether in aircraft or on the ground, and on the installation of launching ramps. Later we took under our own command our air-defence system and the system for the control of aircraft overflying our territory. As our North African units were gradually brought back to metropolitan France, we did not transfer them to Allied command. On September 16, 1959, I inspected the centers for strategic and tactical studies at the Ecole Militaire. Afterwards I brought together the instructors and their pupils and delivered an address which laid down for the benefit of the public authorities and the military high command the new directives of the State on the subject of national security.

"The defence of France must be in French hands," I said. "If a nation like France is obliged to make war, it must be its own war; its effort must be its own effort. No doubt the defense of France might, in certain circumstances, be concerted with that of other countries. But it is imperative that it should remain our own, that France should defend herself by herself, for herself and in her own way." Then I showed that, in the course of our history, the State had never had and could never have any justification, and *a fortiori* any durability, unless it assumed direct responsibility for national defense, and that the military high command enjoyed authority, dignity and prestige in the eyes of the nation and the armed forces only if it was itself answerable on the field of battle for the country's fate. "This means that for France the system known as 'integration', which the free world has followed up to now, has had its day. . . . It goes without saying that our strategy must be combined with that of others. For it is more than likely that in the event of a conflict we should find ourselves side by side with allies. . . . But let each play his own part!" Having invited my listeners henceforth to make this conception the basis of their philosophy and their labors, I declared: "The consequence is that we must provide ourselves, over the next few years, with a force capable of acting on our own behalf, with what is commonly known as a 'strike force',[1] capable of being deployed at any moment and in any place. The basis of this force must obviously be atomic weapons."

These remarks, which I had published, and these first steps towards disengagement had world-wide repercussions. And as time went on, further opportunities arose to demonstrate that the Fifth Republic had its own policies. For instance, when the British and the Americans landed forces in Jordan and Lebanon respectively, with the alleged intention of protecting these States from a possible aggression by the United Arab Republic, we held aloof from their joint expedition and sent a cruiser to Beirut to establish our separate presence. Again, once the independence of the ex-Belgian Congo had been

[1] *Force de frappe.*

recognized and Patrice Lumumba's government formed, we openly disapproved of the action instigated by Washington under the umbrella of the General Assembly of the United Nations which led that organization, contrary to its own charter, to intervene militarily and financially in the internal affairs of the new State. By the same token, the United States having broken off relations with Cuba and requested us to forbid our ships to go there, we retained our embassy in Havana and refused to join in the embargo; we censured the American take-over in South Vietnam; and we refused to allocate forces for the possible use of the South East Asia Treaty Organization.

Last but not least, in the current international debate on disarmament, we put forward our own thesis. This aimed at nothing less than a total ban on the manufacture, the possession and the use of any means of atomic destruction. But since it was evident that such an all-embracing condemnation might well lead nowhere, in view of the reservations of the two nuclear rivals and the insuperable difficulties of a comprehensive control system, we proposed that there should be at least a ban on the construction of launching ramps and means of delivery: rockets, submarines and aircraft. Discovering their whereabouts and supervising their removal would, after all, be in the realm of the possible. And if both sides were deprived of the means of launching atomic missiles, they would doubtless stop ruining themselves manufacturing them. This was the position which I adopted once and for all, and which Jules Moch, our representative, put forward in the committees which, first in New York and then in Geneva, endlessly discussed the subject. Such, however, was not the aim of the Americans. Basically their intention was to conclude with the Soviets, under cover of a world-wide agreement, a direct arrangement which would sanction the monopoly of the two super-powers, would limit contractually the frenzy of their expenditure and would prevent any State which was not yet equipped with missiles from manufacturing or acquiring them. But since this consolidation of the world dyarchy did not correspond to our aims, and in no way contributed towards general disarmament, we parted company from the Americans on this matter while the rest of the Western world continued to follow them willy-nilly.

This new attitude of a France ready to take responsibility for her own destiny provoked a variety of reactions. At home, the political parties and the newspapers were full of disapproval and suspicion. Our partners in the Community were annoyed to see us taking up a position so different from theirs. In Washington and London, this rupture in the general subservience produced a mixture of surprise, irritation and understanding, which expressed itself in a stream of articles and speeches. In this connection, the same newspapers and the same microphones which, before 1958, had scarcely mentioned France except occasionally to commiserate with her, were now ceaselessly preoccupied with our country. Whatever France said and did, especially in the person of her Head of State, her presumed situation in the world, her alleged intentions, were the subject of innumerable appreciations, either bitter and sarcastic, or friendly and eulogistic, but never indifferent. In the eyes of the world, our country had suddenly become one of the principal actors in a play in which hitherto she had been regarded as a supernumerary. And foreign governments, whether those of the allied camp or the Communist bloc or the Third World, realized that we had entered a phase of politics in which France was once more in control of her own destiny and they had no alternative but to make the best of it.

It must be said that, by contrast with the aberrancies to which they had hitherto been accustomed, these foreign governments saw a strong, homogeneous and self-confident regime in office and at work in Paris. Their representatives – for example, the Papal Nuncio and doyen of the Diplomatic Corps, Monsignor Morella (later succeeded by Monsignor Bertoli), Amery Houghton and then James Gavin of the United States, Sir Gladwyn Jebb and Sir Pierson Dixon of Great Britain, Sergei Vinogradov of the Soviet Union, Herbert Blankenhorn of Germany, Leonardo Vitteti and Manlio Brosio of Italy, Tetsuro Furukaki of Japan – although, as usual in our country, they read in our press or heard from the lips of superannuated politicians a great deal of criticism of the government, were no longer able to regale their chancelleries with reports of French political crises. Receiving each of these shrewd diplomatists in turn, I showed them how France was pursuing her line with continuity, and when they left the Elysée to go to the Hôtel Matignon or the Quai d'Orsay or any other ministry, they heard the same story and detected no discordant note. As for our ambassadors, such as Eric de Carbonnel, Secretary-General for Foreign Affairs, Hervé Alphand in Washington, Jean Chauvel followed by Geoffroy de Courcel in London, Gaston Palewski in Rome, Roland de Margerie at the Vatican and then in Madrid, François Seydoux de Clausonne in Bonn, Maurice Dejean in Moscow, Etienne Dennery in Tokyo, Armand Bérard at the United Nations – who, incidentally, formed a team of the highest quality – they now spoke loud and clear, proud to be the representatives of a country that was not afraid to assert itself, asked nothing of anybody and never contradicted itself.

The respectful attention shown us on all sides persuaded me to increase our contacts with the outside world. This led to an active interchange of visits, all of them occasions for mutual exchanges of view if not always mutual persuasion, for the furtherance of relations, for the conclusion of agreements, for the ventilation of news and opinions and for the manifestation of public sentiment. I attached the highest importance to them, knowing what reverberations such encounters often produce. True, they no longer have the same dramatic character as of old, and the facilities of modern travel have deprived them of some of their glamour. Nevertheless, during these years when France was resuming her rightful place in the world, the visits to Paris of so many foreign rulers and statesmen, and my own journeys and those of my ministers to other countries, formed the weft and woof and the visible illustration of our global recovery.

Soon after I had resumed the direction of affairs, the American Secretary of State Foster Dulles came to visit me.

This apostle of containment and the Western deterrent explained to me with deep conviction the principles which guided the policies of his great country under his direction. For Dulles, it was simply a question of stemming the tide and if necessary breaking the back of Soviet imperialism such as it had developed as a result of the world-wide ambitions of Communism. Already the Communist bloc numbered a thousand million people in Europe and Asia and, thanks to the means of total dictatorship, it had the advantage of being able to exploit to the full the human material at its disposal with a view to the production of armaments and the launching of prestige enterprises such as the conquest of space. According to Foster Dulles, it was for the United States to lead the resistance against it. He himself was devoting all his energy to the building of breakwaters in whatever part of the world the ideological, political or military irruption of the adversary seemed most menacing. Hence the creation of NATO in Europe, of CENTO in the Middle East, of SEATO in South-East Asia, and the alliances in the Pacific protecting South Korea, Formosa, Hong Kong, and even Japan. NATO was naturally the principal object of his efforts, not only to bar the route to potential aggressors, but also because he saw it as the best means of circumscribing Germany and preventing her from doing harm. The Secretary of State spoke to me with feeling of America's friendship for France and her keen desire, for sentimental as well as practical reasons, to see us play an active part in the system of mutual security established on the old continent. In this connection he said to me: "We know that you are about to equip yourselves with atomic weapons. Would it not be better, instead of testing and manufacturing them yourselves at vast expense, to let us provide you with them?"

I replied to Foster Dulles that I too believed it necessary to take firm political and military precautions against possible Soviet aggression. If such an aggression occurred, there was no doubt that my country would be at America's side. But the fact was that it had not occurred. To my mind, the behavior of Moscow was governed by the interests of Russia at least as much as the interests of Communism. And Russia's true interest was peace. It seemed to me, therefore, that without neglecting the means of defending ourselves, we should turn our attention towards contacts with the Kremlin. "Is this not in fact what your government is doing in the nuclear field?" I asked him. The Secretary of State agreed. "France," I said, "intends to work towards a *détente* while at the same time preparing for the worst. But in either case, without in any way repudiating her alliance with you, she intends to remain herself and to conduct her own policy. A France without world responsibility would be unworthy of herself, especially in the eyes of Frenchmen. It is for this reason that she disapproves of NATO, which denies her a share in decision-making and which is confined to Europe. It is for this reason too that she intends to provide herself with an atomic armament. Only in this way can our defense and foreign policy be independent, which is something that we prize above everything else. If you agree to sell us bombs, we shall be happy to buy them, provided that they belong to us entirely and unreservedly." Foster Dulles said no more. With this frank exchange of French and American viewpoints, we parted. I was to see him again in February 1959, still as firm and direct as ever, but knowing himself to be marked by death, which was to strike him down three months later.

President Eisenhower felt deeply the loss of his Secretary of State, who had been his right-hand man and intimate associate for more than seven years. His own conception of United States policy would not be radically altered, although it was to be less rigorously expressed. In this field, I found General Eisenhower very much as I had known and respected him when he was in command of the Allied forces during the war. No doubt he shared the somewhat elementary conviction which inspired the American people as to the primordial mission which had devolved upon the United States as though by a decree of providence and gave them the right to predominance. But the President's faith was not ostentatious, and his manner was not intransigent. He was a deeply conscientious man, resolved to make judgments only with full knowledge of the facts and to take decisions only on the advice of qualified experts. He was cautious, did not like risky speculations, and applied the brakes as soon as things began to move too fast. He was conciliatory, seeking always to avoid clashes and to find a way out of any impasse. Nevertheless, this circumspection, extremely praiseworthy in the leader of a country whose power impelled it towards domination, in a Head of State endowed with the most wide-ranging powers and enjoying great popularity, did not preclude a strength and firmness which he was apt to reveal when occasion demanded. Up to the end of his term of office in January 1961, Dwight Eisenhower and I corresponded regularly. We met on three great occasions and each time spent long hours together. We kept each other constantly informed of our intentions, and our dealings were always on a basis of friendly sincerity.

At my invitation, he came to France on a State visit in the month of September 1959. The authorities and the people of Paris did their best to make the occasion a worthy and a popular one. At each of the President's public appearances – the welcome at Orly, the drive through Paris to his residence at the Quai d'Orsay, the salute at the Tomb of the Unknown Soldier, the visit to the Hôtel de Ville, etc. – large and enthusiastic crowds were there to greet him. It was obvious that the Franco-American brotherhood-in-arms, of which our visitor was the most glorious symbol, remained very much alive in the minds of our people. Eisenhower himself was visibly impressed. "What was the total number of people on my route this morning?" he asked me on the evening of his first day. I answered, "A million at least," which was true. "I did not expect half as many," he said, deeply moved.

Our conversations began at the Elysée and ended at Rambouillet. I had developed a liking for the latter as a site for such meetings, Versailles, Compiègne and Fontainebleau, by reason of their size, being unsuitable for restricted gatherings. Housed in the medieval tower where so many of our kings had stayed, passing through the apartments once occupied by our Valois, our Bourbons, our emperors, our presidents, deliberating in the ancient hall of marble with the French Head of State and his ministers, admiring the grandeur of the ornamental lakes stretched out before their eyes, strolling through the park and the forest in which for ten centuries the rites of official shooting and hunting parties had been performed, our guests were made to feel the nobility behind the geniality, the permanence beyond the vicissitudes, of the nation which was their host.

We talked both alone and in the presence of our ministers and ambassadors: Christian Herter and James Gavin on Eisenhower's side, Michel Debré, Maurice Couve de Murville and Hervé Alphand on mine. It was clear that the President of the United States was chiefly preoccupied by the question of his country's relations with Soviet Russia. For him, whatever happened anywhere in the world was considered exclusively in relation to this problem. It was, moreover, taken for granted that in the free world, whether in the realm of security, economics, finance, science, technology or anything else, the fundamental if not the sole reality was that of America. The rest, while putting forward their points of view, simply had to go along with her. For this reason NATO, a system whereby the Allies contributed their forces to a strategy drawn up in Washington, gave every satisfaction to General Eisenhower.

Nevertheless, he repeated over and over again that the United States had no warlike intentions and indeed looked forward to an eventual agreement with the Soviets if only to limit their gigantic military expenditure. Only recently he had sent Vice-President Richard Nixon to Moscow, and now Nikita Khrushchev was about to visit America. "It is my intention," the President told me, "to try to enter into constructive negotiations with him, to show him what life in our country is like, and thus to give him cause to reflect on the achievements of our respective regimes." Referring to the steel workers' strike which was still going on in the United States, he added with his tongue in his cheek: "I shall even show him an American strike."

I explained to Eisenhower that in my view relations between

East and West should not be treated solely from the angle of rivalry between ideologies and political systems. True, Communism loomed large in the present international tension. But beneath its dictatorship, the nations of Russia, Poland, Hungary, Czechoslovakia, Bulgaria, Rumania, Yugoslavia, Albania, Prussia and Saxony still existed, as well as China, Mongolia, Korea and Tonking. "After what has happened to Russia during the two world wars," I said, "do you believe that a Peter the Great would have settled the matter of frontiers and territories any differently from Stalin?" No *détente*, I suggested, would be valid unless it were based on national realities. While recognizing that a technical deal on armaments between Washington and Moscow might help matters, I felt that it could not be a real solution, any more than would an agreement, however spectacular, of mutual give and take concluded by the two camps each assembled in its entirety under the aegis of its protector. For this would serve only to perpetuate the two blocs, whose very existence precluded a true peace. On the other hand, a *rapprochement* between one European nation and another, brought about on the basis of existing realities and confined, at the outset, to economic, cultural, technical and touristic matters, would offer a far better chance of dismantling the Iron Curtain piece by piece, of toning down the frenzy of the arms race little by little, and even of bringing the totalitarians to relax step by step the severity of their regimes. France, who had taken nothing and had nothing to take from the Russian people or from any of those now associated with them, who had been familiar to them from time immemorial, and for whom, through the centuries, they had always felt a special attraction, could and must give an example. This was her intention. I told Eisenhower that I too intended to issue an invitation to Khrushchev, who I knew would be delighted, and that I was sure he would speak to me mainly about Germany and the need to keep her divided. I added that I would not at present contradict him on this point. Indeed, I felt that there could be no satisfactory future for Germany, and in particular no chance of her ever being reunified, in the absence of a general European settlement. Meanwhile, without more ado, I proposed to discuss with the Soviet Premier Franco-Russian co-operation in various practical spheres.

Eisenhower remarked that, following a suggestion from London, feelers were being put out from Moscow as regards a summit conference between Russia, America, Great Britain and France. He himself was inclined to favor it. I replied that I had no objection in principle, but that the negative outcome of a recent meeting in Geneva of the four Foreign Ministers seemed to suggest that we should not be in too much of a hurry and that in any case I wanted to see Khrushchev first.

The President of the United States spoke to me earnestly about NATO, and France's attitude towards it. What worried him most was our decision to equip ourselves with atomic weapons. Returning to the proposal which Dulles had touched on, he offered to provide them to us on condition that the Americans retained control of them, in other words retained the keys, so that the missiles could not be used except by order of the NATO Commander-in-Chief. When I replied that that was precisely what we objected to, that we did not want any bombs on French territory unless we ourselves controlled them, he saw this as a sign of mistrust towards the United States. Whereupon I said to him: "If Russia attacks us, we are your allies and you are ours. But in this eventuality, and in any other for that matter, we want to hold our fate in our own hands, and that fate would depend above all upon whether or not we were the victims of nuclear attack. We must, therefore, have the means to deter any potential aggressor from striking directly at us, which means that we must be capable of striking back at him and that he must know that we would do so without waiting for permission from outside. In a conflict between East and West, you Americans certainly have the means of annihilating the enemy on his own territory. But he has the means to blow you to pieces on yours. How could we French be sure that, unless you yourselves were bombed directly on your own soil, you would invite your own destruction even if, as you breathed your last, you were able to believe that the Russian people were being annihilated at the same time as you? The converse is also true, so that, for Russia and for America, the deterrent is real. But it does not exist for their respective allies. What, after all, is there to prevent Russia and America from wiping out what lies between their own vitals, in other words the European battlefield? Is this not, in fact, what NATO is preparing for? Moreover, in this eventuality France would be doomed first and foremost, for a number of reasons, geographical, political and strategical, as the two world wars have already shown. Thus she is determined to give herself a chance of survival, no matter what or whence the danger that may threaten her."

"How can you doubt," Eisenhower asked, "that the United States identifies her fate with that of Europe?" I answered: "If Europe, sliding to disaster, were one day to be completely conquered by your rivals, it is true that the United States would soon be in trouble. Hence your current ideological slogans – 'the cause of freedom' and 'Atlantic solidarity' – which as usual conceal vital interests. But before the day of reckoning, what would become of my country? In the course of the two world wars, America was France's ally, and France – it has just been brought home to you as you drove up the Champs-Elysées – has not forgotten what she owes to American help. But neither has she forgotten that during the First World War, that help came only after three long years of struggle which nearly proved mortal for her, and that during the Second she had already been crushed before you intervened. In saying this, I intend not the slightest reproach. For I know, as you yourself know, what a nation is, with its geography, its interests, its political system, its public opinion, its passions, its fears, its errors. It can help another, but it cannot identify itself with another. That is why, although remaining faithful to our alliance, I cannot accept France's integration into NATO. As for harmonizing – if one may apply a celestial word to an infernal subject – the possible use of our bombs and yours in so far as this might be feasible, we could do so within the framework of direct co-operation between the three atomic powers which I have already proposed to you. Until you accept this, we shall, like you, retain complete freedom of action."

"But," the President objected, "in view of the cost of this sort of armaments, France will never get anywhere near the Soviet level. In that case, what will be the value of her own deterrent?"

"As you well know," I replied, "in the scale of megatons, only a few volleys of bombs would be needed to demolish any country in the world. In order for our deterrent to be effective, it is enough to be able to kill the enemy once, even if he possesses the means to kill us ten times over."

We took leave of each other, Eisenhower and I, having made it absolutely clear what the Franco-American alliance was and should remain. Subsequently, the action taken by France to arm herself as she pleased and to extricate herself from the system of integration were to earn her a great deal of reproach and invective in many quarters in America, but never led to a rupture or even an estrangement between the two governments.

On February 13, 1960, the first French atomic bomb was successfully tested at Reggan. The event was preceded, on the international plane, by all manner of warnings, inspired by the Anglo-Saxons, relating to the risks of atmospheric contamination to which the explosion might give rise. The United Nations had called upon us to abandon the tests, several African governments protested against the use of the Sahara for them, and Nigeria went so far as to break off relations. It was with a certain degree of irony that we observed this coalition of alarm on the part of so many States which had watched without the slightest indignation while the Americans, the British and the Soviets had exploded some two hundred atomic devices. But once the thing was done, with every possible precaution and without causing a single casualty, the agitation died down. There remained the proof given by France that she had been able – since, alas, it had been necessary – to accomplish on her own, with no outside help, the series of scientific, technological and industrial exploits which had led to this successful outcome, and that she had indubitably recovered her independence.

The accession of our country to the supreme realm of force, while it upset the premises on which Washington's strategy was based, did not fail to arouse, if not satisfaction, at least a great deal of interest in London. In the midst of a changing world, England was uneasy and despondent. The victory which the free world owed to the courage of her people had eliminated her from the front rank. The huge empire on which her power was based had vanished bit by bit. The seas on which she reigned supreme were now dominated by others. Her economy, her finances, her currency, had lost their preponderance. Ever since the dark days when, to avoid being submerged in spite of all her sacrifices, she had accepted Roosevelt's offer of lend-lease, she had found herself under American hegemony. At a time when she needed peace and leisure to adapt herself internally to the conditions of an age of upheaval, she saw mankind torn apart under a storm-tossed sky. In short, her situation seemed to her both unjust and alarming. But since she had not ceased to be ambitious and enterprising, she was casting around for ways and means of carving out a new career for herself. Two courses were open to her. One was the permanent acceptance of American supremacy which at present, in exchange for her docility, provided her with nuclear secrets, helped her to maintain her economic links with her old dominions, and enabled her to keep bases on the oceans of the world: Singapore, Hong Kong, Aden, Bahrein, Trinidad, Cyprus, Tobruk, Malta, Gibraltar. The other led her towards Europe, which hitherto she had always striven to divide, but whose union today, if she agreed to join it while accepting certain restrictions, could ensure her the outstanding role to which her gifts and her experience entitled her.

These looming dangers and dilemmas haunted the mind of the British Prime Minister. In the course of the numerous discussions which we had at this time, he did not conceal from me his anxiety and his perplexity. We were, of course, old friends, ever since the period during the war when, as Churchill's minister, he was attached to me and my "Committee" in Algiers. These memories, combined with the respect which I had for his character and the interest and enjoyment which I derived from his company, caused me to listen to him with confidence and speak to him with sincerity. Besides, I admired England, still young in spite of her ancient trappings, thanks to her genius for adapting the modern to the traditional, and indomitable in the face of danger, as she had recently proved for her own salvation as well as that of Europe. As soon as I returned to power, I had made a point of expressing my appreciation by inviting Churchill, aged but still loyal to the history which had united us, to Paris to decorate him with the Cross of the Liberation. Thus, Harold Macmillan found me disposed to reach agreement with him, provided that it was possible for his country and mine to follow the same path.

This was indeed the case as regards a *détente* with the Soviets. On this subject the British government seemed to me to be on the right lines, on condition, however, that it did not push conciliation to the point of surrender. As early as 1955, Khrushchev had made an exploratory journey to London. In February 1959, Macmillan had paid a return visit to Moscow which demonstrated his goodwill, the more so in view of the quirkish behavior of his host which had made communication somewhat painful. Among the interlocutors who now contemplated with me the prospect of a Third World War, none dreaded it more than the British Prime Minister, convinced as he was that his country, in spite of its island position, would be in danger of sinking with all hands. Thus he was unsympathetic to Germany's grievances, reserved as to the measures to be taken to break a new blockade of Berlin if the need arose, and decidedly cool as regards the tendency to "roll back" the Soviets which was spasmodically manifested by American policy.

But it was about Europe that Harold Macmillan spoke to me most often. At first, he took up an attitude of passionate hostility towards the embryonic union represented by the Common Market. Later, his government endeavored to persuade the Brussels organization to broaden itself, in other words dissolve itself, into a general free-trade system. Having failed in this, the British then seemed content to set up as a counterpoise to the Six an association of the Seven. Later still, they were to apply point-blank for membership of the Community. Yet, whatever the apparent fluctuations, Macmillan never made any secret of the fact that Great Britain must choose her own destiny and that he himself had set his mind on union with the Continent. No doubt he knew what obstacles must be overcome to bring this about. But he was confident of his ability to surmount any that arose on the British side and begged me to lower the barriers on the side of the Community.

"The economic problem certainly presents difficulties," the Prime Minister told me. "But it is the political significance of the operation which has won me over. Believe me, we are no longer the England of Queen Victoria, of Kipling, of the British Empire, of 'splendid isolation'. Many of our people, especially among the young, feel that it is time we opened a new chapter in our history. The two world wars showed us to what an extent our fate is bound up with what happens not only, as of old, on the Rhine and in the Alps, but on the Danube, the Vistula, and even the Volga. The recent cataclysm, which brought into being the vast Soviet bloc and weakened the other powers of the Old World, has put all of us West Europeans in a situation of permanent danger. We must restore the balance. It is true that for the moment the American presence guarantees our security. But it is doubtful whether it will last indefinitely. Moreover, it has placed the Europeans in a position of painful subservience, from which you French would like to free yourselves, and which we English endure only with reluctance. Let us bring Europe together, my dear friend! There are three men who can do it: you, Adenauer and I. If, while the three of us are still alive and in power, we let this historic opportunity pass us by, God knows if, when and to whom it will ever present itself again."

These words struck a sympathetic chord in me. No one was more convinced than I that it would be highly desirable for England to belong to an organized and independent grouping of the States of Western Europe, and any steps she took in this

direction would be extremely welcome. But was she yet prepared to submit to the constraints inseparable from such an
association, one so alien to her historic nature and to what was
still the basis of her existence? For, if an edifice is to hold up, it
requires solid foundations and not merely the good intentions of
its designers. "From the economic point of view," I said to the
Prime Minister, "could you British, who depend mainly on
extensive trade with the United States and a system of preferential imports and exports with the Commonwealth, really agree
to enclose yourselves with the Continentals behind a tariff
wall which would gravely impede your American trade and
exclude your former dominions and colonies? You who live
cheaply on Canadian wheat, New Zealand mutton, Irish beef
and potatoes, Australian butter, fruit and vegetables, Jamaican
sugar, etc., could you ever consider feeding yourselves on
Continental agricultural produce, in particular French, which
would be necessarily more costly? How could you disentangle
your currency, which covers the vast sterling area, from the
mortgages, debts and obligations which this internationalism
entails, and reduce it to the modest status of a simple English
pound?"

Macmillan recognized that the Common Market would
have to make concessions and that in addition a long transition
period would be needed. "Once these concessions were granted
and this transition period was over," I said to him, "what would
remain of the Community? And what is the point of your
joining it if it would mean destroying it? Wouldn't it be better
for you to wait until you are in a position to participate in it as
it is? And wouldn't the same apply to a political union?
Such a union could not, after all, have any real justification
and scope unless it established a European Europe at present,
it is true, allied with the United States, but with its own defense
and foreign policy. But in view of your privileged ties with
America, would you ever come into such a Europe, and if you
did, wouldn't it be in order to persuade it to integrate and
submerge itself in some sort of Atlanticism?" The Prime Minister protested, no doubt very sincerely, his desire for European

independence. But nothing indicated that he was willing to take the consequences *vis-à-vis* the United States.

Macmillan and I spent many hours together, either alone or accompanied by our ministers: in his case the distinguished Foreign Secretaries, Douglas-Home and later Selwyn Lloyd, and the very shrewd Edward Heath; in mine, Debré and Couve de Murville, as always precise and self-assured. We discussed this great subject in Paris and in London, at Rambouillet, Birch Grove and the Château de Champs, without my ever being able to believe, in spite of my wish to do so, that his country was ready to become a new England who would moor herself to the Continent. Later, the day was to come when a certain special agreement concerning the provision of American rockets and underlining the subordination of Britain's nuclear means, concluded separately at Nassau with John Kennedy, was to justify my circumspection.

We had not yet reached this point at the end of 1959, when the world scene was dominated by the prospect of a *détente* between East and West, which had been opened up by Nikita Khrushchev. The ice had undoubtedly been broken by the lively, colorful and prolonged visit he had paid to the United States in November. Since the Communist Party scarcely exists for the Americans, the arrival of the Soviet Premier in their towns and villages caused no local political strains. Indeed, because of the anxiety aroused by the international tension, his presence at the side of the President was generally welcomed. Moreover his jovial and spontaneous personality was anything but alarming. His speeches, which extolled peaceful co-existence, were reassuring. And the zeal for competition which he displayed in matters of production, mechanization, technology, the conquest of space, seemed to be inspired by a genuine sporting spirit. His conversations with Eisenhower, apart from platitudes about peace, had dealt exclusively with subjects which were of equal importance to the two countries and concerned ways and means of consolidating their nuclear monopoly. As a result of this tour, the idea of a Four-Power summit conference became embedded in people's minds.

Although I myself was not convinced that the time was yet ripe, I could not refuse to respond to such a universal desire. I explained my attitude on November 10 to the world's press. "It seems," I said, "that after years of international tension, signs of relaxation are appearing among the Soviets." Then I gave the reasons for this: the certainty on the part of the Russians that any conflict would lead to world-wide destruction; an abatement of the severity of the Communist regime under pressure from the people, who demanded freedom and a better life; centrifugal national tendencies in the satellite countries which Moscow ruled without having won over; and finally, the emergence of China. "Faced with the latter, Soviet Russia realizes that nothing can alter the fact that she herself is a white European nation which has conquered a large part of Asia, and is on the whole well endowed with land, mines, factories and wealth of every sort, confronting the yellow multitude, vast, poverty-stricken, indestructible and ambitious, building up immeasurable power by dint of painful effort and gazing around at the vast empty spaces over which it will one day have to spill." Finally, "and perhaps above all," I ascribed the origins of the new direction which the Kremlin was taking to "the personality of the present leader of Soviet Russia, who realizes that at the highest echelons of power and responsibility, to serve the peace and well-being of the human race is the most realistic realism, the most politic policy." I then observed "that from all this has emerged the idea of a conference of Heads of State with world responsibilities; that in principle there is no objection from any quarter to such a meeting; that France is in favor of it; but that precisely because she wishes the encounter to lead to positive results, she believes it advisable not to be over-hasty. If," I went on to say, "it was simply a question of organizing between four or five leaders a concert of mutual assurances of goodwill and reciprocal effusions . . . the summit conference would serve little purpose. If, on the other hand, it is felt that such an areopagus might open the door to a practical settlement of the problems which beset the world – the arms race, the poverty of the underdeveloped countries, interference in the affairs of others, the future of Germany, the dangerous situation in the Middle East, Africa and Asia – then certain conditions must be fulfilled before the meeting." I enumerated these: the improvement of international relations over the next few months, a preliminary agreement between the Western Heads of State who would be attending the summit conference, and personal contact between Mr Khrushchev and myself, M Debré and our government, so that Russia and France could discuss the problems of the world direct. In this connection, I announced that Mr Khrushchev would be coming to France in March. I concluded: "Thus it would seem that the pressure of all the imponderables, together with the desires of the leaders, is about to produce a sort of confrontation of the modern world with itself. We face this prospect with faith and with hope, though not without caution and not without diffidence."

On December 19 I invited Eisenhower, Macmillan and Adenauer to meet me in Paris. Later we moved to Rambouillet. This Western conference was a dual one. Sometimes it was carried on between three partners, the Frenchman, the American and the Englishman, sometimes between four when the German was brought in. In addition, during all the meetings, Debré was at my side. What happened during these talks was hardly calculated to dispel my apprehensions. For the Anglo-Saxons proved to be highly indecisive. Not, of course, as regards the invitation to be issued to Khrushchev, for on this point, public opinion having been aroused and shown itself keenly interested, there could be no question, in these democracies, of disappointing it. But what agenda were we to propose to the Kremlin? When I suggested that there were two un-avoidable subjects – Germany and disarmament – and that a third, aid to the underdeveloped countries, might provide a starting-point for practical co-operation with the Russians, nobody contradicted me. But the discussions showed that on each of these problems the positions of Washington and London were not firmly fixed.

On the question of Berlin, Eisenhower and Macmillan

inclined towards a compromise but without specifying what it should be. The President and the Prime Minister believed that Khrushchev, in spite of his well-intentioned airs, was really determined to ensure that the city was cut off from the West and would, if necessary, take active steps to bring this about. They agreed that in such an eventuality decisions would have to be taken. But they were extremely reluctant to define them, and made no secret of the fact that if it came to the point they would be even less willing to put them into effect. Fundamentally, both were inclined to do anything to avoid the worst. Macmillan, in particular, declared with feeling that he could not conceive of himself taking the responsibility for leading his country to appalling destruction simply for the sake of the future – in any case highly problematical – of a German city. I for my part considered that if we yielded to the threat, the psychological balance would be upset. Then the natural trend of things would lead the Soviets to demand more and more, and the Western powers to make more and more concessions, until the moment when, withdrawal becoming unacceptable for the latter and conciliation impossible for the former, flash-point was reached. "You do not wish to die for Berlin," I told my two friends, "but you may be sure that the Russians do not wish to either. If they see us determined to maintain the *status quo*, why should they take the initiative in bringing about confrontation and chaos? Moreover, even if any complaisance on our part did not lead immediately to a general aggravation of the crisis, the final consequence might be the defection of Germany, who would go and seek in the East a future which she despaired of being guaranteed in the West."

As it happened, Adenauer, who was naturally not a witness to these tergiversations, but who was well aware of the state of mind of the American and British leaders, came to confer with me and begged me to stand out against surrender. Invited to express his views at a plenary meeting, he declared: "If Berlin were to be lost, my political position would at once become untenable. The Socialists would take over power in Bonn. They would proceed to make a direct arrangement with Moscow, and that would be the end of Europe." The Chancellor's anguish, perhaps excessive but certainly sincere, together with my observations, rekindled some firmness of purpose, without, however, any precise formula being worked out to deal with the situation which would arise at the summit if Khrushchev demanded a settlement of the Berlin question.

Nor did we succeed in working out a common position on disarmament. While Eisenhower, supported by Macmillan, wanted the summit conference to seal the Russo-American agreement then in gestation on an atomic test ban and a veto on the manufacture or the acquisition of nuclear weapons by States not already equipped with them – in other words a final affirmation of the monopoly of the two super-powers – I reserved France's complete freedom of action in this matter. Conversely, my proposal for the controlled destruction of launching vehicles was too far from the intentions of the United States for the President to adopt it at this stage.

Finally, the French proposal to set up a Four-Power organization for the advancement of the developing countries, to which London, Paris, Washington and Moscow would each automatically contribute a percentage of the national income, aroused apprehensions among the Americans, fearful of seeing the Kremlin intruding on their aid operations under cover of such a project. Even our plan to focus joint action on specified objectives, such as the development of the Nile Valley, the feeding of India, the struggle against cancer or leukaemia, did not win their approval. At the end of it all we separated in a spirit of cordiality, but without having resolved the uncertainty as to what we should jointly say to the Soviet Prime Minister, or even as to the agenda for the conference. It was simply agreed, at Eisenhower's request, that if Khrushchev was willing the conference should take place in Paris.

On March 23, 1960, the microphones at Orly airport broadcast my address of welcome to the Head of the Soviet Government, the first to have been received in France. I emphasized that in his person we were welcoming the leader of a great country whose people had from time immemorial been the friends of the French people, which had been our ally in two world wars, which by its valor and its sacrifices had ensured final victory and which today was indispensable to the peace of the world. On the journey to the Quai d'Orsay, the Parisian public, which had turned out in fair numbers, watched our guest pass by with some curiosity, their comparative reserve contrasting with the noisy demonstrations of a few groups of Communists scattered here and there. Later, as the visit proceeded, the atmosphere of Paris warmed up considerably. Indeed, Khrushchev made great efforts to ensure that this was so. Adopting the air of a good-natured family man, he had arrived with his wife, their son, their two daughters, and their son-in-law. Wherever he went, he appeared friendly, alert and nimble in spite of his rotundity, full of laughter and friendly gestures. After three days in the capital, going through the customary program of meetings, receptions and official banquets; of public ceremonies – the Arc de Triomphe, the Hôtel de Ville, Mont Valérien; and of visits – Versailles, Lenin's house, the Renault works at Flins, the atomic center at Saclay, the Chamber of Commerce, etc., the Soviet Premier, accompanied variously by Louis Joxe, Louis Jacquinot and Jean-Marcel Jeanneney, visited Bordeaux, Lacq, Arles, Nîmes, Marseilles, Dijon, Verdun, Rheims and Rouen. For I was anxious that he should go to the provinces and meet the French people. There, as in Paris, he showed himself cheerful and homely, mainly interested in technique and output, and never failing, whatever he was shown, to proclaim Soviet successes in the same field. Finally, he came to Rambouillet, where we spent two quiet days with our families, he and I conferring at leisure, while my wife showed the Russian ladies round the sights of the Ile de France.

Both at the Elysée and at Rambouillet we spent a good deal of time together and had much to say to each other, and not by way of idle chatter. I began by coming straight to the point: "I look on you simply as the present Head of the established government of Russia. Please regard me simply as the

President of the French Republic. We shall therefore only discuss the national interests of our two countries and the ways in which we can reconcile them." "You are right," he replied. "I came here to do just that and I know who I am dealing with." There was nothing unexpected about the subjects of our discussions and of the meetings we held with our ministers, Kosygin and Gromyko on the one hand, Debré and Couve de Murville on the other, and with the ambassadors Vinogradov and Dejean, and if they revealed many divergences of view, they did not provoke any serious clashes. Moreover, Khrushchev, a very voluble talker, was extremely relaxed and easy-going in conversation, especially when we were alone save for our interpreters. However great the differences between us in origin, training and conviction, we established a genuine man-to-man contact.

On the subject of Germany, my interlocutor expressed passionate mistrust. This of course stemmed from the still vivid memories of the German invasions in the course of two world wars, the calamities which had almost destroyed Russia, the mortal dangers which had faced the Soviet regime, and the appalling ordeals inflicted on the population. But it also contained an element of political calculation. For, in order to justify the maintenance of the situation imposed by Moscow on central and eastern Europe thanks to the endorsement given by the Anglo-Saxons at Yalta, the postulate of German revanchism was obviously necessary. When I pointed out to Khrushchev that there was no comparison between the relative power of Hitler's Reich and that of the Federal Republic, and that the military, economic, and political capacity of the Russia of today was incomparably greater than what it had been in the past, he of course agreed, but he nevertheless affirmed that the threat remained because the Bonn government fomented anti-Sovietism among the Western powers, with the consequent risk of producing a conflagration at any moment. It was for this reason that the division of Germany into two States was essential. "After all," Khrushchev declared, "this division is also in the interests of France, which paid dearly for German unity. Why then do you not recognize the East German Republic?"

I observed that my country had indeed suffered terribly from German aggression, and was in a better position than any other to decide what precautions should be taken against a renewal of it. I reminded Khrushchev – who had been introduced to me in Moscow in 1944 – of the solution I had then proposed to Stalin, which consisted of restoring to Germany, without destroying the German people, the political structure which was natural to her and under which she had lived up to the time when Prussia created the German Empire as a result of the defeat of France. Each region would have recovered its former autonomous statehood, and together, on an equal footing, they would have organized a confederation, to the exclusion of a centralized Reich. As for international control, instead of being organized in separate zones, it would have been exercised jointly by the victors, with particular reference to the Ruhr. This would have enabled us to levy at source the reparations which Germany owed and prevent her from manufacturing dangerous weapons. Such a program, if Russia and France had adopted it, would have been the basis of the settlement. But Stalin would have none of it. He preferred to help himself, directly and greedily, by tearing Prussia and Saxony from the body of the Reich and installing there by force a subservient regime, leaving the rest of Germany at the disposal of the West. From that moment, was it not inevitable that the Federal Republic, embittered and fearful of one day being annexed in its turn, should set itself up as a unitary State, make reunification the goal of its policies, and foster ill-feeling against the Soviets in the West? As for France, who certainly had the best of reasons for preventing her principal neighbor from becoming warlike again, but also good reasons for co-operating with her, she bowed to the realities and saw to it that Bonn, contained within a sensible European grouping, remained as closely linked to her as possible.

"I understand your position," Khrushchev said to me. "But let me assure you that the East German Republic will continue to exist and will never be absorbed by West Germany. Would it not be realistic on your part to maintain relations with both? Especially as you are certainly not in any hurry to see Germany reunited." Recalling the various notes which Moscow had already addressed to Washington, London and Paris on this subject, he declared that it was time to settle the German question by concluding a formal peace treaty with the two republics. If the West refused to accept this proposal, Moscow would sign a separate peace with the East Germans. Then, having recognized the full sovereignty of Pankow, the Soviet Government would hand over to the East German Republic the control of its frontiers, and this would involve a complete change in the arrangements for communications between the Federal Republic and Berlin, and would subject the movements of the French, American and British troops stationed in the former capital to the control of Walter Ulbricht's government. Should these new arrangements give rise to acts of force by the Western powers against the East German Republic, the provisions of its alliance with the Soviet Union would automatically come into play. To avoid grave complications, the best thing to do would be to convert West Berlin into a free city which would be evacuated by Western forces, and which would settle the modalities of its existence with Pankow direct. Russia for her part was prepared to recognize its status as a free city. But the Western powers must make up their minds promptly because the Soviet Union would not wait much longer before taking unilateral action.

Icily I gave Khrushchev to understand that the threat he was brandishing did not impress me much. "No one," I told him, "can prevent you from signing what you call a treaty with Pankow which would merely be a document drawn up among Communists and which you would be addressing to yourself. But when you had done so, the German problem would still remain unresolved. Moreover, everyone would know that the difficulties created by your initiative for the French, American and British occupation forces in Berlin stemmed from you. The three Western powers will never allow their troops to be insulted. If it leads to war, it will be entirely your fault. And yet you never stop talking about peaceful co-existence; at home you retrospectively condemn Stalin; only three months ago you were Eisenhower's guest, and today you are mine. If you do not want war, do not take the road that leads to war. The question at issue is not how to stir up conflict but how to organize peace. In this respect, I am in agreement with you in thinking that Germany must never again be in a position to do harm, that her present frontiers must not be called in question, and that she must never have atomic weapons at her disposal. But you must agree with me that it would not be any more conducive to peace if this great people were to be kept in an intolerable national situation. The solution must be sought not in raising two monolithic blocs, one against the other, but on the contrary in working step by step towards *détente*, understanding and co-operation within a European framework. In this way, we shall create among Europeans, from the Atlantic to the Urals, new relationships, new ties, a new atmosphere, which will first of all take the sting out of the German problems, including that of Berlin, then lead the Federal Republic and your Eastern Republic to join forces, and finally enclose the whole of Germany within a Europe based on peace and progress where she can make a fresh start."

This prospect seemed to interest Khrushchev. Mollified, he told me he was very much in favor of a *détente* and even claimed that his plan for a peace treaty was intended to promote it. In any case, he had no intention of precipitating matters, and was prepared to wait a couple of years before concluding the treaty. As for European co-operation, he was anxious to work towards it, and suggested as a start a comprehensive program of exchanges between Russia and France. Nevertheless, he warned me not to have any illusions on the subject of Germany. "How do you know," he asked me, "that the East German Republic will never absorb West Germany? And how do you know that one day the Bonn Government will not come to a direct agreement with the Soviet Union?" I answered that, if the German people were to change sides, the European balance would be upset and this could be the signal for war. "Lenin, Stalin, yourself, the historic leaders of Russian Bolshevism, what were you all if not the disciples of the Rhenish Prussian Karl Marx?" I asked him. "Into what extremes of imperialism and tyranny might not totalitarian Russia be led were she ever to make common cause with a completely Communized Germany possessed of all her instincts of conquest and domination?"

Khrushchev was at pains to prove to me that the actions of his government throughout the world were resolutely peaceful. He cited the good relations which it had established with India, Turkey and Iran after the tensions of the Stalin period. If it provided considerable aid to certain non-Communist States in Africa and Asia, such as Egypt, Ghana, Guinea, Somalia, Afghanistan, Pakistan and Indonesia, this was not with any imperialist or ideological design, but because there was no reason to leave them to the tender mercies of the United States, as was the case, in his opinion, with Latin America and, at this very moment, with the ex-Belgian Congo. When I observed that the French government devoted a larger proportion of its national income to the Third World than any other country, that it would not allow others to interfere with its operations in this field, and that, in particular, it condemned the relations which Moscow maintained with Ferhat Abbas's committee, the Soviet Premier avouched his respect for France's world-wide activity and influence, affirmed that Russia's relations with the Algerian organization were purely *de facto*, and declared that, since my declaration on self-determination in September, he was convinced that France would solve the problem.

To the questions which I put to him about China and Mao Tse-tung, he replied with an optimism which was obviously feigned: "All is well between Moscow and Peking. It is true that there are many people who believe that the huge Chinese population, with neither enough room nor enough resources in its own country, will sooner or later be forced to seek them in neighboring countries, and that this will lead to conflict with Soviet Russia, whose vast territories in Siberia and Central

Asia have a common border with China six thousand kilo-meters long. But those who make these predictions fail to take into account the possibilities presented by modern progress. In fact, China contains within her own borders vast desert regions and other under-exploited areas which have only to be irrigated, reclaimed and populated in order to be rendered fertile. More-over, industrialization has scarcely begun. When it really develops it will procure a livelihood for hundreds of millions of people. It is with this in view that we Russians are helping China with all the means at our disposal. There too we are working for peace."

"Perhaps you really want it," I said. "The Americans say they want it too. Nevertheless, both your countries have pro-vided themselves with colossal powers of destruction, which moreover, they continue to reinforce. So long as this double threat of sudden death hangs over the world, how can the spirit of peace ever be made to reign there?"

Khrushchev vehemently expounded to me the thesis which his government had tirelessly argued at the Geneva conference, and which he had already unfolded to me through a flood of dialectic in the numerous letters and notes he had addressed to me since my return to office. Briefly, he proposed that all atomic weapons should be destroyed, but he was opposed to inspection and control, without which, obviously, the ban would be useless. My own view was that, while neglecting no oppor-tunity of vociferously denouncing the weapons of terror, he had no intention of divesting himself of them. This was also, by and large, the position of the Americans. I pointed out that on the French side there were no illusions on the subject. Neverthe-less, in case there might be some degree of sincerity in the pro-fessed intention of the two rivals to forswear these monstrous instruments of their power, France had taken up a position which I recalled to the Soviet Prime Minister. While believ-ing it necessary to prohibit unreservedly the manufacture and possession of nuclear missiles, and to organize to this end a system of rigorous international control and inspec-tion, we maintained that, short of this total solution, the means of delivering these weapons should at least be destroyed, since this could be verified on the spot.

Although our proposal had been known to him for some time and we had often corresponded about it, Khrushchev affected to be hearing about it for the first time. Indeed, on his return to Moscow, he was to declare publicly that "General de Gaulle's ideas on disarmament correspond to those of the Soviet Union." But things did not go any further; the Russians and the Americans were equally determined to maintain the crushing supremacy conferred upon them by their missiles and their bombs and jointly to ensure that no one else acquired them.

I made it clear to Khrushchev, as I had recently done to Eisenhower, that France, determined to be independent, would have nothing to do with their schemes and intended, as far as lay within her means, to equip herself with a full-scale nuclear armory. It so happened that on April 1 our second atomic test was to be carried out in the Sahara. A report of its successful conclusion reached me at Rambouillet that morning. I gave the news to Nikita Khrushchev, adding that I was anxious for him not to learn of it from the news agencies. He replied to me affably and with a characteristic human touch: "Thank you for your consideration. I understand your joy. We felt it too not so long ago." Then, after a moment: "But you know, it's very expensive!"

From the beginning of their stay in France, the Russian leaders had discussed at length with our ministers practical ways in which the two countries might co-operate. The subject was brought up at a plenary meeting when Debré and Couve de Murville, Kosygin and Gromyko outlined the results of their negotiations. An important cultural and technical agreement was concluded there and then. But in the economic field there was still a long way to go. Russia, with her enormous need for industrial equipment, offered to buy it from us on a large scale provided we placed orders with her of equivalent value. But what she mainly had to offer were raw materials – minerals, coal, oil, etc. – which our existing trade agreements obliged us to purchase elsewhere. Our Russian interlocutors also made great play with the possibility of selling us finished products, in particular machine tools, which we had also hitherto acquired from other sources. At all events, there were considerable prospects of improvement in the field of commercial relations. But this would entail the breaking-down of many old habits and prejudices and, in consequence, the initiation of studies, contacts and exchanges of information. This is what was decided on, and indeed from then on things progressed at a steadily accelerating rhythm.

Alexei Kosygin argued passionately in favor of these developments. This engineer and planning minister impressed me with his intelligence, his deep knowledge of the resources and the needs of his country, and in particular the enthusiasm with which he spoke of Siberia, which from his accounts was for the Russians not unlike what the Far West had been for the Americans. Khrushchev supported him in his disquisitions on the subject, but when the conversation ceased to be official, bombarded him with banter and jibes. "He works too hard." the Soviet Prime Minister declared. During a walk in the park, we got into a rowing-boat which was moored at the edge of a lake. Khrushchev shouted: "Kosygin, you can do the rowing, as usual." Kosygin seized the oars. Jokingly, I asked the Soviet Prime Minister: "By the way, when do you work yourself? We constantly hear that you're travelling either in Russia or abroad. You're always giving long interviews to all sorts of people. When do you find time for desk work?" To which he replied: "But I don't work! A decree of our Central Committee has ordained that after sixty-five – and I'm sixty-six – one should only work six hours a day and four days a week. That's just enough for my journeys and my audiences." "How do the affairs of State get settled, then?" "They don't need me. The Plan settles them in advance!" Then, pointing to Kosygin, who was rowing the boat, he added: "He's the Plan!" Was this said purely as a joke? Or did the remark suggest some obscure rivalry between the two men?

At the end of our discussion, the Soviet Premier promised me his enthusiastic presence at the Four-Power conference and left it to me to arrange the date, the place and the program. He also promised me a magnificent welcome in Moscow, where I had, in principle, agreed to go at his invitation. We exchanged the customary gifts. One of his was a model of the famous Sputnik. On the last evening, by way of compensation for the benign attitudes he had displayed during his trip, he broadcast a speech which was that of a harshly doctrinaire Communist. He left on April 3, friendly and cheerful once more, leaving me, I must confess, impressed by the strength and resilience of his personality, disposed to believe that, after all, there was a chance of peace in the world and a future for Europe, and reflecting that something of profound importance had occurred in the time-honored relationship between Russia and France.

Now it was my turn to go visiting. On April 5, 1960, I was received in Britain, with great splendor. Everything had been prepared in such a way as to ensure that the visit of General de Gaulle was something out of the ordinary. It was clear that the United Kingdom was bent on showing as strikingly as possible that it had not forgotten how Free France had remained faithful to the alliance, that it appreciated what an historic feat it had been on France's part to participate throughout the war and the victory after being initially laid low, and that it was impressed by our national recovery over the past two years. At the same time, on the part of the French visitors, myself in particular, not a word was to be uttered nor a gesture made which did not testify to our respect for the British people, our admiration for the way they had borne themselves during a crisis in which they had suddenly found themselves alone, and our confidence, for the future, in their virtues and in their friendship. These mutual feelings were to give a lofty and unprecedented significance to the occasion. Queen Elizabeth set the tone. On our arrival, she came to Victoria Station with Prince Philip to welcome me and my wife and those who accompanied us, and as we drove through London side by side in her open carriage, the Sovereign went out of her way to encourage with gestures and smiles the enthusiasm of the crowd massed along the route. To give an exceptional cachet to the dinner and reception at Buckingham Palace, she arranged for the first time a glittering firework display around the Palace, and in the midst of the illuminations stood for a long time on the balcony by my side acknowledging the cheers of the vast crowd below. For the gala performance at Covent Garden, the Opera House was garlanded from top to bottom with carnations by her orders. At the dinner which I gave at the French Embassy, the entire royal family was present with the Queen. At her invitation, I had the unusual honor of reviewing the Household troops. With the Duke of Edinburgh at my side, and in the presence of the general staffs of the British Army, Navy, and Air Force, I took the salute, inspected the ranks, and watched the march-past of these troops whose bearing and turn-out were the visible symbol of loyalty, discipline and tradition.

In the conversations, official or private, which I had with the Sovereign at Buckingham Palace, where my wife and I stayed, I came to realize that she was well-informed about everything, that her judgments on people and events were as clear-cut as they were thoughtful, that no one was more preoccupied by the cares and problems of our storm-tossed age. When she asked me what I thought of her own role in the midst of such uncertainties, I answered: "In that station to which God has called you, be who you are, Madam; that is to say the person in relation to whom, by virtue of the principle of legitimacy, everything in your kingdom is ordered, in whom your people perceives its own nationhood, and by whose presence and dignity the national unity is upheld."

I was provided with a living proof of the stability and equilibrium which are the special attributes of the British political system when I was received by Parliament. In the great hall at Westminster were gathered the Lords, the Commons, the Ministers, the principal dignitaries, the highest officials, the representatives of industry, the trade unions, the universities and the press – in short, all those who in every field are called upon to run the country. After the speeches of welcome by the Lord Chancellor and the Speaker of the House of Commons, I addressed this assembly of the most eminent Britons. I began by paying tribute to the England which, not long since, "heroic and alone, took upon its shoulders the freedom of the world," and then recalled my last sojourn in Great Britain: "When from your shores the armies of the West once more set foot on the soil of France in order to liberate Europe, this event proclaimed the resounding martial triumph of your kingdom and the Commonwealth, glorified the unstinting efforts and sacrifices of your people in battles on land, at sea and in the air as well as in the factories, the mines, the fields and the offices, requited all the anxieties and all the tears secretly held back, and invested Winston Churchill with the immortal glory of having been the leader and the inspiration not only of England in the sternest test she has ever known, but also of many others. . . . This outstanding role in the midst of the storm, you owe not only to your profound national qualities but also to the value of your institutions." There followed a eulogy of the British political system, which, "with your almost unconscious self-assurance, you operate in a framework of liberty. . . . So powerful are the forces of tradition, loyalty and the rules of the game in your country that your government is quite naturally endowed with cohesion and durability, your Parliament has an assured majority throughout each legislature . . . your executive and legislative powers balance each other and co-operate as it were by definition. . . . The proof of it is that only four statesmen, my friends Sir Winston Churchill, Lord Attlee, Sir Anthony Eden and Mr Harold Macmillan – all of whom are present here side by side – have conducted your affairs during these twenty extraordinary years." I then went on to say that "this England inspires the confidence of France," and that "Englishmen and Frenchmen, assured of their worth, but in no danger of losing their heads as giants sometimes do, are destined to act together to assist in building world peace." I outlined the basic conditions of such a peace: the achievement of nuclear disarmament, the prevention of a widening of divisions and a festering of wounds, "including those suffered by the German people," the establishment of understanding and co-operation between the two halves of Europe, and the organization of aid on the part of the peoples who lack nothing for those who lack everything. Finally, referring to the forth-coming summit conference, "which will have owed a great deal to the actions of your Prime Minister Mr Harold Mac-millan," and to which the Big Four would come "in the state of mind of travellers undertaking a long and difficult voyage," I affirmed that France on this occasion stood shoulder to shoulder with England and I asked in conclusion: "What peoples know better than France and Great Britain that nothing can save the world except those qualities with which they are pre-eminently endowed: wisdom and firmness?"

I had spoken in French and, as usual, without notes. Many of my listeners understood me direct. The others had followed my speech from a translation which had been distributed in advance. It can happen that a premeditated detail may count for something in a serious matter. In any case, although I had not said a word about the European Community, my remarks were greeted with an overwhelming approval which seemed to be a sign of the desire of the British people to reach accord with France as she had revealed herself and given voice that day.

Nor could one interpret otherwise the enthusiasm and the cheers of the people of London wherever I went, as planned, accompanied by Maurice Couve de Murville and our excellent ambassador Jean Chauvel: the Tomb of the Unknown Soldier, which the English, in accordance with the Nordic spirit, have buried in an abbey instead of exhibiting in a public place in the Latin manner; the Royal Hospital in Chelsea, where, after I had inspected the Pensioners, we were received by the government; the Guildhall, which serves as a traditional setting for the banquet given by the Lord Mayor, Sir Edmund Stockdale, for contacts with the leaders of British industry and commerce and for the picturesque procession of the City guilds; the Franco-British Society, to which I was eloquently intro-duced by its President, Lord Harvey; the French Institute and Lycée, which I found flourishing; Carlton Gardens, which was the headquarters of Free France and to which I made a pilgrimage in the midst of a crowd brimming over with emotion; and Clarence House, where I went to pay a visit to the Queen Mother. The same sentiments were expressed to me by Harold Macmillan in the course of our conversations, as by all the ministers, the innumerable Members of Parliament and the many other personalities whom I met. Churchill – a light that was going out – nevertheless attended the receptions and ceremonies. When I went to call on him at his home, he repeated to me: "Vive la France," the last words I was to hear from his lips.

Some days later, I began my American journey with a visit to Canada. We arrived in Ottawa on April 19. I had already paid two official visits to this country. France had given birth to it four centuries ago and then withdrawn, after two hundred years of praiseworthy effort, on account of European commitments. In our day, by a veritable miracle of fecundity and fidelity, the substance of France remained very much alive there in the form of a population of five million inhabitants concentrated in Quebec and on the shores of the St Lawrence, and two million others spread over the rest of the territory. During my previous visits, in 1944 and 1945, when everything was obscured by the apparatus of war, I had no more than glimpsed the underlying realities which make the Canadian Federation a State that is perpetually uneasy, ambivalent and artificial. This time I was to discern these realities clearly, although still under a subdued light.

My friend General Vannier received us in his capacity as Governor-General. He was a man in the highest degree respect-worthy and respected. He fulfilled his functions with the greatest dignity and the utmost loyalty. He went out of his way to make us feel that everything was as it should be. But in spite of his efforts, the contradictions inherent in the Federation could not fail to make themselves felt. Indeed, he himself could not escape them. He was titular Head of State, but was appointed by the Queen of England, while the territory aspired to complete independence. He and his wife were entirely French in origin, mentality and taste, although his race had only maintained itself by struggling unremittingly against every form of oppression or seduction wielded by the conquerors in order to reduce and dissolve it. He presided over the destinies of a boundless but barely populated country, a country full of resources but without capital, its security apparently guaranteed by its immense size, but confronted along the shores of the Arctic Ocean by the Siberian and Russian coasts, while the United States, with which it had a common frontier stretching for three thousand miles, overflowed with men, money and power. Beneath the warmth of its welcome and the impressive façade of its economic achievement, Canada could not conceal from me the weaknesses of its structure and its situation.

This was certainly the case in the Federal capital. Whether during the ceremonies organized in my honor, or at the receptions which took place at the Governor-General's residence, or in parliament, or at the French Embassy, where I was introduced to the leading Canadian personalities by our ambassador Francis Lacoste, or in the Cabinet meeting which the Prime Minister, John Diefenbaker, invited me to attend together with Couve de Murville, it was impossible to ignore the underlying fact that Canada is split into two radically different ethnic communities. No doubt both sides had more or less adapted themselves to the situation, by reason of the exigencies of living in the same geographical space, the memories of the two world wars in which they had fought valiantly together (and moreover in France only), the blandishments and special favors which were meted out from the English Canadian side to the political and intellectual personalities on the other side who were prepared to play the Federation game, and finally the calculated self-interest which impelled a large proportion of the French-speaking upper classes to operate the system. But it was clear that it was all a matter of compromise and resignation, with no real national unity.

John Diefenbaker spoke to me of his preoccupations and his plans. In the duality between the two peoples cohabiting under his administration, he affected to see chiefly a problem of language which bilingualism would gradually resolve. He himself endeavored to set a good example by expressing himself occasionally and with great difficulty in French. In order to check the economic, technological and financial penetration of the United States, he was anxious for Europe, and especially France, to contribute as much as possible to the development of Canada, and to this end declared himself ready to conclude agreements with Paris, and even to allow the province of Quebec to make its own arrangements in this field. The Prime Minister was also extremely preoccupied about the security of his country which, because of the vast areas of the American continent which it covered in the north, was forced to submit to military control from Washington. Thus nuclear disarmament was the keystone of his foreign policy, since, in the event of war, the Canadian skies would be the shortest route for strategic missiles between the Soviet Union and the New World over the Polar region, and moreover, by eliminating this threat, Canada might be able to disengage herself from the "Yankee".

I told the Prime Minister that France now attached considerable importance to Canada, in contrast to the relative indifference which she had so often shown towards that country. In the first place, her own revival had rekindled her feelings and redirected her attention towards the branch of herself which had maintained and developed itself on the other side of the Atlantic. The fate of Quebec and the French communities settled in other provinces was close to her heart. Moreover, while remaining the friend and ally of the United States, she refused to submit to its hegemony, which might cause serious dangers to the world and America herself. For this reason, while she herself was breaking free from American control in Europe, she would be glad to see some countervailing influence in the Western hemisphere. Hence she was opposed to any suggestion of Canada being absorbed by her southern neighbor, and was more than willing to increase her industrial, technical and cultural investments there. We concluded that there was a case for drawing up agreements to this end, and I invited the Prime Minister to come to Paris to discuss them. Finally, as regards nuclear armaments, I reminded Diefenbaker of France's ideas on the subject. "If, as we propose," I said, "there were to be a preliminary ban on launching-ramps, rockets, missile-carrying bombers and submarines, the security and at the same time the independence of Canada would certainly benefit therefrom. In spite of the Atlantic conformity which binds you to other schemes, I hope for your sake that you will support ours." In conclusion, I told the Prime Minister, whose intentions were certainly highly estimable, that France was willing to enter into much closer relations with his country. But if we were to do so wholeheartedly, and if Canada as a whole were to have the necessary strength and weight, she must have the will and the capacity to solve the problem posed by the existence within her borders of two peoples, one of which was French and must, like any other, have the right to self-determination.

This was certainly the reality that emerged in Quebec through all the fictions and precautions. There too I was the guest of the Federal government, and my visit was organized with a view to contacts with notables, military ceremonies, and visits to historical sites, in such a way that there was no opportunity for popular demonstrations. Nevertheless, a sort of effervescence among the crowds that gathered wherever I went, the fervent cries of "Vive la France!" and "Vive de Gaulle!" which were the only ones to be heard, the fact that a profusion of emblems with the fleur-de-lis of Quebec appeared everywhere beside the very rare Federal flags, revealed to me that since my previous journeys a new climate had developed. Moreover, the Governor of Quebec, Onésime Gagnon, and the Prime Minister, Antoine Barrette, both extremely erudite in the history of Champlain and the illustrious battles of Montcalm and Lévis, were not at all put out by it. At the official dinner, glasses were raised "to France!" Whereupon I observed: "Each of you, I am sure, is thinking: 'the country from which I came.'" An unmistakable tremor ran through the assembled company.

Montreal made the same impression as Quebec, though

accentuated by the massive and populous character of this urban agglomeration, by the widespread anxiety caused by the ever-increasing hold of the Anglo-Saxons on the ownership and management of factories, banks, shops and offices, by the resultant economic, social and linguistic subordination of the French, and by the policy of the Federal administration in automatically anglicizing all immigrants. Fournier, the Mayor, taking me on a tour of the great city, showed me innumerable buildings and enterprises sprouting up under the pressure of American capital and lamented the fact that so little investment came from the home country towards "the second largest French city in the world". Never had it been brought home to me more clearly than it was that day how essential overseas expansion is to France's world position and how much she has suffered from her old-fashioned commercial methods.

My Canadian journey ended at Toronto. Here, in the capital of Ontario, I saw, as it were, the English counterpart of French Montreal. Industry was very active, building was thriving, the university was flourishing. But one sensed a fear of becoming an appendage of the giant neighbor across the great lake. The Governor, Keiller Mackay, a disabled hero of Vimy Ridge, and the Prime Minister, Leslie Frost, found that the process of osmosis with the United States contributed materially to the progress of the province. But it also aroused in them a great deal of melancholy. On leaving this country, I wondered whether the establishment of a State of French origin side by side with another of British origin, the two co-operating with each other in every sphere freely and by choice, uniting their twin nationhoods in order to safeguard them, might not be the only way for Canada eventually to obliterate the historic injustice on which it was based, to develop in conformity with its own true realities, and thus to remain Canadian.

In Washington on April 22 we were plunged into the maelstrom of American enthusiasm. All the way from the airport to Blair House I drove beside President Eisenhower to a deafening accompaniment of cheers, sirens and brass bands,

amid a forest of banners and flags. A similar welcome, expressing in the most conclusive possible way the extraordinary
strength of popular feeling, was to greet the French guests from
one end of their journey to the other. It was an emotional
demonstration of such clarity and magnitude that it amounted
to a major political factor. I had already been struck by it
during my previous visits to the United States, but those were
during the war and in judging the welcome I received, I had
to take into account the heroic circumstances of the moment.
This time, it clearly represented something fundamental and
to me all the more impressive in that it contrasted with what I
usually read and heard about France and my own person in
most American newspapers and broadcasts. At all events, the
cordial atmosphere that reigned on our arrival in the Federal
capital and during the public ceremonies at Arlington cemetery
and the Lafayette monument also enveloped our official
activities.

These first of all consisted of two days of talks at the White
House, in which Secretary of State Herter and Ambassador
Houghton, as well as Couve de Murville and Alphand, inter-
mittently joined. On the 23rd, there was a vast press conference
at the National Press Club where most of the questions put
to me concerned the projected meeting of the Big Four. On
Sunday the 24th, Mrs Eisenhower took the ladies for a trip on
the Potomac and the President drove me to his farm at Gettys-
burg. There we chatted together in the closest intimacy. As
old soldiers, we visited the battlefield which, nearly a hundred
years earlier, had been the scene of the decisive victory of the
northern forces. We returned to Washington via Camp David,
a group of hutments in the middle of the woods, where Eisenhower was especially fond of conferring with his guests. He
told me how he had tried to indoctrinate Khrushchev there. In
all our conversations, the President constantly reverted to the
subject of the forthcoming summit conference. "I am very
keen on it," he told me. "My term of office ends this year and
I shall not run for another. What a splendid exit it would be
for me to end up, without any sacrifice of principle, with an

agreement between East and West!" I told Dwight Eisenhower that whatever happened at the conference, he would carry away the esteem of all on leaving office. Personally, I expected few positive results from the Big Four meeting. Peaceful co-existence was too recent and too limited. The German problem was not yet ripe for solution. But whatever the outcome of the confrontation in Paris, I would work for bilateral *détente* and co-operation with Russia, and do my best to transfer it on to a European plane by gradually bringing in, independently of existing blocs and hegemonies, all the countries that bordered the Rhine, the Danube and the Vistula.

The President agreed that the United States should not try to do everything, that it was for Europe to settle its own problems by itself if it could, that in this connection France had the right to take the initiative and that her revival was a crucial event for the old continent, for the West and for the world as a whole. Nevertheless, he urged me to bear in mind that America was by nature inclined to stay at home, and that in the present state of the globe it might be disastrous if, disgruntled and disillusioned with the very people who needed her help, she returned to isolationism. I confessed to Eisenhower that, while believing America to be indispensable to the world, I did not wish to see her setting herself up as a universal judge and policeman. As for the opposite eventuality, her drawing in on herself, I regarded it as highly unlikely. At the level of power to which she had attained, her strongest temptations were towards intervention, and besides, how could she remain detached in the event of a world conflict, when at any moment and from any point of the compass she could be dealt a death-blow?

My conversations with the President were complemented by those I had with Richard Nixon. In his somewhat curious post of Vice-President, he struck me as one of those frank and steady personalities on whom one feels one could rely in the great affairs of State if ever they were to reach the highest office.

On April 25, the Capitol! There I was received by Congress.

All the senators and all the representatives were present, bursting with cordiality and curiosity. The Speaker, Sam Rayburn, delivered an admirable speech of welcome. As at Westminster, my own speech had been translated and distributed in advance. What I expounded therein was the policy of France. What I showed was that she had one. And I expatiated on its aims: in face of the danger of a war which would destroy our species, to bring about an easing of international tension; to create thereby a peaceful atmosphere which gradually reduced hostility between regimes and from which might emerge the conditions for a settlement of existing problems, above all that of Germany; to organize aid to the underdeveloped countries through co-operation between East and West; and to achieve disarmament, first of all through the destruction of all the means of delivering atomic missiles, in the absence of which my country was being compelled to equip itself with nuclear weapons. I made a cautious allusion to the imminent meeting of the Four: "The mere fact that Messrs Eisenhower, Macmillan, Khrushchev and I find ourselves together will not bring about an immediate solution to problems of such magnitude. But perhaps we shall be able to decide what road to follow, however long and arduous the stages may be." I concluded by affirming that "in any case France's intentions and hopes are firmly fixed."

The ovation I received from Congress, and the remarks which a number of my listeners made to me during the reception that followed, showed me that the satisfaction my speech had caused them was not unmixed with surprise. Hitherto, of course, they had known little of my policies except through the reports, analyses and comments of the news media, and these, by and large, were invariably disparaging with regard to the supposed "Machiavellianism" of General de Gaulle. "How do you explain that?" Richard Nixon asked me. I replied: "It is, perhaps, because everything I have said and tried to do since June 1940 has always been as clear and straightforward as possible. Since many professional politicians and journalists cannot conceive of public action without deceit and betrayal, they see nothing but guile in my frankness and sincerity."

It was certainly not guile which New York acclaimed in my person in an unbelievable surge of excitement as I drove up Broadway beneath showers of tickertape from the rooftops and windows, or as I addressed the crowd in front of City Hall, or drove through the avenues to the various receptions. I may say that Governor Nelson Rockefeller and Mayor Robert Wagner went out of their way to see that nothing inhibited the gigantic enthusiasm of the gigantic city. Crossing to the other side of the United States, accompanied by Douglas Dillon, I found San Francisco also brimming over with warmth and hospitality. California was in any case caught up in the euphoria of its extraordinary growth. It was referred to constantly by the Governor Edmund Brown, by the Mayor George Christopher, and by the presidents of the various associations who greeted me one after another. I could see it for myself as I drove through the industrial zone and was taken for a tour of the harbor. What a future awaited the America of the Pacific when the vast Chinese market was opened to its trade!

My journey to the United States came to an end in New Orleans. There, the excited demonstrations of the multitude moved me all the more because of the reminders of French Louisiana which loomed up on every side. Arriving at Moisant airport, driving through the city the center of which had remained just as it was in "royal times", invited by the Governor, Earl Long, to review his troops in the very square on which ours used to drill, attending a *Te Deum* in the ancient cathedral thronged with people weeping with emotion, hearing so many French voices among the cheering crowd of Whites and Blacks around the Bienville monument, sailing up the Mississippi which was once the splendid artery of "New France," listening to the speeches of Mayor de Lesseps, of the auxiliary bishop and the "President of the Creoles", both of whom were called Bezou, and of the spokesman of the Acadians whose name was d'Arescaux, I felt overwhelmed by the grandeur of the past, but convinced too that its legacy could in future contribute towards our prestige. If what we had sown had remained such a hardy plant, let us cultivate it across the ocean! I returned to our capital via Guiana, Martinique and Guadeloupe. The explosion of feeling in these three *départements* on the occasion of my presence there showed once more how passionately their people wished to remain French, all the more so because of their situation on the edge of the New World.

On my return, I found universal attention concentrated on Paris, where the summit conference was to meet. I had informed Macmillan while in London, and Eisenhower while in Washington, and I had written from Cayenne to inform Khrushchev that I had arranged the first session for May 16. But the very day on which my letter was winging its way towards Moscow, the curtain went up on the bad comedy which was to make the whole thing abortive. On May 1, an American U2 photographic reconnaissance aircraft was shot down over the Russian missile-launching complex in the region of the Aral Sea, and its pilot taken prisoner. There was no question that this was an absurdly ill-timed violation of Soviet air space on the part of the US secret services. But the State Department put out a statement – perhaps half wanting to believe it? – to the effect that it could only have been due to a navigational error. Then the White House made it known, with some humility, that steps were being taken to ensure that such flights did not occur again. But it soon became clear that the Kremlin was determined to build the incident up to dramatic proportions, and that, as a result, the work of the conference would inevitably be compromised. On May 5, the Soviet Premier, replying to my letter, unleashed the most bitter recriminations against the Americans. In remarks made in public, and in a note addressed to Washington he accused them of aggression, criminal espionage and bad faith. However, he informed me that he would be present at the rendezvous I had given him in Paris.

I did in fact welcome him on May 15 at the Elysée. But he was accompanied not only by Gromyko and Vinogradov, but also by Malinovsky, the "rocket marshal". After expressing his respect and confidence for me personally, Khrushchev handed me the text of a statement in which he declared that he could take no part in the conference unless Eisenhower made a public apology to the Soviet Union, condemned the aggression committed by the United States, announced what punishment would be meted out to those responsible, and gave an undertaking that no American spy plane would ever fly over Soviet territory again. It was clear that the Soviets wanted either to inflict a spectacular humiliation on the United States or to extricate themselves from a conference which they now no longer desired after having clamored so loudly for it.

I pointed out to Khrushchev that the business of the reconnaissance plane was only an incident in the Cold War and the arms race between the Soviet Union and the United States, that it was precisely because of this state of tension that there were acts of espionage on the American side, as there had also been on the Russian side; that the real question was to discover whether the two sides were willing to put an end to this state of affairs and bring about a *détente*; that such was indeed the object of the summit conference, and that nothing could have shown more clearly how useful it could be than what had just occurred. If, because of the Soviet attitude, the meeting failed to take place, France would resign herself to the inevitable, however much she regretted it, especially on behalf of the two rivals, since it was they rather than she who had for so long been calling for such a conference. At this, the Soviet Prime Minister, still with a show of furious indignation, affirmed that his country's honor was at stake, that it would not tolerate such outrages, that it had the means to crush its enemies and that, in particular, it could at any moment destroy their bases wherever they might be. "I know," he said, "that France has had no hand in the American provocations. But she is the ally of the United States, whose forces are stationed on her territory. Think what calamities might befall her, without our wishing to do her harm!" I retorted sharply that it was useless to predict what might happen in the event of a conflict, and that already twice in my lifetime I had witnessed the defeat of a country which had taken the risk of going to war in the certainty of winning it. I concluded the interview by saying: "It was not to talk about war that I convened the conference in Paris, but to try and ensure peace. With this end in view, the first meeting will take place tomorrow morning."

That afternoon, I held a meeting at the Elysée with Eisenhower and Macmillan, who had been apprised of the Soviet statement. The immediate object of this meeting was to listen to the views of Adenauer, who had also come to Paris full of anxiety about the possible concessions which the Western powers might be induced to make over Berlin. The Chancellor feared that Khrushchev, taking advantage of the fact that the American President had put himself in the wrong, might procure some changes in the status of the former German capital by way of compensation. It must be said that the Anglo-Saxons, especially the British, did not seem very determined to resist such a deal. Macmillan even seemed favorable to an arrangement on the lines which Khrushchev had recently proposed, whereby Berlin would be declared a "free city" and the British, French and American forces would be withdrawn, the full implications of the operation being disguised to some extent by a "guarantee" from the United Nations. Naturally enough, Adenauer protested against such a "solution". I too was opposed to it, for reasons which I had already explained to them all. To abandon Berlin in the present state of tension would be a confession of weakness and might unleash all the demons of crisis. It would only be possible to seek a solution to the problems of Germany after some measure of *détente* and co-operation had been established. This approach seemed to meet with general agreement, and Adenauer returned to Bonn.

Meanwhile, the President and the Prime Minister seemed far from sure as to the attitude to adopt towards Khrushchev the next day. Eisenhower, very upset by the turn which events had taken, announced his intention to make a conciliatory statement at the first meeting of the Four in reply to the harsh statement which the Soviet Premier had read out to me. Macmillan, who had just been to see the latter, felt that his intransigence might be due to a sudden change of heart on the part of the leadership in Moscow. Khrushchev, criticized for the apparent weakness of his policy of peaceful co-existence, might have seized the opportunity provided by the U2 affair to change course momentarily. The Prime Minister felt it would be best to play for time, and instead of replying direct to the Soviet ultimatum, to spin things out over a series of Four-Power meetings as well as bilateral talks. Then, in my turn, I announced the position which I intended to take up at the plenary meeting. "I refuse," I said, "to allow the conference to degenerate into an exchange of invective between the Russians and the Americans. I intend to put matters on the only basis which is both dignified and may possibly be fruitful. Are we all prepared to tackle the great questions which are the object of this meeting: disarmament, Germany, aid to the under-developed countries? If so, the debate can begin. If not, the conference has no immediate purpose and is adjourned *sine die*."

On May 16, the four delegations took their places around the conference table. I had put the English on my right, the Soviets on my left and the Americans opposite. I was flanked by Debré and Couve de Murville, Eisenhower by Herter and Thomas Gates, Macmillan by Selwyn Lloyd and Hoyar Millar, Khrushchev by Malinovsky and Gromyko. Khrushchev at once took the floor. He made a statement similar to the one he had read out to me the day before, demanding that the United States should acknowledge and publicly condemn their aggression, apologize for it, and punish the guilty men. Failing this, he himself would take no further part in the discussions. He further announced that the visit of the President of the United States to the Soviet Union planned for June 15 could not now take place. While Khrushchev was speaking, Marshal Malinovsky could be seen punctuating the speech with peremptory gestures and warlike grimaces. Then Eisenhower in his turn read a long statement, claiming that the over-flying of Soviet territory by an American aircraft was in no way an act of aggression, that it was simply a defensive measure, and that in any case it would not happen again. Macmillan exuded anxiety and distress. In his view, it was absolutely essential to save the conference, and he therefore proposed that we should give ourselves time for reflection, that we should examine at leisure the two declarations which had just been made, that the door should be left open for bilateral meetings, in particular between the American President and the Soviet Premier, that we should refrain from publishing what had just been stated on either side, and that we should meet again after two or three days.

Having allowed the others to put forward their views, I now took the floor. Addressing myself to Khrushchev, I observed that since the U2 incident had occurred on May 1 and the conference had been convened for the 16th, it should have been possible during the intervening fortnight for him to settle the affair with the Americans direct if he deemed it necessary, or to let it be known that he would not be coming to the conference. It was extremely tiresome to allow two other Heads of State or of Government to come to Paris, and to arrive there oneself simply in order to put forward demands which threatened to paralyze the work of the conference. "In any case, all four of us are here, and what brings us here is the common desire to achieve a relaxation in international tension and examine together the obstacles to such a *détente*. Why not make a start? Espionage is undoubtedly a deplorable practice. But how can it be avoided when two rival powers, heavily over-armed, give each other the impression that they may reach for their guns at any moment? An American aircraft has flown over Russia. At this very moment a Soviet satellite is passing over France eighteen times in every twenty-four hours. How do we know that it is not taking photographs? How can we be sure that all the machines of every sort now flitting across the skies may not suddenly rain down terrible projectiles on any country in the world? The only possible guarantee would be a peaceful *détente* backed up by adequate measures of disarmament. That is precisely the object of our conference. I therefore propose to open the debate. Since two statements have just been made on the U2 incident, let us give the two interested parties time to ponder the matter and settle it between themselves, and let us all meet again tomorrow to tackle resolutely the problems on our agenda. Meanwhile, it is obviously essential that the statements read out this morning should not be made public."

Khrushchev thereupon declared that, anxious though he was to see the work of the conference begin, he would take no part in it until he had publicly received from President Eisenhower the requisite apologies and undertakings. Furthermore, he intended to publish at once the text of his declaration. The honor and the sovereignty of the Soviet Union were at stake, and public opinion in his country would not tolerate the idea of his discussing any other matters with the Western powers, "all three closely allied in NATO," without having obtained redress. "What devil drove the Americans to commit this heinous act?" he exclaimed. To which I observed that "there are many devils in the world who spoil international relations," and brought the session to an end, saying that I would keep in touch with the delegations and that if it proved possible to hold another session to start on the agenda, it would take place next day.

What followed were mere formalities. Early on May 17, the Soviet Prime Minister held an improvised press conference on the pavement outside his Embassy in the Rue de Grenelle at which he disclosed his demands, pending a more detailed exposition the following day to some five hundred journalists. The three Western leaders gathered at the Elysée, where Eisenhower revealed himself to be deeply distressed by Khrushchev's abuse, which had now been made public, and under no illusions as to the future of the conference. I sent a formal invitation to the four delegations to meet in the afternoon "to see whether it is possible for the conference to begin its work". Khrushchev declined, orally and then in writing, saying that he could not come until the obstacles had been removed by the President of the United States. There was a solemn dirge from Macmillan about the "collapse of two years of peace-making efforts" and "the worst crisis his country had experienced since the war". A joint communiqué was published by the French, the British and the Americans declaring that the conference was breaking up without having been able to begin. On May 18, I received a farewell visit from the Soviet Prime Minister who, while bitterly denouncing the President of the United States, "a second-rate fellow, a pawn in the hands of his services, incapable of commanding," seemed worried about what might ensue. Finally, there was a chorus of praise and thanks addressed to me by all the participants. Eisenhower wrote: "I carry away with me from Paris the warmth and strength of our friendship, which I appreciate more than ever . . . and I cherish for you personally a respect and admiration which I have felt for very few men." Macmillan declared: "I should like to thank the General for the masterful way in which he presided over the discussions. . . . The three Western powers have met with a grave disappointment . . . but their friendship has been strengthened." Khrushchev cabled: "I thank you sincerely for the warm and hospitable welcome which you accorded me. . . . Allow me to express the hope that the personal contacts established between us in March and April and our conversations during the past few days will lead to greater understanding between the Soviet Union and France, to the fruitful development of their relations, and to the consolidation of peace in the world." Adenauer sent word: "How delighted I am that it was General de Gaulle who presided over the discussions in Paris! Thanks to the firmness and strength of his personality the West has avoided a grave retreat for which Germany would have been the first to pay the price." Without wishing to turn up my nose at the friendly sentiments which my correspondents were kind enough to address to me, I could not help feeling that they contained an element of relief at having emerged unscathed from a dangerous crisis, and a comforting realization that it was something, after all, to be able to go on living, even under the *status quo*.

The Soviet leaders, having moved heaven and earth to intimidate everyone, adopted an attitude of moderation during the succeeding months. Up to the end of 1960, the Kremlin made no further mention of obtaining from the White House the redress which it had demanded at the time of the Paris meeting, and also played down the plan for a separate peace treaty with East Germany. Khrushchev confined himself to making disobliging comments about the then American President, appealing in advance to whosoever might replace him.

The successor was John Kennedy. Chosen to get things done, but elected only by the skin of his teeth; placed at the head of a vast and wealthy country, but one with grave internal problems; by nature inclined to act swiftly and boldly, but hampered by the cumbersome machinery of Federal administration; entering upon the scene in a world in which American power and glory had spread far and wide, but whose every wound was suppurating and in which a hostile monolithic bloc stood opposed to America; enjoying the advantages of youth, but suffering the drawbacks of a novice – in spite of so many obstacles, the new President was determined to devote himself to the cause of freedom, justice and progress. It is true that, persuaded that it was the duty of the United States and himself to redress wrongs, he was to be drawn into ill-advised interventions. But the experience of the statesman would no doubt have gradually restrained the impulsiveness of the idealist. John Kennedy had the ability, and had it not been for the crime which killed him, might have had the time to leave his mark on our age.

Scarcely was he in office, still somewhat fumbling and over-eager, than he entered into correspondence with me – in February, to ask me to support his government in its proposal to get the United Nations to take over military, political and administrative control of the ex-Belgian Congo, a request which I was obliged to refuse; in March, to persuade me to back his plan to place Laos under the protectorship of SEATO, which I could not accept either; in April, to tell me how delighted he was to accept my invitation to Paris in the near future; and in May, to inform me that he planned to meet Khrushchev in Vienna after having seen me. In the meantime, he had sanctioned the unfortunate expedition against Cuba of the exiles in Florida. On May 31, 1961, he arrived in Paris brimming over with dynamism, he and his dazzling and cultivated wife forming a remarkably attractive couple. They were surrounded by an atmosphere of lively curiosity, and the welcome they were given by the public was enthusiastic in the extreme. The official receptions in the capital and at Versailles were of the greatest splendor. But the main thing, of course, was the series of meetings between the President, seconded by Dean Rusk and Gavin, and myself accompanied by Debré, Couve de Murville and Alphand.

From these it emerged that the attitude of the United States towards France had undergone a very decided change. The day was long past when – traditional friendship aside – Washington insisted on regarding Paris as just another of its protégés, to be dealt with, like everyone else, in the context of the various collective organizations: NATO, SEATO, UNO, OECD, IMF, etc. Now the Americans acknowledged our independence and dealt with us directly and specially. But for all that, they could not conceive of their policy ceasing to be predominant or of ours diverging from it. Basically, what Kennedy offered me in every case was a share in his projects. What he heard from me in reply was that Paris was by all means disposed to collaborate closely with Washington, but that whatever France did she did of her own accord.

When the President reverted to the question of the Congo where, at the instigation of the United States, the UN Secretary-General, Dag Hammarskjöld, was setting up a government to replace that of Patrice Lumumba, I declined to have anything to do with the operation. But it was above all on the subject of Indo-China that I pointed out to Kennedy how far apart our policies were. He made no secret of the fact that the United States were planning to intervene. In Siam, thanks to the virtually exclusive influence they exercised over the government of Marshal Sarit, they were setting up air bases. In Laos, whose neutrality was about to be reaffirmed at a conference in Geneva, they were nonetheless introducing their "military advisers" in collusion with some of the local chiefs, in spite of the reservations of Prince Souvanna Phouma and the neutralist party. In South Vietnam, after having encouraged the seizure of dictatorial power by Ngo Dinh Diem and hastened the departure of the French advisers, they were beginning to install the first elements of an expeditionary corps under cover of economic aid. John Kennedy gave me to understand that the American aim was to establish a bulwark against the Soviets in the Indo-Chinese peninsula. But instead of giving him the approval he wanted, I told the President that he was taking the wrong road.

"You will find," I said to him, "that intervention in this area will be an endless entanglement. Once a nation has been aroused, no foreign power, however strong, can impose its will upon it. You will discover this for yourselves. For even if you find local leaders who in their own interests are prepared to obey you, the people will not agree to it, and indeed do not want you. The ideology which you invoke will make no difference. Indeed, in the eyes of the masses it will become identified with your will to power. That is why the more you become involved out there against Communism, the more the Communists will appear as the champions of national independence, and the more support they will receive, if only from despair. We French have had experience of it. You Americans wanted to take our place in Indo-China. Now you want to take over where we left off and revive a war which we brought to an end. I predict that you will sink step by step into a bottomless military and political quagmire, however much you spend in men and money. What you, we and others ought to do for unhappy Asia is not to take over the running of these States ourselves, but to provide them with the means to escape from the misery and humiliation which, there as elsewhere, are the causes of totalitarian regimes. I tell you this in the name of the West."

Kennedy listened to me. But events were to prove that I had failed to convince him. On the other hand, as far as Latin America was concerned, he had adopted a policy which seemed to approximate to the one which I had outlined to him. He emphasized the importance which his government attached to a plan for an alliance concluded under the badge of progress, whereby the United States would lend massive support to the development of the other countries of the New World. However, conscious of the drawbacks which this quasi-monopoly might entail, and the abuses and repercussions which might result from it, he was anxious for Europe, and in particular France, to make its presence and influence felt more actively in Central and South America. He even asked me to arrange for the Common Market to send observers to the forthcoming Pan-American conference to be held at Punta del Este. I complimented the President on adopting a policy so out of keeping with the principle of exclusivity enshrined in the Monroe Doctrine, and told him that it was indeed my intention to strengthen existing ties between France and the Latin American states. At the same time, I reminded him of the position which France had taken up in the current world debate on international trade. My government had recommended that the prices of the raw materials and tropical produce which were the principal exports of the developing countries, notably of Latin America, and which enabled them to purchase the capital equipment which they needed, should be officially stabilized at an adequate level instead of being constantly at the mercy of harmful speculation. But on this subject, which closely affected the business interests of the United States, John Kennedy did not seem inclined to change direction.

What he had set his heart on above all else was the maintenance of his country's dominant situation in the defense of the West. He did everything he could to find ways of maintaining it without appearing to run counter to French independence. As regards the possible use of atomic weapons, he affirmed that America would certainly resort to them rather than allow Western Europe to fall into the hands of the Soviets. But in answer to the specific questions I put to him, he was unable to tell me at what point and against what targets, far or near, strategic or tactical, inside or outside Russia itself, the missiles would in fact be launched. "I am not surprised," I told him. "General Norstad, the Allied Commander-in-Chief, whom I hold in the highest esteem and who has shown me every confidence, has never been able to enlighten me on these points, which are vital to my country." Furthermore, in his desire to stop France from manufacturing her own bombs, the President proposed to commit to NATO submarines armed with Polaris rockets, new long-range atomic missiles which in his view would represent a genuinely European deterrent. Having heard him out, I could only reaffirm France's determination to become a nuclear power, since it was her only means of ensuring that no one could attempt to destroy her without the risk of self-destruction. As for the Polaris submarines, handing a few of them over to NATO would simply mean transferring them from one American command to another, leaving the decision as to the launching of the rockets in the hands of the President of the United States alone.

John Kennedy seemed somewhat anxious about what might happen at his meeting with Nikita Khrushchev. "I am going to Vienna," he told me, "to show willingness, make contact and exchange views." This caution seemed to me to be wise. I said so to the President, and added: "Since there is no fighting and the Cold War is very expensive, peace may be on the way. But it can only be based on a general and prolonged relaxation of tension. This presupposes the maintenance of the balance of power. Anything that upsets it, and in particular the German situation, would plunge the world into serious danger. Therefore, when Khrushchev summons you to change the status of Berlin, in other words to hand the city over to him, stand fast! That is the most useful service you can render to the whole world, Russia included."

Kennedy left Paris. I had been dealing with a man whose ability, whose age and whose justifiable ambition inspired immense hopes. He seemed to me to be on the point of taking off into the heights, like some great bird that beats its wings as it approaches the mountain tops. For his part, on his return to Washington he was to say in a "report to the American people" on June 6 that he had found General de Gaulle "a wise counsellor for the future and an informative guide to the history that he had helped to make. . . . I could not have more confidence in any man." Having taken stock of one another, we continued on our road, each carrying his burden and marching towards his own destiny.

As was to be foreseen, the meeting between Khrushchev and Kennedy was concerned with Berlin. Like a sea-serpent emerging from the waves, the Soviet plan for a so-called free city was brought to light once more. The American President did not allow himself to be pushed into endorsing it then and there, but he was visibly overawed by the aggressive assurance of his interlocutor. The latter had noticed this, and a few days later, in two solemn speeches, proclaimed Russia's intention of signing a separate peace treaty with East Germany and recognizing her full territorial sovereignty, including frontier control. From this John Kennedy inferred that a grave crisis was about to break out. He went on believing it and wrote to me month after month telling me that in order to avoid disaster we should have to agree to negotiate with the Soviets about Germany. Meanwhile, he intended to reinforce the defenses of Western Europe. On this last point I was in agreement with him, and as far as we ourselves were concerned, ostentatiously brought our forces on the Rhine up to strength both in manpower and material. For the rest, I outlined my position – which was neither that of Washington nor of London – in a letter to the President of the United States on July 6, and in a broadcast to the nation on the 12th.

"In the event of a crisis provoked by the Soviets," I wrote to Kennedy, "only an attitude of firmness and solidarity, adopted and affirmed in good time by America, Britain and France, will prevent unpleasant consequences. . . . Only after a long period of international *détente* – which depends entirely on Moscow – can we enter into negotiations with Russia on the German problem as a whole." Speaking to the French people over the air about the internal and external situation of our country, I declared: "The prospect of a crisis looms once more on the horizon. Of course, the trouble has been started by the Soviets. . . . They have renewed their claim to settle the fate of Berlin unilaterally, by threatening the communications of the former German capital and the situation of the American, British and French troops stationed there, unless Washington, London and Paris abandon the present status of the city in accordance with the wishes of Moscow. . . . There is no question of this being accepted. . . . As I have often had occasion to point out – in particular last year to Mr Khrushchev – if, as they proclaim, the Soviets really want peaceful co-existence, let them begin by abandoning their threats. . . . In an international atmosphere based on co-operation among States and reconciliation among peoples, a problem such as that of Germany would lose something of its urgency, and could eventually be discussed objectively by the interested powers. But with all this thundering in the wings to indicate their intention to dispose of Berlin, as though the rights of three great powers can be ignored and as though the Berliners have no right to be their own masters, the Soviets are accepting in advance the responsibility for the grave consequences which might ensue."

On the German side, Adenauer informed me that he was overwhelmed with confidence and joy by such unqualified support for Germany in her hour of danger. On the Anglo-Saxon side, Kennedy and Macmillan decided that they could not disregard France's views, and although in their correspondence they continued to harp on the possible advantages of negotiations with Khrushchev, refrained from taking active steps in this direction. On the Soviet side, the obvious inferences were drawn and there was a sudden change of attitude on the subject of Berlin. In August 1961, a wall arose which separated the sector of the city occupied by the Russians from the sectors occupied by the three Western Powers. This at once stemmed the tide of fugitives from East Germany to the West which had been gravely detrimental to the former's economic life. At the same time, however, the edifice provided physical proof of the fact that the Kremlin had given up hope of frightening the Americans, the British and the French into allowing them to lay hands on the city.

The actions of a France who was not afraid to be herself

attracted the attention of the peoples of the Third World. It is true that some of them still maintained an attitude of disapproval towards us because of the Algerian affair. Naturally enough, this was especially the case with the Moslems – the Arab countries, the Mohammedan regions of Africa outside the Community, the Islamic countries of Asia. But it was also the case with certain other States which were either "non-aligned" or anxious to be so. However, estrangement from our country was so contrary to the traditions of all these countries, and so great was their desire to see other powers besides the two big rivals among the leaders of modern civilization, that they looked with favor on the reappearance of the "Franks" – especially when our policy of colonial disengagement gradually allayed their grievances. Thus we became the object of new or renewed popular sympathies, and a number of governments decided to establish or re-establish close links with ours. The change in the political, diplomatic and material situation of France attracted an ever-increasing number of important visitors to Paris, contributing towards making our capital a more active center of world politics than it had been for generations.

In addition to twelve Black African Presidents and the President of Madagascar, all of whom were received officially, and King Hassan II of Morocco and President Bourguiba of Tunisia, who came to settle questions connected with the newly-won independence of their countries, a number of Heads of State and of Government who did not belong either to NATO or to the Warsaw Pact were our guests during this period. Indeed, several of them – the Emperor of Ethiopia, the President of Peru, the President of Argentina, Prince Rainier of Monaco, the King of Thailand, the Shah of Iran – insisted on providing us with a public token of their friendship by paying us formal State visits. Thus, independently of our relations with our allies, of the contacts which we were establishing in Eastern Europe, of the ties which united us to our former overseas dependencies, there gradually developed between us and many other countries a network of relations and agreements which placed France in a situation of growing influence and opened extensive new fields of economic and cultural activity.

Pandit Nehru came to see me twice. After a lifetime divided between rebellion and prison, he was the incarnation of independent and united India. He had changed the Gandhian mystique of patience and non-violence into an active policy of progress. This great man, for whom the cause of humanity was inseparable from the cause of the Indian people, his plans continually disappointed by the magnitude of the task, but unshakable in his faith and unwearying in his efforts, outlined to me the gigantic problems of subsistence and unity with which his country was faced, and the ways in which mine might help to alleviate them, not without ultimate benefit to herself. To India, that sea of poverty and illusion but also of values and virtues, a land eternally bedevilled by the caste system and the ravages of nature, but capable of double harvests and substantial manufactures, France was indeed in a position to provide technical, nutritional, medical and cultural aid on a considerable scale. She would find there, in return, an audience and a market from which she had been cut off since the days of La Bourdonnais, Dupleix and Lally-Tollendal. Furthermore, as upholders of the balance of power, we had every reason to wish to see India stand up to her powerful neighbor China. We gave a positive response to Pandit Nehru's appeal, as we also did, on the occasion of his visit to Paris, to the modest demands of King Mamendra of Nepal, the tiny country perched between the Indian and Chinese giants on the slopes of the Himalayas.

From Japan, one after the other, I welcomed the two successive Heads of Government, Nobusuke Kishi and Hayato Ikeda, and then Eisaku Sato, who was cut out for the leading role and was indeed later to assume it. In the name of a great nation – which had suffered terribly from the disaster it had brought upon itself but whose vitality was still intact; which had made the most of its enforced submission but was now impatient of the American yoke; whose national effort was for the time being restricted to the economic sphere, but which had displayed extraordinary qualities of industry and discipline in order to reach a pre-eminent position within that sphere – these very shrewd leaders proposed that France should extend her commercial, intellectual and cultural exchanges with a people which had hitherto been a closed book to her. Their request did not fall on deaf ears. Franco-Nipponese relations were to take on a new dimension.

The young King of Thailand, Bhumibol Adulyadej, paid an official visit to Paris, anxious to restore the atmosphere of trust which had characterized the relations which his country had established and maintained with France since the century of Louis XIV. The Sovereign told me how concerned he was at the external pressures which the Indo-Chinese crisis had brought upon his country; but he hoped to see a revival of our former active friendship. I told him that such was likewise our intention, provided that Thailand remained its own master.

Then there was the cautious and intelligent Prince Souvanna Phouma, who, after suffering several eclipses, had become Prime Minister of Laos, where our schools, our administrative advisers, our military mission and our economic enterprises played an important part in development. He spoke to me periodically about the threat to the unity and integrity of his country from the premonitory rumblings of the Vietnam war. In the north, the guerrilla dictatorship of the Pathet Lao, the movement led by Prince Souphanouvong, had established itself and was being used by Hanoi to counter American penetration. In the rest of the territory, among official, military and land-owning circles, there was a movement under the aegis of Prince Boun Oum in favor of United States intervention. Souvanna Phouma himself was in favor of a policy of neutrality. We supported him, both on the spot and internationally. We urged him to maintain his position whatever happened, since it was the only one compatible with Laos's independence and with the international agreement arrived at in Geneva. We encouraged him to emulate the attitude which Norodom Sihanouk, head of the neighboring state of Cambodia, had maintained with great energy and extreme skill. In fact, the Vietnamese tragedy was to unfold on the frontiers of these two countries and over-flow into their own territory, without either of them forfeiting their sovereignty as long as I myself was in office.

In the Middle East, our affairs were initially at the lowest ebb. The Algerian crisis and the Suez affair had shut us out of the Arab world. I naturally intended to re-establish our position in this region, where there had always been an active French presence, especially since the great political and strategic importance of the basins of the Nile, the Euphrates and the Tigris, of the Red Sea and the Persian Gulf, was now matched by economic power based on oil. It was essential for us to re-establish ourselves in Cairo, Damascus, Amman, Baghdad and Khartoum, as we had remained in Beirut, as friends and collaborators. Meanwhile, the heads of the three States bordering on the Arab world came to inquire what France was planning to do now that she was back on the scene.

I had frequent discussions with the Negus Haile Selassie. We had known each other for many years. During the war he had been the heart and soul of his people, crushed at first but finally victorious. Now he wanted to transform Ethiopia into a modern country. He played a prominent part in the efforts of emancipated Africa to organize itself. Since he ruled over a Christian State surrounded by Moslem lands, since Ethiopia's main outlet to the sea was the French port of Djibouti, since American and Soviet aid had many strings attached, the Emperor was anxious to see an increase in the many-sided help provided by France. We ourselves considered it desirable to support friendly, reasonable, time-honored Ethiopia. We were to conclude far-reaching agreements with her.

Every year I saw the Shah of Iran. During the Second World War I had met him in Teheran when, as a youthful monarch, he had inherited an empire which was prey to rival foreign pressures and the plots of domestic factions. Having maintained the unity and safeguarded the independence of his country, Reza Pahlavi was now in the process of directing the economic, intellectual and social transformation of Persia, a nation as ancient as the history of the world. How often, listening to him discoursing on the problems of development, had I admired his deep knowledge of all the realities of his country! With its considerable oil and mineral resources and its great industrial and agricultural potentialities, the vast empire of Iran, bordering on Russia, was constantly exposed to the encroachments of the Anglo-Saxons, and was anxious to find support from other quarters. The Shah was therefore prepared to offer France a preferential position in business, education, and mineral research. Appreciating the wisdom of this course, France developed a co-operative relationship with Iran which was to grow apace.

David Ben Gurion came to see me more than once. I had developed an immediate liking and respect for this doughty warrior and champion. He was the personification of Israel, which he now ruled, having presided over her foundation and her war of independence. Although France had not formally participated in the creation of this State, which was born of a joint decision by the British, the Americans and the Soviets, she had warmly approved it. I could not fail to be attracted by the grandeur of an enterprise which consisted in re-establishing an autonomous Jewish nation in a land which bore the traces of its fabulous history, and which it had owned nineteen centuries earlier. Humanly, I was gratified that the Jewish people had found a national home, and I saw it as some compensation for all the sufferings which they had endured through the ages, and which had reached a hideous climax in the massacres perpetrated by Hitler's Germany. But while the existence of Israel seemed to me to be more than justified, I considered that a great deal of caution was called for in her handling of the Arabs. The latter were her neighbors, and would always remain so. It was at their expense and on their lands that Israel had set herself up as a sovereign State. In doing so, she had wounded them in their religion and their pride. For this reason, when Ben Gurion spoke to me of his plan to settle four or five million Jews in Israel, which could not contain them within her present frontiers, and revealed to me his intention of extending these frontiers at the earliest opportunity, I urged him not to do so.

"France," I said "will help you to survive in the future as she has helped you in the past, whatever happens. But she is not prepared to provide you with the means of conquering new territory. You have brought off a remarkable achievement. Do not overdo it now. Suppress the pride which, according to Aeschylus, 'is the son of happiness and devours its father.' Rather than pursue ambitions which would plunge the East into terrible upheavals and would gradually lose you international sympathy, devote yourselves to pursuing the astonishing exploitation of a country that was until recently a desert, and to establishing harmonious relations with your neighbors." While offering these words of advice to Ben Gurion, I put a stop to irregular dealings which had developed between Tel Aviv and Paris on the military plane since the Suez expedition, whereby Israelis had become permanently attached at all levels to French military staffs and services. In particular, French co-operation in the construction of a factory near Beersheba for the transformation of uranium into plutonium – from which, one fine day, atomic bombs might emerge – was brought to an end.

Manuel Prado, the President of Peru, was anxious to make his official visit a symbol of the intellectual and emotional attachment which his country cherished for France, and which had led it, before all the other States of North and South America, to recognize Free France during the Second World War. This wise statesman, who was tormented by internal intrigues and external pressures, brought home to me the importance which the organized support of the Latin countries of the Old World, in particular France, might have for the States which had grown out of the Spanish and Portuguese empires. This confirmed me in my conviction that a united Europe, provided it was genuinely European and included the Iberians and the Lusitanians, could accomplish a task as immense as the world itself. The same thought occurred to me on the occasion of the State visit to Paris of President Arturo Frondizi, when he described to me what Argentina had already achieved, what its potentialities were, and what it needed to establish its economic life and, consequently, its foreign policy on solid foundations. The smoldering lava of Peronism was only too easily explained. Since the Buenos Aires government rejected the tutelage of the United States, it was towards Europe, and, in particular, towards France and Italy, that Frondizi turned for aid. By granting Argentina the help which she asked of us, we were adding something to the hopes of the Latin world.

As it happened – a new and momentous event – Spain had twice sent her Foreign Minister, Fernando Castiella, to France officially, and meanwhile he had met Maurice Couve de Murville with some degree of pomp on Pheasant Island on the Bidassoa. The moment had indeed arrived to restore to the relations between the two peoples something of their former scale and prestige. For General Franco's government was anxious to emerge from the isolation into which it had been plunged by its own doing as well as that of others, as a result of the Civil War and certain episodes in the Second World War. Moreover, the peace which he had re-established at home and maintained abroad had enabled modern Spain to develop her resources and her capacities, and it was in the nature of things that she should combine them with those of her familiar and complementary neighbor France. I for my part was conscious of the significance and value of the *rapprochement* which we were being invited to enter into by this, in many respects, great people to whom we were so closely akin. Our political relations were, therefore, re-established on a more cordial plane, while economic and cultural links were encouraged.

The Austrian Federal Chancellor, Alfons Gorbach, had no special arrangements to propose to us. But he was anxious to be reassured that France, in associating herself with Federal Germany, was no less staunchly in favor of the independence of his country. He received the most express assurances on this point. For in undertaking to ensure that the solidarity of the Gauls and the Teutons replaced their former enmity, I had made it a condition that there must never be another Anschluss for our neighbors across the Rhine, any more, indeed, than there should be any revision of their eastern frontiers or any encroachment of Bohemia. The treaty of 1955, by virtue of which the Russians, the French, the British and the Americans had recognized the sovereignty and the neutrality of Austria, remained one of the cornerstones of an ever-precarious but ever-essential structure: the European balance of power.

For reasons of a similar nature, combined with an immemorial friendship, we welcomed the visits of the Prime Minister of Greece. This people, whose political life is as intricate as its coastline and as jagged as its contours, was now successfully governed by Constantin Karamanlis, under whose Premiership its economy and standard of living had made considerable strides. Karamanlis naturally hoped that France would take a more active part in furthering this progress, and he asked us to help Greece to obtain from the Common Market a treaty of association whereby trade would be increased. Moreover, as Prime Minister of a kingdom which was constantly exposed to the designs of its neighbors, continually apprehensive of Russia's possible Balkan ambitions, irritated by the excessive solicitude of the Anglo-Saxons and concerned about what was happening in Cyprus, he was anxious to regain the traditional support of Paris. His desires would be met.

I also received – with some emotion – Jean Lesage who had become Prime Minister of Quebec. He came to discuss matters which were unmistakably French. For his main purpose was to arrange for direct aid from France to the Canadian branch of her people, lost to her sovereignty but, pressed on all sides on American soil by elements of other origins, anxious to remain faithful to its language and its identity and, for this purpose, to have its own means of livelihood and education. There was no precedent for Jean Lesage's mission. It testified to the apprehensions of the French Canadian community in Canada and the hope which the revival of the former motherland had rekindled among them. It must be said that Quebec was making a great effort on its own behalf, building more and more schools, developing technical education, expanding the universities of Quebec, Montreal and Sherbrooke, setting up a gigantic hydro-electric scheme, Hydro-Quebec, and endeavoring to provide itself with factories that were not foreign-owned. The Quebec government and the Paris government settled directly between themselves the details of the aid program which France was henceforth to devote to the French people of Canada.

Thus, from every part of the world, people's attentions and preoccupations were now directed towards us. At the same time, on the Continent, the initiatives and actions that might lead towards unity emanated from us: Franco-German solidarity, the plan for an exclusively European grouping of the Six, the beginnings of co-operation with the Soviet Union. Besides this, when the peace of the world was at stake, it was to our country that the leaders of East and West came to thrash things out. Our independence responded not only to the aspirations and the self-respect of our own people, but also to what the whole world expected of us. For France, it brought with it powerful reasons for pride and at the same time a heavy burden of obligations. But is that not her destiny? For me, it offered the attraction, and also the strain, of an onerous responsibility. But what else was I there for?

The Head of State

❦

The new institutions were in place. From the summit of the State, how was I to shape them? To a large extent it was incumbent upon me to do so. For the reasons which had led me to this position, and the conditions in which I exercised it, did not derive from written texts. Moreover, they had no precedent in our history. Under the monarchy, by virtue of a traditional principle accepted by all, including those who rebelled, the King was by heredity the sole source of authority, even when he bestowed rights or delegated functions. The plebiscites which installed each of our two Emperors conferred upon them total authority for life, whatever the institutional framework which surrounded them. On the other hand, under the Third and Fourth Republics, the President, elected for seven years by parliament alone, had the power of ultimate decision solely for the purpose of commuting the death penalty, although he was partially invested with the appearances of sovereignty and could exercise his influence in certain eventualities, and although everything was decreed or promulgated in his name. But in my case, it was without hereditary right, without a plebiscite, without an election, but simply in response to the silent but imperative call of France, that I had formerly been led to take the responsibility for her defense, her unity, and her destiny. If I had now assumed the country's highest office, it was because, since then, I had come to be accepted as its final refuge. This was a fact which, alongside the literal provisions of the

Constitution, had inevitably to be taken into account. Whatever interpretation might be given to such and such an Article, it was in any case to de Gaulle that Frenchmen turned. It was from him that they expected the solution of their problems. It was in him that they placed their trust, to him that they addressed their reproaches. For confirmation of the way in which people laid all their hopes as well as their disappointments at his door, one had only to listen to speeches, conversations, songs, hear the shouts and the murmurs, read what was printed in the newspapers or plastered on the walls. For my part, I felt the right and the duty to uphold the national interest to be intrinsic to my very being.

It is true that the Constitution which I had had adopted by the country defined the functions of the various authorities, but without contradicting the idea which the people and I shared as to my obligations. That the President should be, as was laid down, "the protector of the independence of the nation, of the integrity of its territory and of respect for treaties, and provide, by his arbitration, for the regular functioning of the public authorities and the continuity of the State" – this was no more than the verbal expression of the essential role which was mine in my own eyes and in those of the citizens. True, there was a government which "decides the policy of the nation". But everyone knew and expected that it would proceed from my choice and would act only with my blessing. True, there was a parliament, one of whose two Houses had the power to censure the government. But for the mass of the nation and myself there was nothing in this to limit my responsibility, the more so since I was legally empowered to dissolve the recalcitrant assembly if need be, to appeal to the country over and above parliament by way of referendum, and, in the event of national crisis, to take any measures which I deemed necessary. Nevertheless, precisely because my office, as now constituted, was the product of my own initiative and the sentiment which existed towards me in the national consciousness, it was essential that a fundamental accord should exist and be maintained between the people and me. And this accord was plainly expressed in the referenda which were held in order to reply to what I requested. In short, nothing, either in my own mind or in public feeling or in the text of the Constitution, affected what events had established not long since as to the nature and extent of my task. Thus it was for me to settle the terms on which I should discharge it, without in any way disregarding the wording of the sacred texts.

Apart from exceptional situations which demanded unexpectedly a positive reaction from the State and for which I accepted direct responsibility, my activities consisted mainly in laying down guide-lines, determining goals and issuing directives for the benefit of the organ of prognosis, preparation and execution which the government constituted. This normally took place in Cabinet. Once a week, seldom more often, always under my chairmanship, the Cabinet met. All the ministers attended, as well as the state secretaries, for a government can have only one policy and for those who assume it, solidarity is indivisible. Opposite me was Michel Debré. On my right, then as always, was André Malraux. The presence at my side of this inspired friend, this devotee of lofty destinies, gave me a sense of being insured against the commonplace. The conception which this incomparable witness to our age had formed of me did much to fortify me. I knew that, in debate, when the subject was grave, his flashing judgments would help to dispel the shadows. The session would proceed in accordance with the agenda which I had drawn up and circulated in advance, normally on the basis of what the Prime Minister had requested and what the Secretary-General to the Presidency, Geoffroy de Courcel, and the Secretary-General to the Government, Roger Belin, had jointly presented to me. These two high officials, at the center of affairs and conversant with everything that went on, were the silent spectators of the meeting and recorded the decisions taken. By means of "briefs" from each of the ministers, every question that concerned the public authorities was submitted to the Cabinet in turn, some giving rise to lengthy statements and general discussions, others calling for the adoption of a draft bill or decree or communiqué, and others necessitating an immediate solution. Anyone could ask leave to speak; it was always granted. In the most important cases, I invited all the members of the Cabinet to express their views. In any event the Prime Minister would present his arguments and proposals. Finally, I would give my own view of the matter and formulate a conclusion. After which, the "summary of decisions" was drawn up by me, and the Minister of Information came to me to receive his directives as to what he was to tell the public about the meeting which had just closed. I may add that not a week passed without my giving audience to the Prime Minister at least once, and discussing with him at leisure the progress of affairs. In addition to this, I received him before opening each Cabinet meeting in order to establish what decisions were to be taken. Moreover, the members of the government all came to see me in rotation, each of them giving me an account of what he was doing and planning to do and taking cognizance of my intentions. Finally, unless there was extreme urgency, restricted Cabinets grouping the ministers concerned and their principal officials, examined with me the problems of the moment. Whatever decisions were taken, rightly or wrongly, at my orders during this period, I do not believe they were ever taken lightly.

Although no sphere of public affairs was neglected by me or made my exclusive preserve, I naturally concentrated on the questions which were of the greatest general importance. From the political point of view they were basically those affecting national unity, such as the Algerian problem, the new relationships of association which were replacing our sovereignty in the French Union, the status of private education which put an end to sixty years of scholastic warfare, the measures to be taken in the agricultural sphere, either by ourselves or in the framework of the Common Market, or the first steps towards participation in the running of enterprises represented by the profit-sharing scheme. In the economic and financial fields, it was above all in connection with the Plan, the budget, the monetary situation, that I had to intervene, for these were all-important, and moreover demanded indisputable arbitration which naturally devolved on me. Our foreign policy also required my attention, since it committed our country in the long term and in a crucial manner. Indeed the Constitution explicitly states that the President of the Republic is "the protector of the independence of the nation," and lays it down that it is for him to negotiate and ratify treaties, that our ambassadors are his personal representatives and those of foreign States are accredited to him. Finally, needless to say, I set my seal on our defense, the transformation of which followed lines laid down by me and whose morale and discipline came under my purview – this for obvious reasons arising from my background, but also because in our new institutions the President is responsible for the "integrity of the territory," is "the head of the armed forces," and presides over "the councils and committees of national defence."

My relationships with my government were thus continuous and extensive. Nevertheless, its role was not usurped by mine. It is true of course that, having heard its views, it was for me to determine the overall direction which it must follow. But the conduct of the administration was left entirely to the ministers and I never gave orders to officials over their heads. It is true that the Cabinet meetings which I held gave rise to decisions. But all those who took part could express themselves freely and fully, and besides, no one becomes a minister unless he wants to, and he can always cease to be one of his own free will. It is true that, whereas I sometimes telephoned Michel Debré or one of his colleagues, I was never called to the telephone by any of them, my staff intercepting all calls. But any member of the government, when he sent me a report, was sure that I would read it, and when he asked for an audience was certain that I would receive him. In short, I kept myself at a distance, but by no means in an ivory tower.

In view of the importance and the extent of the duties of the Prime Minister, he could not but be "my man." So he was, chosen expressly, maintained for a long time in office, collaborating closely and constantly with me. But since our respective activities were not of course separate but distinct, since for every problem that arose, the political and administrative factors involved must be presented to me without disguise, since it was right for the ideas and the policies of the Head of State to be complemented, reinforced and even at times counterbalanced by an initiative, a capacity, a will other than his own, it was essential for the Prime Minister to assert his own personality. Michel Debré did so vigorously, whether in the conception, in which he shared, the planning, which he organized, or the execution, which he directed, of governmental policies. Just as, on board a ship, the time-honored experience of mariners demands that the chief officer should have his part to play alongside the captain, so in our new Republic the executive comprised, after the President who was dedicated to all that was basic and permanent, a Prime Minister concerned with day-to-day matters. Moreover, I felt it advisable for the latter to carry the burden of his office, more onerous and exhausting than any other, for a specified period in the life of the administration, and thereafter to be placed in reserve. On appointing Michel Debré, I had made known to him my intention in this respect. When the new institutions, of which he was one of the principal architects, had proved themselves, when the economic, financial and monetary recovery of the country was assured, when the new association between France and its former dependencies was established, when the Algerian problem was settled, when the National Assembly elected in 1958 had accomplished the far-reaching legislative program expected of it, when all the dangers were past and a very different political period was about to open, I judged that the moment had come to relieve my distinguished Prime Minister of the present in anticipation of the future. In April 1962, Georges Pompidou took his place.

Throughout these forty months, just as there was no decline in the ability, diligence and devotion of Michel Debré, so there was no gap in the cohesion of the government appointed on his recommendation. Of course, as time went on, there were changes in the composition of this body of twenty-seven persons. The following left it: Félix Houphouët-Boigny, when the Ivory Coast elected him President; Antoine Pinay, after he had refused to be Minister of State on leaving the Ministry of Finance;

Max Fléchet, who followed him; Jean Berthoin and Félix Chatenet, one after the other, for reasons of health; André Boulloche, who, having introduced the private education bill, preferred not to put it into execution himself; Jacques Soustelle and Bernard Cornut-Gentille, because of Algeria; Roger Houdet who, after a period at the Ministry of Agriculture, decided to resume his seat in the Senate; and Robert Lecourt and Henri Rochereau, to become respectively the President of the High Court of Justice and a member of the Commission of the European Economic Community. The following entered the Government: Wilfrid Baumgartner, who, however, resigned before the end of his term for private reasons, Pierre Messmer, Louis Terrenoire, Jean Foyer, Lucien Paye, Edgard Pisani, Robert Boulin, François Missoffe, Jean de Broglie and Christian de la Malène. But if there were certain changes of personnel, André Malraux, Edmond Michelet, Maurice Couve de Murville, Roger Frey, Louis Joxe, Pierre Guillaumat, Jean-Marcel Jeanneney, Robert Buron, Paul Bacon, Bernard Chenot, Pierre Sudreau, Maurice Bokanowski, Raymond Triboulet, Mademoiselle Nafissa Sid Cara, Joseph Fontanet and Valéry Giscard d'Estaing remained members of the government from first to last. Of course, all these ministers were very different from one another. While many of them came from various parliamentary groups, a number of others were recruited direct from the public service. If they were all equally attracted by the call of office, zealous in their duty, devoted to the national interest, they were not all equal in sagacity and ability. While the eldest was nearing his seventies, the youngest was only thirty-two. But seeing them at grips with problems as urgent and complicated as any which ever presented themselves to the State, and moreover always hampered by limited means, I considered them as a whole comparable to the finest ministries in the history of France. As long as they were in office, they could count upon my sincere esteem and friendship. From all of them I received proof of loyal attachment. In all of them I sensed a conviction of the historic nature of the task of national renewal in which they were engaged.

This unity and stability, contrasting so strikingly with the previous chaos, infuriated the various pressure groups in national and international organs of opinion. But public authority certainly benefited therefrom, the more so because, at the same time, parliament had undergone changes in its activities and procedures which separated its powers from those of the executive and, by eliminating the chronic confusion, established them on a stable basis. No doubt many parliamentarians suffered under the constraints imposed upon them by the new rules and resented the fact that the government had ceased to be continually at their mercy. No doubt those who in the past could hope to become ministers again and again as a result of governmental crises now felt somewhat thwarted. No doubt, too, as a result of this, a certain ferment disappeared which used to animate the life and the oratory of parliament and without which its debates lost something of their dramatic attraction. Moreover, the complexity of the modern society for which the Chambers now had to legislate had made their task more and more complicated. The subjects of their deliberations were so many and varied that discussion proliferated. But since the sessions and sittings were limited, the result was that "speaking time" was greatly reduced. Because of this, and because of the primacy of technical considerations and the regimentation of opinions, debates were no longer interspersed with the impassioned generalities, exhortations and flights of eloquence with which the great orators of the past used to stir and charm their audiences. A sort of morose mechanization reigned over the assemblies. Since I had always revered the oratorical talents which enlivened the French parliamentary scene, this eclipse of rhetoric inspired in me a certain melancholy. But I consoled myself by reflecting on the disorder created by the parliamentary "games, poisons and delights" which were the keynote of the Third and Fourth Republics and which destroyed them both.

On taking up office, I sent a message to parliament explaining that this was how things must be: "The nature of our age and the peril incurred by the State as a result of its failure to

discern it, have led the French people to effect a profound reform of the parliamentary institution. This has now been enshrined in the new Constitution. It remains to put into practice
the great changes introduced in the functioning of the assemblies
and the relationship between the powers. In doing this, the
National Assembly will ensure within its own sphere the efficacy,
the stability and the continuity of the republican State which
are essential to the recovery of France . . . . That will be the
decisive test of parliament." Subsequently, I did my best to see
that there was no gradual and piecemeal dilution of the basic
reform of the representative system whereby parliament, while
debating and voting the laws and supervising the executive,
had ceased to be the fountainhead of policy and government.
Hence the messages which I addressed to the two Houses on
several occasions, notifying them of major initiatives which I
had taken on my own authority without reference to them.
Hence, on the formation of the Debré ministry and then of its
successor, I refrained from consulting the parliamentary groups
because this would have been, as of old, to bring them into an
operation which was no longer within their province. Hence I
invited a number of personalities who were not members of
parliament to become members of the government. Hence I requested the government to refer to the Constitutional Council
certain rules of procedure which the two Houses were trying to
arrogate to themselves and which exceeded their powers; by
this means, the rules were in effect amended. Hence, in three
and a half years, I authorized the Prime Minister to ask for a
vote of confidence only four times, since the right of censure
sufficed. Hence, in March 1960, I refused to allow a special
session to be called to discuss agricultural problems, a session
which, although it was requested, for obvious motives of electoral
propaganda, by more than half of the deputies and senators,
could only take place under the terms of the Constitution if I
decreed it. Hence, finally, considering that Georges Pompidou
was qualified to become my Prime Minister in his turn, I
appointed him to this office although he was neither a member
of parliament nor in any way connected with it.

Nevertheless, while preventing the institution from returning by roundabout ways to the abuses which had compromised it and threatened to destroy the State, I showed it the respect which I felt to be its due, convinced as I was that it was indispensable to our country provided that it did not go beyond the limits laid down for it. Indeed, in default of being able to make direct contact with the two Houses, I kept myself regularly informed about what was happening there. Jacques Chaban-Delmas, President of the National Assembly, often came to see me. I had a high opinion of his subtle understanding of affairs and his affability with people which marked him out as a model administrator of the affairs of the Chamber, whether from the chair or in the handling of men, groups and committees. Having leapt to the forefront of action in the Resistance at a very youthful age, he had remained prominent in politics without the years seeming to affect either his enthusiasm or his looks. But if he appeared open to influence, eclectic in his ideas, flexible in his dealings, Chaban-Delmas had made up his mind to follow me ever since 1940 and had remained attached to the cause of national salvation and renewal. As long as I directed this struggle, I found that his adroitness matched his talents without blurring his integrity.

The President of the Senate, Gaston Monnerville, also confided to me what he thought about political matters. He had not yet taken up the attitude which was eventually to estrange him from me. This clever Antillean[1] was well suited to his functions. He was passionately concerned about everything to do with the attributions and the prestige of the Assembly over which he had presided literally since its foundation. He was dogmatic in the conception he had long ago formed of the republican regime. At the time of Vichy and the Occupation, this conception, combined with his patriotism, had led him into the Resistance. But now, set in a rigid mould, it tended to make him misprize a necessary evolution and judge it unfairly.

In addition to my discussions with the two Presidents, I had many other links with parliament. The secretariats of both

[1] *Antillais*: from the Antilles, or French West Indies.

Chambers, and those of the parliamentary groups and commissions, were regularly received at the Elysée. Innumerable individual audiences brought a variety of deputies and senators into my presence, and most of the time I took a great interest in the remarks of these men who represented a sounding-board for the anxieties and wishes of the electorate. Besides, my brother Pierre had been Senator for the Seine and Chairman of the Paris Municipal Council, and my brother-in-law Jacques Vendroux was Deputy for and Mayor of Calais. My visits to the provinces always included meetings with the local members of parliament to discuss the local situation. No official ceremony or reception failed to find the representatives of the people at the side of the Head of State. Finally, I made a careful and to a large extent rewarding study of the principal debates in parliament, for their results were on the whole positive. It is true that, as long as the Algerian drama lasted, the parties more or less resigned themselves to self-imposed silence; it is true that the rules laid down by the Constitution were such that a ministerial crisis was difficult to provoke; it is true that members were aware that a dissolution would be pronounced as soon as a motion of censure was passed; it is true that there existed in the National Assembly a group of more than two hundred members elected to support de Gaulle and, consequently, his government and who, apart from a few dissidents who could be counted on the fingers of two hands, remained compact and resolute; and it is true, finally, that the Prime Minister, who arranged the timetable of the two Assemblies, organized their co-operation with the executive and took part in their debates, enjoyed among members of parliament the respect which his talents deserved. At all events, the legislative task achieved during this period was a very considerable one.

Independently of the budgets which, regularly discussed and always voted on time, maintained the finances of the State in equilibrium and helped to bring order into the economic, administrative and social spheres, a considerable corpus of reforms was accomplished by the law. For example, national development programs were put in hand as regards basic industries, universities, schools, public health and hospitals, scientific research, housing and sport. A new framework for our agriculture was decided on, together with the means necessary for its transformation in terms of direction, investment, markets, social insurance, training, irrigation, etc. The upgrading of workers was facilitated by vocational training, adaptation to new jobs, the creation of university institutes of labor, and promotion to the rank of technician and engineer. On the basis of the report of the Commission presided over by Pierre-Olivier Lapie and reflecting a wide range of experience and opinion, the question of State aid to private schools, the control to be exercised over them and the obligations imposed on them was settled. Steps were taken to ensure the protection of historical monuments and the carrying out of work to restore the most important of them to their original splendor. The Paris conurbation was established as a "region" and a "district" was created setting it up as a unit for planning purposes. The rational development of the overseas *départements* and territories was put in hand. The pernicious privilege of the private distillers[1] was limited. A plan for the modernization of national defense was adopted whereby it would henceforth be based on three elements: an atomic force destined to act on land, at sea and in the air; a combined force of large units of the Army, the Navy and the Air Force trained for attack, maneuver and intervention; and an overall system of territorial defense.

The national ordeals which shattered the executive and legislative powers had not left the judicial power unscathed. On resuming the leadership, I found it in a state of acute depression. This was true above all as regards recruitment to it. Although the standard of entry for the judiciary had been lowered, although it had been thrown open to women, and although lawyers and professors of law were admitted to it more or less automatically, it was becoming impossible to fill all the vacancies and there was a danger that those who eventually filled them might include a considerable number of incompetents. The fact was that this pre-eminently honorable and disinterested

[1] *Bouilleurs de cru.*

profession offered few material advantages at a time when business seemed to offer a great many. In addition, the moral strains which events had inflicted on a body more susceptible to them than most had reduced at once its attractiveness and its cohesion. Such were the cumulative consequences of the oaths of allegiance imposed by Vichy, of the pressures which that regime and the enemy had exerted on it to ensure the condemnation of resisters and opposition elements, of the sanctions taken against judges who refused to comply – all of which had been followed by the inevitable purge carried out at the time of the Liberation. More recently, the judicial career, which demands independence, had suffered from the intrusion of politics into its administration, since under the terms of the 1946 Constitution several members of the Higher Council of the Judiciary had been appointed by the National Assembly, in other words by the parties. Finally, the malaise of the judiciary was aggravated by its antiquated structure – the courts being badly distributed and too numerous for a population now more and more concentrated in the towns – and by the inadequacy of its technical and material resources at a time when its function had taken on a growing complexity.

A thoroughgoing judicial reform was thus essential. On December 22, 1958 I put it into effect, on the basis of proposals by Michel Debré, then Minister of Justice, in two ordinances outlining organic laws linked to the new Constitution, one relating to the status of the judiciary, the other to its Higher Council. In order to rationalize the recruitment and training of judges, magistrates and public prosecutors and give them a preliminary training, a Center for Judicial Studies was set up in Bordeaux which would represent for the judiciary what the National School of Administration was to the civil service. In order that members of the judiciary should enjoy a material and moral situation worthy of their status, the hierarchy was reduced to two grades, thus regularizing and accelerating promotion, salaries were considerably increased, and the Higher Council of the Judiciary was removed from politics by changes in its composition and its functions. To adapt the administration of justice to the present structure of the country, the small local courts[1] were abolished and replaced by a much smaller number of higher courts[2] while the assize courts were reinforced, and procedures simplified from top to bottom of the system.

At the Elysée I presided over the Higher Council of the Judiciary, whose secretariat was run by Pierre Chabrand. There, the proposals of the Keeper of the Seals[3] or the Supreme Court of Appeal[4] were submitted to me with a view to nominations, postings or honors; appeals against the death sentence were presented to me; and the views of the Minister and the nine other members were expressed to me on every subject whether general or particular. To ensure that nothing was said that was in any way influenced by my own way of seeing things, I did not formulate my decisions until the end of the session.

Outside the Council, I followed the application of the great reform through the reports made to me by the Minister, Edmond Michelet, an open-hearted, generous-minded, loyal companion whose illusions had been darkened by the strains of the Resistance, the horrors of deportation and the bruises of the political struggle but whose natural humanity had remained unimpaired. I listened to Nicolas Battestini, First President of the Supreme Court of Appeal, and my friend Maurice Patin, President of the Criminal Chamber. I sought the advice of the First Presidents of the Assize Courts and the public prosecutors whom I received periodically in Paris, and with whom I made contact during my provincial journeys. Thus I was able to see the members of the French judiciary emerging from the doubt and bitterness into which they had often been plunged, though remaining exposed to the tribulations of our age. I found the great majority of them modest in their way of life, dignified and upright in their conduct, but for that reason somewhat isolated in the midst of a materially grasping and morally confused society. I found them scrupulous in their investigations

[1] *Juges de paix* and *tribunaux d'arrondissement*.

[2] *Tribunaux de grande instance*.

[3] *Garde des Sceaux* – the Minister of Justice in his formal capacity as head of the judiciary.

[4] *Cour de Cassation*.

and judgments, but browbeaten and upset by the uproar of the specialists in the manipulation of public opinion, who invariably seek after scandal and take the side of impunity. In short, I found them wedded to their exacting duties which they performed conscientiously and often with distinction, but at the mercy of a *Zeitgeist* in which the prevailing trends were those of laxness and mediocrity. However, the effort of renovation undertaken in this field as in others was beginning to bear fruit. As a result of the reform, the position of judges and the functioning of the courts improved gradually, the number and the quality of young candidates for the Bench increased, and the judicial power on which the human condition and the foundations of the State in so many respects depend was strengthened.

All in all, I exercised my functions in such a way as to lead the executive, to maintain the legislature within the limits laid down for it, and to guarantee the independence and dignity of the judiciary. But in addition to this I was actively involved with the great advisory councils, instead of having merely formal and conventional relations with them. The Constitutional Council, which had just been created, was in regular liaison with me, notably in the person of its president, Léon Noël. He brought to the task of advising me on the functioning of our new institutions not only a vast experience, juridical, administrative, diplomatic and political, but a wide-ranging mind and the ardor of a patriot. In the Economic and Social Council, the representatives of the country's principal activities examined government proposals relating to progress and development, in particular the national Plan. I consulted their principal spokesmen: the President, Emile Roche, well-informed about everything, Robert Bothereau and Gabriel Ventejol of the CGTFO,[1] Maurice Bouladoux and Georges Levard of the CFTC,[2] Georges Lebrun of the CGT,[3] André Malterre and Roger Millot of the CGC,[4] Léon Gingembre of the PME,[5] Joseph Courau and

[1] *Force Ouvrière:* Socialist trade unions.
[2] *Confédération française des travailleurs chrétiens:* Catholic trade unions.
[3] *Confédération générale du travail:* Communist-led trade unions.
[4] *Confédération générale des cadres:* white collar and supervisory staffs' union.
[5] *Petites et moyennes entreprises:* small-business pressure group.

Albert Génin of the FNSEA,[1] Marcel Deneux and Michel Debatisse of the Young Farmers, René Blondelle of the Chamber of Agriculture, Georges Villiers of the Employers' Federation, Georges Desbrière of the Chamber of Commerce, etc. I listened with interest to these qualified men, all the more readily because of the restrained tone of their remarks during our discussions, by contrast with the violence of their public declarations. Uncompromising as they were in asserting their opposing points of view, they knew that the State was the arbiter and often the dispenser, and it was upon the State that each of them focused his grievances and his demands.

The *Conseil d'Etat* was as always an intellectual elite trained in the study of law and economics, the youngest of whom had recently emerged from the National School of Administration. In its juridical investigations and its settling of disputes, many of its members, of whatever age, remained faithful to the principles of impartiality which are its justification and which made its reputation. Several of them who were attached to me, and a number of others seconded to administrative posts or to various ministries displayed remarkable ability. But there were some who allowed themselves to be influenced by the currents of politics. This was particularly the case with those who, having left the Council to become members of parliament and even ministers, had rejoined it after electoral defeat. As a result, the "advices" formulated in the Palais-Royal on the decrees and bills prepared by the government were sometimes influenced by political considerations. René Cassin, who both in war and peace was a champion of democracy and an apostle of the rights of man, and later Alexandre Parodi, who was held in high honor for the great services he had rendered to the Republic when danger was at its height, were the successive directors of the Council. They explained its workings to me with a clarity that enabled me to distinguish what to take and what to leave. The situation of the judiciary, its needs and its wishes, and the functioning of the Court of Cassation, still composed of eminent judges but snowed under with an accumulation of

[1] *Fédération nationale des syndicats des exploitants agricoles:* main peasant union.

cases and lacking means and manpower, were the subjects on which I was enlightened by the First President Battestini and the Attorney-General Besson. The role of the Board of Audit[1] was restored to its old prestige, as soon as some budgetary stability and order had been restored to government expenditure. Its First President Roger Léonard and Procurator-General Vincent Bourrel, when they came to submit to me the results of the auditing of parliament, knew that I would use them myself, all the more so because, the long-standing arrears having been made up, they applied to the current financial year.

The Delegates-General for Scientific Research, first Pierre Piganiol then André Maréchal, kept me informed of the more and more extensive work in that field, of the ever-increasing desires and aspirations of scientists and the ever-increasing needs of the laboratories. I followed closely the activities of the Atomic Energy Commissariat through the reports of the High Commissioner Francis Perrin, the General Administrator Pierre Couture and the Director of the military application division, Jacques Robert, the last-named being the moving spirit behind the research, building and testing from which our nuclear armament emerged. What was happening in the armed forces was expounded to me regularly by the Head of the Joint Chiefs of Staff, a position occupied successively by Generals Ely, Olié and Ailleret, as well as the Chief of Staff and the Inspector-General of each of the three services. Their reports for my guidance usefully complemented those which I received from the Minister. Finally, I had frequent dealings with General Catroux, Grand Chancellor of the Legion of Honor. To crown his magnificent career, he drew up the new code whereby the Order would be cured of its inflation sickness and prepared the bill which was soon to inaugurate the National Order of Merit. As for the Order of the Liberation, the exemplary life which it led, and with which its Chancellor, General Ingold, succeeded by General Claude Hettier de Boislambert, kept me conversant, was a great comfort to me.

On a completely different plane, but one which I set much

[1] *Cour des Comptes.*

store by, I received several discreet but very interesting visits from the Comte de Paris. High-principled and punctilious, the heir of our kings was solely concerned with the unity, the social progress, and the prestige of our country, and spoke to me about these matters in the same remarkable way as they were dealt with in the *Bulletin* which was the mouthpiece for his ideas. I may say that I drew profit and encouragement from each of my meetings with the Head of the House of France.

The men who, in the top ranks of the civil service, were responsible for the implementation of government policy, also came to see me, at my summons, to give me an account of their actions and their problems. First of all the heads of the various government departments: their task was a growing one as the administrative domain expanded. Likewise the directors of the public services and the nationalized industries: no doubt they were spared the pangs of competition, but, on the other hand, they were subject to the control of the Ministry of Finance and, at the same time, the costly claims of the unions. Likewise the prefects: they were answerable for everything that happened in the *départements,* notably as regards economic and social matters which were now very much to the fore, but the fact was that their authority was universally recognized and they were the effective leaders of local life. Likewise our ambassadors: for them too, practical, technical and commercial questions had become a vital part of their function, and in this respect as in others they were able to gauge the importance of the restoration of France's political credit. Likewise the educational authorities[1]: they were gratified to see new universities, colleges and schools springing up, and an influx of new teachers, but they had a premonition of the upheavals which the rising tide of student numbers would sooner or later bring in its wake, and they were concerned about the crisis which would eventually break out in their establishments, where part of the teaching body was continually at odds with authority, whatever it might be, and compromised its traditional prestige by repeated strikes which scandalized its disciples. Likewise the commanders of the

[1] *Recteurs d'Académie:* heads of academic regions.

military, naval and air regions: none of them had been led astray by events in Algeria though they had been sorely tried by them; all were anxious above all to see French power restored.

By and large, the various corps of the French civil service[1] formed a capable and dignified whole. Thanks to the practical sense and organizing ability which inspired the original architects of the edifice, it had lasted since Napoleon in spite of all our trials and the incredible instability of our regimes and governments. True, the methods of recruitment needed to be made more flexible, the administrative divisions widened, to adapt these bodies to the changing pattern which had brought economic, social and educational factors to the forefront of public activity and was transforming France from a rural and village existence to an industrial and urban one. But their original conception, and the experience they had acquired over the years, remained valid, and the nation as a whole, while ready to carp and jibe at them, had no inclination to destroy them. They for their part appreciated the quasi-revolution which had given the Republic a head. An atmosphere of cheerful contentment pervaded the gatherings at which their representatives congregated around General de Gaulle, as at the Elysée for the celebration of the New Year, or in the provinces on the occasion of my visits. All were delighted to see that the edifice of the State now had its keystone, cementing the pillars together.

But it was to the people themselves, and not only the notables, that I wished to be linked both visually and aurally. The French people must see me and hear me, and I must see and hear them. Television and public journeys gave me the opportunity to do so.

During the war, I had made much use of radio. Whatever I had been able to say and disseminate by this means had certainly contributed towards strengthening national unity against the enemy. After my departure, since I was not allowed on the air, my voice had been heard only in local gatherings. But now the combination of the microphone and the screen presented

[1] *Les Corps constitués.*

itself to me at the very moment when this innovation was beginning its lightning development. Here, suddenly, was an unprecedented means of being present everywhere. Provided, of course, that these appearances were successful. The risk was not the first or the only one I had taken, but it was considerable.

If, since the heroic days, I had always forced myself when making speeches in public to do so without consulting notes, when speaking in the studio it had been my habit to read from a script. But now the televiewers could see de Gaulle on the screen while listening to him over the air. In order to remain faithful to my image, I would have to address them as though we were face to face, without paper and without spectacles. However, since my talks to the nation were delivered *ex cathedra,* and were inevitably the subject of all sorts of analyses and exegeses, I wrote them with care, and had to make a considerable effort to ensure that what I said in front of the cameras was exactly what I had prepared in advance. This septuagenarian, sitting alone behind a table under relentless lights, had to appear animated and spontaneous enough to seize and hold attention, without compromising himself by excessive gestures and misplaced grimaces.

Many times in those four years the French people by the million met General de Gaulle in this way. Always I spoke to them less about themselves than about France. Taking care not to encourage some among them at the expense of others, to indulge one or other of their various components, to flatter this or that particular interest, in other words not to use the time-honored recipes of demagogy, I endeavored on the contrary to unite hearts and minds on the basis of what they had in common, to make them all feel that they belonged to the same whole, to rouse the national spirit. On each occasion I aimed to show where we stood collectively as regards the problem of the moment, to indicate how we could and should resolve it, to bolster our will and confidence. The talk would last approximately twenty minutes. That evening, the show would appear on the universal stage without any mutterings or applause to give me an indication of what the vast and mysterious audience thought of it. But later there would arise from the news media, alongside the modest choir of favorable voices, the noisy chorus of doubt, criticism and persiflage, stigmatizing my "self-satisfaction." On the other hand, it would transpire that, in the depths of the national consciousness, the impression produced could be summed up by such remarks as "It's the real thing!" or "De Gaulle never changes!" or "France is really something, after all!" Thus the required effect was achieved, since the people had lifted up their heads and looked towards the heights.

However, my talks were necessarily too brief for me to deal in detail with major questions. For this purpose, I used the press conference, also televised and broadcast, and reported verbatim in most of the newspapers. Twice a year, the delegates of every French publication, the representatives of all the international agencies and the correspondents of the entire foreign press were invited to the Elysée, together with a few specialized officials from the ministries and embassies. The government would be there, grouped beside me. A thousand spectators would be seated in the banqueting hall to take part in this species of ritual ceremony, to which the memories of the past and the curiosity of the present gave a world-wide appeal. It was the most elusive kind of audience, made up of people whose sensitivity to human values is blunted by their profession, whose judgments make no impression unless they are caustic, and who often, with an eye to headlines, circulation, sensation, hope to have failures rather than successes to report. Nevertheless, beneath their coldness, their irony, their scepticism, I could detect the eagerness of these communicators and the respect of these connoisseurs. The interest they showed me was reciprocated on my part. As a result, an atmosphere of sustained attention pervaded the assembly and made it, each time, even more of an event.

In any case I always saw to it that these press conferences were an occasion for announcing major decisions, as well as for a survey of current problems. The subjects were naturally dictated by circumstances. What I intended to say about each of them was prepared in advance as regards basic essentials. Moreover, my press officer saw to it before the meeting that questions would be put to me thereon. These I would answer one by one, in such a way that the whole added up to the affirmation of a policy. Of course there was no lack of malicious questions aimed at embarrassing me. I would put a stop to these attempts with a few sallies which raised a laugh. For an hour and a half, the actions and intentions of France as regards her institutions, her economy, her finances, social questions, decolonization, Algeria, foreign affairs, defense, etc. were brought to light, more frankly and completely, I genuinely believe, than they had ever been before. No sooner had I finished than there was a rush towards the teleprinters, the telephones, the news rooms. The following day would appear the declarations which the spokesmen of all shades of opinion invariably lavished on my remarks, the comments and interpretations given by the French and foreign radios, and the articles about them, generally hostile, or at least sharp and malicious, which appeared in every organ of the press. Then the media, having shown by their own uproar that my declarations had "got across", reassured themselves by concluding: "He said nothing new."

Through sound and pictures I was close to the nation, but as it were in the abstract. On the other hand, the public ceremonies, the parades, the inaugurations, to which of course I gave all the requisite pomp but where I appeared surrounded by the obligatory ritual, did not bring me into direct contact with people. In order to establish a living bond between us, I decided to visit every *département* in France. Between the beginning and the middle of this seven-year term, independently of my trips overseas, I was to cover sixty-seven of the ninety-three *départements* in metropolitan France in three and a half years. These were spread out over nineteen journeys each lasting four, five or six days. During the year 1959 I visited, in February the Haute-Garonne, Gers, Ariège, Pyrénées-Orientales, Hautes-Pyrénées and Basses-Pyrénées; in April the Yonne, Nièvre, Allier, Saône-et-Loire and Côte-d'Or; in May the Cher, Indre, Loiret-et-Cher and Indre-et-Loire; in June Cantal, Haute-Loire, Puy-de-Dôme and Loire; in September the Pas-de-Calais and the Nord; in November the Territoire de Belfort, the

Haut-Rhin and Bas-Rhin. During 1960 I visited, in February the Tarn, Aude, Gard and Hérault; in July the Manche, Orne, Calvados, Eure and Seine-Maritime; in September Finistère, Côtes-du-Nord, Morbihan, Loire-Atlantique and Ille-et-Vilaine; in early October the Isère, Haute-Savoie and Savoie; at the end of the same month the Hautes-Alpes, Basses-Alpes and Alpes-Maritimes. During 1961, in April the Landes, Tarn-et-Garonne, Lot-et-Garonne, Dordogne and Gironde; at the end of June and the beginning of July the Meuse, Vosges, Meurthe-et-Moselle and Moselle; in September the Aveyron, Lozère and Ardèche, and in November Corsica, the Var and the Bouches-du-Rhône. During the first half of 1962, in May the Lot, Corrèze, Creuse and Haute-Vienne; in June the Haute-Saône, Jura and Doubs.

Each *département* was traversed in its entirety from morning to night. The program changed little from one to the next: a big reception in the departmental capital consisting of a review of the troops on the esplanade; meetings with the local members of parliament, the departmental council, the administrative corps and the mayors of all the communes at the prefecture, and audiences given to various delegations, the bishop of the diocese, the Protestant pastor, the Rabbi, the principal officials, the general officers; the presentation of the municipal council and the notabilities at the town hall; an address to the population in the main square where a considerable crowd would gather in the midst of general enthusiasm; meanwhile, if it was Sunday, mass at the cathedral, and in any event, a banquet at the prefecture for the elected representatives and the notables. There would be similar ceremonies in the sub-prefectures and other main towns, always including a visit to the town hall, a formal address from the municipality, and a speech to the assembled inhabitants. There would be brief stops in a number of small towns and villages where the mayor would greet General de Gaulle before the assembled population and he would reply. Along the route there would be visits to factories, workshops, mines, agricultural developments, universities, laboratories, schools, military establishments, etc. In every locality, large or small, where I stopped, the popular turn-out would be considerable, the atmosphere joyful, the display of flags touching. On every road I took, people came out in large numbers to applaud. Wherever I spoke in public there were resounding cheers. When I broke into the *Marseillaise*, it was invariably taken up by the entire audience. When I mixed with the crowd or went through the streets, faces lit up, voices were raised in delight, hands stretched out towards me. In seventy days I saw twelve million Frenchmen, travelled forty thousand kilometers, spoke six hundred times in councils or official gatherings, four hundred times from public platforms, shook hundreds of thousands of hands. During the same time my wife quietly went to visit some three hundred hospitals, maternity centers, old people's homes, orphanages, homes for handicapped children. Throughout my journeys there were only two discordant episodes: very few people turned out in Grenoble to listen to me in front of the prefecture; and my visit to the port of Marseilles coincided with a strike of dock workers who waved banners inscribed with their claims at the end of the jetties. All in all, I was greeted from one end of the country to the other by a striking demonstration of national sentiment which deeply moved the participants, greatly impressed observers, and afterwards appeared everywhere thanks to television. In each of its regions, our country thus gave itself a spectacular proof of its rediscovered unity. It was moved and heartened by it, and I was filled with joy.

In addition to all this, a host of impressions and a great deal of practical information was gathered in the course of these tours. On the immutable surface of France and the abiding bedrock of its human substance, I saw with my own eyes the transformation that was being wrought by the rapid development of industry, the mechanization of agriculture, the growing birthrate, the bulging student population, the proliferation of motorized transport. Although our country, compared to others such as Germany, Britain, Belgium and the Netherlands, is particularly resistant to change, on account of its geography, its lack of raw materials, the low density of its population, and its contentious and at the same time conservative character, this necessary transformation was nonetheless everywhere in progress, though with considerable differences in speed and scale between the regions, which are also much more diverse than elsewhere. Wherever I went, once the memory of the Liberation had been duly evoked in the formal addresses, the prefects, the elected representatives, the delegates, the officials, spoke to me almost exclusively about building, urbanization, the creation of industrial zones for the expanding cities; about credits, markets, consolidation of scattered holdings, irrigation, road improvements, for the modernization of farming; of faculties, schools, technical colleges, which were never numerous enough or big enough; of roads to be widened, canals to be dug, airfields to be built, in order that life should flow more freely and prosperity come more quickly. What I heard and saw brought home to me on the spot, in all their severity and magnitude, the three vital necessities for the nation: the equipment and development of the territory; the creation of regions and the merging of communes with a view to enlarging administrative units which were too small for our time; and the direct participation from the highest to the lowest of the economic and social organisms in the study and application of plans, which were still the responsibility of politically elected councils. On my return to Paris, the conclusion which I drew from my journeys and the observations which the ministers who accompanied me brought back with them did much to clarify government policy.

Aside from my official travels at home and abroad, conferences at Rambouillet and visits to Colombey-les-deux-Eglises, which together accounted for approximately a quarter of my time, my life was naturally spent at the Elysée. The determinism of history had placed me in this palace which, though I appreciated its somewhat antiquated charm and reasonably convenient situation in relation to the various ministries, in my view presented certain drawbacks. At one time on the outskirts of Paris, the Elysée is now wedged in the middle of the capital, and as a result, what with the combined constraints imposed upon me by security, protocol, traffic and public curiosity, I was virtually imprisoned there unless, duly escorted down avenues cleared of cars and lined with enthusiastic spectators, I went to some ceremony, public monument or exhibition. The building contained a number of extremely handsome rooms decorated with period furniture which were more or less adequate for the inevitable receptions, but it offered very little space for the various services of a now very active Presidency. Moreover, ever since the palace became the property of the State by virtue of Madame de Pompadour's bequest to the King, few great events had left their mark on it, with the not wholly propitious exceptions of the final abdication of Napoleon I and the launching by his nephew of the *coup d'état* of December 2, 1851. For all these reasons, I wondered whether it would not be advisable to set up my residence and my offices elsewhere. But since the great houses which had once been adapted to such a purpose had disappeared in 1871, the Tuileries burnt down by the Commune and Saint-Cloud by the Prussians, since Versailles would have been excessive, the Trianon was in danger of collapse, Fontainebleau, Rambouillet and Compiègne were too far away, and Vincennes – which I considered – was in process of restoration, I settled for what was immediately available and had, moreover, become adapted to time-honored Parisian administrative habits. The new Republic, then, so far as its functioning and its reputation were concerned, would make the most of the old Elysée.

Work went on there methodically and peacefully. I arrived in my office, which I had installed in the principal room on the first floor, at half past nine every day, having already acquainted myself with the latest news and glanced through the morning papers. My mornings were spent in reading diplomatic despatches and various memoranda concerning domestic affairs; drafting any necessary comments or replies, which were transmitted at once to those concerned; presiding in Cabinet every Wednesday, at special ministerial meetings once or twice a week, most often to discuss Algeria, the economy or foreign affairs, and periodically the Higher Council of National Defence and the Higher Council of the Judiciary; receiving the Prime

Minister or another member of the government, a visting statesman from abroad, an ambassador or an academician. After
luncheon, whether or not there were guests, work was resumed
forthwith. Various senior civil servants, delegations or leading
personalities were received in audience. An hour or two would
be devoted to papers connected with forthcoming Cabinet
meetings. Finally, I would hear the reports of my principal
assistants: the Secretary-General to the Presidency, Geoffroy de
Courcel, the head of my personal secretariat, René Brouillet,
the Chief of Staff to the President, General de Beaufort, later
General Olié and lastly General Dodelier, and the Secretary-
General for the Community and African and Malagasy Affairs,
Jacques Foccart. These would sometimes be joined by one or
other of the special advisers or *chargés de mission:* Olivier
Guichard, and later Pierre Lefranc for political affairs, Jean-
Marc Boegner, then Pierre Maillard for Foreign Affairs, André
de Lattre, then Jean-Maxime Levesque and Jean Méo for
Finance and Economy, Bernard Tricot, then Jacques Boitreaud
for constitutional and legislative matters, Jean-Jacques de
Bresson for Algeria and questions of legal administration,
Pierre Lelong and Guy Camus for Education and Scientific
Research, Jean Chauveau for Information, Xavier de Beaulain-
court for private correspondence. Such was my entourage, few
in number but high in quality. Having listened to their reports,
I formulated my decisions and signed State papers and correspondence. At eight o'clock in the evening I left my desk. It
was extremely rare for me to return to it before the following
day. On principle and from experience, I knew well that at my
level one must not be in too much of a hurry in conducting
affairs.

The presidential palace was naturally the setting for continual visits, parties and ceremonies. Since nothing is too trivial
when it comes to upholding the prestige of the State, I felt it
important that in this respect things should be done liberally
but with moderation, affably but with dignity. My wife, as
hostess, felt the same way, and the Head of Protocol, Ludovic
Chancel, succeeded by Pierre Siraud, saw to everything

efficiently. Our receptions were therefore frequent and we tried to give them a certain style. Over and above my four thousand guests in every prefecture in France, fifteen thousand French and foreign guests graced our table at the Elysée during this period. As many again attended other functions. Regardless of the occasion or the scale of these gatherings, ranging from a formal banquet or ceremonious *soirée* for a Head of State to an intimate dinner for a few chosen guests, through all sorts of meals and receptions for members of the government, parliament, the advisory councils, the diplomatic corps, the civil service, the judiciary, the armed services, the educational authorities, the business and trade-union world, the world of letters, arts, sciences, sport, etc., these representational duties, while enabling me to meet face to face a fair number of able and gifted people, added greatly to the mental and physical burdens of my office.

The time – all too short – not taken up by the exercise of my functions I spent quietly alone with my wife. In the evenings, television and occasionally the cinema brought our contemporaries before our eyes instead of the other way round. On Sundays, our children and grandchildren would come to see us if they were in Paris and if my duties permitted. My son and my son-in-law, having fought hard and brilliantly in the Free French forces, had pursued their careers as regular officers, one in the Fleet Air Arm, the other in the Armored Corps. While their father and father-in-law was completing the first four years of his renewed mission, Lieutenant-Commander, later Commander, de Gaulle, having taken a course at the School of Naval Warfare, successively served on board the destroyer *Duperre,* was posted to the Naval General Staff, commanded the fast frigate *Le Picard,* which cruised along the Algerian coast stopping and examining suspect vessels, and was finally appointed to the Headquarters of the Joint Chiefs of Staff; and Colonel Alain de Boissieu commanded the 4th Light Cavalry Regiment at Châteaudun-du-Rummel in the Constantine region, then became head of the military staff of Delegate-General Delouvrier in Algiers, and later Chief of Staff of the

Armored Corps Inspectorate, before going on from there to the Center for Advanced Military Studies and the Institute for National Defense. Both of them, as well as our daughter, our daughter-in-law and their children, saw France as I did. The same was true of our brothers and sisters and our nephews and nieces. This family harmony was precious to me. Whenever possible, we went to La Boisserie. There I withdrew into seclusion to think. There I wrote the speeches which were a painful and perpetual labor for me. There I read some of the books that were sent to me. There, gazing at the distant horizon or the immensity of the sky, I restored my peace of mind.

How could it help but be affected by the strains to which I was subjected, the obstacles I encountered, the question-mark poised over the future of my undertaking? In particular, I had to face the fact that the evidence of France's revival merely exacerbated the opposition of those who until recently regarded themselves and were regarded as the leaders of political opinion. Across the spectrum of parties and newspapers, nowhere did my efforts find favor, and no sooner was the solution of the Algerian problem in sight than the chorus of malevolence redoubled. As François Mauriac, whose devotion to France combined with his understanding of history, his patriotic and aesthetic appraisal of greatness, his gift for probing and analysing the springs of human passions, made him an incomparable observer of our times, remarked in his weekly column on March 12, 1962: "What is not a dream is the incredible strength of this old man, for whose downfall every political group of any significance, whether of the right or the left, is hoping, waiting, preparing, once peace is attained, and whose very isolation, one feels, fortifies him against this impotent, growling pack which surrounds him."

To tell the truth, although I sometimes resented the hostile coalition of caucuses and scribblers, it did not affect me very profoundly. I knew that there is nothing that paper will not print or the microphone transmit. I knew how much the provocative phrase tempts the professional stylist. I knew the extent to which the new institutions, my presence at the head of the State, my way of conducting affairs, had reduced the power and influence of certain groups which had been dominant under the former regime and were mortified at having lost their position. I knew, in particular, how much they resented the distance at which, not out of disdain but on principle, I felt obliged to keep them. When their rancor overstepped all bounds I consoled myself by repeating the words which Corneille puts into the mouth of Octave:

Quoi! Tu veux qu'on t'épargne et n'as rien épargné![1]

Yet, impervious though I was to personal attacks in speech and in writing, I was more susceptible to the impression that, through me, it was the very idea of national revival which inspired such resistance and fury in the country's leading circles. It was as though the ruling groups of yesterday, irrespective of their activities, their labels, their ideologies, had opted for decadence, either out of vertigo in face of the precipices to be negotiated in order to avert it, or because, having persuaded themselves that it was unavoidable, they erected it into a defiant intellectual doctrine, or, finally, because their routines and their weaknesses might find therein a chance of survival and a semblance of justification. All this raised in the most disturbing way the question of what would become of the country, once my departure saw the disappearance of the phenomenon represented by an effective authority at the head of the State, legitimized by events and identified with the faith and the hopes of the French people.

However, before tackling this problem "of the succession", I must say that the results achieved four years after my return seemed to me encouraging. Instead of our country remaining immersed in the humiliating political confusion in which it had been floundering, I had sought to persuade it to choose a State with a head, a government, some stability and authority. It had done so. Rather than allow it to spill its blood, squander its

---

[1] "What! You expect to be spared when you yourself have spared no one!"

money, tear itself apart by clinging to an outworn and unjustifiable colonial domination, I had sought to replace the old
empire with a friendly and practical association between the
peoples who belonged to it. This had been achieved. At a time
when economic drift, financial insolvency, the chronic weakness
of the franc and social stagnation were impeding the progress
essential to France's prosperity and power, I had sought to ensure that her economy was planned on modern lines, that her
budgets were balanced, that her currency should have a sound
and indisputable value, that the door should be opened to a
change in the relations between her sons by steps towards the
participation of all in the running of enterprises. We had
accomplished these things. In order that Europe should cease
to be a battleground of hatreds and dangers, to flaunt its
economic and political divisions on either side of the Rhine and
the Alps, to set its eastern and western peoples at one another's
throats on ideological grounds, I had sought to make France
and Germany good neighbors, to see the Common Market of
the Six take shape, to create a framework in which they could
concert their actions *vis-à-vis* the outside world, to revive the
natural affection and trust between the Slavs and the French.
All this was well under way. Whereas France had been betray-
ing her own past by straying among insidious supranational
clouds, abandoning her defence, her foreign policy, her destiny
to the Atlantic hegemony, leaving to others the fields of influence, co-operation and friendship with which she had once
been familiar in the Third World, I had sought to ensure that
she asserted her own personality among her neighbors while
respecting theirs, that without rejecting alliance she refused
protectorship, that she provided herself with a force capable of
deterring any aggression and consisting in the first place of a
nuclear armament, that she reappeared in the thoughts, the
activities and the hopes of the world, in short that she recovered
her independence and her radiance. This was indeed what was
happening.

On the slope which France was scaling, my mission was
always to guide her upwards, while all the voices below con-

tinued to call her down. Having once more chosen to listen to me, she had dragged herself out of the morass and had now passed through the stage of renewal; but thenceforward, today as yesterday, I had no other goal to offer her but the summit, no other road but that of endeavor.

Part II

ENDEAVOR

1962 –

Chapter 1

꿎

In the year of grace 1962, France's revival was in full flower. She had been threatened by civil war; bankruptcy had stared her in the face; the world had forgotten her voice. Now she was out of danger. The State had succeeded in rescuing her by virtue of a complete change whereby it now incorporated a supreme authority legitimized by events and backed by the confidence of the people. But the present does not guarantee the future. An edifice whose soundness depends on the presence of a single man is necessarily fragile. Since danger was no longer in sight, many of our countrymen were immediately tempted to return to their easy-going ways. Some, in particular, found it more and more difficult to accept a government which governed. Tomorrow, unless the dyke was well cemented, the tide might sweep away what now seemed firmly established. All the more so because in the course of time storms would inevitably rage, whether blowing in from outside, or rising within the confines of a country which, since the Gauls, has been periodically the stage for those "sudden and unexpected upheavals" which astonished Caesar. In order that France should recapture and preserve, not for a brief period only, but on a lasting basis, the unity, the power and the status without which she would be doomed, the regime which governed her must remain steadfast and coherent. Having never ceased to think and act in accordance with this national imperative, it was clear to me that the State, at present well-ordered, must remain so in the future. This required that it must never again become a prey to the multifarious, divergent and devouring factions which had dominated, debased and paralyzed it for so long.

The old monarchy had achieved continuity at the cost of a centuries-long struggle against the vassals, but nothing less than heredity, anointment and absolutism had sufficed. The two empires had succeeded for a time in preventing disintegration, but only by means of dictatorship. Thereafter the Republic, although it originally incorporated a few theoretical safeguards, abandoned itself to the parties and became a perpetual power vacuum. Its ultimate dereliction in face of national crisis and the fact that I chanced to have been pre-ordained as the country's savior, had enabled me, with the direct concurrence of the people – that is to say on a pre-eminently democratic basis – to establish institutions designed to span the future. For the higher and permanent interests of France had their instrument and guarantor therein in the person of the Head of State. Yet how could one doubt that this profound transformation, which had given the Republic a Head that organically it had never had before, would eventually be undermined by all the vested interests? How was it to be endowed with a distinctive enough character to enable it to be maintained in law and in practice when the dramatic circumstances and the exceptional person that had imposed it in the first place had disappeared?

For a long time I had felt that the only way was the election of the President of the Republic by the people. If he alone was chosen by Frenchmen as a whole, he would be "the nation's man", invested thereby in the eyes of all, and in his own eyes, with a paramount responsibility precisely corresponding to the role assigned to him in the Constitution. In addition, of course, he would need the will and the capacity to fulfil this charge. That, obviously, the law could not guarantee. For the virtues of an institution have never at any time or in any sphere been able to compensate for the irremediable infirmity of a leader. Conversely, success is possible only if talent is provided with its instrument, and nothing is worse than a system in which quality wastes away in impotence.

It is true that, speaking at Bayeux in 1946 about the regime which France needed, and then directing the proceedings and debates in which the Constitution was elaborated in 1958, I had not yet specified that the Head of State should be elected by universal suffrage, and had at first been content to have him chosen by a broadly-based electoral college which on the national level would be similar to those by which senators were elected on the departmental level. For it seemed to me desirable not to do everything at once. Since I was asking the country to wrest the State from the control of the parties, by deciding that the President instead of parliament should henceforth be the wellspring of power and policy, it would be as well to postpone the final completion of this vast mutation. I may add that, at the time, in order not to alienate the almost unanimous movement of national support, I deemed it advisable to take into consideration the passionate prejudices which, since Louis-Napoleon, the idea of a plebiscite aroused in many sectors of opinion. When experience of the new Constitution had shown that the supreme authority wielded power under its terms without any suggestion of dictatorship, it would be time to propose the ultimate reform to the people. Moreover, I myself intended at the outset to assume the functions of Head of State, and, by reason of past history and present circumstances, the manner of my accession would be no more than a formality with no bearing on my role. However, for the sake of the future, I was determined to finish off the edifice in this respect before the end of my seven-year term.

Meanwhile, the instinct of self-preservation was keeping the parties on the alert. Suspecting my design, they felt that it was yet another reason for getting rid of me before I had accomplished it, or at least weakening me enough to force me to abandon it. Hence, gradually, as the problem of Algeria was settled, as the loyalty of the Army was incontrovertibly affirmed, as terrorist subversion was suppressed, the various strands of opposition began to combine and reinforce one another. It became evident that the relative neutrality which they had observed up to then was about to cease, that more and more obstacles would be raised at every turn, and that the actions and intentions of General de Gaulle would become the target of their recriminations. There was reason to believe that all the political factions would patch up their differences and connive to bring the latent crisis to the boil. Continual harassment, a well-timed censure motion in the National Assembly against the government, and if need be against any other which might succeed it; general elections, either at the normal time or following a dissolution, bringing back to the Palais-Bourbon their disparate but unanimously hostile majority, the launching of campaigns in different directions, but all equally disparaging, by virtually all the newspapers and networks – by these various means they would aim to put me in grave difficulties, to persuade me to abjure either my functions or my supremacy, to undermine in the public mind the idea that the Head of State should actually be one, and, in any event, to place future presidents in the situation which was formerly that of a "guest in the Elysée".

If they succeeded, once more it would be as though the revival of the State was to be but a temporary phenomenon destined to cease when the danger was past. Once more, in the face of a national emergency whose primary cause was the incapacity of the regime of the parties, the latter would have made a show of abdicating in favor of a demiurge entrusted overnight with the country's salvation: in 1914 Joffre; in 1917 Clemenceau; in 1940 Pétain, and then, the error having been recognized, de Gaulle; in 1958 de Gaulle again – with the intention, the crisis over, of reappearing armed with pretensions and demands commensurate with the degree of their erstwhile discredit and humiliation. Once more, exploiting the limitless capacity for forgetfulness of the electoral clienteles, the time-honored French proclivity for splitting up into garrulous factions and indulging in political games – as though they were circus tricks or fairground competitions – and the aversion of organized interests for a strong central power, the parties would re-establish their supremacy and resume the downward path. Needless to say, I was determined to foil their attempt. But this presupposed that the French people gave me their backing against them all.

They could do so, and thereby resolve both the political problem and the constitutional question, if, at my request, they voted for the election of the Head of State by universal suffrage. In this way they could give the lie to the parties as a whole in the immediate context, and consolidate the new institutions for the future. It was only from the mass of the nation, and certainly not from parliament, that it was possible to hope for the adoption of such a measure, for two-thirds of the deputies and nine-tenths of the senators would not accept it at any price. And in any case it was a basic principle of the Fifth Republic and of my own doctrine that the French people must themselves decide in matters that concerned their future. I therefore intended to propose this decisive confirmation to them directly, and I must do so without delay since, with the sole exception of the UNR,[1] all the parliamentary groups had opened hostilities.

From the beginning of 1962, before I had revealed my plan, I was already under fire. The application of Article 16 of the Constitution, which I had invoked at the time of the rebellion of the four generals in Algiers, had already aroused a great deal of feigned alarm and artificial agitation in political circles, until the liquidation of the OAS induced me to decide on a return to normal. In March, on the eve of the Evian negotiations, the National Defence Committee of the Palais-Bourbon took up the cudgels and loudly expressed its disapproval of the recall of two Army divisions and all the Air Force combat units from Africa to metropolitan France at my orders. Immediately after the referendum on Algerian independence, the attack sharpened and spread. On April 17 the Pompidou ministry, in which no fault could have been found since it had only just come into being, obtained a vote of confidence from only 259 deputies, while 247 voted against it or abstained. On May 15, five MRP[2] ministers withdrew from the government, using as their pretext a press conference in which, once again, I had

---

[1] *Union pour la nouvelle république:* Gaullist party.

[2] *Mouvement républicain populaire:* Christian Democratic party.

advocated the union of Europe through organized co-operation between States, and rejected integration. It is true that two of them, Pierre Pflimlin and Maurice Schuman, who had only been in it for a month and, in fact, were to opt that very day between their ministerial portfolios and their seats in parliament, could claim to have been surprised by my remarks. But the other three, Robert Buron, Paul Bacon and Joseph Fontanet, had been members of my government from the beginning, and had accepted quite happily both the form and substance of the directives which I had always given to the policy of France. The truth of the matter was that if the five were suddenly parting company with me, it was because their party in turn was joining the hostile coalition. On May 22 the Independents followed suit, summoning the four ministers who were members of their group to tender their resignations and expelling them when they refused.

To cut short the war of attrition, I decided to take the initiative and the offensive. Speaking on the radio on June 9 I announced to the nation that "by means of universal suffrage, we must eventually ensure that in the future, over and above the men who come and go, the Republic can remain strong, orderly and continuous." No political soothsayer could fail to understand what this meant. Consequently, on the 13th of the same month, as a deliberate demonstration against me, 296 deputies in the National Assembly, who described themselves as "Europeans" signed a declaration condemning the plan for political co-operation, which I had proposed to the member States of the Common Market and which had just been rejected by Holland, Belgium and Italy, and demanding the supranational "solution" instead. The signatories represented a large majority in the House, and moreover the ten Communist deputies, who did not subscribe to the declaration, condemned me no less strongly. Scarcely had this wave broken than another arose. The day after the final Algerian referendum, I recognized the independence of Algeria in the name of France, in accordance with the solemn pledges we had undertaken. Consequently, the mandate of the Algerian members of the French parliament having no further object, I put an end to it by ordinance, under the powers with which I had been formally vested by the referendum law. A storm of protest at once broke out in the Palais-Bourbon and the Luxembourg which had not the slightest justification in law but was simply an expression of the hostile attitude of the majority. There could be no doubt that a merciless struggle would begin as soon as I had formulated my constitutional proposal.

The opportunity to join battle, and a warning that there might not be much time to lose were suddenly provided by the assassination attempt at Petit-Clamart on August 22. This, after the previous one near Pont-sur-Seine which had almost succeeded, and with the prospect of further attempts in the offing, brought home to an alarmed and agitated public the question of what might become of the State if de Gaulle were suddenly to disappear, and made it clear to me that the eventuality could arise at any moment. I therefore deemed it desirable to hasten matters. On August 29 the Cabinet was informed that "I contemplate proposing an amendment to the Constitution with a view to ensuring the continuity of the State," and the news was published. However, in order not to confuse matters, I did not finally show my hand until after my State visit to Germany. But as soon as this was over, a communiqué was issued on September 12, after the weekly Cabinet meeting, announcing that "General de Gaulle has confirmed his intention to submit to a referendum a proposal that the President of the Republic should henceforth be elected by universal suffrage."

On September 20, in a radio and television talk, I explained to the nation why I was asking it to carry out this essential reform, and how it would be enabled to do so. I observed that "the institutions in force for nearly four years have replaced the chronic confusion and perpetual crises which bedevilled the action of the State by continuity, stability, efficacy and balance in the powers of government"; that "no one doubts that our country would soon be plunged into the depths of disaster if, unhappily, we were to abandon it once more to the sterile and contemptible games of yesterday"; and that "the keystone of our regime is the institution of a President of the Republic chosen by the reason and sentiment of the French people to be the Head of State and the guide of France." Having recalled the functions and responsibilities which were his under the terms of the Constitution, I declared that "in order that he may effectively fulfill such a charge, he needs the explicit trust of the nation." As far as I myself was concerned, I went on to say, "I felt on resuming the leadership of the State in 1958 that events had already done what was required, and for that reason I agreed to be elected otherwise. But the question will be very different for those who, not having received the same national distinction, come after me one after the other to assume the position which I at present occupy . . . . In order that they should be fully empowered and totally bound to carry the supreme burden, however onerous, and in order that our Republic should thus continue to have a good chance of remaining sound, effective and popular in spite of the demons of our divisions, they must receive a direct mandate from the citizens as a whole." Then came the statement of the proposal I was putting to the country: "When my own seven-year term is over, or if death or illness interrupt it before it runs out, the President of the Republic will thenceforward be elected by universal suffrage." But by what means should the country express its decision? I answered: "by the most democratic means, the referendum, which the Constitution provides for in a very simple and clear manner by laying it down that 'the President of the Republic may submit to a referendum any bill', I repeat any bill, 'dealing with the organization of the public authorities.'" I ended by saying to the French people: "As always, I can and will do nothing without your support. As always, I shall soon be asking you for it. As always, it will be for you to decide."

But as always, too, the very principle of a direct decision by the people was anathema to all the old political groups. Moreover, my possible success would, for the moment, put paid to the hopes they cherished of seeing me depart. Above all, the adoption of my proposal would greatly reduce their chances of returning to the old ways. For there was no doubt that once I had gone, unless my successors enjoyed a unique mandate by virtue of the fact that they had received it from the nation as a whole, the parties intended to find ways and means of reverting to the previous system. Their pressures and their influence on the college of notables which elected the President, the pledges they would be able to extract from the presidential candidates, and then, once the victor was installed, a particular way of interpreting the constitutional texts, a little juridical sleight of hand, a few amendments effected through parliament, would quietly restore them to complete possession of the Republic. But first of all they would have to defeat me. Hence, in the struggle which was now beginning, not a single political faction, whether of the Left, the Right or the Center, was missing from the opposition camp, and there was to be no abatement in the concerted virulence of their actions and speeches.

As is so often the case in our political battles, the question at issue was not in itself the subject of the debate. Since to the mass of the French people the idea that they themselves should elect the President of the Republic seemed perfectly natural, since it also seemed to them quite normal for the Head of the State actually to run it, and since they thought that de Gaulle was right to prepare for his succession, the army of the "Noes" was careful not to challenge the actual principle of a reform which was so evidently popular. Their accusations were directed against the juridical conditions in which I was proposing it and which were inevitably obscure to the majority of the people. So the country was to witness a frenetic campaign, apparently inspired by the defence of the law, but in reality directed against me personally and aiming to prove, by a flood of imputations stemming from every point of the political compass, supported by all kinds of committed jurists, repeated *ad nauseam* by virtually the entire press, that General de Gaulle was violating the Constitution in order to set up a dictatorship. The argument put forward was this: Article 89 provides for the possibility of constitutional revision through parliamentary channels; no other article is specifically devoted to revision; to initiate it through a referendum is, therefore, contrary to the law.

Inured as I was to the specious charges which had been levelled against me for so long, it seemed to me that this one overstepped all bounds. For in submitting the reform to a direct popular vote, I was merely applying a constitutional provision as glaringly simple and clear-cut as it could possibly be. What, after all, could be plainer or more categorical than Article 11 which prescribed that "the President of the Republic may, at the proposal of the government, submit to referendum any bill dealing with the organization of the public authorities"? Was there anything which, by nature and by definition, could have a more obvious bearing on the organization of the public authorities than the Constitution, and, in particular, what it laid down as regards the method of electing the Head of State? Had this not always been admitted in legal doctrine and parlance, so much so that the Constitution of 1875 which inaugurated the Republic was precisely called: "Law concerning the organization of the public authorities"? Why, in this Article 11 which covered the constitutional sphere no less unquestionably, should it have been necessary to mention what was self-evident, to wit, that it might open the way to revision? If, by an extraordinary denial of his own text, the legislator intended the opposite, how could he have failed to specify it? In what way could the power to resort to a referendum in order to amend the constitutional law be regarded as inconsistent with the procedure laid down in Article 89, the latter being operative when the public authorities deemed it preferable to use parliamentary channels? Did it not stand to reason, moreover, that in such a grave matter both should be available depending on the circumstances, and was this not the meaning of Article 3 which stated: "National sovereignty belongs to the people who exercise it through their representative and by way of referendum"? Finally and above all, since the 1958 Constitution derived from the direct suffrage of the people, by what authority were they to be denied the power to alter what they had themselves created?

I must say that the stubborn insistence of the parties on interpreting the Constitution in such a way as to deny the people a right which belonged to them, seemed to me all the more high-handed in that I myself was the principal inspirer of the new institutions, and it really was the height of effrontery to challenge me on what they meant. In particular, if the referendum system existed in our law, it was because I had had it adopted in 1945 by universal suffrage. If it had been applied in order to call the 1958 Constitution into being, it was because I had imposed this testamentary clause on the dying Fourth Republic. If there was an Article 11, it was because, being legally and expressly mandated to draw up and submit the Constitution to the country, I had wanted it to include just such an article, in that place with that meaning and scope. Moreover, when I examined this part of the draft on June 26 and 30, 1958, at a meeting attended by Michel Debré, the Minister of Justice, who was in charge of drawing up the Constitution, and the Ministers of State Guy Mollet, Pierre Pflimlin, Louis Jacquinot and Félix Houphouët-Boigny, I had insisted that the country as a whole must be given all the power which the referendum enabled it to exercise in every sphere and, above all, that of constitutional amendment. All of them had pointed out, and I had acknowledged, that the text of Article 11 gave me complete satisfaction on this point. The fact that the former political leadership now shamelessly concurred in ignoring the principles, the spirit and the origin of the Constitution, in refusing to read what was written therein or, having read it, in refusing to admit that the words meant what they said, would finally have enlightened me, had I needed enlightening, not, of course, on their good faith since I expected none from them, but on the unquenchable nostalgia which an absurd past inspired in them.

Meanwhile, my talk on September 20, which made matters absolutely plain, put an end to the preliminary skirmishes and opened the pitched battle. It is true that, almost at the same time, elections on a restricted suffrage to renew a third of the Senate seats took place with no apparent emotion. But notwithstanding the calm which surrounded this formality, all the parties were entering the fray and closing ranks with an eye to the forthcoming national consultation. On the 23rd the

Socialists announced: "A new and glaring violation of the Constitution is about to be consummated . . . . The election of the President of the Republic by universal suffrage is simply a demagogic means of giving plebiscitary sanction to the successive encroachments on the prerogatives of government and parliament." On the same day the Communists called for "the union of all republicans to fight the common enemy, personal power, which is gradually evolving towards a *de facto* dictatorship." On the 25th, the PSU[1] proclaimed "its unanimous hostility to the President of the Republic's plan for a plebiscitary referendum." On the 30th, the Radicals, meeting at Vichy for their annual congress, gave an enthusiastic ovation to a fiery speech by Gaston Monnerville who declared: "To the attempt at a plebiscite which is about to develop, my answer is No! . . . . To allow the violation of the Constitution is to allow anything." And the President of the Senate urged the National Assembly to pass a motion of censure, adding: "This would be a direct, legal and constitutional retort to what I consider an abuse of power." Without waiting for October 8 and 9, the dates theoretically fixed by the MRP and the Independents to announce their decisions, everyone knew that they had thrown in their lot with the opposition. Even the Republican Center, the Poujade Movement, the Algerian Repatriates[2], joined the "Noes."

In the midst of all this, the bill to be submitted to the nation, which was drawn up in accordance with my directives under the auspices of the Prime Minister, was submitted in the normal way for examination by the *Conseil d'Etat*. The latter, instead of confining itself to proposing any textual amendments which it considered desirable, set itself up improperly as judge of the way in which the Head of State, the protector of the Constitution, had decided to apply it, and formulated an opinion which was unfavorable to the appeal to Article 11 and the use of the referendum. Now this body, composed of officials who held their appointments by governmental decree and not by election, was

---

[1] *Parti socialiste unifié:* left-wing socialist group.

[2] *Rapatriés d'Algérie:* party formed by French settlers repatriated to France after independence.

qualified to give the executive power the legal opinions which were requested of it, but in no way to intervene in political matters nor *a fortiori* in the constitutional sphere. Knowing the views of the Council, whose meetings, in the absence of those of its members who had been seconded to me or the government, were noisily dominated by notorious and avowed partisans, former ministers or members of parliament and future political candidates, I was not in the least surprised by the attitude of its assembly. Nor was I surprised to learn that in defiance of all the obligations and traditions of the Council, the secrecy of its deliberations and its vote was betrayed the moment the sitting was over; for without the slightest delay the news agencies published its conclusions, and the parties seized on them as ammunition for their campaign. For this reason, when the Vice-President, Alexandre Parodi, came to convey them to me after I had already read them in the newspapers, I replied that I would pay no attention to an "opinion" of this sort, which in any case was not legally binding. The following day the Cabinet adopted the text of the bill. I asked each member in turn whether he endorsed it. All of them did so unreservedly with the exception of Pierre Sudreau, who, consequently, left the government.

So that the proprieties should be observed to the uttermost on my side, on October 2 I addressed a message to parliament in which I formally made known the decision I had taken and the reasons which justified it. After pointing to the fact that "the institutions which the French people adopted four years ago, in the aftermath of a grave crisis and on the eve of further perils, have succeeded, thanks to the stability of government and the continuity of its policies . . . . in resolving difficult problems and overcoming severe trials," I declared: "We must now see to it that these institutions remain. This means that, in the future and over and above the men who come and go, the State must have at its head an effective guarantor of the fate of France and the Republic. Such a role presupposes . . . . that the man who fulfills it should enjoy the direct and explicit confidence of the nation." I pointed out the corollary – a bill providing for the election of the President of the Republic by universal suffrage which was to be submitted to a referendum – and added: "I consider that there is no better means of effecting the amendment which is called for in the text adopted by the French people in 1958, an amendment which affects each individual citizen." Finally, referring to the recent assassination attempts, I concluded: "The nation, which has just been brought abruptly face to face with an alarming prospect, will thus have the opportunity to confer on our institutions a new and solemn guarantee."

My message having been listened to in complete silence by both Houses, all the parties, Right, Left and Center, at once launched their declaration of war. A motion of censure on the government was put down in the National Assembly, signed jointly by the delegates of the Socialists, the Radicals and their associates, the MRP and the Independents. Although the Communists were not signatories, it was certain that they would vote in favour of the motion. In accordance with the law, the debate would open two days later. No one could doubt that a crisis was about to explode, that the country would have to decide, and that it could mean either the end of de Gaulle, his historic role, his policies and his Republic, or else a new lease of life for them.

On October 4, without waiting for the debate and the vote on the motion of censure, the decrees concerning the referendum – the text of my proposal and the summons to the electors – were published in the *Journal Officiel*. That same day, before the deputies began their sitting, I addressed the French people directly by radio and television. I expressed myself in the most categorical terms. Recalling that it was the people themselves who had chosen the new Constitution "in the aftermath of a crisis which all but plunged France into disaster and destroyed the Republic," I compared the striking results which it had enabled us to achieve to the bankruptcy of the regime of the parties: "Our public life, which yesterday presented the spectacle of the intrigues, maneuverings and crises with which everyone is familiar, today bears the stamp of stability and efficiency. Instead of a sick currency, finances in deficit, a threatened economy being a constant source of anxiety and humiliation, we are now advancing along the road of prosperity and social progress on the basis of a sound franc, an external trade surplus and balanced budgets. Whereas we were in the process of destroying our national unity and squandering the elements of our military power as a result of the failure to achieve decolonization, to put an end to the Algerian conflict and to crush the subversive movement which was planning to overthrow the State, we have now established co-operation between France and her former colonies, Algeria has joined this association in its turn, we can set about modernizing our Army, and the dire conspiracies which threatened the Republic have been reduced to the shameful and futile expedients of robbery, blackmail and assassination. Finally, if until recently our country was regarded as the 'sick man' of Europe, today its influences and prestige are recognized throughout the world."

Emphasizing that this beneficent Constitution made the President of the Republic the effective "Head of State and guide of France," that it was this essential character "which the partisans of the discredited regime are naturally anxious to deprive him of," because then we would relapse into the conditions of yesterday, I went on to declare that "in order to be, *vis-à-vis* himself as well as others, in a position to fulfill such a mission, the President needs the direct confidence of the nation . . . ." This confidence, "which I myself implicitly enjoyed in 1958 for exceptional historic reasons," must henceforth be expressed through universal suffrage.

I did not hesitate to draw attention to the dramatic circumstances in which the people were being invited to adopt my plan. "From the beginning," I said, "I knew that I should have to propose this change to the country before the end of my seven-year term. But pressing reasons have induced me to take the initiative here and now, as is my right and duty." And I recalled "the attempts against my life, either perpetrated or planned, which make it incumbent upon me to ensure to the best of my ability that the Republic is established on a firm basis."

I described "the general disquiet provoked by the dangers of chaos which France might suddenly incur" and which must prompt the nation to show by a massive vote "that it intends to maintain its institutions, and has no desire after de Gaulle's departure to see the State once more delivered over to political practices which would lead to a hideous catastrophe, this time without hope of redemption." I outlined what we were accomplishing, internally in terms of the economic and social progress of our country, externally in terms of world peace and co-operation between East and West; "this whole immense enterprise requiring that the French people themselves be provided in the years to come with the means of choosing those who one after the other, at the head of the State, shall be answerable for their destiny."

Finally, as to my "clear, simple and straightforward" proposal on the subject of which they were about to avail themselves of the referendum procedure, I asked all Frenchmen and Frenchwomen to give me a vote of confidence: "It is your answer on October 28 which will tell me if I can and if I must pursue my task in the service of France."

I had spoken at one o'clock in the afternoon. Two hours later the session opened in the Palais-Bourbon. The position of the parties revealed itself to be as completely hostile towards me as mine was firm towards them. Paul Reynaud and Bertrand Motte on behalf of the Independents, Guy Mollet and Francis Leenhardt on behalf of the Socialists, Paul Coste-Floret on behalf of the MRP, Maurice Faure on behalf of the Radicals, Jean-Paul David on behalf of the other Center parties, and Waldeck Rochet on behalf of the Communists, all addressed the House in identical terms. Whatever Georges Pompidou and the orators of my persuasion, Lucien Neuwirth and Michel Habib-Deloncle, might say, everyone's mind was made up. Basically it was a clash between two Republics, the Republic of yesterday whose hopes of a re-birth were discernible behind the bitter diatribes of the partisans, and the Republic of today which was personified by me and whose survival I was endeavoring to ensure. But I had seen to it that the decision would not be taken in those precincts, and the censure motion, which was carried by 280 votes out of 480 deputies, in no way affected my determination to achieve victory elsewhere.

Yet such were the habits and illusions in political circles and the organs of information that, judging by what they said and wrote, it might have been thought that the Assembly's vote represented a defeat for me. Glancing through the Parisian press, I found it to all intents and purposes unanimous on this point. Thus *L'Aurore* affirmed, in the words of Jules Romains: "The Republic is saved!"; *Le Figaro* proclaimed with André François-Ponçet: "Parliamentary democracy is the only true democracy"; *Paris-Jour* warned me of the risks I would incur if I dissolved the Assembly; *Combat* considered that proof had been given that I could not dispense with the parties, and that I must draw the obvious conclusions; and *Le Monde* predicted "a constitutional crisis" unless I gave in. All this made me more than ever inclined to demonstrate that it was the National Assembly itself which would suffer the consequences of what it had just done against me. Deliberately ignoring the crisis, I spent the whole of October 5 attending military maneuvers in the Mourmelon area. It was not until noon on the 6th that I received Georges Pompidou, who in conformity with the Constitution came to tender his resignation and whom I forthwith invited to continue in office together with all his colleagues. Publicly, of course, I made ready to pronounce the dissolution of parliament and, as the Constitution enjoined, consulted the presidents of the two Houses to this end. My meeting with Jacques Chaban-Delmas was cordial and lasted half an hour; that with Gaston Monnerville took two minutes without even a handshake. On October 10 my decision was published, together with the decree which fixed the general elections for November 18 and 25. Just as in 1958, although in circumstances that were clearly very different, I was calling upon the country first of all to pronounce judgment on our institutions, and then to provide itself with a new Chamber.

The referendum campaign was marked by the same unanimity among the parties as they had shown in parliament. It is true that some of their members, while passionately advocating a negative vote, loudly protested – tactics or conviction? – that they had no desire to return to the old ways and put forward proposals which were to all appearances constructive. For example, Paul Reynaud, who in spite of all the vicissitudes, historical, political and personal, of his long career had never ceased to place the life, the oratory and the preponderance of the Palais-Bourbon above everything else, but who seemed to admit that its vices needed to be kept under control, ventilated the idea of "one parliament, one government". In his view, whenever the National Assembly was elected, a ministry would be formed on the basis of the majority and reflecting its composition and would remain in office for as long as the deputies themselves retained their seats. If they happened to overthrow the government, the Assembly would be *ipso facto* dissolved and new elections would be held. The former Prime Minister considered that this would suffice to avoid the endemic ministerial crises which had brought the Third and Fourth Republics into disrepute. But what Paul Reynaud, no doubt, had in mind was that the right of dissolution would thereby be abolished, together with any possibility of intervention by the President, and that parliament would thus once more become sovereign. It was my conviction, however, that under such a system, as a result of the eclipse of the Head of State, the sole means of asserting and, if necessary, imposing the higher permanent interests of the country would once more disappear. As for believing that wisdom would prevail in the Assembly once it knew that it would be condemned to present itself for re-election if it explicitly withheld its confidence from the government, this would be to disregard the adroit subterfuges which the parties would use to get rid of ministers without overthrowing the government or provoking a dissolution. For what sort of cohesion could a government formed of their own delegates and on the basis of their maneuverings possibly have, if they thought fit to disown or withdraw those of their members whom they had seconded to it? The ingenuity of the caciques would be applied to settling political crises by the breaking up of ministries rather than by the dismissal of the deputies. This would provide plenty of fodder for the intrigues of the caucuses, but what would become of the efficacy and dignity of government?

Other political tacticians, equally theoretical, for instance Paul Coste-Floret and Gaston Defferre, also professed their anxiety to remedy the abuses which the impotent omnipotence of parliament formerly displayed for all to see; but, anxious above all to make the National Assembly inviolable, they advocated the so-called "presidential system" on the American pattern. According to them the Head of State, who would be at the same time the Head of Government, could be elected directly by the people. But he would not have the power to dissolve the Assembly, any more than the Assembly would have the power to overthrow him. Executive and legislature would thus go through the whole duration of their respective mandates without either of them ever being able to coerce the other. For my part I was convinced that such a system, which is in any case known to have its drawbacks in the United States, would be at variance with the political nature and the character of the French people, which make them disinclined to tolerate a real government except in times of crisis and which, in the absence of indisputable safety valves, impel their representatives to strive to subdue it, in other words to annihilate it.

Since becoming an independent State, America has been through one civil war – more than a century ago – but has never suffered revolution or foreign invasion and, thus, never experienced the chronic divisions which such tragedies leave in the depths of the national consciousness and which make government a permanent object of suspicion and prejudice in the eyes of many categories of people. It has only two parties, which are opposed on none of the fundamental issues – nationhood, moral law, institutions, defense, freedom, ownership. It is a federation of States each of which, with its governor, its representatives, its judges and its officials – all elected – takes upon itself responsibility for a large part of the immediate business of politics, administration, justice, public order, economy, health, education, etc., while the central government and Congress normally confine themselves to larger matters: foreign policy, civic rights and duties, defense, currency, overall taxes and tariffs. For these reasons, the system has succeeded in functioning up to now in the north of the New World. But where would it lead France, a country beset by the after-effects of the convulsions inflicted upon it by so many internal and external crises, a country in which everything, in the political, social, moral, religious and national spheres, is always totally in dispute, a country whose people are in the habit of splitting into irreconcilable factions, a country the demands of whose unity coupled with the perpetual threats from outside have induced to centralize its administration to the utmost, thus making it *ipso facto* the target of every grievance? How could one doubt that, with us, the fact that the two powers were erected face to face behind theoretically impregnable ramparts, would lead to intransigence on both sides, parliament refusing to vote the laws and budgets for any recalcitrant government, and the latter, in consequence, over-stepping the bounds of legality for lack of any recognized outlet to their conflicts through dissolution on the one hand or a vote of censure on the other? The inevitable result would be either the submission of the President to the demands of the deputies or else a pronunciamento. How then could one speak of balance? It must be added that, our country being what it is, common sense forbids the merging in a single person of the supreme office of Head of State, responsible for the fate of the nation, in other words the long-term and the continuous, and the secondary role of Prime Minister, whose function it is to run the executive, to direct current policy and to deal with day-to-day contingencies.

In any case, the champions of parliamentary government and those of the presidential system, who indignantly rejected the resort to a popular vote to amend the Constitution, were well aware that neither the Senate nor the Chamber of Deputies would ever adopt either of the two proposals. If they ventilated them, none the less, on the eve of the national ballot, it could only be to create a diversion. For them as for all the other partisans, it was simply a question of foiling my plan, as was proved on October 10 at a joint press conference given by the leaders of what was called "the Cartel of the Noes". Under the prestigious chairmanship of Paul Reynaud, who a few days before had declared that "President de Gaulle has violated the Constitution and insulted parliament," and with the active concurrence of Guy Mollet who for his part had written: "If the people answer 'Yes', de Gaulle will inevitably lead them into civil war," the Independents, the Socialists, the MRP, the Radicals, the Democratic Entente, the Liberal European Party, combined to express their passionate hostility. At the same time the PSU announced a determined "No" to "the Gaullist monarchy". Earlier, Gaston Monnerville, who had been re-elected President of the Senate by a unanimous vote – the UNR group having abstained – declared to frantic applause from the assembly that "the Constitution is being violated," that "the people are being misled," that what de Gaulle was proposing was "not democracy, but at best a sort of enlightened Bonapartism," that it was, in fact, "the negation of democracy," that "the struggle may be long and hard, but the Republic will be saved". Meanwhile Vincent Auriol, making himself the champion of errors which not so long ago he had been the first to recognize and deplore, wrote: "The referendum is an act of absolute power . . . . While ostensibly making obeisance to the sovereignty of the people, it is, in fact, an attempt to deprive the people of its sovereignty for the benefit of one man . . . . I vote 'No!' " At the same time, the Communists called on Frenchmen and Frenchwomen "to answer 'No' in order to prevent de Gaulle from taking a further step on the road to dictatorship, destroying the last vestiges of democracy . . . . and intensifying his policy of reaction and war." Lastly the CNR,[1] created by Georges Bidault and Jacques Soustelle and linked to what remained of the OAS, advised its followers to vote "No."

This joint offensive of all the parties was emulated by a number of professional organizations which, though strictly speaking they had no business to involve themselves in political

[1] *Conseil national de la Résistance.*

debates, hastened to take part in this one. For instance the CGT enjoined its members "to demonstrate by an unequivocal 'No' their rejection of the blank check which de Gaulle was asking the French people to sign"; the Paris branch of the association of *Force Ouvrière* unions announced that, "like its general committee," it was calling on the workers "to answer 'No' in the referendum"; the National Committee of the CFTC, while declaring that it had no intention of influencing the voters, endorsed "the unfavorable verdict on the referendum reached by the Confederal Council"; the *Ligue de l'Enseignement*[1] proclaimed: "In order to remain the master of its destiny and safeguard the future of democracy, the people will answer 'No'"; the *Syndicat national de l'Enseignement technique* declared itself "unanimously in favor of voting 'No' "; the *Syndicat national de l'Enseignement secondaire* urged its members "to answer 'No' to this attempt to destroy basic liberties"; the *Union française universitaire* called on all its members to vote 'No'; the Executive Committee of the FNSEA[2] condemned "the procedure imposed on the country, the project as presented, the underlying objectives of the President of the Republic and the moral pressures exerted by the authorities"; the Central Committee of the MODEF[3] called on farmers "to declare themselves against the government's agricultural policy by voting 'No' in the referendum," etc.

The *Conseil d'Etat* provided a shrill reminder that it was not to be excluded from this chorus of opposition. On October 21, a few days after its ruling against the President of the Republic on the subject of Article 11, it returned to the charge. Its judicial assembly issued a judgment under the terms of which the Military Court of Justice set up by ordinance on June 1, in pursuance of the legislative or rule-making powers conferred on me by the April referendum on Algerian independence, was simply annulled. Created to empower the government

---

[1] Main State teachers' organization.

[2] *Fédération nationale des syndicats d'exploitants agricoles:* main peasant pressure group.

[3] *Mouvement de défense de l'exploitation familiale:* left-wing small-holders' group.

to have the OAS criminals summarily tried, this court had been fulfilling its functions for nearly five months, and had passed sentence in a number of cases without its validity being questioned by the *Conseil d'Etat*. The Council had now suddenly chosen to do so, with the intention of challenging my authority a week before the national consultation. The particular occasion was the case of a certain "Canal", the Treasurer of the OAS, who had just been convicted. The Council proclaimed itself competent in this matter on the ground that it fell within "the administrative sphere"! Having examined the case, it declared that the procedure laid down for the functioning of the court was "not in conformity with the general principles of law" because it did not provide for the right of appeal, and that consequently my ordinance was *ultra vires*. The Council therefore pronounced the Court of Justice dissolved and its sentences quashed.

To accept such an injunction, especially in a matter of this kind, would clearly be to acquiesce in an intolerable usurpation. As Head of State, invested by the stern test of history, by the terms of my office and by the people's vote in a referendum with a legitimacy, a mandate and a legislative mission which were not and could not be amenable to the jurisdiction of a body in no way empowered to question them, I considered the ruling of the *Conseil d'Etat* to be null and void. It was clear that political influences within the Council had caused it to exceed its powers. Besides, in what way were "the general principles of law" violated by the fact that certain cases were not submitted to the Court of Cassation, when the sovereign people had decided that they should be exceptional and expeditious to the extent of empowering me to set up through the law a special tribunal to try them? In circumstances of war or public danger, had not French justice, military or civil, like that of every other country, frequently been organized in such a way as to act swiftly without higher authority being called upon to intervene in each case? Had the *Conseil d'Etat*, in the hundred and sixty-two years of its existence, ever raised any objection to this? Had it even done so in the case of the Military High Court which had preceded the Court of Justice and whose sentences had also not been subject to appeal? Finally, was it not scandalous that this body, created to assist the State, should draw attention to itself in such a way in connection with the cause of a notorious criminal? Three days later the Cabinet roundly condemned "the character of an intervention which clearly lies outside the sphere of administrative justice which is that of the *Conseil d'Etat*, and which both by its object and by the time and circumstances in which it has arisen, is calculated to hinder the action of the public authorities in regard to the criminal subversion which has not yet been suppressed." At the same time it was decided to bring about the reform that was clearly called for in this overweening body. But the position adopted by the areopagus in the Palais-Royal[1] and loudly trumpeted by all the organs of opinion, was exploited to the utmost by the "Cartel".

The latter, indeed, in denouncing de Gaulle's "arbitrary" behavior and the alleged infringement of the Constitution by the resort to a referendum, enjoyed the support of the press in a way that was frequently blatant, sometimes veiled, but on the whole determined. Almost all the Parisian and provincial newspapers sought to persuade public opinion and the electorate to reject my proposal. They did so either by declaring themselves openly in favor of voting "No" or by publishing prominently the views of the spokesmen of the hostile political groups and unions, or by exclusively calling attention to the opinions of politically committed jurists, stuck fast in the notion of the parliamentary system such as it existed when they had read their law, or by producing more and more disparaging appraisals, anecdotes and caricatures concerning me.

In the long run I had become impervious to this attitude on the part of the press. I realized, moreover, that in view of the contumacious, resentful and jaundiced climate of opinion characteristic of our time, criticism of government must seem *a priori* more expedient and more profitable to publishers and editors than support for an arduous and ambitious national

[1] Headquarters of the *Conseil d'Etat*.

enterprise. I realized that those whose job it was to deal with "news" had personal reasons for regretting the departure of the previous regime which, far more than the present one, provided them with contacts, preferment and influence. I realized, also, that as far as I myself was concerned, although I read the newspapers and listened to the radio, although I always took an interest in the talents displayed there, although I used the pen and the microphone as much as anyone, it was part of my nature and a precept of my office invariably to keep my distance, an attitude which did not endear me to the professionals of the media. Yet, armored though I was against their arrows, I was none the less pained by their excesses – for instance, when the journalists of the radio and television service joined in the demonstrations of disapproval which had been mounted against me, by declaring a strike a few days before the ballot. They, too, complained of injustice, on the grounds that broadcasting time allocated to the parties in the referendum campaign was inadequate. Yet these same people had not raised the slightest protest when for more than twelve years the governments of the day had kept de Gaulle off the air.

Truly it was high time to prove that all the political, professional and journalistic vested interests added together did not express the will of the people, any more than they defended its collective interests. That so many men of so many different kinds, by no means lacking in merit, having lived through the atrocious confusion of the recent past, should wish to return to a regime which they knew to be disastrous; that having witnessed the country's evident revival they should do their utmost to halt its progress and set it once more on the downward path; that having seen, heard and known General de Gaulle for a quarter of a century and, whatever schools of thought they belonged to, participated in his national effort at one time or another, and even in some cases been members of his government, they should show nothing but mistrust and aversion towards him as soon as they were no longer afraid – all these were facts which naturally saddened me but nevertheless strengthened my determination. Rationally as well as humanly, the success of their coalition would be fatal to the State and unworthy of France.

It was for this reason that I committed myself to the uttermost. The talk which I delivered to the country on October 18 once more put the issue in the plainest possible terms. Were we to return to the system of the past, or were we to ensure the future of our institutions? Just as I had done at the time of the Algerian question, I indicated point-blank what personal consequences I would draw from the ballot. 'If your answer is 'No,' " I said, "as all the old parties wish, in order to re-establish their calamitous regime, as do also all the agitators in order to launch into subversion, or if the majority in favour of 'Yes' is slender, mediocre, aleatory, it is quite obvious that my task will immediately and irrevocably be brought to an end. For what could I do afterwards without the whole-hearted trust of the nation? But if, as I hope, as I believe, as I am certain, you give me once more a massive 'Yes', then I will be confirmed in the trust which I bear; then the country will be settled, the Republic secure and the horizon clear; then the world will finally be persuaded of France's great future!" On October 26 I repeated to the people that "whether my historic task is brought to an end or allowed to continue" depended on them.

No doubt, at a time when the country had only just emerged from a period of turmoil, and was alarmed by the recent assassination attempts, circumstances may well have seemed disquieting enough to many people for the prospect of my departure to influence their votes. But had I the right to conceal from my fellow-citizens how matters stood as far as I was concerned, since this was obviously an important factor in the verdict they were about to reach? Yet a number of opposition spokesmen complained of "plebiscitary blackmail" and went so far as to deny me the right to withdraw if my proposal was rejected. Of course this way of looking at things was explicable at the level of professional politics, where in any contest the sole aim is to obtain or keep a place, whatever fate may afterwards befall the ideas one has upheld. It was explicable from the viewpoint of the former regime, under which the Head of

State, whatever his own convictions, simply had to put up with what was submitted to him for signature. It was explicable in terms of the conventions of the past, in accordance with which the hero or heroine did not leave the stage until he or she was strangled by "the sultan's janissaries". But on the national plane which was his, how could de Gaulle continue to answer for France if the French people, consulted by him in an urgent and solemn manner on a subject which affected their entire future, were to decide against him? In the unimaginable event of his choosing to stay should such a contingency arise, what would be left of his honor and authority, since he himself had made direct accord between the French people and their guide the origin, the basis, the mainspring of the new Republic?

On the eve of the referendum, interested commentaries proliferated on what precisely would constitute the "slender, mediocre, aleatory" majority with which I would refuse to be satisfied. For among the leaders of public opinion there were cautious and calculating people who did not yet want to see my downfall but who hoped that my success would be as limited as possible, so that I should be placed in a precarious situation and their critical interventions would regain some of the weight they had had in the past. For instance Pierre Brisson, the well-informed editor of *Le Figaro*, was certain, as he wrote to an eminent correspondent, that "if de Gaulle goes now, it will mean disaster," that "the elements which were at large at the time of Clamart, and are still at large, are terrifying," that "arrangements have been made for a total and immediate amnesty, absolving the killers and bringing back Bidault and his henchmen," that "the phrase 'abuse of power' used by Monnerville was a key phrase," and that "to vote 'no' at this time in these circumstances is to vote for the worst." But he nevertheless declared to the readers of his newspaper that he himself was not taking sides and would put a blank voting paper in the ballot box.

On October 28, 1962, the French people decided by a considerable majority that the President of the Republic should henceforth be elected by universal suffrage. Out of 28,185,000 registered voters, 21,695,000 voted. Of these 13,151,000 voted "Yes" – more than sixty-two per cent – 7,974,000 voted "No" and there were 500,000 spoiled papers. Considering that, for the first time since the days of the RPF, and unlike the three previous referenda, the parties had united to join battle with me without reserve and without exception, I had made up my mind that a positive percentage somewhere in the sixties, relegating the "noes" to the thirties, would satisfy me. This was the case. I must, therefore, carry on. However, on the opposition side, it seemed at first that, faced with the published result, people could not believe their eyes and ears. The President of the Senate publicly called upon the Constitutional Council to declare the vote of the French nation null and void. Vincent Auriol, who was an *ex-officio* member of the Council in his capacity as a former President of the Republic, but who up to then had never appeared there, suddenly took his seat in order to support Gaston Monnerville. Their motion was naturally rejected. But that such declared and professional "democrats" should have no hesitation in flouting the will of the people was eloquent proof of the dictatorial lengths to which the spirit of partisanship can lead.

Meanwhile the coalition, swallowing its discomfiture, at once pinned its hopes on the forthcoming general elections. These of course, would be very different from a referendum in which the matter was settled at one stroke between de Gaulle and the nation. The contest would be split up among four hundred and eighty-two constituencies in each of which, in very varied circumstances, the personal standing of candidates, the well-established voting habits of the electoral clienteles, the position of local political notables – senators, deputies, departmental councillors, mayors, mostly linked to the parties – the influence of the local press which was nearly always attached to the customs and the men of yesterday, would all play their part. The majority in the previous National Assembly had been largely made up of opposition elements. Should this majority increase or even hold its own, de Gaulle, through his government, would be faced with severe parliamentary difficulties, aggravated by the fact that under the terms of the Constitution he could not dissolve the new Chamber for a year. In order for a ministry to survive and for a budget to be passed, he would either have to give up the struggle, or surrender to the parties, or take exceptional measures which in the absence of public danger would appear unjustifiable. With this prospect in view, the old political formations, determined on revenge, decided to bury the hatchet and join forces against "the Association for the New Republic". The latter, created under the ardent aegis of André Malraux for the express purpose of upholding my cause, included, in addition to the UNR and the UDT,[1] which were already merged, a few elements detached from several other groups. Since the question at issue in the contest which was about to open, as in the referendum, was the safeguarding of the new institutions and, in particular, of the power of the Head of State, this time I was induced to enter the electoral fray myself. I did so without attacking anyone in particular and without ever naming any of those who heaped personal abuse on me. But I did so vigorously enough to exorcize the system whence the assailants had sprung and to which they would inevitably return if they succeeded in defeating me.

On November 7 I told the nation that the decision it had taken ten days earlier was "of the greatest significance for the future of France." Moreover, I went on, "the referendum has demonstrated beyond the shadow of a doubt a fundamental principle of our time: the fact that the parties of yesterday do not represent the nation. They gave clear and terrible proof of it in 1940, when their regime abdicated in the midst of disaster. They illustrated it once more in 1958, when they ceded power to me on the brink of anarchy, bankruptcy and civil war. They have now confirmed it in 1962."

I then recalled what had recently happened: "Now that the nation was forging ahead, its coffers full, the franc stronger than it had ever been, decolonization finally achieved, the Algerian drama brought to an end, the Army completely restored to discipline, French prestige re-established throughout the

[1] *Union démocratique du travail:* Left Gaullist party 1958–62.

world . . . . we saw the parties of yesterday turn against de Gaulle . . . . we saw them unanimously oppose the referendum. . . we saw them, without a single exception, join forces first of all in parliament to pass a vote of censure on the government, then before the country to persuade it to vote 'No.' Now their coalition has been repudiated by the French people . . . . Thus it is a fact that to identify the parties of yesterday with France and the Republic would today be utterly absurd."

Then I pointed out what must now be done: "By voting 'Yes' in spite of them, the nation has just disclosed a large majority in favor of political renovation . . . . It is absolutely essential that this majority should become enlarged and consolidated and, above all, that it should establish itself in parliament . . . . For if parliament were to reappear tomorrow dominated by the old factions, it would inevitably wallow in obstruction and plunge the public authorities into the sort of confusion with which we are all too familiar, until sooner or later the State became engulfed in a new national crisis . . . . On the other hand, think what a role parliament could play if, shaking off the pretensions and illusions of the partisans, it decided to lend its resolute support to the work of recovery which has been pursued over the past four years!"

Finally I launched my appeal: "Frenchmen, Frenchwomen, on October 28 you sealed the condemnation of the disastrous regime of the parties . . . . But on November 18 and 25 you will be electing the deputies. It is my earnest wish that you ensure that this second confrontation does not contradict the first. In spite of local habits and traditions and sectional considerations, it is my wish that you confirm by your choice of men the decision which in voting 'Yes' you made as to my own destiny . . . . I ask you to do this, taking my stand once more on the only ground which matters to me, namely the good of the State, the fate of the Republic and the future of France."

The first ballot on November 18, 1962 revealed what the commentators called "a Gaullist tidal wave": thirty-two per cent of the electors voted outright for candidates of the UNR and five per cent for those who were explicitly associated with it.

In the previous elections, in 1958, which at the outset had produced what was regarded as a startling success for the grouping which had been put together to support me, the percentage obtained did not exceed twenty-two. As normally happens under a voting system based on a simple majority, the results were massively accentuated at the second ballot, the more so because the parties, unanimous in opposing, were not unanimous in reaching agreement with each other. On November 25 the "Association", receiving forty-three per cent of the votes on the second ballot, won a triumphant victory. Out of four hundred and eighty-two seats in the National Assembly, the UNR, which had gained sixty-four, would now occupy two hundred and thirty-three, constituting the largest group ever seen in the Palais-Bourbon, and it would be regularly reinforced by some forty other deputies who had pledged it their support in order to get elected. To crown all, for the first time in the history of universal suffrage, every Paris constituency – there were now thirty-one of them – was won by the same formation, that which had been created to support the policies of General de Gaulle.

On December 7, once the bureau of the new National Assembly had been elected and its committees set up, I renominated the government as a matter of form. It was to all intents and purposes identical to what it had been before. Georges Pompidou remained Prime Minister, with André Malraux, Louis Jacquinot, Louis Joxe and Gaston Palewski at his side as Ministers of State respectively in charge of Cultural Affairs, Overseas Territories, Administrative Reform and Scientific Research and Atomic and Space questions. The ministerial departments were distributed as follows: Justice: Jean Foyer; Foreign Affairs: Maurice Couve de Murville; Interior: Roger Frey; Armed Forces: Pierre Messmer; Finance and Economic Affairs: Valéry Giscard d'Estaing; Co-operation: Raymond Triboulet; Education: Christian Fouchet; Public Works and Transport: Marc Jacquet; Industry: Maurice Bokanowski; Agriculture: Edgard Pisani; Labour: Gilbert Grandval; Construction: Jacques Maziol; Ex-Servicemen: Jean

Sainteny; Posts and Telecommunications: Jacques Marette; Information: Alain Peyrefitte; Repatriates: François Missoffe. Two State Secretaries attached to the Prime Minister, Jean de Broglie for Algerian Affairs and Pierre Dumas for Relations with Parliament, one attached to the Ministry of Foreign Affairs, Michel Habib-Deloncle, and one for the budget, Robert Boulin, completed the executive. Of its twenty-six members only three were newcomers, Jacquet, Sainteny and Habib-Deloncle. Two former ministers left the government: Roger Dusseaulx, who was elected chairman of the UNR in the National Assembly, and Georges Gorse who became Ambassador to Algeria.

Thus the political storm which the parties had unleashed in vain, with the object of preventing the edifice of our institutions from being consolidated and at the same time of wresting power from my hands, had had no effect on the government. As before, the Head of State had nominated the ministers who composed it so that they could carry out together the task which he himself had laid down. He had chosen the first among them to be his second-in-command. He had appointed the others on the basis of their abilities and their personalities without accepting any conditions. None of them was delegated by any extraneous authority or subject to any outside allegiance. Allowing for inevitable and commendable human divergences, this group of men formed around him and by his choice, linked by the ambition to play a prominent part in the progress of our country, presented a cohesion which had no precedent in the annals of the former Republics. Parliament for its part gave evidence of having undergone an unbelievable transformation, not only theoretically but in actuality. It is true that the Senate, having failed as yet to find a modern economic and social function and hence an effective responsibility, enclosed itself in an attitude of hostility which was as morose as it was futile. But the National Assembly, which alone in the last resort had the power to make law and supervise the government, had become representative of a French public opinion which, in spite of residues of malignancy, gave every indication of having adopted the new regime. There now existed in the Palais-Bourbon a majority, compact, homogeneous and resolute enough to give its steadfast support and confidence to one and the same policy and to give it legislative effect to the exclusion of political crisis until the end of its mandate.

Had the State ever known such continuity and stability without the slightest infringement of our liberties? When had the world last witnessed such an appearance of assurance and serenity in our organs of government? Had I not served France well in leading her people to this profound transformation?

Chapter 2

୶ჯ⅃ঌ

In the fifth year of its life, the Fifth Republic was established
on the foundations I had laid down. Nothing short of a major
upheaval could now prevent it from carrying out the national
task. But what it must do in the future, as well as what it had
already done, and even the recent onslaught against me by the
coalition of its adversaries, underlined the unique duty that
was still incumbent upon me. I was, indeed, deeply conscious
of it. Though I recognized the essentially relative nature of
political authority, however highly esteemed, though I regarded
as excessive the general tendency of public opinion to make me
responsible, be it in praise or blame, for everything that
happened, though I was amused at the extravagant terms in
which some people described my alleged omnipotence – the
English newspapers, for instance, who called me the "Sun-
President" – I knew to what both past and present committed
me. I knew that it was for me alone to pilot the ship. I knew that
there was no respite in the surge of difficulties.

Nevertheless, having steered the fragile craft through rough
water, I felt that I should now be able to guide it for a while
in calmer seas. Our country had completely overhauled its
political institutions, transformed its empire into a vast system
of interdependent States, put down a serious military revolt,
liquidated the sinister terrorist enterprise, put an end to the
Algerian drama, restored to health its economy, finances and
currency, which had been at death's door, and rekindled in

itself a long-forgotten light and warmth; now it had to continue its progress, re-establish its power and ensure its independence. This would mean, at home, an immense effort of work, organization and output, accompanied by inevitable jolts which must be prevented from leading to disaster as in the past. It was to this that I intended that the government should first and foremost direct its energies. At the same time, taking advantage of the crédit and prestige conferred on us by the kind of miracle we had just achieved, I wanted to increase and extend our action in world affairs with a view to playing an independent role. Finally, convinced that beyond what was done and to be done, we must still accomplish the profound human and social reform of participation, though in view of its magnitude and the atmosphere of the time, it would first have to mature, I would continue at least to guide the nation in that direction. In a word, France, having suffered many setbacks and much confusion, from which she had recently emerged only at the cost of dangerous upheavals, must now knuckle down to a harsh period of adjustment if she was to come to terms with the modern age.

This policy, though apparently peaceful enough, was nevertheless destined to encounter many obstacles. For now that the nation had been freed from its afflictions for the first time since the dawn of the century, now that it was no longer threatened by either invasion or ruin, now that it need no longer fire a shot, nor seek outside help, nor face insurrection, the cohesion recently forced upon it by the dangers of civil war and financial collapse was to dissolve into innumerable individual anxieties and grievances. This meant that though the immediate situation did not absorb me in so regular and obvious a way as had the events of the last four years, it none the less demanded my stimulus and intervention. Long-term plans and prospects naturally continued to come under my purview, and I had every reason to feel that should any serious incident occur, safety or shipwreck would once more depend on me. In short, it became desirable that official policy should make the role of the Head of State less prominent in day-to-day matters, that it should bring more openly into play than hitherto the government's role in examining, choosing and applying the numerous measures to be taken on the most varied subjects, but that it should still require any vital decision to be made by me.

Georges Pompidou seemed to me capable and worthy of conducting affairs at my side. Having long put his merit and devotion to the test, I now intended that, as Prime Minister, he should deal with the many complex questions which the period about to open would inevitably raise. While his intelligence and wide culture kept him abreast of ideas of every kind, he was by nature inclined to concentrate on the practical side of things. Though he admired brilliance in action, risk in a venture, and boldness in the exercise of authority, he himself tended towards cautious attitudes and a circumspect approach, while at the same time he excelled in grasping the basic issues in every problem and finding a solution. And so this political neophyte, unknown to the public until he was in his fifties, suddenly found himself – by my doing, and without his having sought it – invested with unlimited responsibility, thrown into the center of public life with all the searchlights of the news media trained upon him. But it was his good fortune to find cordial and vigorous support at the summit of the State, a government of ministers who were devoted to the same cause as himself and unsparing in their co-operation, a compact majority in parliament after the short-lived ordeal of the referendum and the elections, and in the country a great mass of people willing to give their approval to de Gaulle. Thus protected from above and supported from below, but moreover self-confident beneath his circumspection, he grappled with the problems of the day, exercising, as occasion demanded, the powers of comprehension and the tendency to scepticism, the talent for exposition and the inclination to hold his tongue, the desire to reach decisions and the art of temporizing, which made up the various resources of his personality. In the light of my position and my knowledge of the man, I placed Pompidou in office to assist me during a specific phase. Circumstances were to weigh sufficiently heavy for me to keep him there longer than any Head of Government for the past century. Moreover, the relative lull that the situation called for, while responding to the dominant characteristics of the Prime Minister, also suited the mood of the people, who were adapting themselves with difficulty to the conditions of generalized industrial activity. In contrast with the individualistic way of life as country-dwellers, craftsmen, tradesmen and *rentiers* which had been that of their forefathers for so many centuries, Frenchmen now found themselves, not without some distress, forced into a mechanized mass existence. Work, in factories, workshops, mills, dockyards, stores, demanded uniformly mechanical and repetitive movements in well-established grooves and with always the same companions. Nor was there any variety in office work, where jobs and fellow-workers remained unchanged, following the lines laid down by a matter-of-fact plan or a computer program. Apart from the hazards of bad weather, agriculture had become no more than the setting in motion of automatic motorized machinery, with a view to turning out rigidly standardized products. As for commerce, it was carried on in identical supermarkets, with shelves full of mass-produced goods and aggressive advertising. Everyone now lived in a kind of cell in a nondescript block. Grey, faceless crowds travelled in public transport, and one could neither drive nor walk along a road or street without being herded into lanes and regimented by signs. Even leisure had become collective and prescribed: rationalized meals handed out in canteens; cheers in unison from the grandstands of sports grounds; holidays spent on crowded sites with trippers, campers and bathers laid out in rows; day or evening relaxation at pre-ordained hours for families in identical flats where, before bedtime, everyone simultaneously watched and heard the same broadcasts on the same wavelengths. All this was due to force of circumstances, but I knew that it weighed more heavily on our people, by reason of their nature and antecedents, than on any other, and felt that some sudden additional provocation might well precipitate them one day into some irrational crisis.

This was all the more true because, as they contemplated their own development, their aspirations grew and kindled. All levels and conditions of the populace, straining to improve their standard of living but thwarted by the ruthless laws of the capitalist system, were in a permanent state of resentment or suspicion towards ill-defined interests which they felt to be determined to keep them down. And then the trade unions, because they took no part in the studies and debates from which decisions stemmed – the chief among them, moreover, being closely associated with the systematic opposition of the Communist Party – devoted themselves exclusively to pay claims. Hence, despite the undoubted rise in wages, full employment for all, basic insurance against illness, unemployment, accident and old age, maternity allowances, subsidies for large families, constant improvement in amenities throughout the country, notably in housing, schools, hospitals, old people's homes, holiday camps, etc. – in short the material progress of the French people – the fact remained that social relationships were still marked by suspicion and bitterness. In spite of the variety and the quality of the food on every table and the clothes on every back, the increasing number of labor-saving devices in homes, of cars on the roads, of aerials on the roofs, everyone resented what he lacked more than he appreciated what he had.

Furthermore France's adjustment to modern economic conditions could not but entail shocks and jolts which inevitably caused some perturbation. Our working activities, long settled in their objects, sites and customs, were now undergoing changes in character, location, techniques, equipment and tempo which affected the situation and the way of life of many people. International competition, to which we were exposed by the lowering of customs barriers within the Common Market, and the liberalization of world trade, confronted our manufacturers with problems which they were formerly spared by protectionism. To the global evolution begun more than a century ago which brought country-dwellers into the manufacturing towns, had now been added a new shift that specifically affected mines, factories and transport. This led, from time to time and from

342

place to place, to crises which were due to insurmountable economic imperatives and which vitally affected the lives of the people concerned – seeing which, the working masses could not escape the anxious feeling that this vast movement of change might jeopardize the job, status and home of every one of them. Amid the general progress, a cloud overshadowed the fate of the individual. The time-honored serenity of a nation of peasants certain of being able to extract from the soil a meager but assured living, had given place, for those born in this century, to the muted anguish of the uprooted.

All in all, what the nation had to do at home for some time to come was to persevere with the radical transformation on which its future depended, and to bind up one by one the wounds it might incur in the process. As far as the State was concerned, this was to be accomplished, not indeed by crushing freedom or the spirit of enterprise, but nevertheless by applying a definite plan – whence, on the part of the government, constant action in a variety of forms through the medium of the law and the administration. I was to head this action, publicly accepting responsibility for it, inspiring or correcting the ministers and officials who would have to carry it out, and imposing such measures of progress or restriction as were demanded by the nation's future but, in the immediate event, ran counter to other interests.

There remained my duty towards society. Doubtless the spiritual sickness resulting from a civilization dominated by materialism could not be cured by any form of government. But, at least, it might one day be assuaged by a change in the moral climate that would make Man a responsible being instead of a mere tool. At the same time, in order that the inevitable inequalities, displacements and taxes entailed by a modern economy should appear to everyone as justified and in order, it must be organized in such a way that each man would be a partner as well as an employee. I had to admit, however, that in cold blood, in the atmosphere of stagnation succeeding dramatic events and the removal of danger, when routine, selfishness and sectarianism were once more becoming entrenched, the peaceful revolution of participation could not be set in motion on the scale it demanded. But after all, it was not overnight that I had succeeded in rallying the country to the cause of the Resistance, or in persuading it to adopt a regime worthy of it, or decolonizing its overseas possessions and emancipating Algeria. I was well aware that the general consent that makes legislation bear fruit seldom appears except in a thunderflash. Though I had no desire for the storm to arise, I would have to take advantage of it if one day it were to break. In politics, as in strategy, business and love, one must of course have the gift. One must also have the opportunity.

Under the aegis of a now stable and coherent regime, the country was working hard and well. It was doing so, at that time, within the framework of the Fourth Plan, which envisaged a vigorous expansion of French production. The average annual increase in gross domestic production, ambitiously pre-estimated at 5·5 per cent, was to be greatly exceeded, reaching 7·2 per cent in 1962, 6·3 per cent in 1963 and 7 per cent in 1964, chiefly by reason of industrial development, which in the course of these three years rose respectively to index points of 122, 128 and 138 in relation to 100 in 1959. What we achieved during the same period in terms of growth rate in comparison with other countries, with the sole exception of Japan, placed us first among all the great nations of the world, including the United States, Germany, Britain and Italy. This had never happened to us before.

Thanks to this national success, household consumption, which is a practical index of the standard of living, had increased by a third in 1964 in relation to 1959. At the same time, our foreign trade soared to an extent hitherto unknown for France. We bought and sold twice as much abroad as five years before. Throughout the world, at trade fairs and exhibitions, French products were now appearing which were very different from the luxury articles that had previously been almost our sole contributions. Among the most powerful machines, the heaviest engines and vehicles, the most complex pieces of apparatus, ours were always on offer, and often did well.

Conversely, foreigners were beginning to regard the French as people who were well able to pay for the best. It is true that in our country people were working regularly and industriously. In the private sector the average working week was forty-six hours, and there were virtually no strikes. For the first time in her existence, France had no more than 24,000 unemployed in the strict sense. Scarcely 110,000 people failed to obtain work immediately they sought it. Yet this was the period when the young people born in great numbers after the war were beginning their working life, when the end of the Algerian conflict and the reduction by half of the period of military service returned 300,000 national servicemen to civilian life, when the economy of the mother country absorbed at one blow 400,000 workers repatriated from Algeria, and when our frontiers were opened to 120,000 new foreign immigrants.

In order to ensure our future development, these increased earnings of the French people were not by any means consumed in their entirety. The upkeep of industrial plant, equipment and machinery, and *a fortiori* their renewal – which competition forced upon our often antiquated concerns – demanded large-scale investment. The Plan set a target of twenty-four per cent of the national product to be put aside for this purpose. In fact we did better, thanks chiefly to savings, which enriched the national coffers by 6,000 million francs in 1962, 6,500 million in 1963 and 8,500 million in 1964. Moreover the State budget, whose revenue was constantly growing with increased prosperity was able to contribute unprecedented sums, in excess of what had been forecast, to the development of the country, both by the financial help and services it provided and by the infra-structure it was building up.

Naturally, the activities and even the lineaments of France were evolving as progress advanced. During these three years, licenses granted for the construction of factories occupying more than 500 square meters amounted to more than 14,000; these were nearly always for installations in the provinces. The drive to concentrate agriculture meant the disappearance of some 150,000 small farms and the consolidation of almost two million hectares. In commerce, a thousand new self-service shops and 207 supermarkets were opened. A million housing units providing accommodation for four million Frenchmen were built, almost all subsidized by public funds and credits. A thousand kilometers of railway line were electrified. Work was everywhere speeded up on canals, ports, airdromes and tele-communications. This included the development of the gigantic enterprise which, by making the Rhône navigable along its entire length and joining it up with the Rhine, was to provide a direct link between the North Sea and the Mediterranean by convoys of large barges. The Moselle was opened up between Apach – soon it was to be Metz – and Trèves for barges of 1,350 tons, thus putting the industry of Lorraine in easy com-munication with the Rhine for heavy loads. In the port of Strasbourg a refinery center to serve the whole of the Rhine region was set up: the oil would now be unloaded near Marseilles at Lavéra and taken to its destination by a "Euro-pean" pipeline 700 kilometers long. Paris Airport, grouping together the airfields at Orly and Le Bourget and eventually Roissy, was organized and equipped for national and inter-national traffic on a scale inferior to none in Europe. Having from the beginning lagged far behind in the matter of telephones we were now gradually catching up, installing 190,000 a year instead of 110,000 as before. The ultra-modern center for space telecommunications at Pleumeur-Bodou was opened. Our quadruple factory for isotope separation rose from the ground at Pierrelatte. The French electricity board built several new atomic power stations.

In addition, this was the time when a start was made to our motorway construction. Whereas five years earlier almost noth-ing had been done, 480 kilometers were in use and 150 more in process of construction in the year 1964, in accordance with the plan adopted in 1959. In this matter it was our intention to pull back the lead which the Germans, the British and the Italians had gained over us. It is fair to say that if they had set to work earlier than we had, this was because when the reign of the motor car began their ordinary road networks were seriously inadequate. We, on the other hand, had at our disposal the matchless system bequeathed to us from the pre-railway era, and scrupulously maintained ever since by our Highways Department. Hence, although we had as many cars as our neighbors, or more, we had been slower to feel the need to build great utilitarian motorways. But in this area of modernization as in others, our decision was made and we had begun to put it into effect.

While this evolution was gathering momentum and accelerating our general development, it inevitably brought in its train a reduction and slowing down in certain individual sectors. For these, the inevitable consequence was diversification or transfer to other branches of industry – a painful reconversion requiring the sudden changeover from one set of skills, procedures and locations to another. In our country, neither men nor things are by nature mobile. Industrial plant does not easily lend itself to the risks attendant on innovation, which also have a distressing effect on personnel as far as their jobs, housing and way of life are concerned. This was the case with our coal-fields, whose output and share in our sources of energy were alike progressively diminishing. But this economic constriction produced a social crisis.

The crisis was all the more serious because it was largely unexpected. In fact the immediate needs of the post-war period had led us to extract the maximum possible output from our mines. Although their best coal seams were exhausted and their running costs often excessive, we had thought it desirable to devote very costly efforts to increasing production and renewing equipment. For if we were to put our iron and steel industry, our factories and our railways on their feet again, and produce electricity, coal provided almost the only source of energy to which we had access in our own right. The mining industry, therefore, as represented by its executives, engineers and miners, had become established as a vital section of our economic life, and was constantly being urged to increase its efforts. But conditions had changed. Oil was now readily available for all kinds of uses. A number of hydro-electric dams had been built during the past twenty years which had replaced power stations as the main source of electricity. Natural gas was coming on the scene. Atomic energy, with its limitless possibilities and ambitions, was making its appearance. Moreover, the restoration of communications, credit facilities and trade with the outside world had made it possible for us to import better coal than our own for various industrial and domestic uses. Finally, our own coal deposits, as a result of having been heavily overworked, increasingly precluded profitable exploitation. The time had come to restrict the tonnage extracted, to concentrate on the most advantageous sites and to close down others. This, of course, meant that new careers must be found for those miners who would cease to be miners, and their children who never would be. This contraction and mutation had been under way since 1960, when the government, following the report by Jean-Marcel Jeanneney, the Minister of Industry, decided that coal production should decrease in five years from fifty-nine to fifty-two million tons, and that help should be given to workers obliged to change jobs and move house.

But miners are proud men. They are proud of their job, whose rugged and dangerous character gives it a special nobility. They are proud of the warm feelings with which, for the same reason, the whole population regards them. They are proud of the part they can play, as outstanding as any in the nation so long as the latter genuinely needs them. It is for these reasons that, however harsh they may find life in the pit where they toil and dig the coal in the dark, threatened by cave-ins, gas explosions and silicosis, any of which might well prove fatal, they are still profoundly loyal to it. The various advantages in wages, pensions and housing which they receive also help to keep them attached to their work. For moral as well as material motives, therefore, they resented the restrictive measures, not only as a wrong inflicted on some of their number, but also as a mistake and as an injustice to their calling. Consequently, they were as a body determined to act in order to make the authorities relent. Seeing this, their unions made preparations for a strike which they intended should be decisive.

The unhappy collision which heralded this unhappy episode occurred at Decazeville. Owing to very unfavorable conditions there, it had been decided to cut down the workings in the area to a minimum, while providing for the introduction of new industries. In September 1962 there began a work stoppage which was to last for more than five months. But just as it seemed that this local dispute was on the way to settlement, the unions extended it to all the coalfields in the country, calling upon managements and, through them, upon the government to grant unacceptable wage increases forthwith, and to reconsider the closures already in operation or contemplated. This time the engineers and white-collar workers joined the movement, which showed it to be truly inspired by the anxiety of the entire industry as regards its future. Despite the government's undertaking to add a fair percentage to wages, having regard to the situation in other public services, and to arrange for an enquiry to be made jointly by the management and representatives of the employees into the future of coal production and the relevant problems of planning, vocational training, re-employment and pensions, the unions unanimously decided on an all-out strike, starting on March 1, 1963.

The winter, which had been very hard that year, was to continue for several weeks longer. This produced a higher than average consumption of coal and left no stocks at the pitheads. The leaders of the movement, therefore, supposed that industry, transport and domestic consumers would be unable to endure being deprived of fuel, and that in order to avert a catastrophe, the authorities would soon be obliged to accept their conditions. But they reckoned in particular that, when it had thus been proved that nothing could replace French coal in France, the running-down program would be abandoned. Now, for my part, I was determined to carry out this program come what might. Not, of course, that I was personally in the least happy to see the diminution of the role that had been imposed on our collieries. I was well aware of the stupendous toil that generations of miners had expended in order to develop a patrimony which I myself had decided to nationalize after the

Liberation. As a man of the north myself, I had a particularly high regard for these workers. Besides, my brothers Xavier and Jacques and my brother-in-law Alfred Cailliau had been mining engineers. But here, too, I must consider only the general good of the country. And then I must admit that I had the illusion that in the last resort the miners would not wish to take the responsibility of inflicting grave damage on the French community by refusing it coal at the very moment when it might have been supposed that the need for it was vital. If the problem was put to them in this way, would they not decide to stay at work while the proposed discussions were going on? Indeed, the management intimated that by intervening in this sense the government might well avert the strike. Hence, when the government submitted to me a recommendation that the work force should be requisitioned, I acceded to their request. Not that I had ever believed that one could force four hundred thousand men to work if they did not agree to do so. But I thought it conceivable that all or part of the work force would regard this decree signed by me as an affirmation of the national interest, and would consider it their duty to obey.

Alas, it was not to be. Except for the servicing of coke plants and safety precautions, the entire coal industry was paralyzed. For reasons of traditional sentiment, combined with the opportunism of political elements, the miners received sympathy and sometimes assistance from the most varied sources. Meanwhile, the attempt by the government to come to an agreement with the strikers through the intermediary of a Commission of Inquiry came to nothing. Week after week the crisis dragged on, showing that my hopes had been mistaken. But it also turned out, contrary to what the miners had supposed, that France was managing without French coal. Doubtless, industry and domestic heating suffered somewhat, but within bearable limits. Moreover, by increased purchases of American, British, Russian and Polish fuel and further recourse to oil and hydro-electric power, the worst deficiencies were made good. The strike, instead of proving to the country that it needed its coal mines, demonstrated, on the contrary, that it could live by other means.

At this, the mining profession was seized with doubt as to its own future, and the movement petered out for want of the stimulus that had set it in motion. After a stoppage lasting thirty-five days, work was resumed on more or less the terms that had been offered at the start. There followed meetings between the representatives of management and the mining employees for a joint study, such as the government had proposed before the crisis, of the true situation of the coal industry, the choice of pits to be closed and the reconversion measures which would accompany the reduction in output and in manpower. From these semi-official round-table discussions there emerged conclusions which were to clarify official decisions in the years to come.

Meanwhile, on all sides, the economic transformation of the country was inflicting other wounds upon it. A *laissez-faire* system would have ignored them, leaving them to bleed. A totalitarian discipline would have cauterized them with a red-hot iron. The planning policy of the new regime intended to heal them. Sometimes it did so on a small scale, in local crises brought about by the stagnation of certain establishments – for instance, the ironworks at Hennebont or the arms factory at Châtellerault – helping in such cases with problems of liquidation and encouraging the opening of new factories in the area to provide employment for redundant workers. Sometimes it was involved in more far-reaching intervention. Thus, at Saint-Nazaire and Nantes, our shipyards had come to be completely re-organized in the face of foreign competition which threatened to become overpowering with the entry of Japan into this field. Obviously, it would be absurd for us to give up shipbuilding since we had qualified engineers and skilled workers in this branch of industry, our country was washed by four seas, sea traffic was continually increasing throughout the world, and oil tankers and ore-ships were needed everywhere. But it was essential that the managements of the enterprises concerned should not shrink from the mergers and closures and re-equipment that would be required, and that employees should adapt themselves to the resulting changes.

Official prompting, in which Marc Jacquet, Minister of Public Works and Transport, played an important part, supported by Jean Morin, the Delegate-General for the Merchant Navy, succeeded in setting in order a first-class French industry. The government supplied the loans and subsidies necessary for the re-equipment of the shipyards and the rehousing of families, but also imposed a program of development. Thus France kept her place in the forefront of shipbuilding.

The people repatriated from Africa presented a problem unprecedented in its numerical magnitude and in national importance. In 1964 a total of more than 1,300,000 persons were estimated to have settled in the mother country in less than three years; of these, 980,000 came from Algeria. As far as the latter were concerned, it might have been supposed that because of the guarantees secured under the Evian agreements the withdrawal would have been less massive and precipitate. But the orders given by the OAS and enforced by terror had encouraged a general and speedy exodus. Perhaps, too, the attitude of the *pieds-noirs* towards the Arabs made it impossible for a sizeable French minority to remain under the Algerian government. At all events, the influx of so great a number of our nationals, uprooted from their homes, deprived of their jobs and full of bitterness, but whose return brought to the country an appreciable accession of population and of talent, required that my government should produce a policy and not merely stop-gap measures. The law of December 26, 1961, had laid down in good time, in general terms, the task of national solidarity which must and, indeed, would be carried out.

This task concerned all that must be done to welcome, integrate and compensate these French citizens who were returning to their ancestral land. Since the resources that the State could devote thereto, though substantial, were of necessity limited and would have to be spread over a considerable time, it was decided that public action and public funds should in the first place be directed towards the reception and then the resettlement and employment of the people concerned. Accordingly, much of the compensation for losses suffered was deferred to a later date. With humane efficiency, François Missoffe undertook the duties of Minister for Repatriation. Thanks to the extensive arrangements for providing food and shelter for this deprived and disorientated multitude, their arrival passed off in a seemly fashion. Then a whole series of measures was put into effect, some dealing with the finding of a job for each individual according to his profession, rehousing him according to his wishes and arranging for social security as required; some with help for families and the aged; some with grants and loans which made it possible to acquire or to set up industrial, agricultural or commercial enterprises. Moreover, by ordinances adopted under the powers conferred on me by the referendum law, one hundred and twenty thousand dwellings were allocated to the repatriates: these were built under the controlled rent scheme,[1] or prefabricated, or subsidized, or requisitioned. In three years, ten thousand million new francs were spent by the State on the people repatriated from Africa, not counting what was contributed by local communities and by many private individuals. Obviously, this vast operation could not dispose of grievances or comfort sorrow. But it did achieve its object, which was the resettlement in a worthy and useful manner of more than a million Frenchmen in their ancestral homeland.

Their resettlement, it is true, was facilitated by the general economic progress. But though this was in many ways synonymous with industrialization, it did not mean that French agriculture was to be trodden underfoot. The means of ensuring this existed under the *Loi d'orientation* of 1960 and the *Loi complémentaire* of 1962. They must now be put into effect. The minister Edgard Pisani applied himself to it with all his ability, clear-sightedness and vigor. Accordingly there was a general speeding up in the extension of profitable farms, the elimination of unviable holdings, the consolidation of scattered holdings, the improvement of rural amenities, and the pensioning-off of aged farmworkers. In July 1963, the Forestry Law made the State responsible for the safeguard of our woodlands, and

[1] HLM (*habitations à loyer modéré*): council flats.

organized its control over deforestation and its subsidies for replanting. A decree of May 1964 imposed new regulations on the wine-growing industry regarding production, with the object of placing a reasonable limit on the quantity produced while improving the quality. Finally, another decree reorganized the meat market at the level of the stock-breeders, and set up a chain of local modern slaughterhouses to this end. Before all these measures were taken, the minister held lengthy consultation with the professional organizations, among whom, incidentally, he encountered more objections than encouragement. For the rest, these same bodies put an adverse rather than favorable interpretation on the strenuous efforts made by Edgard Pisani on behalf of the government at the Brussels talks, to ensure that the produce of our soil should in practice be admitted to the European Common Market. Even when the agreement reached on this subject with our partners on December 23, 1963 crowned the success of our demands, there were nothing but murmurs of complaint from the Chambers of Agriculture and the Farmers' Unions. But alas! is it not the usual tendency of Frenchmen, whatever their trade, to clamor for progress while hoping that everything will remain the same? At a time when many heads of firms were looking with suspicion at what was being done to modernize industry, when a large number of teachers greeted educational reforms with nothing but criticism, and not a few officers were upset by the modernization of the Army, how could farmers be expected to approve of all the advances in agriculture?

In addition to the periodic troubles caused during this time by the coal industry, the shipyards, the repatriation problem or some rural activity or other, as well as the alarm aroused among tradespeople by the appearance of supermarkets and the regret felt by craftsmen as mass production became more widespread, there were from time to time upheavals affecting the public services; this was not because of their equipment, which except for the delay in telephone installation was generally adequate to the country's needs, but by reason of the chronic discontent of their employees. It must be admitted that the civil servants, officials, technicians, white-collar and manual workers, who serve either the State in various branches of administration or the general public in nationalized concerns, did find, amid the economic transformation of France, that the fairly privileged position they had once enjoyed was being eroded. No doubt in the past their salaries and wages had been calculated to the nearest sou, as they still were. But their value had been stabilized in the days of gold currency, and they and their families were able to live their lives on a solid, albeit modest foundation. Moreover, they had the advantage, exceptional in the society of that time, of a statute which guaranteed their job and their promotion, and a retirement pension to set their minds at rest when their career was over. They also valued the honorable status they enjoyed in the eyes of their friends and neighbors. But now these advantages were disappearing. For workers in the public sectors, whose incomes were fixed by budgets and scales that were necessarily rigorous, inflation fostered a constant anxiety as to how much their earnings were worth from one month to the next, whereas private industry, as it expanded, was continually raising wages and bonuses. Moreover, now that all branches of industry enjoyed full employment and were on the lookout for qualified applicants, their security of tenure no longer had the same relative attraction. As for the much-prized pension, once their prerogative, social security now provided one for everybody. All this had produced in the administration and the public services a state of mind that favored wage claims. As it was for the government to decide whether to implement them or not, it was to the government that the staffs which it controlled, directly or indirectly, applied, or against which they complained. During these years of lively economic expansion, the government had accordingly to deal with continued agitation, accompanied by work stoppages, in the fields of education, railways, electricity and gas, posts and telecommunications, hospitals, public transport in Paris, etc.

But quite clearly a strike in a public service assumes a very different character from one in a private firm. For it is an attack directed against the community as a whole by the very people who, by virtue of the profession they have chosen and which offers them security, have undertaken to provide it with an element essential to its activity and even to its existence. In refusing to teach in school, in cutting off electricity, gas and water, in holding up communications by post, telegram and telephone, the effect of their action is not to prevent an employer from getting richer but to jeopardize the interests of all in order to put pressure on the responsible authorities. This is indeed a powerful *de facto* argument for those who are making a claim. But it is also, from the government's point of view, a powerful reason for not allowing itself to be coerced. Moreover, an ordinary employer can grant wage increases by reducing profits, raising prices and cutting down his work force. But the state cannot use these methods. It cannot, at a moment's notice, reduce its costs in one department without deducting from what it owes to another payee; it cannot increase taxes without contravening the laws governing the level of taxation, or increase charges without affecting the cost-of-living index to the detriment of all; it cannot modify the number or the deployment of its servants without breaking their contracts, and it cannot, because of the "grid"[1] system, give something to someone without giving it to everyone. In short, unless it is to destroy the balance of the budget and start printing more banknotes, the government is in principle bound to resist strikes in the public sector. By the same token, such strikes represent a form of bullying directed against the community as well as ultimatums delivered to the government. Despite this they continue to occur. For the disruption of national services weighs heavily on the life of every individual, while workers in this category of employment run no risk of losing their jobs. Furthermore, the unions chiefly concerned are those of the CGT, which is allied to the Communist Party and which uses them as a weapon in its political and social struggle.

In order to prevent as far as possible work stoppages in the public sector, and to limit the consequences if they should

[1] Wage structure based on fixed differentials.

nevertheless occur, my government acted in two ways. First, it
endeavored to ensure that consultation became a regular
practice. To this end, the Toutée and Grégoire Commissions
brought together the various interest groups concerned, to
establish the facts of the situation in public enterprise and to
decide how the "wage fund" should be divided among the
different levels of employees. With the same object, Pierre
Massé, the Commissioner-General, held official consultations
with trade-union organizations to draw up the Fifth Plan,
which proposed to lay down rules as to what share of the
national product each category of workers should receive, in
other words to inaugurate an "incomes policy". But these steps
towards participation went hand in hand with measures concerning the exercise of the right to strike. In accordance with
the Constitution, the government passed a bill through parliament in July 1963 which, without challenging this right in
public services, put certain limits on its misuse. Henceforth,
any union decision involving a work stoppage must be formally
notified to the management at least five days before being put
into effect. Furthermore, such decisions could not be successively
applied to different sections of the work force. Lightning strikes
which disrupted the life of the population without warning were
thus proscribed, as were "staggered" strikes[1] which, while
ostensibly involving only one group at a time, in fact brought the
whole concern to a halt.

Settling difficulties of this kind as they occurred was essentially the business of Georges Pompidou and those of his colleagues who were immediately concerned. They dealt with them
competently and level-headedly. In case after case I left matters
to them. But it was I who decided, either in Cabinet or in
private, on the general line to be taken: that the budget should
regulate salaries and wages in the public sector, so that they
increased in accordance with the growth of the national product;
that employees should be statutorily entitled to fuller information and consultation with managements and also with ministers
but that the government should not allow itself to yield to

[1] *Grèves tournantes.*

ultimatums – this was what I insisted upon. Taken as a whole, the incidents which occurred in the public services were tiresome but not ruinous. Yet I saw in them yet another proof of the sickness and instability of our social structure. They would finally have convinced me, had I needed convincing, that to cure this fundamental evil, it was essential that those who by their toil produce the wealth of the nation should be directly associated with the conduct and progress of the activity in which they are involved, and so become responsible for it. Short of having to hammer out this reform in the fire of war or revolution, I would propose it to the people as soon as I had reason to believe that events had made them ready to accept it.

This would undoubtedly be the case in education. But when? In what circumstances? At the moment, this institution was in the throes of a vast travail. For the same evolution which, thanks to industrialization, was providing the mass of the people with a better life materially, and which would no doubt lead it one day, through participation, to a better state of mind, was bringing about an enormous development in the education of the French people. From the starting-point created long ago at the primary level by compulsory schooling, reinforced by free secondary education and completed in higher education by the extension of grants, an elemental thrust was impelling boys and girls towards wider knowledge. In a world whose highest echelons had become accessible to all, the desire for knowledge went hand in hand with the realization that the more one learned, the higher one might rise. Conversely, the general progress demanded more and more skills at every level of society. Hence, a tidal wave of willing learners was engulfing schools, colleges, lycées and universities, especially as the birthrate, fortunately re-established after the Liberation, had now almost doubled the potential school population compared with its pre-war level. Since the State had rightly taken on the responsibility of teaching the young, it was for the State to provide the means. Moreover, in such matters as the access of pupils to different levels of education, the appointment of teachers, subjects studied, syllabuses, examinations and diplomas, the diversity which had formerly existed in our country was now more or less impossible, though freedom of education was still granted. Government and parliament were, therefore, constantly and urgently at grips with these vital and reverberating problems, as, for their part, were families and public opinion.

It was a particularly thorny task for the government, since this is a field in which there is a clash not only of pedagogical theories but also of ideologies, and in which politics is passionately involved. It was a particularly onerous one because running costs, building and recruitment of staff alone imposed constantly increasing burdens on the budget. It was a particularly troublesome one because teachers were discouraged from taking initiative by the centralization rigorously imposed on the educational system since the days of Napoleon and Fontanes and at the same time disposed by the spirit of the age towards relentlessly critical and contentious attitudes. It was a particularly lively one because the teachers' and students' organizations invariably indulged in the most extreme theories, advanced the most outrageous solutions, split up into every possible category of Marxism and anarchy, and agreed only in their desire to use education as a means to destroy present-day society.

I, on the contrary, in the office I held and with the ambition I cherished for France, regarded education as a pre-eminent public service endued with exceptional importance and distinction. In my view, the mission of the men and women who guide the young into the realm of knowledge entails a sovereign responsibility on the human level. The powerful influence they exert on our destiny by teaching the flower of the people constitutes a unique national duty. Doubtless, my lofty conception of the teacher's role is in part due to the memory of my father who, throughout his long life, lavished his ability and devotion on generations of pupils. Indeed, in all the sayings and writings that have accompanied my actions, what else have I myself ever been but someone endeavoring to teach? But the views which I brought to bear on this subject, however imbued with idealism, were none the less political. Since in our time France must be transformed in order to survive, she would depend as much as ever on the quality of mind of her children as they came to assume responsibility for her existence, her role and her prestige. It was therefore essential that, without indoctrinating them in the totalitarian manner as to what they must think and believe, we should, on the contrary, be careful not to nip their enthusiasm and hopes in the bud. We must also ensure that the teaching they received, while developing their powers of reasoning and reflection as hitherto, should be relevant to contemporary conditions, which are utilitarian, scientific and technical. In short, a massive and popular training, founded on time-honored experience but looking to new horizons, must now be dispensed to our youth.

To achieve this, a host of problems had to be faced simultaneously. There was the problem of the numbers of schoolchildren, amounting to seven million in 1958 and due to rise to nine million in 1964, not counting the two million who were being taught in private schools. There was the problem of the number of teachers, which in the same period rose from 350,000 to 500,000. There was the question of new classrooms in schools, colleges and lycées: 100,000 of them would have to be opened. There was the problem of the universities which, starting with 160,000 students, would have as many as 350,000, with a teaching staff of 30,000 increasing to 75,000, a growth which would demand the construction of eighty-two institutions of higher education, the expansion of many others and the allocation of modern equipment to all of them. There was the problem of the financing of the educational program which was to double in six years, and from eleven per cent of the total national budget in 1959, would rise to eighteen per cent in 1964. And dominating all other considerations, there was the problem of the principles which were to govern the aims as well as the organization of this gigantic apparatus. On this last point, two basic and opposing facts existed side by side. One was the elemental impulse towards giving all young people of every social class free access to all levels of education. The other was the necessity for constant and regular intervention by the teachers, so that this irruption should be orderly and profitable. But to this the teachers, bearing in mind the philosophy by which they were generally inspired, were not in the least disposed.

This was soon brought home to me. As early as March 6, 1959 I had raised the school-leaving age by ordinance from fourteen to sixteen. Of course this measure did not in itself offend the teaching profession. But the text of the decree also recommended the beginning of a streaming process, so that every pupil should be guided by his teachers in the direction and towards the goal that best corresponded to his aptitudes. But this proposal, which to my mind was organically linked to the first, met with universal hostility and remained a dead letter. For this reason a succession of ministers – Jean Berthoin, André Boulloche, Louis Joxe, Lucien Paye, Pierre Sudreau – the extreme difficulty of whose task made their time in office short-lived, exhausted themselves in their attempts to regulate the mounting and turbulent flow of pupils in most establishments. However, in 1963, once the problems of our institutions, Algeria, the economy and external recovery were decisively settled, I set about fixing the policy for education. This gave rise to a series of Cabinet meetings, some restricted and some not, in which I always had before me Georges Pompidou, himself a former graduate teacher and a *normalien*[1] and at my side the Minister Christian Fouchet, who had no intention of being in turn unseated by his unruly mount, and who was to remain in the saddle longer than any predecessor had succeeded in doing for a hundred years.

As matters still stood at the time, the scholastic careers of the vast majority of young people were predetermined about the age of eleven. At that stage, they either went on to pursue their education in a lycée until they sat the *baccalauréat* examination, successfully or not; or they stayed in primary school until they began the apprenticeship for their working life. Only a few, having finished their primary education, went to technical colleges to receive the rudiments of a vocational training. For

[1] Graduate of the *Ecole Normale Supérieure*.

some others, secondary education took the form of entering a technical high school where they received both general and practical instruction. The decrees issued that year, which complemented the statute of 1959, modified this system considerably. Equality of opportunity was initiated. We had already created in 1960 the *Collèges d'enseignement général,* in which the cycle of primary education was completed in a three-year course. But now we established, within the precincts of the lycées themselves, *Collèges d'enseignement secondaire,* open to all who wished to enter them, provided that the authorities judged their abilities sufficient. In these comprehensive establishments pupils would receive a secondary education varied according to their aptitudes but based on the same syllabus. From there they could, at the statutory school-leaving age of sixteen, either leave, or continue their studies in a secondary school, or else go to technical schools or colleges. This meant that, while primary and secondary education remained distinct, the barriers separating them were lowered. It also put an end to the long-established system of predetermination, which settled from the outset and with few exceptions the educational and, to a large extent, the social fate of every child in France. Thus young people were offered a free education in which all paths were open to each according to his ability.

It then became necessary to canalize the river which was overflowing the banks of the secondary school system. This meant, in the first place, that those pupils who were acknowledged to be unsuitable for a particular course of study should be streamed off elsewhere. It also meant that among the subjects included in the curriculum, in an age when the sciences, modern languages and technical subjects were claiming a place beside the arts, alternatives must be organized to suit differing abilities. Why should some be left to languish in studies to which they were unsuited? Why should those who are capable of pursuing these studies but whose aptitudes naturally varied, all receive identical tuition? Streaming of pupils, therefore, became a vital necessity, and intervention by the teachers an obligation inherent in their vocation.

If this was true for secondary schooling, how much more obviously so was it for higher education! From the reports I received in Cabinet meetings during the course of 1963, it emerged that a general laxity had opened the universities to a spate of unsuitable applicants. Already the proportion of students graduating was barely thirty per cent, the lowest in the world. To allow the system to be swamped meant either accepting the wastage of a large number of young careers, or consenting to a derisory lowering of the standards of courses and examinations, and the awarding of meaningless diplomas – in short it would bring the whole institution of higher learning to ruin. On the other hand, the universities could regain their prestige and effectiveness on two conditions: in the first place, if an attempt was made to stem the inflationary tide; and then, if the traditional disciplines of arts, sciences and law were broken up, and new ones created, so as to diversify the options available for varying aptitudes, linking the teaching in the faculties to the practical concerns of the modern world, and preparing the young French elite to distribute themselves among the various branches in which they would make their living.

Accordingly, having personally taken steps to widen the scope of public education to the utmost, I was determined to see that streaming and selection were introduced from top to bottom of the system. But the fact was that, in this matter, my requests, even my orders, met with a stubborn passive resistance from those concerned. Once again it was brought home to me that, unless a clean sweep is made by dictatorship or revolution, no institution can really be reformed without its members' consent. This was certainly true of the teaching profession. While they readily accepted "democratization", which corresponded to the basic ideological stance they had come to adopt, and gave them the impression that the more pupils they had the more important their role; while they were prepared to keep all the flood-gates open, even at the cost of lowering pass-standards in examinations and especially in the *baccalauréat;* while they exerted themselves by every possible means to ensure that their own numbers were increased and new premises built, they were not in the least prepared to wield authority and accept the burden of responsibility. To guide their pupils in a particular direction as a matter of course, to take the initiative in closing doors to some of them, to involve themselves in the future of them all – such things seemed incompatible, not, indeed, with the capacities of the members of the teaching profession taken as a whole, but with their attitudes and traditions. Many of them greeted the changes with a sort of languid scepticism, when they saw that they themselves were involved in them and that the changes had been ordained by the government. In this, of course, these pre-eminent representatives of French intellectual life were demonstrating a general attitude of mind, the result of the accumulated distractions of two centuries, which in my view would sooner or later overwhelm society unless it was rebuilt under a renewed discipline.

For this reason, while striving to introduce into the educational system some palliative measures to stem the tidal wave that might well engulf the whole edifice, I fully intended to build up another one day, of such a kind that all who dwelt in it or made use of it – teachers, administrators, pupils, students, parents – would have a direct share in the management, progress, discipline, punishments and results of educational establishments which, being now autonomous, would be obliged to function efficiently or to close down and stop wasting the time of teachers and learners and the funds of the State. But here, too, I was well aware that such a project would have no chance of success unless some tempestuous wind were to disperse the vaporous clouds among which the persons most concerned were straying. That hurricane was indeed to blow in 1968. After it was over, without having swept away de Gaulle and his regime, the educational system, under the guidance of the great ministers I was to call upon for the purpose, would be reformed by law from top to bottom on the hitherto unacceptable basis of participation.

The same attitude of mind which delayed this outcome in

education also held up much-needed changes in the administrative structure of our country. It was all too obvious that the system adopted by the Revolution, codified by Napoleon and operated without modification ever since, by which the country as a whole was divided into ninety segments, and municipal life broken up into thirty-six thousand units, did not meet the needs of today. It is true that at the outset there had been some justification for this system. In the France of the eighteenth century – made up of country parishes – with which the Convention was confronted, it was convenient to have a large number of communes, each in its own setting, with its plots of land, its character and its parish church. In any case, since the ambitions of the smallest of them, as far as collective enterprises were concerned, did not go beyond the upkeep of the road, the exploitation of a wood, or the building of a wash-place, they did not exceed their resources. Moreover, as the Assembly, in its political zeal, had abolished the old provinces and, with mathematical exactitude, wanted each of the new components to have the same area, the division into *départements* was not lacking in logic. This was the period when the new State, suddenly rising from the ruins, intended that its local authority should become uniform, centralized and accessible to the population, when industry was still almost entirely in the hands of individual craftsmen, when the farmworker in his field saw nothing beyond his own horizon, when what was bought and sold at village markets travelled slowly, for short distances, by cart or boat. Consequently, it suited the circumstances to install the central power, in other words the Prefecture, in the principal town in an area sufficiently large to continue its immemorial existence from day to day, and sufficiently small for every mayor, litigant, ratepayer and gendarme to be able to reach the seat of authority by horse or carriage. Later on, with the appearance of large factories, the invention of the railway, the telegraph system, the telephone and the motor car, the increasingly frequent and widespread movement of men and materials, in short the relative shrinking of distances, caused the *département* to be outgrown. But people had become used to it.

In this connection, the Senate, elected by the communes at departmental level, became the privileged chamber in the parliamentary regime that succeeded the Second Empire, with sufficient political influence, legislative power and conservative spirit to ensure that nothing should happen to change the established order as far as local government units were concerned. Indeed, at the birth of the Fifth Republic, these remained exactly as they had been created at the end of the *Ancien Régime*.

This meant that they were much too small for the modern world which is dominated by economics with its ever-increasing demands for extensive planned development and improvement. Three-quarters of our communes lacked the necessary resources to provide for these needs, because by far the greater part of the wealth of France, formerly to be found in the villages, was now in the towns, as were all its most important activities and the mass of its population. It was only by getting rid of a large number of municipalities through the merging of communes that the basic unit of local government could be raised to the desired level. But, obviously, such a transformation must be part of a whole and incorporated in the great reform which would enlarge administrative areas between the ministries in Paris on the one hand and the communes on the other in accordance with the requirements of economic life and progress. Since the old provinces still retained their meaning in human terms, despite their official abolition and the subsequent shifts of population, all that was needed was to revive them on the economic plane over and above the *départements*, in the shape and under the title of regions, each of sufficient size to provide the framework for a specific activity.

This implied that the head of the local administration – the prefect – should have the authority and the means commensurate with a unit of such a size and with such a purpose; that the discussion of regional plans, the voting of regional budgets and the supervision of the regional executive should be in the hands of a new council, on which politically elected members would be joined by spokesmen for professional and social organizations; and that the Senate, once the symbol and strong-hold of the aberrancies of the Third Republic, and reduced since the latter's demise to a subordinate parliamentary role, should bring together the representatives of local communities and the delegates of the various branches of the country's economic life, instead of the former kicking their heels in the Luxembourg, in the futile pretense of exercising a legislative power they no longer possessed, and the latter being confined in a consultative council which was naturally seldom consulted. In this way, the great economic and social assembly, which would work out the details of French legislation in this hence-forth all-important field would be brought into being; at the highest levels in the State, participation would be at work; the administrative structure essential to the modern age would be directly linked to the reform of the human condition and human relations; and the constitutional task outlined at Bayeux soon after the Liberation, in the light of the lesson learned in two centuries of history, and with a view to a long future, would be finally completed.

Such, indeed, was my intention. Whenever I spoke to the nation, either on television and radio or at press conferences, or in public speeches in the course of my travels, I constantly proclaimed it. Meanwhile, until events indicated the right moment to attain this end, we could at least make a start. As early as 1960, a decree had brought the twenty-one "planning regions" into being and integrated them into the overall plan for national development. At the end of 1963, irreversible decisions were taken. In each region, a prefect with an expert staff of officials was given effective powers over his colleagues in the *départements* in all matters relating to development and expansion. At the same time, a Regional Economic Develop-ment Commission (CODER) was set up alongside him, in which spokesmen for various interest groups joined with local elected representatives in the preparation of all economic measures. It was not long before the regional spirit began to blow through these commissions which, however embryonic, reflected the present-day realities and aspirations of our provinces. Areas that were thriving economically but frustrated by being artificially broken up, such as Lorraine, Alsace, Nord, Pas-de-Calais, the Rhône and the Alps, Upper and Lower Normandy and Franche-Comté, found in them an appropriate framework for the discussion of their problems and furtherance of projects commensurate with their size. Others, such as Provence, Languedoc-Roussillon, Aquitaine, the South-West, the Loire country, the Center, Picardy and Champagne, which were eager to expand in various directions, saw them as the means of uniting many disparate impulses into an ordered whole. And others still, Brittany, Auvergne, Limousin, Charentes-Poitou and Corsica, which because of their geographical position had for long been cut off from the great trends of the industrial era, and were in the grip of a sad decline, discovered thereby a new vitality and a resolve to make the most of the conditions of their revival. That the spirit of modern times should rekindle these flames which had been kept under a bushel – that it should renew in our regions an enthusiasm and competitiveness which, as a result of excessive centralization, had hitherto remained the monopoly of the capital – could not but further the effort, the stability and the unity of our country.

Meanwhile, as it happened, the hypertrophy of the Paris conurbation had given rise to profound problems. From the administrative point of view, the Seine *département,* which included Paris and its suburbs, was an enormous body which, despite its fifty thousand officials and its many services, could not adequately sustain the life of such a human agglomeration. It is true that the capital itself, with its Prefect of Police, its *arrondissements,* its town halls, its municipal council, its abundant wealth, the unity which characterized it within its changing boundaries, the aid which the State had always lavished on it, had retained its personality despite the overflow of population. But most of the surrounding communes, which had sprung up rapidly and haphazardly, represented a disorganized jumble of problems and needs. To these must be added a fair number of equally problem-ridden places in the Seine-et-Oise, Oise and Seine-et-Marne, which were also officially linked with the Parisian monster. In such a thickly populated area, the authorities could neither function nor ensure public services in a satisfactory manner. Such administrative short-comings weighed heavily enough on everyday life; they had become intolerable in matters of development. Housing, roads, schools, hospitals, factory-building, green spaces, sports grounds, traffic control, etc., required unified planning and control. Moreover, there was every reason to suppose that the conurbation, whose population had increased by a million and a half souls in ten years, and had now reached ten million, would continue to grow in numbers and in extent, whatever might be done to revitalize the provinces. The Fifth Republic had no intention of allowing future growth to be carried out in the same confusion as in the past. In the same series of Cabinet meetings at the Elysée in which the measures to initiate regional organization were taken, I promulgated those which would tackle root and branch the problem of the Paris area.

Roger Frey, the Minister of the Interior, proposed both sets of measures. This was all the more desirable because the administration for which he was responsible was not predisposed towards structural reform in its own sphere. The prefectoral corps had adapted themselves over the years to existing administrative divisions, duties and functions. Not of course – and with good reason! – that they were unaware of the shortcomings of the system. But experience and skill had taught them to make the best of it. It was not without some apprehension that they envisaged the changes to be introduced in the long-established balance of local appointments and practices, as well as in the ranks of their own hierarchy. For the rest, the prospect of radical transformation in a conglomeration as huge, as hidebound and as subject to political influences as the Paris area, aroused the most passionate feelings on all sides, and gave rise to countless pressures, debates, objections and criticisms from the parties, the press and the various interest groups. But Roger Frey's dedication to the national interest, which he had shown in the Resistance struggle and then in the

days of the RPF, and which was his guiding principle today as
a member of the government, made him determined on reform.
Moreover, in the plans he put forward concerning the capital
and its environs he was backed by two men of great ability:
Raymond Haas-Picard, the Prefect of the Seine, a wise counsellor in the matter of administrative organization; and Paul
Delouvrier, Delegate-General to the Paris District, the enthusiastic inspirer of the Plan which was to shape the future of
Greater Paris in harmony with that of a modernized France.

After a great deal of study and discussion, a decision had to
be made. I made it. Thereafter, the Paris Region was created
and organized by law in 1964. It was to have its own prefect,
with responsibility for town-planning, development and public
services throughout the conurbation. It was to have its own
governing bodies: a Council of Administration and an Economic and Social Committee, the one made up of representatives of the departmental and municipal councils, the other of
delegates from professional organizations. It was to have its
own budget, financed by a share in its own rates, loans that
it would negotiate and State subsidies. Under this umbrella
there were to be seven *départements,* Ville de Paris, Hauts-de-
Seine, Seine-Saint-Denis, Val-d'Oise, Val-de-Marne, Essonne
and Yvelines, through which public action and protection would
penetrate the hitherto compact and isolated mass of citizens.
At the same time, a "Master Town Planning and Development
Scheme for the Paris region"[1] was drawn up, which would
control its growth and progress up to the end of the century.
Rather than allow industry and population to pile up con-
centrically, as it had always done from earliest times, the over-
spill would now be directed along well-separated natural
arteries – the Seine valley downstream towards Rouen, the
Marne valley upstream towards Meaux, and the Oise valley
towards Pontoise – on which new urban centers would be built
in an orderly and rational manner. A network of communications adequate to this colossus was decided upon and immediately begun: motorways, boulevards, ring-roads, riverside

[1] *Schéma directeur d'urbanisme et d'aménagement de la région parisienne.*

roads, extensions of the metropolitan railway into the outer sub-urbs, etc. Finally, all necessary steps were taken to give the administration powers to purchase the necessary land and to prevent any building not in accordance with the Plan.

Thanks to the new Republic, then, the country was over-coming without serious disturbance the trials inseparable from its own transformation, notably those arising from the coal industry, the shipyards, the repatriates, agriculture and the public services. These were, in a sense, the reverse side of a coin whose obverse showed a picture of satisfactory general progress and peace completely restored. The government could deal with them without being shaken, whereas in earlier days it would have been thrown into a sterile succession of crises. In the same way, it was able to initiate, in particular in education, local government and regional development, reforms which formerly would have been endlessly discussed without any decision being taken, and which interminable controversies would still have prevented from getting under way today, had there not been an effective authority to set them in motion. For the rest, all this was happening amid an economic expansion which was also the result of the country's auspicious situation, but from whose effervescence, as always happens, the monster of inflation was now beginning to emerge. Under the regime of old, this monster would once more have eaten up much of France's substance. Now it was to be repulsed by virtue of the determination shown at the summit of the State.

Already in 1962, the stability achieved three years earlier had begun to be shaken. There were three main contributory causes for this. In the first place, there was the monumentally over-privileged position that the world had conceded to the American currency since the two world wars had left it standing alone amid the ruins of the others, the pound sterling alone being temporarily reprieved. At the same time, the world's entire stock of gold was piling up in the United States. The countries of the West, and those more or less attached to them, had no choice but to accept the international monetary system known as the "gold exchange standard," according to which the dollar was automatically regarded as the equivalent of gold. It was so, in fact, as long as the Federal Government limited its issue of banknotes in direct proportion to its gold reserves, and paid back its creditors on demand either in currency or in precious metal. But the vast sums lavished abroad by Washington after the victory for purposes of power, prestige and aid, together with the calls upon its funds from all the countries which were forced to rebuild or eager to develop, had drawn America, in the fifties, into a process of galloping inflation. The reluctance of the United States to forgo its hegemony led it continually to create nominal capital, in other words to issue dollars, which it used for lending to other countries, for paying its debts, or for buying foreign goods, well in excess of the true value of its reserves. Moreover, America carried sufficient political and economic weight for the International Monetary Fund, responsible since Bretton Woods for keeping an eye on the balance, not to insist that it be maintained, and for a number of foreign countries who had a favorable balance of payments with her to be willing to accept payment in notes and bonds drawn on the Federal Bank, and not in gold. In France itself, the surplus dollars which the United States exported to us by virtue of the gold exchange standard, either to acquire shares in certain of our industries or to provide them with credit at our banks so that they could buy equipment, put a strain on our currency. For since this foreign capital was naturally converted into francs on the spot, it resulted in an artificial increase in our total money supply.

Another cause of trouble was the actual deficit which was appearing in our budget. It was true that the report of the Rueff Commission and the rigorous plan that had emerged from it, had allowed for a "shortfall" which, in the expectation of growth in the resources of the State, it was thought would normally be made good from year to year by short- or medium-term credit. Moreover, for some three years ordinary revenue had been so considerable that the "shortfall" never reached the total allowed for in the budget. But in 1962 the massive aid given to French citizens repatriated from Africa had reversed this trend. In addition to this, the private sector having exceeded the wage-levels laid down in the Fourth Plan, the State had had no option but to do the same in the public sector. We had even seen the nationalized Régie Renault, to the surprise of the Minister for Industry, suddenly decide to give their employees an extra week's paid holiday, a concession which, spreading throughout all branches of industry, resulted in a general reduction in hours of work for the same wage bill. Finally, in the development programs adopted for education, research, housing, armaments, hospitals, etc., a mysterious urge speeded up the decisions of the departments and the work of the contractors, and at the same time the forecast tempo for the financing of these programs. So many little streams trickling from these sources of deficit finally became a river. The Finance Ministry in the rue de Rivoli had no difficulty in guarding against it in the short term by issuing quantities of treasury bonds. But this merely accentuated further the symptoms of an unhealthy tension.

Above all, the psychological attitude inseparable from modern expansion, and which might one day prove its ruin, just as optimism of people in good health leads them to overtax their strength, was unleashing the canker of inflation on to the economy. The better things went, the more easy-going people became, with everyone staking on the future a little more than he possessed. In the business world, there was no hesitation in resorting to large-scale credit, a lavish attitude prevailed as regards salaries and bonuses, and expense accounts were exaggeratedly high. On the trade-union side, there was a correspondingly powerful tendency towards higher wage demands, which were seldom disputed but which gave the unions added prestige. In government departments and State-run concerns, there was a less rigorous attitude towards pay, as well as towards public works and government contracts. Among the public at large, hire purchase was on the increase. In short, a kind of general imperceptible impulse was gradually allowing expenditure to run ahead of earnings. Whence an excessive increase in the means of payment in relation to what was produced, a steady rise in prices, and an insidious deterioration in the trade balance.

The fact was that in the summer of 1963, although in the previous year the growth in the national product had barely reached 5·8 per cent, the total money supply – banknote treasury bonds, bank deposits and postal checks – had gone up from 123,000 million to 142,000 million, that wage increases had been of the order of ten per cent, the price index had risen by six per cent, and though exports were up by 11·5 per cent imports had increased by twenty-three per cent. If this deterioration in economic equilibrium were to continue, the franc would soon be in danger.

I had to acknowledge, however, that the desirability, not to say the absolute necessity, of an unshakable currency did not exercise many people's minds. In particular, in the circles responsible for the conduct of the nation's business, while lip-service to these principles was sometimes paid, there was widespread readiness to make the most of the advantages that inflation offered in its early days. Industry enjoyed the tempo imparted to its affairs, even if it was somewhat hectic. The unions found that price rises provided an impetus for rises in wages, however vicious the spiral might become. Even the Treasury temporarily benefited from the collection of unpaid arrears of taxes. But this drug-induced euphoria could only conceal for a short while the erosion of the organism, in other words the damage inflicted on our currency. Now the strength of a country's currency is an index to the world of the true effectiveness of its economy, on which its policy depends. At home it is the essential condition of honesty in relationships, moderation in desires, serene acceptance of one's lot, and the whole social and moral order. For the State which stamps its effigy on its coins – king, emperor, republic – it is the proof of its capacity, the justification of the authority it exercises and the confidence it demands, the argument it needs in order to ask for effort, impose sacrifice, or put down abuses. In these circumstances, I was determined, as I always had been and always would be, to maintain the franc at the rate I had fixed, when I took it upon myself to set France on the road to recovery.

The appropriate means were well-known. All that was needed was to apply them. In the spring of 1963 I called upon the government to do so. Then in August, since I could see that the good resolutions seemed to be losing their edge, I decided to precipitate matters by taking sterner measures. It is true that Georges Pompidou seemed less convinced than I was of the prime importance of the stability of the franc from the national and the international point of view, and was above all concerned that nothing should be done to jeopardize the existing expansion. It is true that Valéry Giscard d'Estaing, the young Minister of Economy and Finance, who certainly condemned inflation in the name of financial orthodoxy, but who would have the chief responsibility for carrying out the policy, was somewhat shaken by the realization that his task of promoting the general interest would entail firmness and severity towards each particular interest. Yet both of them fully and unreservedly endorsed my resolution. On September 12, 1963, the Stabilization Plan, drawn up in the course of our discussions, in consultation with the senior officials concerned, was agreed by the Cabinet and at once put into operation. Budget economies, credit restriction and price stabilization were naturally the chief fields of government action in which the gifts of the Prime Minister and the keeper of the purse were deployed. At the same time, the Bank of France was instructed to demand from the Americans that eighty per cent of what they owed us by virtue of the balance of payments should henceforth be repaid in gold.

At the end of a year, after a few minor jolts, the desired result was achieved. The increase in total money supply had been brought down from twenty thousand million to thirteen thousand million. Wholesale prices were back to the level they had been at twelve months earlier. Retail prices had risen by only 2·5 per cent. The trade balance was once again favorable. Despite the dire predictions of a chorus of Cassandras, expansion which had scarcely slowed down while the Plan was in course of execution, resumed its vigorous upward movement.

As for the slight symptoms of unemployment that appeared here and there, they soon disappeared. In any case, the National Employment Fund, set up by the law in 1963, had begun to do its work. For the second time, then, the new Republic had set the economy in order without halting the progress towards prosperity, indeed quite the reverse. It is true that few voices were raised to acknowledge the overall benefit of the operation, while many were heard in recriminations and complaints provoked by partial and short-lived strikes. But how could I not have learned by now that what is good for the nation is not achieved without disapproval from public opinion and losses in elections?

Appendix

༄

Letter dated May 30, 1970 from General de Gaulle to M. Pierre-Louis Blanc, commissioned by the author to assemble the documents for *Memoirs of Hope*. This letter outlines the scheme of the second volume. Later, the author was to indicate that in the final chapter he intended to evoke the great figures of French history.

30 May 1970

Mon cher ami,

I intend to write seven chapters for "Endeavor".

Two will be "political", devoted respectively to the *referendum* of October 1962 (the formation of the Pompidou government, the vote of censure, the dissolution of Parliament, the referendum itself, and the elections) and the *re-election* of December 1965 (the all-out offensive by the parties, etc.).

Two will be economic and social. In these I want to deal with *problems* (for example, the miners' strike of 1963; the stabilization plan; the agricultural crisis, etc.) and *progress* (the development of industry, agriculture, trade, education, technology and communications – with figures).

Two chapters will be concerned with foreign affairs: the *crises* (Cuba, the veto on Britain's entry into the Common Market, the assassination of Kennedy, Vietnam, the British elections, the departure of Adenauer, etc.); *decisions* (the Franco-German treaty, our tough line in Brussels, our withdrawal from

377

NATO, our attitude on the monetary question, our recognition of Peking, etc.) and *visits* (those I made, and those I received).

Finally, a chapter of a "philosophical" nature, in which I shall give my personal view on the situation of France, Europe and the world.

This is for your guidance as regards the documents.

Croyez, mon cher Blanc, à ma sincère amitié.

C. de Gaulle

Index

༺⚜༻

Abbas, Ferhat, 60, 71, 88, 97, 103, 119–20, 230
Abidjan, 54
Aden, 216
Adenauer, Konrad, character of, 173–4; and meeting with de Gaulle (Sept. 1958), 174–9, 181; and meeting with de Gaulle (Nov. 1958), 179–80; official visit to France of (July 1962), 180; and Common Market, 187, 194, 195, 197; and Berlin question, 223–4, 249, 260; mentioned, 218, 222, 253, 377
Afghanistan, 230
Agadir, 53
agriculture, in Algeria, 42, 61, 76; and farm prices, 140, 147; expansion of production in, 134, 149, 158–9, 281, 293–4, 377; and *Loi d'orientation agricole* (1960), 157, 353; and *Loi complémentaire* (1962), 157, 353; and Common Market policy, 159, 178, 182, 185–9, 219, 273, 354; and trade unions, 285, 326; mechanization of, 341, 354; and disappearance of small farms, 345–6, 353; mentioned, 9, 10, 29, 133, 144, 156, 160–1, 276, 278, 335, 371, 377
Ahidjo, Ahmandou, 68
Ailleret, General Pierre Marie Jean, 108, 122, 286
Aïn-Temouchent, 93
Air-Afrique, 66
Akbou, 93
Albania, 212
Algeria, and Algerian Statute (1947), 13–14, 45; outbreak of fighting in (1954), 14–15, 85; and May 13 movement (1958), 17–25, 42, 47; activities of Committees of Public

Safety in, 20, 23, 24, 47, 49, 59; de Gaulle's policy towards, 40–53, 69–71, 74–7, 80–4, 87–92, 104–5, 115–16, 123–6; de Gaulle's visit to (June 1958), 47–53; de Gaulle's visit to (July 1958), 53; de Gaulle's visit to (Aug. 1958), 57, 59; constitutional referendum held in (1958), 58; activities of Electoral Control Commission in (1958), 58; and Constantine Plan, 61–2, 113; offensive against rebel strongholds in (1959), 63, 71–4; revolt of the Barricades in (Jan. 1960), 78–81, 83–5, 92, 103, 110; dissolution of Territorial Defence Units in, 85; suppression of Psychological Warfare Bureaux in, 85; de Gaulle's visit to (Mar. 1960), 86; cantonal elections in (May 1960), 86–7; de Gaulle's visit to (Dec. 1960), 93–4; referendum on (Jan. 8, 1961), 95–8; and relations with Tunisia, 99–101, 103; and relations with Morocco, 102–3; OAS terrorist campaign in, 103, 120–2, 127–30; Challe's military coup in (April 1961), 105–11, 309; and FLN negotiations with French government (1961–2), 111–15, 119–21, 125; and Evian agreements, 125, 129; referendum on (April 8, 1962), 127, 326; referendum on (July 1, 1962), 129–30, 310; independence attained by, 130, 310, 316, 319, 344–5; as source of oil supplies, 154; and relations with Soviet Union, 230; Gorse appointed as ambassador to, 336; emigration to France from, 352–3; mentioned, 12, 16, 29, 30, 33, 60, 145, 166, 193, 203, 261, 264, 272,

379

United States of America—*cont.*
231-2, 240; and relations with Britain, 216-20; and Berlin question, 222-3, 228, 249, 258-60; activities in Latin America of, 230; natural resources of, 233; and relations with Canada, 239, 240, 242; de Gaulle's visit to (April 1960), 242-7; and U2 incident, 247-54; and Paris Summit Conference (May 1960), 247-53; activities in Laos of, 255-6, 263; and relations with Japan, 262; and relations with Ethiopia, 264; and relations with Israel, 265; and relations with Argentina, 267; and relations with Austria, 268; presidential system in, 323; and international finance, 371-2, 375; mentioned, 38, 138, 168-9, 177, 189, 195-6, 204, 350
UNR, 309, 325, 333-6
Upper Volta, 39, 55, 65, 68
Ural Mountains, 173, 229
U2 incident, 247-54

Vannier, General Georges, 238
Vendroux, Jacques, 280
Ventejol, Gabriel, 284
Verdun, 225
Versailles, 11, 210, 225, 255, 295
Versailles, Treaty of, 168
Vézinet, General Adolphe, 94, 105, 108
Vichy, 316
Vichy regime, 7, 71, 78, 169, 279, 282
Victoria I, 218
Vienna, 254, 258
Vietnam, 40, 82, 120, 205, 256, 263, 377
Vignaux, Charles Merveilleux du, 26

Villacoublay, 130
Villiers, Georges, 285
Vimy Ridge, 242
Vincennes, 103, 295
Vinogradov, Sergei, 206, 226, 247
Vistula, River, 218, 244
Vitteti, Leonardo, 206
Volga, River, 218

Wagner, Robert, 246
Wallis, 39
Warsaw Pact, 261
Washington, de Gaulle's visit to (April 1960), 242-5, 247
Washington, Treaty of, 178
Werner, Pierre, 194, 195
West Germany, and Common Market, 173, 177-9, 183-7, 190, 195, 197; desire for reunification in, 174-7, 226-30; and status of Berlin, 180, 217, 222-4, 228-30, 249, 258-60; and NATO, 200, 208; and relations with Austria, 267; economy of, 344; motorways in, 346; mentioned, 166, 181, 206, 253, 269, 300, 311, 377
Weygand, General Maxime, 78
Wigny, Pierre, 195
Yalta, 199, 226
Yameogo, Maurice, 68
Youlou, Abbé Fulbert, 54, 68
Yugoslavia, 212

Zarifete, 86
Zeddine, 93
Zeller, General André, 105, 110, 111
Zenata, 86
Zeralda, 110